TO THE HAPPY FEW
SELECTED LETTERS OF STE[

Stendhal was one of the many pen-names us[
born at Grenoble in 1783, and educated there. ___ ___ ___
was seven; he detested his father and the rest of his family, and the devout,
Royalist atmosphere in which they lived. In Paris by 1799, he procured
an army commission in 1800 which took him to Milan. In Italy, he fell
in love and discovered his spiritual home. Between 1806 and 1813 the
victualling of Napoleon's armies in Germany, Russia and Austria constituted much of his work. He left the army at the end of this period, his
health impaired largely through his own excesses. He refused office under
the Bourbons and spent seven years in Italy, absorbed by a shattering
unrequited passion which was the main event of his life. Unjustly accused
of spying, he was forced to leave and from 1821 to 1830 he was mostly
in Paris, living frugally, writing, and frequenting literary *salons*. He
published *Of Love* (1822) and *The Red and the Black* (1830) during this
period. Under the July monarchy he was appointed French consul at
Trieste, but was soon transferred to Civitavecchia, a dreary, unhealthy
port, 45 miles outside Rome. He held this office until his sudden death
from apoplexy, in a Paris street in 1842. His masterpiece *The Charterhouse
of Parma*, which he wrote in 52 days, appeared in 1839. Stendhal was not
a conscious stylist, and was prepared to sacrifice harmony and rhythm
to the lucidity with which he expressed his often complicated ideas. He
had an ironical attitude to life, and the behaviour of his characters, and
even their virtue, springs from their passions. His ideal was what he called
Beylism: a worship of magnificent, all-conquering energy in the pursuit
of happiness.

Stendhal's life resembled that of his novels. If his heroes were on the
whole younger and better looking than he was, they were less mature; in
many of these letters it is the poet who did not die young who writes, in a
poetry of ideas. The three persistent themes of the novels, the love affairs,
the life of action, and the precise analysis of the various forms of passion
he distilled from these, are also the persistent themes of his correspondence. Here Stendhal courts Metilde, delineates the anatomy of love and
struggles through the snow, retreating from Russia.

John Norman Cameron (1905–1953), poet and translator, was educated
in Edinburgh and at Oriel College, Oxford. He worked as an Educational
Officer in Southern Nigeria until the Second World War. After the war
he joined the J. Walter Thompson advertising agency. His Collected
Poems, edited by Alan Hodge, were published by The Hogarth Press in
1967.

STENDHAL

TO THE HAPPY FEW

SELECTED LETTERS

EDITED BY E. BOUDOT-LAMOTTE
TRANSLATED BY NORMAN CAMERON
WITH AN INTRODUCTION
BY CYRIL CONNOLLY

PRIVATE CORRESPONDENCE

PUBLISHED BY THE SOHO BOOK COMPANY
1 BREWER STREET   LONDON W1

MCMLXXXVI

Published by
THE SOHO BOOK COMPANY
1/3 Brewer Street, London WIR 3FN
1986
First published in this translation by John Lehmann in 1952
Based on the readings established by Henri Martineau
Translation © Estate of Norman Cameron 1986
Introduction taken from *Previous Convictions* by Cyril Connolly
by kind permission of The Hogarth Press
© Estate of Cyril Connolly

British Library Cataloguing in Publication Data

Stendhal
    To the happy few: Stendhal's letters.
    1. Stendhal—Biography
    2. Authors, French—19th century—Biography
    Rn: Marie-Henri, Beyle   I. Title
    843'.7   PQ2436.A2

ISBN 0-948166-09-6

Printed and bound in Great Britain
by Redwood Burn Ltd, Trowbridge, Wilts
Cover design, title page and introductory material
© THE SOHO BOOK COMPANY LTD 1986
Set in 11pt Fournier 1pt leaded
Designed by Sally McKay at Graham Rawle Designs

INTRODUCTION

Cyril Connolly

THERE should be a pale blue wrapper round certain books meaning 'You can read your way out of anything with this. It is another world and a better.' A red wrapper would mean, 'Another world, but a sadder.' Thus the letters of Flaubert are magnificent but harrowing, the correspondence of Baudelaire slow torture—only in the world of Stendhal do we sail away to forty years of good-humour. 'Apart from this everything goes well: we have not seen a woman since the post-mistresses of Poland, but by way of compensation we are great connoisseurs of fires,' so he begins the Retreat from Moscow. 'I, too, have had a grapple with the void. It is only the immediate experience which is disagreeable, and the horror of it comes from all the silly nonsense that is put into our heads at the age of three'—so he announces his last illness, with the strange prophecy of his end: 'There is nothing ridiculous about dying in the street, provided one does not do it on purpose.'

Though he considered himself an unhappy man and knew boredom as only artists know it, he had a sunny and optimistic disposition and he had imbibed from his grandfather (like George Sand) something of the rational art of happiness of the eighteenth century. Of the three writers in the age of transition who grew up under Napoleon and led the way to modern literature, Stendhal is the most solid and indestructible. Constant could not fertilise a whole generation by 'Adolphe' alone; Chateaubriand formed a sombre leaf-mould round Flaubert and Baudelaire. The writers influenced by Beyle's 'On me lira vers 1880' are still emerging.

'My habitual state of being is that of one unhappily in love who adores music and painting. I have set an exquisite sensibility to seek out beautiful landscapes. That has been the only object of my travels. I have valued contemplation above everything else, even a reputation for wit.' Such is the romantic Stendhal's definition of himself. But there are two others: the realist and the man of action. The realist could observe the unhappy love affairs of the romantic while conducting his consulship at Civita Vecchia, enjoying Roman balls, analysing political trends and satirising social follies. The man of action had the makings of a hero and fell with Napoleon in 1815.

In every work by Stendhal we can perceive the fusion of these personalities which exist in rather different proportions in Balzac and Delacroix. On the whole the realist predominates and gives a somewhat flinty aroma, a whiff of the garrulous and lonely old bachelor to the correspondence; but the inclusion of many love letters in this book redeems the *côté boulevard* by a *côté salon*; Stendhal was fortunate to live at a time when love still had its dangers and drawing-rooms their magic so that his abandonment of the pursuit of glory was not embittering. He wrote very few letters about his books and the three drafts of his acknowledgment of Balzac's great tribute to the *Chartreuse de Parme* form almost an autobiography. His correspondents were chiefly worldly and beautiful women or worldly and cynical men. It is regrettable that the superb exchange with Mérimée published by 'Fontaine' is not included but in the letters to Di Fiore we find a charming relationship with a cultivated younger man which went on until his death.

I am not a Beylolater, I need a *fond noir à contenter* in my heroes, but of all those who lack it, the seed of Epicurus, Stendhal is the least stupid. We can never dismiss him as insensitive or shallow. He had the quality which Norman Douglas in his travel books inherited from him of a serene acceptance of himself and of the universe, coupled with a prickly wit, critical curiosity and an unchanging admiration for love and youth and courage. It was right he should know Byron or dig up Etruscan tombs and find a bust of Tiberius. Could Horace have said good-bye better? 'I have great hopes of recovery. Nevertheless I want to say farewell to you, in case this letter may be the *ultima*. I truly love you, and you are not one of a crowd. Farewell, take events cheerfully as they come.'

BIOGRAPHICAL NOTE ON STENDHAL

Jean Stewart

Henri beyle, better known as Stendhal, was born at Grenoble in 1783. Of his family, childhood and youth he has left an incomparable picture in the *Vie de Henri Brulard*. As a schoolboy he reacted violently against the conventional piety of his home and studied mathematics because *selon moi, l'hypocrisie était impossible en mathématiques*; he dreamed of a career at the Ecole Polytechnique in Paris—*les mathématiques me sortiront de Grenoble*. But Napoleon's seizure of power in 1799 diverted his ambition, and in 1800, together with his cousins the Daru brothers, he joined Napoleon's army in Italy. Here he discovered his spiritual home; Italy meant for him music, gaiety, passion, *l'art de jouir de la vie avec tranquillité*, and he fell in love with Milan and with a Milanese woman. But the end of the campaign brought him back to Paris, where, living on an allowance from his father, he haunted theatres, tried his hand at play-writing, and loved an actress, Mélanie Guilbert; for her sake he moved to Marseilles, taking a job in a grocery business. The affair petered out and within a year we find him bored with Marseilles, appealing to his cousins for a job in Paris. War with Prussia in 1806 brought employment, and Henri followed Napoleon's armies to Germany; in 1809 he was in Vienna, attending Haydn's funeral. 1810 saw him back in Paris, having been appointed Auditor to the State Council; 1811 brought leave, and a flying visit to Milan. But not peace; Napoleon's disastrous Russian campaign involved Beyle in fresh adventures, and as official courier he witnessed the fire of Moscow and the retreat of the Grande Armée. Napoleon's fall and the restoration of the Bourbons cut short his official career. He settled in his beloved Milan, and wrote, partly for pleasure, partly to pay his debts. In the *Vies de Haydn, Mozart et Metastase* (1814) he borrowed shamelessly and without acknowledgement from German and Italian authors, from one of whom he had to face a charge of plagiarism. Here, as in the *Histoire de la Peinture en Italie* (1817), second-hand material is shot through with original observation and feeling. But it was his own emotional experience, his affair with the magnificent but faithless Pietragrua, his hopeless passion for Métilde Dembowski, that inspired the highly original *De L'Amour* (1822).

Meanwhile in his travel-book, *Rome, Naples et Florence* (1817) he had mingled personal impressions and social and aesthetic commentary with acute criticism of the tyranny of Church and Emperor in Italy. This, together with his reputation for free speaking and his friendship with Italian liberals and patriots, brought the Austrian police on his tracks; the Milanese meanwhile suspected him of being a French spy, and Milan became uncomfortable.

In 1821 he returned to Paris, and spent the next nine years in its most brilliant intellectual society, enjoying music, the theatre, friendship, freedom, and, from 1824 to 1826, a romantic affair with the Countess Curial, " Menta "—but, alas, neither fame nor fortune. He eked out his precarious pension with journalism, chiefly literary articles in English newspapers for which journeys to England in 1821 and 1826 ensured him contacts. Twice he paid secret visits to Italy, dodging the police. Meanwhile he wrote unappreciated books: the *Vie de Rossini* (1823) on which Berlioz poured scorn; the two pamphlets on *Racine et Shakespeare* (1823 and 1825) which were his contribution to the battle of Romanticism then raging; *Armance* (1827), an enigmatic novel whose unprintable clue is given in a letter to Mérimée, written in an effort to combat the black depression following his break with Clementine Curial. *Promenades dans Rome* (1827), providing the double pleasure of research and reminiscence, restored his spirits. Then, in 1830, came *Le Rouge et Le Noir*; a provincial *crime passionel* had suggested the theme of this masterpiece, amazingly swift and rich, profoundly original in its psychological and social observation. It made some sensation, mainly scandalous; it seemed immoral, irreligious, subversive. Fame seemed further off than ever.

Meanwhile the Revolution of 1830 had expelled the hated Bourbons and brought back a liberal government. Beyle sought an appointment, in Italy if possible; he was sent as consul to Trieste, despite protests from the Austrian authorities. Here he was unutterably bored; in 1831 he was transferred to Civita Vecchia, *un trou abominable*, where *ennui* reigned even more completely. To distract himself he wrote books that, as a civil servant, he dared not publish; those admirable autobiographical fragments, *Souvenirs d'Égotisme* and *Henri Brulard*: another novel, scathing in its social criticism, *Lucien Leuwen*, to be left unfinished. In 1836 he was granted leave to go to Paris, and, thanks to his friend Count Molé, then minister, that leave was prolonged for three years of freedom, of keen intellectual activity, of emotional experience. He wrote copiously and for pleasure; *Mémoires d'un Touriste* (1838), a curious and delightful travel-book, *Chroniques Italiennes*, retelling the melodramatic Renaissance stories with which he had beguiled the tedium of his consular days, and the great *Chartreuse de Parme*, that rich and subtle picture of Italian life, love and society into which he distilled all his deepest feelings, his maturest thoughts. The fall of his protector Molé sent him back to his post at Civita Vecchia; here he began work immediately on another novel, *Lamiel*, the ironical story of a feminine Sorel; and here, in 1840, he read and replied to Balzac's brilliant appreciation of the newly published *Chartreuse*. This recognition of his genius by that very different genius whom he had called King of Novelists touched him deeply, but fame had come too late. He had already felt the hand of death; "*je me suis colleté avec le néant*", he wrote in 1841; and death overtook him suddenly, the following year, in Paris.

TABLE OF CONTENTS

THE LETTERS

TO HIS SISTER PAULINE[1]

Paris, 18th of Ventôse, Year VIII[2]
(Sunday, March 9th, 1800)

I can't think what kind of a creature I am, my dear Pauline, when I reflect that I have been capable of spending five months without writing to you. For some time now I have been thinking of it, but the variety of my occupations has always prevented me from carrying out my desire. First of all, I want you to write to me every week without fail: otherwise I shall scold you. Secondly, I don't want you to show either your letters or mine to anybody: I don't like to be embarrassed when I am writing from the heart. Tell me how the piano is going, and whether you are taking dancing lessons. Have you danced at all this winter? I expect you have. Are you learning to draw? Old Nick, who keeps on interfering with my affairs, has been preventing me from taking drawing-lessons since I have been here. I have been taking dancing lessons of a dancer

---

[1] This letter, addressed : " To Citizeness Pauline Beyle, Grande-Rue, No. 60, Grenoble (Department of the Isère) ", is the earliest-known letter from the writer who was later to be Stendhal. Pauline Beyle was born at Grenoble on March 21st, 1786.

[2] In an obituary which he had the fanciful idea of writing himself, on April 30th, 1837, Stendhal sums up the first years of his life as follows: " Beyle (Henri), born at Grenoble on January 23rd, 1783, died at—— on ——. His parents were well-to-do members of the upper middle class. His father, advocate to the Parliament of the Dauphiné, adopted a title of nobility. His grandfather was a physician, an intelligent man and a friend, or at least an admirer, of Voltaire. M. Gagnon—such was his name—was a man of the utmost refinement, much respected at Grenoble, and leader in all projects of reform. Young Beyle witnessed the first bloodshed of the Frence Revolution, on the occasion of the famous ' Day of Tiles ' (17—). The people revolted against the government and threw tiles at the soldiers from the roofs. Young Beyle's parents were devoutly religious and became ardent aristocrats, whilst he himself turned into an exaggerated patriot. His mother, an intelligent woman who read Dante, died very young. M. Gagnon, who was inconsolable at the loss of this beloved daughter, undertook the education of her only son. The family had exaggerated sentiments of honour and pride, and communicated these to the young man. M. Gagnon probably had an income of between eight and nine thousand francs a year, which at Grenoble in 1789

from the Opéra. His style is not at all like Beler's. Since the style that I am being taught is the right one, and since it will therefore reach the provinces sooner or later, I advise you to practise yourself in it, by bending deeply in all steps and especially exercising the instep[1]. I dance with Adèle Rebuffel[2], who is full of talents and intelligence, although she is only eleven years of age. One of the things that have done most to bestow these gifts upon her is her wide reading. I wish you would follow the same course, for I am convinced it is the only right one. Your reading, if well chosen, will soon interest you to the point of fascination, and will introduce you to true philosophy. And philosophy, that inexhaustible source of supreme delights, is what gives us the capacity and strength of soul that we must have if we are to appreciate and worship genius. With its help everything is made smooth; difficulties disappear; the soul expands, it has greater grasp and greater love. But I am speaking to you in an unknown language: I wish you were capable of understanding it.

I advise you to pray grandfather to ask Chalvet[3] for La Harpe's *Cours de Littérature* which he is bound to have, and I advise you to read it. Perhaps you will find it a little boring, but it will give you polish, and I promise that in the end you will be well rewarded. I also advise you to look out my literature note-books, in which you will find the same things as you will be simultaneously reading in La Harpe. Such study is indispensable: you will find it so when you enter any circles of

---

meant that he was a rich man. In his house, to speak of 'money', or even to refer to the metal, was regarded as a vulgarity.

"Young Beyle conceived a horror of this town which persisted until his death. It was here that he came to know human beings and their low qualities. He passionately desired to go to Paris and live there by writing books and comedies. His father informed him that he did not wish his son's morals to be corrupted, and that the latter would not see Paris until he was thirty.

"From 1796 to 1799 young Beyle interested himself only in mathematics. He hoped to enter the École Polytechnique [a college of engineering], and to see Paris. In 1799 he took the first prize at the École Centrale [a school of engineering] (master, M. Dupuy). The eight pupils who took the second prize were admitted to the École Polytechnique two months later. The aristocratic party were expecting the arrival of the Russians in Grenoble. They used to exclaim:

'*O Rus, quando ego te aspiciam!*'

"This year the examiner, Louis Monge, did not come. At Paris everything was going to the devil.

"All the youngsters went off to Paris to take their examinations at the École Polytechnique itself. Beyle arrived in Paris on November 10th, 1799, the day after the eighteenth of Brumaire. Napoleon had just seized power."

[1] "In the original, *en exerçant particulièrement le coup de pried*, the last three words seem to be a mistake, by Beyle or a copyist, for *cou de pied*.

[2] "Mme Rebuffel, my cousin, had a daughter, Adèle, who showed signs of great intelligence. It seems to me, however, that she did not live up to her promise. After we had been a little in love with one another—a childhood's affair—these childish sentiments gave way to hatred and then to indifference, and since 1804 I have entirely lost sight of her." (*Vie de Henri Brulard*.)

[3] Grenoble's city librarian.

society that are worthy of the name. I wish you could sometimes go to the theatre, to well chosen pieces, for I am convinced that nothing does more to form good taste. I wish especially that you could see the best light operas: it would give you a taste for music and would cause you infinite pleasure. But be sure to remember that you can never go there without father. I would be delighted if he could appreciate my reasons for giving all this advice. I shall speak to him about it when I come to Grenoble. I advise you to try to read Plutarch's *Lives of the Great Men of Greece*: when you are further advanced in literature, you will realise that it was the reading of this work which formed the character of the man who possessed the fairest soul and greatest genius of them all, J. J. Rousseau. You might read Racine and the tragedies of Voltaire, if you are permitted. Ask grandfather to read you *Zadig* in the same way as he read it to me two years ago. I think it would also be a good idea for you to read *Le Siècle de Louis XIV*, if nobody objects. I know what you'll say: "What a lot of reading!" But, my dearest girl, it is by reading thoughtful works that one in turn discovers how to think and feel. In any case, read La Harpe. Farewell. I have no room on this sheet of paper for any more. I preferred to make the attempt this evening rather than not do so for several days.

———— 2 ————

TO HIS SISTER PAULINE

Paris, the 20th of Germinal, Year VIII
(Thursday, April 10th, 1800)

I cannot at all understand your silence, my dear Pauline. What can be the occupations that prevent you from writing to me? Dancing, I would suppose, were we not in Lent. But I'll wager you one thing: you are thinking to yourself that you must carefully prepare your letter and make a rough draft of it. That's the stupidest folly that can possess one, for, to have a good epistolary style, one must write exactly what one would say to the person if one saw him, only being careful not to write down repetitions to which, in conversation, a tone of voice or gesture might give some value. Have you started on La Harpe? I suppose you have, but I expect you haven't dared to tackle Plutarch: nevertheless I think you would do well to read him. You'll find in him the very picture of the daily life of the ancients, and that is most essential, because people are always talking about it, and talking about it very foolishly. In due course, and when you have finished Plutarch, you will be able to read Demoustier's *Lettres à Émilie sur la Mythologie*. I beg you, when you are studying M. Dubois's[1] *Cours de Littérature*, which is amongst my papers, to look carefully to see whether you can find a note-book entitled *Selmours*. If you find it, I beg you to take it and lock it in some corner where nobody will dig it up. Don't mention this to anybody, and give up the bad habit —if you still have it—of reading my letters to people.

How is the piano going? How are the lessons from the nuns? Try to have yourself taught a little mathematics; nothing could be more essential. If I were at Grenoble I would undertake the task with pleasure. Since I am not, I think that M. David might give you a few lessons: they would not cost papa very much, and would be of great use to you.

I suppose that if you took four or five lessons every ten days, it would cost from six to nine francs a month, and at the end of six months, for some forty francs, you would have learnt to reason better than a lot of men. Tell me what you think about this; and, if the notion attracts you, I'll propose it to papa, or you can ask him yourself. It would be worth more to you than forty years of your nuns and fifty pairs of stockings. A girl who intends to be a good mother should know how to make a stocking and should never touch a needle, especially in the precious days of youth. You will have scarcely any opportunity to educate yourself after you are twenty: meanwhile, when you have spent two hours in knitting, within the same period you could have read two hundred and fifty pages of some useful book, and what a difference! Be sure to remember that a pair of stockings costs six francs, and that nothing can make up for the thirty or forty hours of toil and the ten or twelve hours of tedium that it causes you. Do you ever go to the theatre? Tell me if a piece is being played at Grenoble entitled *L'Abbé de l'Épée*? Here in Paris it has reached its thirtieth performance. How is Caroline[2]? Is she losing some of that tale-bearing, tattling tone she had when I left? If she has the misfortune to have it still, try to make her understand that nothing is more justly detested. She really must be careful about it. She is just at the age at which character is formed; it was at this age that you yourself, cry-baby though you were, became a good and sympathetic person. What is Félicie[3] doing? How does Oronce[4] seem? Always remember that when I ask you a question I want to learn what you think, and not what everybody says.

[1] Dubois-Fontanelle, Professor of Literature at Grenoble École Centrale.
[2] Marie-Zénaïde-Caroline Beyle, younger sister of Henri and Pauline.
[3] Daughter of Romain Gagnon, Henri Beyle's uncle.
[4] Son of Romain Gagnon.

In general, one should never repeat another's opinion, not if it were that of the Pope, without having carefully weighed it: otherwise one is in danger of saying silly things that give a false impression of one's style of judgment. If you have been told something as a fact, it is possible that the person who told it to you may have had some emotional reason for deceiving you: so you must try to verify it when opportunity arises. Think about this a little, and, above all, answer me. If your ideas are in confusion, take my letter and answer it point by point, questioning yourself and setting down your opinion on each matter. I embrace you. Farewell. Greetings to everybody, to Marion and to Antoine[1].

. . . .

—— 3 ——

TO HIS SISTER PAULINE

April or May 1800

It's quite a long time, my sweet sister, since I made up my mind to reply in advance to the letters which you will certainly one day write to me, when you have less to do. But I happen at this moment to be hidden beneath a desk in the course of a game of hide-and-seek, and unfortunately am so well hidden that for ten minutes I have been sought in vain: so I am taking the opportunity of conversing with you. How is the reading? Have you started on La Harpe? I recommend him to you all the more because grandpapa will explain anything you cannot understand. Are you still going to the nuns? I have no great idea of that. I would prefer it if you gave them up, like the stockings.

Spend a lot of time in cultivating your intelligence, and leave manual work to human machines.

A treatise has just been published on the education of girls, by Mrs. Edgeworth, translated by C. Pictet, one of the collaborators of the Bibliothèque Britannique: papa probably knows it, it is said to be interesting, and it would be a good thing for you to read it.

What are your entertainments? Do you ever go to Claix? Do answer, I beg of you. By so doing you will serve two objects: the first, of giving me a great deal of pleasure, and the second, of forming your style.

[1] Family servants.

[37]

Goodness, I'm caught! The noise of my pen gave me away. Since I was the last to be caught, I'm not " it ", and I can go on for a moment. What is Caroline doing? And Gaëtan[1]? And Félicie?

Do you know if they can send me a copy of M. Dubois-Fontanelle's *Cours de Littérature?*

I'm doing nothing but ask you questions, so my letter is easy to answer. Answer it as soon as you can, and at length. I embrace you with all my heart.

———— 4 ————

TO HIS SISTER PAULINE

Milan, the 10th of Messidor[2] Year VIII of the Republic
(Sunday, June 29th, 1800)

I am very grateful, my dear Pauline, for the little letter you have written me. I only wish it were somewhat longer. I don't know when you will choose to put a stop to my complaints in this respect. You know that I'm at Milan, it is a city five times the size of Grenoble and quite well built. There is a church in Gothic style—that is to say, all in filigrees arranged in more than semicircular arches, which is astonishing when one thinks about it, but is not immediately striking like the sublime Pantheon. I think the top of the dome is higher than the gallery of the Pantheon. To have an idea of this latter, you must imagine a circular gallery, fifty or sixty feet long and as tall as four belfries of Saint-André piled one on top of the other. The church is not finished, and probably never will be. Its interior is, on the whole, not beautiful; the only astonishing thing about it is the infinite patience which it presupposes in the various craftsmen who have contributed to its construction. There are perhaps a thousand statues, varying in height from forty feet to six inches. I shall not tell you about the Mont Saint-Bernard; one day you'll read the description of it in one of the *Mille et Un Voyages en Italie.*

[1] Another son of Romain Gagnon.
[2] Henri Beyle set off on May 7th, 1800, to rejoin his cousins Pierre and Martial Daru in the Army of Italy, with no precise mission. Thus it was that he " entered Milan on a delightful morning of spring—and what a spring ! "
" From the end of May until October or November, when I was received as an ensign into the 6th Regiment of Dragoons, at Bagnolo or Romanengo, between Brescie and Cremona, I had five or six months of complete and heavenly happiness. From 1800 to 1821 Milan has been for me the place where I have constantly longed to live." (*Vie de Henri Brulard.*)

All I can tell you is that its difficulty has been extraordinarily exaggerated[1]. There is not a moment's danger to troops. I passed by the fort of Bard, a much more difficult mountain. Imagine a steep valley like that of the Vallée de Saint-Paul, near Claix. In the middle, a hillock; on this hillock, a fort. The road runs along the bottom of the valley, straight towards the fort, and passes beneath it within pistol-shot. We left the road at a distance of three hundred feet from the fort and climbed the hill under continual fire from it[2]. What troubled us most were our horses, which bounded five or six feet at every whistle of a bullet or cannonball. I don't know if you understand all this description, but I want to share with you this truly astonishing spectacle, and I have only a moment in which to write to you. Here in Milan there is a magnificent theatre. Just imagine it, the interior is as large as half of the place Grenette. The same opera is performed for a fortnight. The music is divine and the actors are detestable. All the boxes are reserved, with the result that we have only the pit and the box reserved for the General Staff. I am doing my utmost to learn a little Italian, but I have not been able to find a ———[3], so I am making very slow progress. I have received a far better impression of the Italians than one has of them in France. I have struck up an acquaintance with two or three, who truly amaze me with the wisdom of their ideas and the sense of honour that prevails in their hearts. One thing I was very far from expecting is the delightful amiability of the women of this country. You will not believe me, but truly at this moment I would be in despair if I had to return to Paris. We have spells of extraordinary heat, by which we are dreadfully overcome. At first we thought we could brave these spells by stuffing ourselves with ices, but we found that after refreshing us for a moment they made us hotter. I hope you will answer this long letter. Address your answer to Milan. I hope to be still there, or in the neighbourhood, when your letter arrives.

H. Beyle

. . . .

[1] " What ! The Saint Bernard pass—*is that all it is*? I kept on saying to myself. I was even so ill-mannered as to say it aloud a few times. . . ." (*Vie de Henri Brulard.*)

[2] " We thought that the army was forty leagues before us. Suddenly we found it halted by the fort of Bard. . . . This was how I came under fire for the first time. It was a sort of virginity that was as much of a burden to me as the other." (*Vie de Henri Brulard.*)

[3] A word has been torn off.

TO HIS SISTER PAULINE

July-August 1800

I can't think, my dear Pauline, what can be preventing you from writing to me. How is it that, in the tranquil life you lead, you cannot sacrifice a moment to a brother who loves you tenderly? We are suffering here from spells of heat such as the French cannot endure, we are all overwhelmed by them. Very recently I made a quite agreeable journey, which took me away for several days from the burning squares of this city. I went with Daru to accept the surrender of the fortress of Arona, and thus had occasion to visit the divine Borromaean isles. There are three of them: Isola Bella, Isola Madre, Isola dei Pescatori. Imagine a semicircular lake, about fifteen leagues long: the part of it that points towards Milan, or rather towards Buffatora, is fringed with delightful slopes. The Tessino, a superb river, debouches on this part of the lake. As one advances over these tranquil waters, the slopes turn into mountains, and the part of the lake near Switzerland is surrounded by haughty crags that remind one of the Bernard. These shores are very quiet: few houses, no agriculture, no trace of the detestable pergolas and palings that disfigure the celebrated shores of Lake Leman. Here nature is everywhere in evidence. From time to time we met a small skiff manned by two fishermen; and thus we proceeded for an hour and a half. Suddenly we put to shore and found ourselves at the foot of the fortress and of the town of Arona. I have never seen a more imposing sight. Imagine, on one side, an escarpment like that of the Gate of France at Grenoble; on the other side, a quite gentle slope, and on its summit an impregnable fort surrounded by five rings of fortification that make it impossible to storm, and surmounted by a slender, high tower flying the tricolour. Suddenly a salute of nineteen guns was fired, a rain of earth fell on the lake, for a moment muddying its clear waters. We disembarked, after having struggled for three-quarters of an hour against a fairly strong gale. Next morning, after visiting the fort, we re-embarked on Austrian gunboats. We put out from the shore, and at once our eyes were caught by a statue of good St. Charles: it is sixty-nine feet tall, and its pedestal twenty; with one hand it points majestically to the harbour; with the other hand St. Charles gathers a fold of his surplice—this fold is the doorway into the edifice. A man could stand upright inside the saint's nose; the statue is calm in the middle of the lake. Nothing had disturbed it for a long time until, very recently, at the siege of Arona, a bullet struck it in the chest, happily without damaging it. I have never seen so fair a sight: I cannot find the words to express my feelings. We sailed along peacefully. I was standing beside the admiral of the enemy flotilla, and made conversation with an aide-de-camp, a charming young man, apart from a few prejudices. After three hours' sailing we noticed in the middle of this divine lake a green mountain, and on its right a beach and a small white house. The island on the left was Isola Bella. The one on the right was Isola Madre. But I perceive that I am waxing loquacious: no matter. Now that you are beginning to catch a sight of this romantic situation, you will enjoy exploring its enchanting détours. Above all, do not show this letter to anybody. I still cannot help feeling that it would seem vastly ridiculous to chilly souls. I embrace you.

B.

——— 6 ———

TO HIS SISTER PAULINE

Saluces, the 15th of Frimaire, Year X
(Sunday, December 6th, 1801)

. . . .
I notice with great pleasure that you are reading Voltaire's tragedies. It is right that you should familiarise yourself with the masterpieces of our great writers: they will fashion both your intelligence and your heart. I advise you to read Racine, the shocking Crébillon and the charming La Fontaine. You will see what an immense distance separates Racine from Crébillon and this latter's crowd of imitators. After that you must tell me which of the two you like best, Corneille or Racine. Perhaps, at first, Voltaire will please you as much as either: but you will soon feel how greatly his fluent but empty verse is inferior to the richly furnished verse of tender Racine or majestic Corneille.

You might ask grandpapa for Montesquieu's *Lettres Persanes* and Buffon's *Histoire naturelle*, from the sixth volume onwards—the first five would not amuse you. I think, my dear Pauline, that these works, so various in kind, will afford you much entertainment—and at the same time you will make the acquaintance of their immortal authors,

But that is enough chatter on one subject. Give me full details of your activities with Mlle Lassaigne and of how you spend your time. Perhaps you are a little bored; but remember that in this world we never achieve perfect happiness, and profit by your youth in order to learn. The knowledge we gain follows us all through the remainder of our lives, it is always useful to us, and sometimes causes us to forget a deal of woe. For my part, when I read Racine, Voltaire, Molière, Virgil, *Orlando Furioso*, I forget the rest of the world. By " world " I mean that crowd of people of no consequence who so often vex us, and not my friends, who are always present with me, deep in my heart. It is there, my dear Pauline, that you have imprinted your name in ineffaceable characters. I think of you a thousand times a day. It is a delight to me to think of how I shall find you again—grown, beautiful, educated, lovable and loved by everyone.

. . . .

———— 7 ————

TO HIS SISTER PAULINE

Paris, the 11*th of Nivôse, Year XI*[1]
(*Saturday, January* 1*st*, 1803)

Souvent, las d'être esclave et de boire la lie
De ce calice amer que l'on nomme la vie,
Las du mépris des sots qui suit la pauvretè
Je regarde la tombe, asile souhaité;
Je souris à la mort volontaire et prochaine,
Je me prie en pleurant d'oser rompre ma chaine,
Et puis mon coeur s'écoute et s'ouvre à la faiblesse,
Mes parents, mes amis, l'avenir, ma jeunesse,
Mes écrits imparfaits; car, à ses propres yeux,
L'homme sait se cacher d'un voile spécieux.
A quelque noir destin qu'elle soit asservie,
D'une étreinte invisible il embrasse la vie;

[1] Beyle had resigned his commission and installed himself in Paris, with a promise from his father of an allowance of 150 francs a month. At the date of this letter he had recently taken a room in the rue d'Angiviller, on the sixth floor, overlooking the colonnade of the Louvre.

[42]

Il va chercher bien loin, plutôt que de mourir,
Quelque prétexte ami, pour vivre et pour souffrir.
Il a souffert, il souffre: aveugle d'espérance,
Il se traîne au tombeau, de souffrance en souffrance
Et la mort, de nos maux le remède si doux,
Lui semble un nouveau mal, le plus cruel de tous![1]

Don't you feel these lines sweetly penetrating into your soul, expanding and soon reigning there? For my part, they seem to me the most moving lines I have yet read in any language. My first intention was to copy them out whilst they are still fresh in my mind, in order to send them to you with my next letter; but here I am at my writing-table, I have half an hour to myself, why not write to her with whom I would like continually to speak? I plan to come and see you at the beginning of Thermidor[2]. At first I proposed to travel a month later, but what folly! We have so few days of life in store, and perhaps many fewer to spend together! Let us hasten to enjoy them, let us live together and let our days slip by in the bosom of friendship. I am learning here, no doubt of it; but how cold is knowledge by comparison with feeling! God, seeing that man was not strong enough to feel all the time, decided to give him knowledge, to rest him from his passions in his youth and to occupy him during his last days.

Unhappy and deserving of much sympathy is the chilly heart that knows only how to know! Ah, of what use is it to me to know that the sun goes round the earth, or the earth round the sun, if I waste in learning these things the days that were given me in which to enjoy them? Such is the folly of many a man, my dear Pauline; but it shall not be ours.

I was forgetting to tell you the name of the author of these sweet lines I send you: André Chénier composed them a few days before the Terror that caused his death.

. . . .

[1] Often, weary of being a slave and of drinking the lees of that bitter cup which is known as life, weary of the scorn of fools which pursues poverty, I look towards the tomb, that longed-for refuge; I smile upon death, so willing and so near, and beseech myself, weeping, to dare to break my bonds; and then my heart gives ear and opens itself to weakness—my parents, my friends, the future, my youth, my imperfect writings; for a man can hide himself from his own gaze behind a specious veil. To whatever black destiny his life may be the servant, he clings to it with an invisible embrace; rather than die, he will search very far for some friendly pretext for living and suffering. He has suffered, he continues to suffer: blind with hope, he drags himself to the tomb from suffering to suffering; and death, sweet remedy of our ills, seems to him but a new ill, the cruellest of all !

[2] The eleventh month of the French Republican year, from July 20th to August 18th.

TO ÉDOUARD MOUNIER[1]

Paris, 21st of Nivôse, XI
(Tuesday, January 11th, 1803)

What could I have found to tell you, my dear Mounier, during six months of my life that have been spent in the most utter folly? I at last made the acquaintance of that passion for which my hot youth so ardently yearned. But now when sombre love, the subject of so many jests by my friends, has given place to amiable gallantry, I too can jest about it with you. Yes, my friend, I was in love, and in love in a singular manner, with a young person of whom I had but caught a glimpse, and who requited the most deeply felt passion only with disdain. But at last all that is over: I have no more time for dreams, I dance almost every day. In my quality of madman I put myself under the tutelage of my friends, who were able to find no other means of curing me than to make me fall in love. Thus I have become smitten with the very pretty wife of a banker; I have danced with her several times, I have had myself introduced into her circles, I have just written her my fifth letter, she has sent back three of them unread, the first she tore up: according to all the rules, she is bound to read the fifth, and will answer the sixth or seventh. Six months ago she married the brilliant equipage and the two millions of a lout who is so banal as to be jealous of her—jealous of a woman of Paris! He has chosen a fine time to be jealous; so I count on having good sport with the brute. The day before yesterday he staged me a priceless comedy. Malli had given her handkerchief and money into my safekeeping; then she left sooner than she had told me she would, with the result that Monsieur her husband sought me out, during a quadrille in which I was engaged at the other end of the room, in order to ask me for his wife's " things "! He was so comically serious as he gave me this fine message that everybody burst out laughing: it still tickles me as I write. Yesterday evening he was cool towards me, and when I said that I was

---

[1] Son of Jean-Joseph Mounier, Deputy to the Assemblée Constituante, Édouard Mounier was a childhood's friend of Beyle's whom the latter describes as follows in the *Vie de Henri Brulard*. " Dull, adroit, delicately sly, a typical Dauphinois just like the minister Casimir Périer, but this latter is more Dauphinois than he. Édouard Mounier has a drawling accent, although educated at Weimar, he is a peer of France, a baron and a worthy judge of the Cour de Paris." (December 1835).

delighted to witness the return of the use of the rapier and of embroidered coats, he informed me, with a judicial air, that such things were merely one more opportunity for young idiots to trouble society.

Everybody congratulates me on the rapidity of my progress. I am Mme B's first lover: she has refused men who were worth much more than myself. I keep on telling myself this in order to tickle my conceit, but in truth these joys of vanity are very short-lived. I rejoice for a moment when, leaning on an arm of her chair, I induce her to smile, or when I make a little manikin with the end of her handkerchief; but when my pride seeks to congratulate me on the difference between my success of this year and that of last, I grow absent-minded; I remember the charming smile of her whom I still love despite myself; I feel tears straying into my eyes at the thought that I shall never see her again— you must agree that I'm a terrible fool! Here I am, thrown back on my own resources. After all, what did that girl do to make me love her so much? She would smile at me one day in order to have the pleasure of avoiding me the next; she would never permit me to say a word to her. On one single occasion I tried to write to her, and she scornfully rejected my letter. Finally, of all that violent love, the only token I have left is a fragment of glove. You must agree, dear Mounier, that my friends are right and that for an officer of dragoons I have played a most brilliant rôle in the affair. If she had only loved me—but the cruel fair continually made a sport of tormenting me. No, she is naught but a coquette; so I hereby forget her for ever, and if I were to see her at this moment I should be as indifferent towards her as she was towards me in the days of my most lively ardour.

But forgive me, my dear fellow, I am boring you with my follies. I shall not do so again: I feel that I am forgetting her. Am I not to have the pleasure of embracing you this winter? Come and have a brief look at this Paris of ours, now that it is in its full lustre: I am sure that, philosopher though you are, it will please you much more than in the spring. In any case, hope that we will go wine-harvesting together in our Dauphiné. Come to us, my dear Mounier, and compare our gay valley-peasants with your Bretons. Will not Mlle Victorine[1] be of the party? In any case, present my homage to her, and rest assured of the *endless friendship of*[2]

H. B.

---

[1] Victorine Mounier, the recipient's sister, with whom Beyle was in love. He writes to the brother only in the hope of shining in the eyes of the sister.

[2] In English in the original.

TO HIS SISTER PAULINE

Paris, 1803

Send me a reply quickly, my dear Pauline, or I shall suppose you to be in prison, in solitary confinement or dead. Why do you not write to me in your trouble? Can you answer me that, mademoiselle? Have you no excuse? Is it not somewhat scatterbrained of you to complain that you are unhappy, and then not to seek consolation? Do you know how I shall set about consoling you? I shall set about ceasing to love you at all; and then it will cost you every effort to recapture my friendship. Come now, child! What is the meaning of all this self-torment? Take care, nothing is so ageing as grief; and, just to punish you, I am going to treat you as if you were an old woman: I shall tell you some anecdotes which I read this morning:

M. de Thiers was the friend of Mme d'Erigny. This lady had her arm and left leg very painfully burnt by a cauldron of boiling water. De Thiers did not go to see her for six weeks; and, when he appeared, Mme d'Erigny said to him: " So this is how you forsake your friends! Do you know that, during all these six weeks in which you haven't come to see me, I have been suffering like a poor wretch, that I haven't shut an eye? "

" What! Has it been as long as that? "

" Quite as long. "

" How quickly time passes! "

A fine sketch of an egoist. But to continue, since you probably will not see the pamphlet in which I read the story, here's another:

The King was hunting in the woods of Versailles. At a distance of three or four leagues from the town, a bodyguard fell while galloping, and broke his thigh. The King turned to M. de Rochechouart and said to him: " Monsieur, you have your coach, do me the kindness of taking this young man back to Versailles."

Next day M. de Rochechouart recounted the episode at a house he was visiting. " The poor wretch caused me terrible anguish," he said. " Every movement of the carriage subjected him to frightful pain. He screamed, he ground his teeth; all this put me in a state which you can well imagine. Fortunately, I remembered that I had in my pockets some eau de la reine de Hongrie."

" You gave him some? "

" No, I swallowed a gulp of it, and that kept me going as far as Versailles."[1]

These two sketches are genuine: observe the style of narration, the right tone, simple, easy and concise. A provincial would not have failed to insert pathos, or even horror. He would have described the breaking of the thigh, have spoken of the blood. The name for the talent that frees M. Suard from these faults is subtlety.

In society everything must be said with simplicity and ease. One should say to oneself, and never say it to others, that the company is met for pleasure, and should suppress anything that might diminish whatever pleasure you are capable of giving. To give pleasure to people, you must concern yourself with them, which means talking very little about yourself. Your innuendoes must be lively; and there is a clear sign by which you can tell that you are giving pleasure. In nearly every company, what you have to reckon with is human vanity. A vain man seeks at every instant to discover some new advantage in himself: as soon as he has discovered one, he gives you a clear sign of it—he laughs. Laughter is nothing else but that: the sudden glimpse of an advantage which we did not know we had, or which we had lost from sight.

. . . .

———— 10 ————

TO HIS SISTER PAULINE

May 1804

My dear child, your letter distresses me greatly. I shall write to you every second day to distract you. I am writing today to papa to thank him for the two hundred and four francs he sends me. They could not be more timely: for a week I had holes in my shoes, and I needed all my ingenuity to insert over the hole a small patch blackened with ink.

I am in debt to the pension where I eat, and where I am scarcely known; I am in debt to my janitor; I am in debt to my tailor, who kept on dunning me every morning; I pawned my watch long ago. For a fortnight I have gone nowhere, for lack of a dozen sous in my pocket;

[1] An anecdote repeated in *Lamiel* in 1841.

I am neglecting M. Daru, General Michaud[1], Mlle Duchesnois[2]! What a lot of reasons for despair!

Well, the fact is, I've never laughed so much. Three years ago I would have been in despair: since then I have learnt reason. The life of the most powerful man of all time, Alexander the Great, and the life of the most humble city-dweller are alike in that they are a mixture of a few vivid delights and numerous moments when a man, if he is wise, is happy, or, if he is not, feels bored and is unhappy.

Boredom is excusable only at your age, when one has not yet learnt to avoid it. Later, a man who is bored is a fool and a burden on others, and is consequently shunned by everybody.

Permit yourself today to possess one ounce of boredom, your neighbours will notice it and will shun you; next day you will have a pound of it; the day after that, two, and gradually you become stupid.

I have passed through all these states.

Men have various resources against boredom.

First of all, when one is bored, one must exercise the body, that's the surest method. For this reason I often rode on horseback; I sought to be present at duels—to become passionately interested, in fact. When one has passions, one is never bored; without them, one is stupid.

But this principle requires thorough explanation: on this subject the charming authoress of *Valérie*[3] says a very true thing: "*Whims*" (little passions lasting a fortnight or a month) "*give charm to life: passions kill it.*"

I shall now proceed to tell you that I have discovered this for myself (I often quote myself, because I am the man whose heart I know best.)

Man, as a moral creature, is divided into the *heart*, or centre of the passions, and the *head*, or centre of calculation and judgement. One can succeed, with the help of sincerity, in approximately knowing one's heart: to know one's head, one must have very little pride, and, since one always has pride, one never knows it well. This is the correct meaning of the saying that it is difficult to know oneself.

In Italy and at Paris I have committed follies that might have cost me everything, even honour. For example, for a whole evening I rode behind a coach as a flunkey. I took from a library a book in which I had been told letters were hidden. It all passed off, by good luck and by

[1] Beyle had been his aide-de-camp in Italy.

[2] His friend Crozet had recently introduced him to Mlle. Duchesnois, whom he went to applaud at the Théâtre Français almost every evening. "She has a delightful nature and is much less ugly than I had supposed . . . in future, when I am about to be presented to somebody, I must write down the compliment which I intend to pay. On the spur of the moment, I am at a loss." (*Journal*, April 24th, 1804).

[3] The novel by Mme de Krudener, which had just appeared.

a frank audacity which was inspired in me by passion and makes me shudder to this day.

Nevertheless, it all became known, even matters concerning which I had confided in nobody: I was told that I had been seen on the box of a carriage, with a livery on my back, etc. etc.

Observe the great difference between a man and a woman! A ten-thousandth part of these adventures would have spelt perpetual ruin to Lucrece herself: that is what you must remember. An intelligent man says to women: Be pretty if you can, be respected you must. 'Tis said, and 'tis all too true, that respect is the opinion of the greatest number: the greatest number is an ass; must one therefore commit follies? No, but often one must abstain from being reasonable.

. . . .

——— II ———

TO HIS SISTER PAULINE

June 1804

. . . .

The other day I was talking of M. Rebuffel to one of the friends of that excellent man, one of those who loved him most. He was under many obligations to him; in a word, he cherished him. We came to speak of the matter of mourning. " Why, I wore it a fortnight," said this friend, " as the *Almanach national* prescribed."

I confess I was stupefied, although I was already familiar with this characteristic of the Parisian animal: I had never seen the animal so well in its natural condition, or from so near.

Faced with the alternative of being embarrassed by those who love us or of not being loved at all, I would be compelled to choose love. Perfection certainly lies between, but it is very rare: where is it to be found? Only amongst entirely reasonable people; and how many of them are there?

I hope that you are working a little, and that this will have afforded you distraction—unless your trouble comes from some secret passion: in which case, tell me of it frankly. On this head, you can be sure of the deepest secrecy. Besides, I know almost all the young people of Grenoble, through my friends I can make the acquaintance of the others, and I can be of some service to you. If this is your trouble, we will explore the matter to the end. In any case, never forget that father has provoked envy, and that we will be used more severely than others, especially having the misfortune to have excited the jealousy of our uncle, who would be believed as a member of the family. I became completely convinced of this trait in his character when I was at Échelles with André and Mallein; he expressly turned the conversation upon you, in order to say that you were working too much. If you had not been working, he would have said that you were dissipated. I quickly took this wrongful accusation upon myself, since the occasion was important.

Despite his intention, his malignity turned to your advantage; for since Caroline and you are a sort of anchorites in Grenoble, André (you know whom I mean[1]) became very interested in you both, and especially in you, as a result of an odd circumstance. On the day before my departure I accompanied you to the rue des Vieux-Jésuites. You remember how, as we turned into the street, I heard somebody call out to me: it was André, who had been escorting Mme Rézicourt. That evening you had on your head a veil like the pretty *mezzaro* which Genoese women wear—it gives an air of sweet distress. Perhaps you were, in fact, slightly distressed, with the result that he created for himself a perfectly sweet picture of you: I saw that he had been struck by it. In his eyes, your outward appearance expressed a woman's sweetest characteristic, that tender affliction, that gentle sympathy, which causes a man to think (confusedly): " She will share in my grief. She is kind, simple." It needs less than that to cause love to burgeon: André never stopped talking of your sweet appearance.

Nevertheless I would not have him win your tenderness. For the sake of your happiness, you must not marry a man with whom you are in love, and I'll tell you why: all love comes to an end, however violent it may have been—and the more violent, the more quickly it will end than others. After love comes distaste—nothing could be more natural—whereupon the couple avoid each other for a time. No harm in that; but if one is married one is obliged to remain together, one is surprised to find nothing but vexation in a thousand little things that used to spell happiness. A young man of my acquaintance loved a young lady *e era riamato*[2]. In the little games they played together, this damsel had a habit of stealing his handkerchief. It was charming. She did it a few days ago, and the young man thought the action utterly stupid.

---

[1] M. H. Martineau thinks that the person referred to was François Périer-Lagrange, who was to marry Pauline in 1808. (Cf. letter No. 37.)
[2] And was loved in turn.

They will not see each other for a year, and then they will be friends, they will remember with pleasure the time when they loved each other.

If, on the other hand, they were living together, they would have seen each other every hour of the day. The woman's vanity would have been wounded, the man would have been bored, and all their lives they would have mortally detested one another; instead of which, if one marries for reasons of good sense, one is never irritated, because one gets approximately what one expected. There is a false kind of good sense, professed by all the fools in the world, who use it to reproach people of intelligence; but there is also a true good sense, which one must study because it leads to life's happiness. In general, every ill comes from ignorance of the truth, every sorrow and grief comes from expecting of men that which they are not in a condition to give you.

Think about that, my dear Pauline, and write to me often, telling me whatever chance thoughts occur to you. Send me a character-sketch of Fany du Cont., it will be most useful to me. I believe I have discovered that all your passions, mesdames womankind, come down in the end to nothing but vanity. I wish to investigate this opinion; and if I find it to be true, you will cause me to commit no more follies.

. . . .

———— 12 ————

TO HIS SISTER PAULINE

3rd of Fructidor, Year XII
(*Tuesday, August 21st*, 1804)

I have great need of you here, my dear Pauline: there are moments when the soul, weary of work, seeks to love, attaches itself more and more to the objects of its affection, wraps itself up in them and would give anything in the world to be at their side. For several days I have been overcome by this access of feeling, which returns all too often for my happiness. As long as the soul is cold or but moderately agitated, Paris is the city of happiness; but as soon as it again becomes tender, I yearn for Grenoble, tedious though it is. Could I but see you here, with one other person! How great would be my happiness to be able to pass the evening in your midst, far from all intrigues and worldly cares! Could I but assemble around me a family such as I believe could exist! I very much fear that in our youth we never have this joy; and that is why we shall spend the season of love without entirely tasting its bliss; and it will be only when our enfeebled souls no longer feel but weakly, and our aged faces have grown stiff, that we shall be able to live together.

I shall tell you as a deep secret that today, the 3rd of Fructidor[1], I began taking lessons in rhetoric from La Rive, the celebrated tragic actor. Not that I am still interested in this art; but my physicians have advised me to seek distraction. They told me that I would perish of melancholy if I did not follow this course. I go there with Martial Daru, to whom we shall in future refer as Pacé[2]. So I went this morning. I came home at eleven o'clock to work, but nothing interested me. I needed to be with people whom I could love, I needed to speak to them, to clasp them to my bosom, and not to work at learning new truths. I took down some novels, but all seemed to me silly and inflated instead of tender. I tried to read *La Nouvelle Héloïse*; but I know it by heart. So I spent my whole day in daydreams, and now I am going to the theatre in search of distraction. Not that this state in which I find myself, this superabundance of tenderness, is in any way painful: it would be happiness, if there were anyone to whom I could say: "I love you!" But all I can see here are wits or half-souls. All the young women here bore me: their tenderness is but simpering and studied little graces—nothing that is absolutely free, natural, vigorous. All that I love is at Grenoble, or eighty leagues from here. I can write only to you; the other[3] has perhaps forgotten me: that is the cause of my melancholy. Nevertheless, by dint of meditation, I discovered a way of writing to her; but what will she think of my letter? Will she answer it? Does she not, perhaps, love another? I am hatching a great folly: before returning to Grenoble, I want to go incognito to the town where she lives and sate myself there with the pleasure of seeing her. 'Tis a romantic method, but it will give me much delight and does no harm to anybody; I do not see why I should resist the temptation. I shall shortly set about economising for the purpose. She would indeed be astonished if, whilst taking an evening walk, in the public gardens, at nightfall, she noticed me amongst the trees.

. . . .

[1] August 20th.
[2] "Pacé and I are taking our first lesson from La Rive." (*Journal*, August 21st, 1804.)
[3] Victorine Mounier, at Rennes.

TO HIS SISTER PAULINE

11th of Fructidor, Year XII
(Wednesday, August 29th, 1804)

Your letter dismays me beyond all expression. You are about to commit a folly. Do remember that to go to Voreppe[1] without your father's knowledge will at once degrade you from the position that you are capable of occupying in society, and will demean you to the rank of girls who have gone astray.

Such is the truth in my soul and conscience. I swear to you that I shall not say anything to anyone. Do think that in your place you see only the happiness of a roving life. You disregard all its inconveniences. One of these days you will be receiving a letter which is the best answer to yours of the 5th. You will see from it how sad one sometimes becomes at being isolated, and also what a difference there is between you and me.

Since I am a man, my heart is three or four times less sensitive, because I have three or four times as much power of reason and experience of the world—a thing which you women call hard-heartedness.

As a man, I can take refuge in having mistresses. The more of them I have, and the greater the scandal, the more I acquire reputation and brilliance in society. I left Grenoble when I was seventeen; now I am twenty-one. In this interval I have had as many women as a man well could have. Well, two years ago I began to be disgusted with this manner of life—this to the point at which, despite my age of twenty-one years and my fortunate position of not having twelve francs' income a year, I would marry another Pauline if I found one such who was not my sister, and I would be ready to live by no matter what trade—as a printer, for example, or a maker of newspapers, or something even drearier.

You, for your part, have a much more tender soul, and have not filled it with distaste by four years of life in high society. Before two years were out you would be burning to find a man whom you could love. You would desire this so much that you would end by persuading yourself (like the famous Englishwoman, Mary Wollstonecraft Godwin) that you had found him, and you would have done nothing of the sort. By dint of desiring something, in this matter in which illusion is so easy,

---

[1] A community in the Isère, fourteen kilometres from Grenoble.

one ends by persuading oneself that one has achieved it. *And the irreparable fault of having made a mistake removes for ever the possibility of finding an husband worthy of one.*

Bear in mind this truth: who would wish, even if he were in love with her, to marry a girl who had run away from her parents?

I am the least prejudiced man I have ever met, and I assure you that I would not. If I were in love with her, I would " trifle " with her, and then leave her.

Bear in mind that you will not find in society twenty souls that understand yours; that I, who have had twenty times as much experience as you could ever have, do not know four such. Pay heed to this number. One of them is Mlle Victorine Bigillion[1], who has just done exactly what you would like to do. She lived a solitary life at Saint-Ismier; this strengthened her passions and her will. This latter is so strong that her father became convinced that she was " crazy ". Whereupon she was shut up, almost as if she were a madwoman. The poor child was driven to desperation; she ran away as far as to Moirans; she was caught, and at present, I think, is in prison at the Grande-Chartreuse, where she will remain at the pleasure of her parents, people whom she has offended in every sort of way. Her only way of getting out would be to marry, and who would want her?

Such are the true facts of this adventure. Try to get somebody to tell you about it, and you will see how the public judges strong-willed souls. If it saw them as they are, it would merely be jealous of them; but it does not understand them, and thinks them mad.

There never was a more direct warning to you than that of poor Victorine.

In Italy I knew a woman named Angelina[2], whom I loved beyond all expression. She had exactly your character. She spent her youth free from folly; indeed, she spent at least two years of it shut up in a convent, against her will. Finally she married, and for eight years has been the happiest of women.

Bear in mind that Saint-Preux is an imaginary character, like all the heroes in novels.

. . . .

[1] " Mlle Victorine was possessed of intelligence, and thought much; she was freshness personified. Her face, which was in perfect harmony with the sashed windows of the apartment which she occupied with her two brothers. . . .

" We lived there in all innocence, around this walnut table covered with a cloth of raw canvas.

" We lived at this time like young rabbits playing in a wood and nibbling the wild thyme." (*Vie de Henri Brulard.*)

[2] Signora Pietragrua. (Cf. letters 38, 82 *et passim.*)

TO HIS SISTER PAULINE

Year XIII
(1804)

You will find in society, my dear child, many desiccated souls. Such people have never in their lives had a moment of sorrow, of that anointing sorrow which you and I have so often suffered; as a rule they are susceptible only of two passions, vanity and love of money. This desiccation comes from the soul. To us it often happens, as to other sensitive souls, that we weep at an idea that enters our heads. Just now, whilst returning from purchasing the paper on which I write, I passed through a street named des Orties, and well named[1], for nobody enters it. One of its sides is formed by the majestic gallery of the Museum. This gallery is very high and very black; the street is narrow and silent, and on the other side are very tall houses. I met there a woman of forty, aged by poverty, who carried her child on her back and sang in order to beg. This fact, together with the appearance of the street, which had already begun to affect me, awoke my pity. Lending an ear, I heard that she was singing a song of the guardroom: this gripped my heart and made tears come into my eyes. I quickened my pace, and it was not until I was on the Pont Royal that I realised I had not given her anything. There are so many destitute charlatans in Paris that, when one is not rich, it is necessary to refrain from giving. Nevertheless I regretted not having given to this poor mother. Then it occurred to me that the reason why the song had made tears come into my eyes was that the words, which were lewd, were bound to destroy in the spectators' heart that very sentiment upon which she depended for some charity. If any mother seeing her pass by with her child upon her back took pity on her, thinking: "One day I, too, might be reduced to that", nevertheless, when she heard the song, her pity would cease. "In any case, I would never be immoral," she would say. "This woman certainly is immoral, her song proves it, and it is certainly her immorality that has brought her to this."[2]

. . . .

[1] The street of nettles.

[2] "A poor person who does not say a word to me, who does not emit lamentable and 'tragic' cries, as is customary in Rome, and who eats an apple as he drags himself along the ground, like the legless cripple of a week ago—such a person immediately moves me almost to tears." (*Vie de Henri Brulard.*)

TO HIS SISTER PAULINE

7th of Ventôse, Year XIII (Shrove Tuesday)
(February 26th, 1805)

What of the three hundred francs that were due to arrive at the end of the week? It is three weeks since that week went by.

Fiez-vous, fiez-vous aux vains discours des hommes![1]

I was singing this song this morning, when my tailor came, for the tenth time, to ask for a payment on account. I said to him: " Trust, trust in the vain utterance of men ", etc. etc.

Tell me what has happened in the matter; tell father that if he is willing to grant me an advance, it could not come at a better moment. Can it be that uncle has been visiting Grenoble? Or has my last letter to father failed to remove the sort of coldness he feels towards me?

It is I who can complain, and it is I who am reproached. I have, in truth, no *right* to complain; but still less do I deserve to be scolded. For, after all, my whole crime is to have asked, in Vendémiaire[2], for an advance that I am now promised in Ventôse[3]—and then they speak of sensibility! *O tempora! o mores!* But let us hasten to laugh at it all, for fear of being obliged to weep. Indeed, we do wrong to think men better than they are, and doubly wrong to believe in their words, we who continually repeat that one must believe only in deeds. The fact is that a truly sensitive soul knows men in general, but often, without suspecting it, makes an exception of the man with whom he has to do, especially when that man is his father. The intriguer, on the other hand, has no knowledge of men and passions, but knows by heart the individual whom he seeks to influence: this difference between people is worth noting.

Give me full details of your present life: I reflect that it is eleven months since I left Grenoble. Tell me about the changes that have meanwhile taken place in " local customs "; for mankind is in a continual state of revolution. Where is the family dwelling at present? And, to pick up my thread, what of that promise of three hundred francs? Is it

---

[1] Trust, trust in the vain utterance of men!
[2] First month of the French Republican year, September 22nd to October 21st.
[3] Sixth month of the French Republican year, February 20th to March 20th.

a bad joke? Or is there some good intention behind it? In this case, you can tell father the truth, which is that, in this expectation, I have had clothes made, for the price of which I am now being tormented.

For the rest, apart from these small unpleasantnesses, to which I bend my mind only with distaste, I was never so happy. My existence in society was too vigorous—too brilliant, I make bold to say—to be in any way graceful. When I was present, I was well received; but in my absence people spoke ill of my actions. I have changed all that by doing less to thrust myself forward: let the reader take note.

My attitude is decided; I expect from father only the amount of my portion, which he almost cannot refuse me. I shall put these twenty or thirty thousand francs in the bank, and I shall work like a nigger, leaving Claix, le Cheylas and all fine expectations to Caroline, who will end by laying her hands on them, with the help of her hypocrisy. This, I think, is the only course still open to me. I have the example of MM. Barthelon, Flory, grandfather Périer, etc. In two years I shall return to Paris, and there, perhaps, we shall one day be able to live happily together.

Voilà belle Pauline, à quel point nous en sommes!

Amidst all this worry, yesterday, the 7th of Ventôse, I garnered a delightful day—a day which, when all is weighed, was the finest in all my life.[1] From noon until half-past three I made a public appearance that was positively above the human—something that Molière might have written and Molé acted. After all, you know how ugly I am: women whom I had offended complimented me on the figure I cut! I was in stockings, breeches, black waistcoat, bronze coat, superb cravat and jabot. Eh, what a conceited ass am I to tell you all this! But I am thinking aloud in your company.

Is it not a provoking thing that I am held up in my projects simply because this evening I cannot go to the Français? Perhaps I shall have greater successes, but I shall never display as much talent; I had never in my life done anything approaching it. This is the first time, at the age of twenty-two years and one month, that I have been able to gain enough ascendancy over myself to be amiable from calculation and not from passion.

I shall tell you about it all *viva voce*, and you will perceive that the song I quoted at the beginning of this letter is something much more than a song. Bear that in mind, and take care never to let yourself be carried away by the pretty things that you will find men doing for you.

. . . .

[1] " I displayed great talent. This is the first time I have seen so much of it in myself. It is assuredly a case of finding joy in vanity. Ah, well! . . . it is love alone that makes me find sweetness in the memory of my day. The only happiness I desire is that which I can obtain from the love of Mélanie, all else is of small account." (*Journal*, February 25th, 1805.)

TO HIS SISTER PAULINE

Paris, the 25th of Germinal, Year XIII
(Easter Monday, April 15th, 1805)

That Fate who, at his will, makes us run or halt, leap for joy or perish of languishment, and who manipulates us like jumping-jacks, has for a week prevented me from answering your divine letter. I think Fate does not even take the trouble to pull the strings, that he frankly laughs at us, and that he relies upon our follies to produce the bizarre movements that make him laugh.

Well, let us imitate Fate: it is always profitable to imitate the master. He induced me to show your last letter to one of my friends, whom I know to be a man of much intelligence. He had scarcely read half of it when he wanted to set off post-haste to marry you. He was swept away, enthusiastic, and sought to be physically whisked away in a carriage. I held him back by the sleeve.

" You will create a fine scandal at Grenoble! That's a fine idea!"

" Very fine. You tell me she's pretty! "

" But there are a thousand difficulties. For example, you are married, you are thirty-six," etc. etc.

In short, I sweated blood and water, as Jesus Christ had done exactly 1805 years before, and approximately at the same hour. But I was not crucified, which is why I am writing to you.

Thereupon, to console himself, this gentleman took a pen and a large sheet of paper and set about covering the whole of it with the following words: " Mlle Pauline, sublime! " I send you a sample of it.

When his admiration permitted him to see more clearly, " What a taste for witticism, my friend! " he said. " What distinction, why, it's marvellous! That sort of thing is not taught in the provinces! I see through your affair, it's an appalling intrigue! "

" What d'you mean, an intrigue? "

" Yes, an intrigue. You often see madame R——, who has quarrelled with my wife."

" What d'you mean, quarrelled? "

" All these ' what d'you means ' of yours," said L——, " they'll never cease! Yes, quarrelled. This is all a dark deed of blind-man's-buff."

" Yes, indeed, it is a very sinister game."

" Mme R—— and you, you conspired to fabricate this letter. You sent it to your sister. Whilst copying it out, the child gave it that candid charm of which your black souls are ignorant, and you have read it to me in order to make me get myself divorced. 'Tis mighty good of you; you present yourself in a fine role! "

Mme R. is an old person of twenty-two, as pretty as Raphael's virgins, full of intelligence and of sentiments similar to yours, but nevertheless not nearly approaching you.

He went off to publish it everywhere that I had a sister with more wit and grace than he had ever seen united in a single person.

If ever you come here and enter into this circle, your reputation is made. I shall give some details concerning it, because it is possible that you may allow yourself to be tempted and to set off from Grenoble as soon as you have received my letter.

Six years ago, eight or nine girls were receiving instruction at a school almost as awe-inspiring as that of mademoiselle Lassaigne. Despite the school, they were intelligent; and their intelligence brought them together. They vowed to see each other when they were married, whatever might be the circumstances of their husbands. They kept their word: six of them married men of fairly unequal fortunes: this does not prevent each of them from receiving in her turn. Apart from seven or eight relatives, invited from duty, all the rest of the company is young, gay and witty. (This is a clever way of telling you that I am all of these things.) The atmosphere of the house is lethal for fools, they quickly escape and cry the news everywhere that the place is an abyss, a rendezvous of evil-natured persons who respect nothing and mock at everything since God made the world. They don't say it to our faces, because they live at a long distance from us, but they think it.

If you have not enough money to leave home, the remedy is simple: come and learn banque with Mante[1] and me. There are twenty women here who keep gaming-houses and, in five or six hours of an occupation less arduous than knitting a stocking, earn fifteen or twenty thousand francs. You will do likewise, and at the same time will enjoy that liberty which you so much desire, and the charms of a most attractive circle. Here liberty is at its peak; this is the country for you; I don't understand why you don't at once take the diligence. You are made to have every possible success, and in truth (to speak in terms of our future) this is the

---

[1] " An income of six thousand francs won at banque with a friend as reliable as Mante, will free me from all embarrassments and allow me to enjoy all the pleasures of that sensibility which nobody will ever know." (*Journal*, February 11th, 1805.)

place where you can most advantageously set about the manufacture of happiness.

On the subject of happiness, I shall have the happiness of seeing you when father has sent me the money to pay my debts. Why, the abundance in which he keeps me is beginning to frighten me! I fear that he is putting himself to inconvenience for my sake, and that it is for me to set bounds to his kindnesses, since he himself knows none. Truly, his kindnesses are boundless.

Be prepared, then, to work hard during the fifty or sixty days which I shall have the happiness of spending at your feet. I shall requite you by ceaselessly scolding you. Pending these struggles, I send you an article from a journal, which, contrary to its custom, makes good sense, and will help you to perfect the talent which causes you to make conquests at a range of a hundred and forty leagues.

Write to me soon, and I shall not show anybody any more of your letters. Did you see Mante? Perhaps he will lend you Tracy. What does the family say? When I come, I hope to find that you have eight or ten real-life sketches ready for me, especially the sketch of Flavie, otherwise I shall fall in a rage like the père Duchesne[1], which is so d-mn-d patriotic. 'Tis pity they don't see our letters. Do you know what the boy is teaching his sister, and why he so often writes her those fat letters that cost sixteen sous each? What, he's teaching her to swear? The black-hearted wretch, the villain! The philosopher!

. . . .

——— 17 ———

TO HIS SISTER PAULINE

The 29th of Germinal, Year XIII
(Friday, April 19th, 1805)

This morning I had a need of intimate and tender delights. I re-read your letters, they enraptured me, especially one of the 9th of Messidor[2], in which you are even more yourself than usual. It is true that next day you felt obliged to make excuses for it, since you feared that " it might have bored me ". What a thing to be afraid of!

[1] A virulent newspaper.
[2] Tenth month of the French Republican year, June 20th to July 19th.

. . . The unhappiness of sensitive souls comes of explaining in their own way the words of the desiccated people. These latter tell you that the first of blessings is liberty. This may be true for them, but it is not exactly true for us. There must, of course, be a certain degree of liberty, without which everything turns to poison; but absolute liberty means isolation, and that is the peril of States. Behold yon eighty-year-old beggar who deprives himself of the half of his daily bread in order to feed his little dog!

A thousand things that slide over their desiccated souls without their noticing them, are for a tender soul the makings of happiness or unhappiness; and most of the things that we believe, on the word of the desiccated, that we should desire, are for us not even pleasures—such things as the delights of vanity, for example. A soul like yours, my dear Pauline, derives more pleasure from a beautiful tree that you come upon during a walk than they derive from a brilliant, brand-new equipage in which they intend to cut a dash. They see that, as a rule, they cut much less of a dash than they expected, whereas you, under your tree, dream of happy lovers, of a married couple together taking their two-year-old infant for a walk, of Sappho making the woods resound with her sublime accents, and of the thousands of pictures with which your imagination furnishes your heart.

. . . .

━━━ 18 ━━━

TO MÉLANIE GUILBERT[1]

The 1st of Messidor
(Grenoble, Tuesday, June 20th, 1805)

My charming dear one,

We seem to have become absolute strangers to one another, now that I am exiled in this dreary country[2], and you have become so foreign to

[1] " My solitude in the rue d'Angivillers had ended in my living for a year at Marseilles with a charming actress who possessed the most elevated sentiments, and to whom I never gave a sou." (*Vie de Henri Brulard.*)

Beyle had met Mélanie Guilbert at Dugazon's on December 31st, 1804—the day on which he bought Tracy's *Idéologie*. On May 8th, 1805, they left Paris together by the diligence for Lyons. From there Mélanie proceeded directly to Marseilles, where she had obtained an engagement at the Grand Théâtre on the recommendation of Prefect Thibaudeau. Meanwhile Beyle went to Grenoble, where he spent two months with his family.

[2] " I feel that I am spoiling the pleasure I promise myself from my journey to Marseilles, by the stupid, gloomy and degrading conversations with my father and grandfather to which mention of it gives rise." (*Journal*, June 21st, 1805.)

a heart all of whose sentiments are dictated by you, that you fear to bore me by telling me of your woes. You seek to be sad all by yourself; you tell me nothing of all those little details that would be so precious to me, and which you nevertheless promised, if you remember. They would be my very happiness; at every hour of the day I would imagine what you were doing; I would see you, I would know how your lodging is furnished, at what hour you perform, on which days you perform, and all such small matters that are delightful because they are so close to you. Instead of which, I know nothing. Gradually small events will occur which will seem to you too boring to relate because you have said nothing of the events leading up to them. You will have nothing more to say to me, you will no longer find it anything but tedious to write to me, and soon you will no longer write to me at all. Thus everything will be over, and that Mélanie whom I love so much will no longer wish to be anything to me, and will treat me as a stranger. Ah, my dear one, I cannot endure this part of the world, and I must leave it, even though it were to cost me forty prospective wives.

I used to love my family, before I knew you, and always visited them with renewed pleasure. In the company of the delightful sisters whom Heaven has granted me I forgot all the women I had ever known. Today my sisters' affection seems to me insipid. You have given me a distaste for everything; wherever I go I am filled with gloom. When I receive your letters, I am crazy for half a day—everyone notices the change in my mood. I re-read them twenty times, I remain supported by them for whole hours together. At last I perceive that there is no love in them other than that which I put into them. You do not tell me even things that you would tell a friend: for—if I deserve this title, at least, what though I am not so old and my attachment to you has not lasted as long as that of those whom you so name—pray bear in mind that I adored you from the first moment I saw you, that I love only you, that I have no other friend, that you have separated me from everything in the world, that you alone control my lot. And, after saying all that, I well realise that I would be but too happy to be merely a cold " friend " like the others. I shall have to treat as a stranger this person whom I have so much loved, to pay her polite attentions and receive them from her. You shall be nothing more to me than an acquaintance. Ah, what a harrowing thought, I have a sense of death in my heart! Nothing smiles upon me any more, I have no more desires for the future. I clearly see that I must adopt the language of a " friend ". It is better to do this of myself than to have to be bidden to do so.

I would so much like to know what sort of people are the actors of your company, how they act, whether the principal of them has at least some gleams of talent, no doubt obscured by the affected and exaggerated style of the provinces, or whether he has no traits of naturalness and sensibility and is altogether detestable. How are the actresses, how is the répertoire, what is the attitude of the public? Is it merely talkative and inattentive, as usual, but capable of being stirred, in the middle of its conversation, by the simple and direct expression of profound sentiments —as in those delightful moments you had one day when you recited the first scene from *Phèdre* at Dugazon's, before M. de Castro—or has modern bad taste rendered it utterly inappreciative? It seems to me that the southerners may be utter flibbertigibbets, but must at least in their hearts be capable of feeling. Their character must make them excellent spectators: their actions are never governed by reason, they are almost always passionate; they are bound to recognise themselves in such a perfect and charming imitation of nature; and, once their attention has been caught, they are bound to follow wherever you care to lead them, and to weep or tremble whenever you wish.

I suppose that the actresses have formed cabals against you; that the actors have taken sides in obedience to their mistresses; that the most amiable of them have forsaken their mistresses; that the public is being torn in all directions, and is perhaps revolting against the real or imagined protection of M. Th.[1] I can suppose anything, even the greatest absurdities, because I see from close at hand the brutal stupidities of the gossips of a small town.

My imagination strays amongst all possible sorts of accident, now that I know you are not as happy as you should be, and know also that one or other of these accidents must have befallen you, since you tell me you are not happy. What sort of life do you lead at Marseilles? Do you often go out, or do you live in solitude? Do you often see your fellow actors? Such are the thoughts that have been agitating me during the four days that have gone by since I learnt that you are not happy; and I combine these thoughts in all sorts of ways. I would give my life to know the truth of the matter, for I keep on imagining still graver reasons for your grief, and instead of setting about to find a remedy for whatever ill may in fact exist, my reflections cause me ceaselessly to invent some still greater ill. I dare not concentrate my mind on anything, and I would already have set off from here twenty times were it not that by so doing I would throw away the fortune that my father's assurances permit me to hope will one day be mine.

You have no idea of the torments I have been suffering for four days:

[1] Thibaudeau.

[63]

the worst of all is not to dare reveal to you their cause, for fear you should think me indiscreet, impertinent or even jealous. You know too well whether I have any right to be any of these. As regards the first two imputations, unless you positively love me more than you love M. de Saint-Victor[1], I must appear to you to deserve both of them, and you will throw my letter on the fire; but if, on the contrary, I have succeeded in inspiring you with a little love, or even pity, you will bear in mind that I am lonely, detained far away from you, and by the most disagreeable of motives, isolated amidst beings who cannot understand the griefs that agitate me, or who, if they did understand them, would do so only to mock at them. You know very well whether or not it is my wish to displease you. If I were still in the period in which I was still " playing a part ", I would not suffer from all these disturbances, I would be well able to distinguish between what I might and might not permit myself; but, as it is, what at one moment seems to me reasonable and natural, the next moment appears impertinent and overweening. Ten times since I began this letter I have broken off from it, and I cannot set down a phrase without regretting by its end the idea that I set about expressing to you at its beginning. In all the other disquietudes that I have suffered in my life, I could, by dint of reflection, see the difficulty more clearly and succeed in making up my mind. Here, the more I think, the less I understand. If I may dare tell you what I feel, it is that whereas I see clearly what I might have expected of Séraphine or some other such woman, in your case, Madame, I see absolutely nothing. Sometimes I see you as kind and gentle, as you sometimes have been, although very rarely with me; sometimes as cold and polite, as on certain days at Dugazon's when I thought I no longer loved you, and tried to pay attention only to Félipe.[2] The crowning torture is to think that, whatever my sentiments may be, I must write you a long letter to express them, and that this long letter will seem to you offensive and insipid, and its length will enhance my faults instead of inclining you to forgive them. The worst torment, however, is this dreadful uncertainty: to begin with, I was disquieted by wondering whether you would tolerate my letter. It seems to me that you hate me; I re-read all your letters in the wink of an eye, and I find in them not the slightest expression, I shall not say of love—I am not so fortunate—but of even the coldest friendship.

---

[1] " She told me of her relations with Hochet, editor of the *Publiciste*, and Saint-Victor, the poetaster, author of *L'Espérance*." (*Journal*, February 20th, 1805.)

[2] " I thought I was no longer loved. I went to Dugazon's. . . . I played the fool with Félipe, who let me do it. At last Mélanie arrived, at about one o'clock. I played the fool with her; I embraced her. She replied coldly and politely. I thought that all was over. This did not diminish my gaiety with Félipe." (*Journal*, March 6th, 1805.)

I have not even won a position in your heart such as that of Lalanne.
I would prefer anything to that. Write to me quite honestly, pretending
that I have never loved you and never will. I do not know what I shall
do, but at least I shall frankly abandon myself to my despair, and at least
I shall cease to be perpetually torn between despair and false hopes.
Nothing is worse than that. Help me, I beg of you, to cure myself of a
love which you clearly find importunate, and which therefore can result
in nothing but my unhappiness. Deign just once to tell me openly what
your letters tell me tacitly. Now, when I read them coldly and in sequence,
I think you must have been astonished that I have been so slow in understanding so clear a language. A coldness so constantly sustained has said
all that was necessary, I freely admit. Forgive me, I have re-read these
letters fifty times; but always I thought only of the letter I held in my
hand, and it did not occur to me to compare it with the others.

. . . .

———— 19 ————

TO HIS SISTER PAULINE

Bourg Saint-Andéol, Tuesday, 7.30 p.m.[1]
The 4th of Thermidor, Year XIII
(Tuesday, July 23rd, 1805)

I write to you, my dear Pauline, from a room overlooking the Rhône
and affording a view of more than fifteen leagues. It is furnished in
Italian style, with a gallery outside: all this, together with the inhabitants'
quick and vivacious manner of speech, reminds me of sweet Italy. I
take great pleasure in the inhabitants' southern costumes. This morning
I arrived at six o'clock in Valence. Mademoiselle Revol came with us
as far as the approach to the house. I listened to her with full attention,
because I had seen her with mademoiselle Talencieu. This motive was
natural enough. Old Pythagoras was right in saying that a pretty face
is the best of introductions. The third inmate of the coach was a conceited
fool who had travelled widely and written the history of his life and travels
in seven octavo volumes. Humanity lost this estimable work in a ship-
wreck, in which this great author was not as lucky as Camoëns.

[1] " *After two months and* —— *days* of torpor, dark boredom and *somewhat* of hope, I
finally left for Marseilles on the 3rd of Thermidor, XIII." (*Journal*, July 28th, 1805. Italicised
words in English in original).

Yesterday evening, at Saint-Marcellin, this gentleman—doubtless in a bad humour caused by our bad supper, and to prove before us all the fine things he had told us about his courage—picked a quarrel in the street with three young lawyers. I put myself between them, smoking a cigar, and was rewarded by being appealed to as a witness by both sides, both of whom were equally noisy and equally disinclined to fight. The innkeeper led my fool to the coach, where I went to sleep amidst the din of his exploits. . . . When, at 6 o'clock, we arrived at Valence, a small town with pointed cobbles, facing some mean cliffs, I was informed that I could leave only on the morrow, by the Dervieux diligence, if there were room, or in the evening by the stage-coach. I did not despair for the safety of the Republic; I had myself and my trunk conducted to the harbour, and an hour later there came by a big, ramshackle boat, which ought to be sold at, or rather *in*, Avignon for firewood, and I embarked. Apart from the risk of drowning, I was roasted alive until two o'clock, when the " southerly wind freshened ", a marine term to which you must accustom yourself. I shall often use it in the tales of my great voyages. We rowed as far as Saint-Andéol, we were perishing of thirst and heat, we laughed as we drank and drank as we laughed, we conned the wind until seven o'clock, then we conned the town, and then we went to bed. I would like to tell you everything that has made me laugh since two o'clock, but I have not enough ink. The inn, which is very good (*au Soleil levant*, innkeeper Vaubertrand) is kept by two girls who are rather pretty: one of them, indeed, very much so, with a certain elegance and a certain delicacy in her eyes, which are blue and very attractive. One would scarcely suppose her to be eighteen, she is twenty-one, married, and has had children, who have died; but my lack of ink halts me in the middle of my disquisition.

Ask father to send forty-nine francs to Bigillion, who was so kind as to lend me nineteen francs at . . .[1] and the other thirty at Grenoble. Ask him also to pay Richard the cobbler, rue des Prêtres, and the boot-maker, the German, rue Sainte-Claire. I counted upon seeing father yesterday, but I was obliged to leave before having had this pleasure. Farewell, don't forget me, I expect to find one of your letters at Marseilles, in care of M. Mante, rue Paradis, door 86, no. 8. Lock up everything I left in the wardrobe I used at Grenoble. Cordial greetings to everybody, and tell me what impression you have of the Grande-Chartreuse.

. . . .

[1] A word has been torn off.

TO HIS SISTER PAULINE

Marseilles, 2nd of Fructidor, Year XIII[1]
(Tuesday, August 20th, 1805)

I find your letter charming, my dear Pauline, and anyone else would find it sublime. What charms me especially is its natural and profound depiction of a character that is both sublime and touching. This is exactly what you sought to be. So never again make that mistake in judgment which causes you to believe that the least interesting passages in your letters are those in which you speak of yourself. You are led into this error by an excess of modesty. For me, as you know, such passages are the most interesting. For the public, if your letters were fated to be published, they would be the same. They unfold a character that combines greatness with deep sensibility, and this latter is what moves one most. The other parts of your letters are interesting only in so far as there is something of *yourself* in them. In other words, whatever is mere narrative would be insufficient for the generality of the public, because chance has not yet made you witness of any very interesting events.

The more one delves away into one's own soul, and the more one dares to express some very secret thought, the more one trembles when it is written down: it appears strange, and this strangeness is what constitutes its merit and gives the thought its originality; and if, in addition, it is true, if your words exactly copy what you feel, it is sublime. So write to me exactly what you feel.

In the habit of writing thus—which one must acquire—there is a reef to be avoided. One cannot find in oneself enough talent to depict precisely what one feels; and, having recognised that fact, one behaves as if one did not believe in it. This is a mistake: one must write with equal application at all times. For example, I myself was never less disposed to write than at this present moment. I've worked like a nigger all morning at copying out letters that are horribly bungled in both thought and style; after which I read for a quarter of an hour a book that is horribly

---

[1] Arriving in Marseilles on the evening of July 25th, he met Mélanie at the Grand Théâtre and lodged at the same hotel.

" I start banking," he notes in his *Journal*, date July 27th, to record his entry as a clerk into the house of Meunier and Co., where he was to learn the grocer's trade.

puffed-up (that is to say, its expressions exaggerate the author's thoughts and feelings). In my eyes this fault is the worst of all; it is the fault that does the most to drive out sensibility. One must not write except when one has things to say that are either great or profoundly beautiful; but in this case one must say them with the utmost possible simplicity, as if one were striving to prevent them from being noticed. This is the contrary of what is done by all the fools of this century, but it is what is done by all great men.

This book of which I am speaking, puffed-up though it is, is excellent at bottom. Its title is: *De l'influence des Passions sur le bonheur*, by Mme de Staël. It is her best work. It is well within my range of comprehension, yet to read it I toiled arduously for a fortnight. As soon as I muster the courage, I shall read it again, extracting the fine thoughts and translating them into French. The work has two or three great faults: they can all be ascribed to one cause—the author's exaggeration. Mme de Staël is not a sensitive person, and she has believed herself to be very sensitive; she has sought to be very sensitive, in the secret places of her heart she has made it her pride, a point of honour, an excuse, to be very sensitive; and consequently she has indulged in exaggeration. Thus she has given free rein to her passions (this is a mere supposition, as I scarcely know her except by her works), and has been astonished not to find in them the happiness that they give to truly passionate souls. One of the probable causes of her discontent is that she had predicted happiness for herself (you see how I am acquiring her style) as something different from what it is. Once or twice in a year one has moments when the soul is entirely made up of happiness. She has imagined that such moments are what constitute happiness, and has been unhappy at discovering that they are not. A little study of man as a moral being teaches us the rarity of this delightful state; a little study of man as a physical being also shows how rare it is. To produce it one requires an erethism. (The first string of a violin, when lax, produces *re*. When one tautens it to its natural pitch, it produces *mi*. Tauten it still more, and it produces *fa*; but soon it breaks, it is in a state of erethism.) So it is with our nerves. The state of ecstasy induces in them a condition which cannot endure without causing horrible agonies.

Such, my dear one, is the state into which I fell two years ago. The search for such happiness, which cannot be achieved with bodies such as ours, has pre-disposed me to melancholy and has given me that hatred of boredom for which I am so often reproached. Having experienced this malady, I can clearly make out its symptoms in Mme de Staël. I am cured of mine: hers has thrown her into a terrible humour with the passions. Had not Mme de Staël sought to be more passionate than nature and early education had made her, she would have created masterpieces. She has sought to depart from her natural pitch, she has created works full of excellent thoughts, fruits of a *reflective* character, and they lack everything that depends upon having a *tender* character. Since, however, she has wished to indulge in tenderness, she has lapsed into a farrago of nonsense. After this long preface, I advise you to read this work, at the risk of being a little saddened. She does not feel the happiness of loving, she is interested only in having her love requited. She does not perceive that pleasure can be found in such love as a sensitive soul feels for the spectacle of the Apollo of the Belvedere.

I am very happy. I used not to think that in all nature there was such a beautiful character. You have no idea of Mélanie. She is a Mme Roland[1] with more grace. At present she is reading Mme Roland, and considers that she lacks grace and suffers from pride. My happiness would be assured if I had an income of fifteen thousand francs—the equivalent of four to five thousand at Grenoble. I hope to have it one day, and then nothing will be able to approach the happiness I shall enjoy.

Now that I am happy, I have only one disquiet, that of knowing that you are not as happy as you deserve to be. I have said this to Mélanie, and she is well disposed to love you. She feels as you do. A thousand times she has quoted to me your comparison: "I feel that I am grasping a man's hand," etc. She is like you, she does not dare to give expression to deep matters of sentiment, they seem to her ridiculous. To induce her to do so, one must beseech her for a quarter of an hour. In short, she has the extreme delicacy of artistic souls, the same delicacy as that of Tasso. . . . Farewell. I was not in writing mood, but I broached this letter in order to deserve one from you, of four pages at least. While you are in Claix, keep a journal for me of all that you feel each day. That is what I truly wish: sweet Pauline, let us write to each other daily. Tell papa that I am in the greatest possible need of money, and make it plain to him that, whatever he may care to send, he must send it immediately. Speak to him of my eight hundred francs of debts in Paris—after all, they simply must be paid. Have you shown grandfather the letter in which I spoke to you about this, in such a way as to get eight hundred francs out of papa? Farewell. When shall we all be able to live together in Paris—you, Mélanie, my daughter[2], myself and Mante? Ah, dear Pauline, how happy we shall be! I wish you would get married—to

---

[1] " . . . to be read in 1900 by the souls whom I love, people like Mme Roland, Mélanie Guilbert. . . ." (*Vie de Henri Brulard.*)

[2] Mélanie's daughter, whom he passed off as his own.

Mante, for example. What would you say to that, if we could arrange it? Keep a triple secret. Send me a great number of cravats, the heat here obliges me to change them twice a day. But, above all, some long letters, a diary—letters with a new paragraph added every day. All best wishes to Auntie Gagnon and to Mmes Mollié and Charvet. My respects to Mme Mallein and my charming cousins. Prod Gaëtan. Give him the second volume that you will have found in my wardrobe; but, above all, write to me.

. . . .

──── 21 ────

TO HIS SISTER PAULINE

Marseilles, the 9th of Fructidor, Year XIII
(Tuesday, August 27th, 1805)

My dear Pauline, on Sunday, the day of Saint-Louis, 1805, we made an excursion that I shall remember all my life.[1] The region of Marseilles is dry and arid, so ugly that it hurts the eyes. The air hurts the chest by reason of its extreme dryness. Clouds of dust impede the horses and stifle the travellers. All there is in the way of trees are wretched little shrubs all covered with dust. These shrubs are, in fact, olives, so valuable that there is a local saying: whoever has ten thousand olives has an income of ten thousand crowns. There are, admittedly, a few trees such as one sees on the promenade at Grenoble; but their leaves, which are always white with dust, are half drawn in because of the extreme heat, and, far from their shade giving pleasure, one is pained to see them suffering so, and wishes for them that they had been born in the forest of Fontainebleau.

A league to the east of Marseilles is a little valley formed by two rows of absolutely arid rocks. In the whole chain of them you would not find a patch of grass as big as this sheet of paper. All there is are a few little sprigs of lavender, mint and balsam; but they are not green, and at four paces' distance they blend into the greyness of the rock. At the bottom of the valley is a river which is the size of the Robine and is called the

---

[1] He records in his *Vie de Henri Brulard*: " At Marseilles I had the delicious pleasure of beholding my mistress, who is uncommonly well made, bathing in the Huveaune beneath a crown of trees."

Huveaune. This river brings life to half a league of ground which is called la Pomone, because it is full of appletrees.

The Huveaune runs along one side of the harbour. It is flanked by big trees, and under these trees are charming little paths, and, from time to time, benches lost amongst all this greenery. The place has the verdure and coolness of le Cheylas. Anywhere else it would be merely handsome: here the contrast makes it enchanting. There is a château with high towers, but so densely surrounded by a clump of chestnuts that the towers appear only above the trees. This château really gives one the impression of a sojourn in fairyland: you can imagine these knightly towers emerging from magnificent chestnuts. Before the château, which inspires me with thoughts that are not sombre—the towers are not big enough or black enough—but, rather, melancholy, they have planted a pretty little avenue of plane-trees, which are perhaps five or six years old and are the size of the smallest cherry-trees in les Tilleuls. Their cheerful greenery forms a striking contrast with the château and the great chestnuts.

I seemed to be listening to a work by Cimarosa, in which, amidst great, sombre and terrible melodies and in the midst of a piece that sublimely and forcefully depicts the horrors of revenge, jealousy and unhappy love, this master of the emotions of the heart has inserted a gay little air, with accompaniment on the shepherd's pipes. It is in this fashion that cheerfulness is here found side by side with the deepest gloom. I have just heard a young girl singing a gay ditty: perhaps inside the house her sister, who had just poisoned herself in despair, was sighing out her last breath. Such is the thought that occurs to any hearer of Cimarosa's sublime work who is worthy to feel it and understands the significance of the little melody. Such is the manner in which artists require to be heard. Such is the effect produced upon us by the little lane of plane-trees or sycamores, those trees that have pretty barks of nankeen silk, leaves like those of the vine, and, for fruit, thorny chestnuts hanging in a long tail. Some of these trees are to be found amongst the first fifty trees along the promenade at la Graille.

We had taken with us two partridges and a roast pigeon, a pâté, a fricassee of veal, some peaches and grapes and a bottle of Bordeaux wine. We left at three o'clock and stopped at a little inn which we cherish for your sake. Twenty-five days ago, whilst visiting la Pomone, or rather whilst returning from it, I entered this inn to ask for lemonade or wine. Beside the door I found a pretty child of four, sleeping in the position of an Infant Jesus by Raphael. He had a face which, with its lovely dark eyes and fair hair falling in great curls on his shoulders, might have been painted by Greuze. I brought Mélanie in to look at the child. She was charmed by him. But she commented that his sleep had an expression of its own: the face, and especially the attitude, expressed a serene and tranquil repose, but the eyes expressed grief. We enquired about him: his leg, which he had broken two hours before, had just been put in splints.

18th. Tell my grandfather that today, the 18th, I have still received nothing. Let him form his own opinion on the subject of keeping one's promises. I would dearly like to take a decisive stand in the matter. If he begins like this, what will he do in future? It is simply too expensive to have a son.

Write to me, you ungrateful little wretch.

. . . .

—— 22 ——

TO HIS SISTER PAULINE

Marseilles, the 30th of Fructidor, Year XIII
(Tuesday, September 17th, 1805)

I fear you are vexed about something, my dear child, and I complain at your not telling me about it. Why is it that you never write? I deserve better.

. . . If I were not wildly in love with another woman, the regret I feel at your not writing to me would lead me to believe myself to be in love with you. Indeed, Mélanie, beautiful soul though she is, was caused a moment of jealousy by the sight of the despondency into which I was thrown by your silence.

So *write* to me, I repeat for the thousandth time: write anything that comes into your head: and it is precisely because you won't know what to say to me after the second line that I can be sure that you will not tell me of events of little interest, but of what you think, what you feel—in a word, of all that I am burning to know.

. . . When one is vexed, one must avoid meditating about oneself. One is like a man with jaundice: he must not study the map of the countries he is about to traverse—he would see everything in yellow. Yellow is the colour of Sweden, so he would believe that every country was Sweden, and if by chance the King of Sweden had set a price upon his head, he would be in despair: this despair would be the effect of his jaundice. And such is the effect from which I suffer every time I go to Grenoble; so much so that, on the last occasion, I almost entirely avoided thinking about my future.

I am happy here, my dear one; I am tenderly loved by a woman whom I madly adore. Hers is a beautiful soul—nay, beautiful is not the word, 'tis sublime! Sometimes I have the misfortune to be jealous of her. The study I have made of the passions renders me suspicious, because I see all the possibilities. Since she is less rich than you, and indeed has almost nothing, I am going to buy a sheet of stamped paper in order to make my will and give everything to her, and, after her, to my daughter. I don't think it will be much; but, after all, I shall have done what I could. If it all produced nothing, if I should die, and if one day you were rich, I commend to your care this tender soul, whose only fault is that she allows herself to be too much overwhelmed by misfortune. You know this fault; you know what a consolation it is when a sensitive soul takes pity on you! Therefore, even if you are not rich, bestow, as tears upon my ashes, a tender friendship upon Mélanie Guilbert and my daughter.

What strange beings men are! I am writing this letter to you in the counting-house. My whole soul was taken up with the task, when in came a go-between who employed a mask of sentiment to ask for a payment that the firm was not willing to make him for another six days. Our people, who for two months had been treating him with apparent friendship, haggled sharply with him over his *percentage*. The affair has completely withered me up. Write me, very soon, a long letter. Write me four or five pages.

What is your view of rhetoric? Taken in the manner in which we regard it, it concerns what is most profound both in the *soul* and in the *head*. It lends perceptibility to details that are abstract and difficult to conceive of, and therefore to engrave on the memory. It is therefore the necessary complement to human study. Write soon, soon, soon, write at once. When you receive my letter stretch out your hand to your pen. . . . Europe has just lost a great poet, *Schiller*.

. . . .

23

TO HIS SISTER PAULINE

Marseilles, the 9th of Vendémiaire, Year XIV
(Tuesday, October 1st, 1805)

Dearest, at last I have received one of your letters. Now that my letters to you cannot be opened, I shall write to you much more often—but on one condition, that you answer me. When I receive no letter from you, I feel terribly ill at ease. Because I know you have so many vexations, I need to know that you can still endure them. In order to do this the more easily, you require to know more of this " vale of tears ", as the prophets call it. The truth is, it is a vale in which, if one is endowed with a little sensibility, one always dreams of better things than one possesses. If one strays off from this into thinking oneself unhappy, one will always be so. If, on the other hand, one embraces the excellent philosophy of Scapin, and always expects the worst, one often finds reasons to be joyful. I am beginning to acquire this beneficial habit.

Once you are in society, you will be appalled by the general heedlessness; you will see how all beings are isolated by egoism. You will have the greatest difficulty in finding, I do not say, an heroic, but even a sensitive soul. In Paris, that huge city, even after ten years of careful search you will scarcely succeed in assembling a circle of thirty intelligent and sensitive people. On the other hand, from the very first day you will have all the delights offered by the arts.

Even the most corrupt of men, if he creates a work of art, paints into it the most perfect virtue and sensibility. The only result is to produce melancholy in sensitive souls, who are so simple as to suppose that the world resembles these inaccurate images of it. That is my great fault, my dearest: a fault what I cannot strive too much to overcome. I think it is yours, too, for our souls are much alike.

Two things can cure one of this fault: experience, and reading *Memoirs*. I cannot too strongly advise you to read Retz's. If they do not interest you, postpone the reading of them for a year. You will find in them the tragedy of nature, described by one of the most intelligent and interesting men who ever lived. His face was a mirror of his genius. I have never seen a face that was so gay and witty.

Saint-Aubin, an excellent engraver of portraits, has done engravings of sixty famous men, which Herhan sells for twenty francs. As soon as I have some money, I shall send you a small collection of those which I know to be good. Molière and Retz are perhaps the best.

Continually read and re-read Saint-Simon[1], in seven volumes. The history of the Regency—the most interesting of them, because it depicts the French character, which was developed to perfection in Regent Philippe himself—is, by a happy chance, the easiest of all sections of history to study.

Duclos, who is a very clever man, wrote his *Memoirs* on this period. Saint-Simon, a man of genius, has written his own. Marmontel, a man enlightened by scholarship, has just published the history of the Regency, in which he alternately quotes and criticises Saint-Simon. Finally, Chamfort, a man of right principles and a satirical and very subtle wit, published a long piece on the Memoirs of the trenchant Duclos at the time of their appearance—in 1782, I think. So we have a most interesting period presented to us by four men, Saint-Simon, Duclos, Chamfort and Marmontel, of whom the first has genius, the two next a very rare wit, and the fourth great learning. Voltaire was brought up in the customs of the Regency: in a thousand passages in his work you will find typical observations on the French character at this period. One of his great achievements has been the undoing of pedantry. *People began to examine, instead of piously believing, the books of the examiners.*

This trend was strengthened by the Revolution. Anyone who has talent is a philosopher; which is the reason why we are by far the first people in the world. This war, if only it lasts, will enhance this happy state of affairs and make it that of Europe, by spreading our light, at present in Naples and over Germany and Holland, and soon over Spain and Portugal—countries at present so absurd in their superstition and pride. I do not know whether you will be able to read this scribble: I am writing to you in haste, in order to earn a second letter from you.

Yesterday I chanced to read the notebooks I wrote at Paris, in Messidor[2], year *XII*, concerning the head and the heart, and the division of the passions, with which I was occupied at the time. I found the principle correct, but all the rest *gisquet*[3], conceited, empty, ill-considered —resembling an article by Geoffrey, especially in its presumption and ignorance. This has caused me to reflect seriously.

. . . .

1 " I worshipped Saint-Simon in 1800 as much as I did in 1836. Spinach and Saint-Simon are the only two tastes I have had all my life—second only, of course, to a taste for living in Paris with an income of a hundred louis, and writing books." (*Vie de Henri Brulard.*)

2 Tenth month of the French Republican year, June 20th to July 19th.

3 Possibly a reference to an acquaintance of this name?

24

TO HIS SISTER PAULINE

Marseilles, Saturday the 22nd of March 1806

I have received your letter of Monday. You would not believe what pleasure it has given me: ever since this morning I had been seeking to distract myself from the over-sensibility that seemed to be pursuing me. Your letter, which I received at two o'clock, put me in the happy state of thinking about what one loves. Eugénie came in at a very bad moment for me. It is all very well for your letter to contain the promise: " until to-morrow ". You wrote the same thing two months ago, and this letter of yours is the first I have received since then. I might sing, like Grégoire: "The oath we take today, will it hold good tomorrow?" I am vexed that in your letter you do not strike the chord of sensibility. You do not speak enough of yourself, you tell me nothing of your welfare, or of what you think of the long philosophic pieces that I send you. Discourse to me at length on all these matters; tell me whether you have read Tracy. . . . I say! Do you know how useful you are to me as an ambassadress? It was you who wrote the letter about the eaux-de-vie, it is you have explained its effectiveness, and have shown me that I touched the chord of sensibility. It is what we call " using the cushion ", a metaphor taken from billiards.

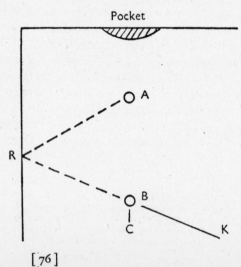

If one struck the ball B in the direction CB, one would pocket ball A, but B would be pocketed with it. Instead, one uses the cushion: that is to say, one strikes in the direction KB, and the ball rebounds from point R in the direction RA.

That, pussy, is a very long and clumsy explanation of a clumsy term, but you will understand that "using the cushion" means setting in play the passion that one knows to exist in another person rather than directly approaching that person.

This is a universal principle; for when a person loves you, to approach him or her directly is precisely to set his or her love in play. You will observe that I am doing all I can to explain to you the subtleties of society: if I were dealing with a person like Séraphie[1], you would end by being a Merteuil[2]. But, since I know you to have an excellent heart, I wish to prevent you from being a Delphine[3]; which is exactly the fate that awaited the pair of us in society, if we had not properly ordered the matter. You will therefore realise that one must acquire the habit of "using the cushion" very early. This is one of the great principles of which I have spoken to you: our intelligence soon taught us the truth of it, but our "moral personalities" (our desire for happiness) have not yet grown accustomed to it. I hope that the success of the letter in question will have two good results: firstly, that of giving you the habit of "cushioning", and secondly, that of giving you the habit of writing: both are necessary to my happiness. So let us write to one another, my dearest: we are each other's best friends. I love you with all my soul, I shall never love a mistress as much as I love you. When we are both weary of society, we shall take a little house in Paris or in the vicinity, where we shall spend our life together and await its end in the bosom of the fine arts and of the tenderest friendship. I am getting excited and displaying—and I know it—too much sensibility. I break off my letter until tomorrow morning. Farewell.[4]

. . . .

[1] Mlle Gagnon: "This Aunt Séraphie had all the acidity of a religious old maid—that female devil—my bad genius throughout all my childhood." (*Vie de Henri Brulard.*)

[2] "*Les Liaisons dangereuses* had been written at Grenoble by M. Choderlos de Laclos, an artillery officer, and depicted life in the town. I actually knew 'Mme de Merteuil'. Her real name was Mme de Montmaure, and she used to give me candied nuts." (*Vie de Henri Brulard.*)

[3] Mme de Staël's heroine.

[4] Her theatrical engagement having ended, Mélanie Guilbert had left Marseilles. Beyle notes in his *Journal*, in an entry dated March 25th: "The slavery in which Mélanie held me often weighed upon me; the abandonment in which I am left by her departure vexes me."

TO MARTIAL DARU

Grenoble, the 1st of June 1806

My dear cousin,

Here I am at Grenoble[1], but not from inconstancy. The only reason for my suddenly leaving Marseilles was that I had received terrible letters from my grandfather. My father finds commerce humiliating: he will do nothing for a son who shifts hogsheads of eau-de-vie; and he would do everything for a son whose name he saw in the newspapers. That is why M.D.[2] and you have been receiving so many letters.

Do you think that M.D. is willing to help me? Does he believe that I have matured a little since I resigned my commission? If he is still at all interested in me, I ask for two years in which to prove myself; after which he will be able to judge.

You know, my dear cousin, for how many millions of reasons I would prefer copying out reviews in your office to a post worth six thousand francs but two hundred leagues away. Do not think that what I am longing for is Paris: it is the life of the Casa d'Adda[3], the kindnesses you lavish upon me, and the hope of being able to acquire some of those qualities which make for happiness and cause you, in particular, to be adored by all around you. Forgive me for the trouble I am causing you; but an instant is about to decide, once and for all, whether I shall be able to see you sometimes, or whether I shall remain stuck in this country of self-importance and crudity.

If you need a man who works ten hours a day, here you have him! If he is at your side, he has no need to speak of his constancy; and, above all, he asks for two years in which to prove himself.

Farewell, my dear cousin. I wonder if you could find time to write me a few words.

. . . .

[1] "On receipt of a letter from my uncle, I have resolved to go to Grenoble." (*Journal*, May 18th, 1806.) He left Marseilles on May 20th, for Toulon, having "formed the design of going to Grenoble by the little route: Aix, Manosque, Sisteron, Gap, La Mure, etc."
[2] Pierre Daru.
[3] The house at Milan where his cousin had given him hospitality in 1800: "The Casa d'Adda, those words remain sacred for me."

"Martial was perfect, and really always has been perfect, in his treatment of me. I am vexed that I did not realise this better during his life-time." (*Vie de Henri Brulard.*)

TO HIS SISTER PAULINE

Saturday, 18*th October* 1806[1]
2 *p.m.*, *Metz*.

My dearest, we set off from Paris on the 16th at three minutes past six o'clock in the evening. This is the first moment we have had for writing. We were quite sad at leaving Paris, so we decided that we must laugh more than ever.

I am absolutely delighted with Martial's manner towards me. I embrace you with all my heart, likewise the rest of the family.

You have doubtless learnt of the death of Prince Ferdinand.[2] We are going to Coburg, but the Emperor must be well forward of there. We are going from here to Mainz, from Mainz to Wurzburg, from Wurzburg to Bamberg, thence to Coburg, and thence to a career of glory.

. . . .

27

TO HIS SISTER PAULINE

Berlin, Monday, the 3rd of November 1806

My dearest, I think we shall go to Brunswick. It is said to be a handsome city, with a French theatre. Here, as is proper, there is a German one: the celebrated Iffland is playing there. I have seen him several times; he seems to me to have great naturalness in the sentimental style and great simplicity in the comic style. What I mean is that when he is playing a comic part and has something ridiculous to say, he does not show that he thinks it ridiculous—he says it guilelessly, as fools say foolish things in real life. I am told he has written tragedies.

The day before yesterday the weather was cold and damp. We went

[1] Arriving at Paris in July 10th, Beyle set out again on October 16th, accompanying Martial Daru on the track of the Grande Armée.
[2] Ludwig-Ferdinand of Prussia, killed at the battle of Saalfeld on October 10th, 1806. (Note by M. Martineau.)

to an inspection at Charlottenburg, which was held at 9 o'clock. I had been on the go since seven, and was somewhat affected by the cold. Yesterday evening I perceived that I was chilled, that I felt very queer. This evening I felt the same symptoms; so that, instead of going up to dinner, I am writing to you.

I fear this may be a recurrence of my slight fever of two years back. I want to be rid of it quickly: it plunged me every evening into horrible gloom. It is true that at that time I had nothing to be happy about, except my intellectual faculties. I was in Paris without fire, light or a coat, and with broken boots. Here things are very different. I am to be paid three or four hundred louis; I am fairly well clad, although not in all respects; I am ill-lodged and well-fed.

. . . My room faces the arsenal, a superb building beside the King's palace. We are separated from it by a branch of the Spree, whose waters have the colour of green oil. Berlin lies upon a tract of sand that begins a little beyond Leipzig.

Wherever there is no paving, one sinks to the ankles. All this sand makes a desert of the city's outskirts, which produce nothing but trees and some turf.

I do not know who had the idea of planting a city in the middle of this sand. It has 159,000 inhabitants, or so they say.

· ·

———— 28 ————

TO HIS SISTER PAULINE

Grande-Armée, the 24th of March 1807

· ·

A passion is the perseverance of a desire: this desire is aroused by the idea of the happiness one would enjoy if one possessed the desired object (which idea is at the same time that of the unhappiness of one's present state, in which one does not possess the object), and by the hope of achieving one's aim; for, as Corneille has so well said of Love:

Si l'amour vit d'espoir, il s'éteint avec lui.[1]

The more one reflects on all the passions, from Caesar's passion for dominion over the Roman Republic to Werther's passion for Lotte,

[1] If love doth live by hope, with hope it must go out.

[80]

the more one sees that the analysis of each of them is an exact description of what takes place in the heart of a passionate man.

Well, then, how the deuce is one to find in the union of a man and a woman the necessary conditions for engendering or sustaining a passion? No such conditions exist. This theoretical conclusion seems to be refuted by the spectacle of some happy marriages; but most often that member of the couple who is the more intelligent becomes a play-actor for the other's benefit, and both for the benefit of the public.

Generally speaking, everybody only play-acts at happiness: we know some individual who assures everybody that he is never bored—his conduct proves the opposite.

When love really is present in a marriage, it is a conflagration that goes out, and goes out all the more rapidly the more brightly it has blazed.

This I have observed in fifty or sixty couples whom I have had opportunity to study from close at hand. What sort of happiness, then, can be found in marriage? Friendship? But that is exceedingly difficult. It is scarcely possible, except for a man of fifty who marries a widow of thirty. If they are sufficiently intelligent, custom and the knowledge that the world is watching them will have made them indulgent.

Between married people, even such happiness as is found in friendship has too much passion in it to be a sure foundation for happiness. What cements friendship in this world is the possibility of separating at any moment: a friend is aware of the possibility of never seeing his friend again.

I think, therefore, that you should seek for happiness in an easy-going husband whom you can manage. You will contract towards him that sort of benevolence which, if one is good-hearted, one always feels towards benefactors. This manageable husband will make you mother of children, whom you will adore: thus your life will be filled, not with the emotions of a novel, which are physically impossible—by reason of the nature of the nerves, which cannot always be stretched to the same degree, and because every repeated impression becomes *more* facile and *less* felt—but with a reasonable contentment.

I wanted to tell you all this, despite the fact that at present I feel very weak, as a result of my illness. These ideas are the foundation of whatever happiness is possible for a young woman. If I were dead, I would feel that my greatest regret was that I had not developed them as I feel they might be developed.

In conclusion,

1. You must get married;
2. To a man who is kind, and fairly rich.

But seek for no transports of joy in marriage. Remember the moral drawn by Scapin: one must expect nothing, in order to enjoy the little one gets.

The odds are a thousand to one that your husband's soul will seem vulgar to you, and his intelligence will seem ridiculous. Your happiness will depend, not only upon how carefully you hide these opinions from him, but also upon how carefully you persuade him that he is very much superior to you. There will surely be some matter on which he stakes his pride: on drawing up a document, on acquitting himself well in the sports of society, on being good at the game of " Petit Bonhomme vit encore "[1], or at catching butterflies. You must see to it that everything about you, even to the words you utter in dreams, proves to him your profound veneration for these gifts of his.

From the moment of marriage, you must become a hypocrite. Some piece of society tattle may estrange you from your husband. Those who give orders love foolishness in those who obey. You must become, not devoutly religious—the leap would be too great, and the rôle is too boring—but reasonably pious, going to confession once a month.

You will have to conceal from your husband any too lively friendship that you may feel towards some woman friend or towards me: otherwise he would decide that you loved him less than you loved this person, and would be annoyed. If you had more pettiness of spirit, you would attach importance to many details which, as it is, you neglect. You might even go so far as to keep your husband constantly in love with you. To do this is a woman's master-stroke; but your character is too elevated to possess this degree of coquetry.

The pleasures of such souls as ours either are not understood or are detested by the vulgar souls who populate society: remember this, as a guiding principle. If my letter is too badly written for you to read it fluently, copy it out.

You must hide your superiority, and must enjoy in solitude, in your boudoir, the reading of a book that entertains you or the pleasure you take in an evening party. Do not deliver yourself up to the enthusiasm that may on occasion come over you. Bear in mind that, however you may outwardly appear, you have at your side a dead weight that either will fail to understand your pleasures or else will envy them. One wastes one's ardour in trying to communicate it to these blocks of ice. One must find enjoyment in one's own solitary company, and, as regards one's friends, reveal one's thoughts to them only *in proportion* to the degree of intelligence one finds in them. Otherwise you run

[1] A children's game.

the risk of their thinking you superior: from that moment, you are lost.

Perhaps you don't believe all this: within four years you will believe it as I do. Experience will have taught you this painful habit.

I beg of you, meditate on this letter, and accustom yourself to the idea of having a dull and mediocre husband: you absolutely must not remain a spinster.

Today I saw an excellent image, of death—a young rook that I saw fall and perish in the Ocker, a small river that runs through Brunswick.

. . . .

——— *29* ———

TO HIS SISTER PAULINE

Brunswick, the 30th of April 1807

. . . .

A conflict going on within me between honour, on the one hand, and love and ambitious interest, on the other, has on seven or eight occasions in the present month brought me to a peak both of unhappy agitation and of glowing happiness. On the 5th of March, considerations of honour involved me in a quarrel with Martial; on the 5th of April, they brought about our reconciliation. I was due to leave for Thorn. I conquered love, with infinite distress and, I must confess, with tears. I was so agitated that at seven o'clock in the evening, at the moment when I was about to take my decision concerning the question of departure, I ran through the streets of Brunswick like a madman. I passed before the windows of the girl[1] to whom I had taken a fancy: I felt that I was being torn asunder. Nevertheless, honour proved the stronger. I went to inform Martial that I was willing to go. He did not wish me to: he counted on my love to detain me, and he told me all that was necessary to make me stay.

I am staying; I believe myself to be happy. I do not know why Minette is resolved to make me " sit up and beg ": politics, vanity and compassion all bid me concern myself no more with her. At a famous ball I paid court to another: astonishment, wretchedness, disappointment on Minette's part. This other offers an easy and victorious retreat.

[1] Wilhelmine von Griesheim. Of all the women with whom Beyle fell in love, "the poorest was Mina von Griesheim, youngest daughter of a general who had no fortune and was the favourite of a fallen prince ". (*Vie de Henri Brulard.*)

'Then, in order to effect a reconciliation with Mina, I carried out a superb manoeuvre. On the promenade I saw from a distance a man of great wit who has a proper contempt for the human rabble: he also has fifty years' experience, and an income of a hundred thousand francs: the very personification of good company. I fell into conversation with this man, and for two hours displayed so much wit, in his own style, that finally he invited me to an evening party at his house that same day— a party at which no French were to be present. What a triumph! I arrived full of happiness at his house, knowing that all the Fräulein von Gries-heim were coming. Minette had decided not to come: all I found there were her sisters and Fräulein von Treuenfels, her rival. I obtained an assignation with this latter. As I was leaving the house, I was told: " If you go this evening to such-and-such a house, you will find Wilhel-mine there." I cut short my assignation: I seized upon a moment at which Fräulein von Treuenfels had gone out to make tea for me, and I decamped. I arrived at the house indicated, where I found no Minette, but two of the most ugly and desiccated females in Brunswick.

Finally, yesterday, Minette and I were reconciled. I could fill two or three volumes with an account of such stupid trifles; but I do not wish to abuse your friendship by boring you. Yesterday Minette *clasped my hand*—no more than that. You will laugh at me, but after the life I have been leading for six years, this affair has kept me in a turmoil for the past month.[1]

I shall spare you all the intermediate embarrassments. My only con-fidant, the only Frenchman here with whom I can converse, is jealous of the talent and energy that he sees me display in this intrigue, of which he knew the background; he has almost ceased to speak to me, and for a week has not come to see me.

I have been suffering from a severe pain in the chest. It has been painful to utter the slightest word. Amidst so many agitations caused by such small matters, Wisdom continually scolded (reinforced by the unhappi-ness that luckily attended step by step upon all my faults), and finally emerged victorious, having succeeded in slaying Love.

I no longer have any fancy for Minette—that blonde and charming Minette, that Northern soul such as I have never seen in France or in Italy. The proof of this is that I am going to try to go to Falkenstein, which is Army Headquarters. Following upon what grandfather told me

[1] " I was much madder, but also much happier when, without saying a word to anyone, and when I was already a grown man and appending my signature to official documents, I kept on thinking of the passions that I was on the eve of experiencing, feeling and perhaps inspiring. The details of a hand-clasp beneath tall trees at night caused me to indulge in daydreams for hours on end." (*Voyage dans le Midi de la France.*)

concerning M. Daru's letter, ask grandfather to tell him—*if he has occasion to write to him*: I say "if", for I must not be impatient—that I wish to *serve with the Army in the field*: do not forget to do this.

A strong soul who succeeded in doing all that reason dictated would be master of his entire surroundings.

During the past two months I have had striking evidence of this. Remember that, in addition to the little I have told you of my recent disturbances, I have undertaken eight or ten journeys of fifteen or twenty leagues, have done ten hours of work in two, and—what is much more of an affliction, but is very good for strengthening the soul—I have had *no confidant*, have always been alone.

This evening at the ball there will be a battle royal: I shall find myself between the two rivals. Perhaps tomorrow I shall be in the same state of agitation as I was in two days ago; but my mind is made up, I shall go to the Army if I can. What attracts me is the desire to see from close at hand the mighty sports of those basement-area dogs who are known as men.

I have been reading two books that you should read: an *Histoire de la Pologne* by Rhulière, and *Histoire de la Réformation* by Ch. Villiers, a work that won the prize awarded by the National Institute in the year XIII. *Father*[1] has it, get Bigillion to ask him for it.

The great Father[1] is very pleased with you. I see that at last you are progressing in wisdom, the only road to happiness. When you wish to be happy, you will be so. For this, you must first achieve tranquillity: the beauty and goodness of your soul will supply you with enough pleasures. A lentil falling in a turbulent sea causes no movement in it: in a calm sea it creates millions of circles.

Once nothing can disturb your soul, you will achieve your happiness with an ease that will enchant you. For this, one must entirely conquer vanity. What matter whether Mme Augustin Périer has said of you: " That stout Mlle B . . . looks like a hen-turkey when she walks ", or " nobody could be more graceful than dear Pauline! "? *Tutto costena*[2] for the vulgarities and stupidities of all who blame or praise: their opinions will soon be a matter of indifference to you. But do not reveal this lofty quality. People would say: " What! So here is somebody who escapes our domination? Perhaps in her heart she rightly prefers herself to us? " And then, like my friend here in Brunswick, they would hate you.

[1] In English [*sic*] in the original.
[2] Possibly *costena* is an error for *costenza*, constancy, in which case the phrase might be an equivalent in bad Italian for a French phrase meaning: " Accept everything with equanimity."

According to what *the great father*[1] tells me, age does not put an end to agriculturomania. You will never get married, my poor lass: a merino is much superior to a son-in-law. So be reasonable! Think of a husband as a thing, and not as a being. A dragoon must have a horse, in order to live, and a girl must have a husband. I suggest you take M. Badon. He's a good fellow, who will feel that you are doing him a favour by marrying him. You, for your part, will persuade him that you are very happy with him, and he will let you live peacefully and independently. You will have children whom you will adore. The good fellow will keep merinos, like his father-in-law; and he will take you to see Paris. Gradually we shall attract him to the place, and you will be happy—more so, perhaps, than with Périer, but ten million times more so than with Faure, Fleuron or any of the others. Perhaps Penet has a sufficient degree of wit and feeling to be happy in loving his wife; but, even though I know him, I would wager ten to one that after the first three years Badon's wife will be happier than Mme Penet.

Reflect a little on what I have said, young woman of twenty-two.

. . . .

30

TO HIS SISTER PAULINE

Brunswick, 1807

People are right when they say that all emotional disturbances are greater in solitude. I wrote to you three days ago—and I distinctly felt—that my fancy for Minette had entirely passed. I sacrificed her to Fräulein von Treuenfels, whom I do not love at all; I was amused by the agitation of the two rivals. In short, I demanded of philosophy the emotions that love no longer gave me: love has revenged itself.

Fräulein von Treuenfels has almost told me that she loves me. It was on Thursday last, and this avowal of love took the form of confessing to me the love that she had and no longer has for Herr L . . . I have reason to believe that on that same evening she was reconciled with Herr L . . . I saw for the first time at Minette's side a suitor who has courted her for four years and in order to marry her is waiting only for the consent or death of his father. Even without loving him, she must prefer him to me,

[1] In English [*sic*] in the original.

who have no desire to marry her. On this particular evening she held the balance between the two of us; but yesterday she had an appearance of loving him. Would you believe it that for four mortal days I have been thinking of nothing else? When my mind is not distracted by the turmoil in my soul, it is entirely occupied with the question of how to induce her to love me without getting her into trouble with her future husband; and I am quite sure that, the day after I have become certain of her love, I shall find her almost insupportable. Yesterday, at last, with rage in my heart, I remembered the influence of the physical upon the moral: I took a great deal of tea, and partially recovered my reason—enough, at least, to be amiable. But she is too intelligent and too passionate to be very appreciative of this sort of merit. In my distress I sought to distract myself by indulging all my tastes and going on little journeys. The letter I have written to father will tell you what my reading was, and where. My books bored me. This morning I held an inspection of them. My eye fell on a volume of diverse thoughts by Helvetius. I took horse and galloped as far as Richemonde—a very pretty English garden, as far distant from Brunswick as the bridge of Piquepierre from Grenoble, set in open country covered with pale vegetation. Richemonde reminds me of the Belvedere: it has a small château. When I arrived beneath the cool shade, I flung myself on the grass. For two hours Helvetius gave me consolation.

Such is my life, dear one: how is yours? Are you thinking at all seriously of getting married? What I mean is, are you cured of believing you can find a Saint-Preux or an Émile for a husband? You will find neither, my dear, but only a conceited man whom you will manage, a man neither good nor bad, whose character will change every ten years with his physique. I shall not be at ease until I know that you are married: it is the proper employment for a girl, and you would not believe how pleased I am with myself for having found employment—if only in order to learn how to do without it. Do not hope to find solid happiness in celibacy: the image of marriage will always come to trouble you. I passionately want to know what you think concerning this important and urgent matter.

Remember that time is precious: my adventure of this week should prove it to you. I had Minette's heart almost in my hand; it depended only on me whether she would love me deeply. I vaguely said to myself: " It cannot fail! " But it *has* failed, and cruelly.

Speak every day to father on my behalf concerning money: I have great need of it. Speak about it daily, I count on you for that; but I confess that I begrudge the time you will spend in speaking on my behalf, and would rather that you employed it in writing to me,

Give me all possible details of the death of Mme de Rézicourt, and of the effect that this death—which, for my part, I consider moving—has had upon (1) her good friend, the fair and frail Blanchet, (2) upon *tutti gli altri*[1]. *Farewell and love me ever as thine best friend. The German tongue*[2] causes me to forget all my English.

HENRI.

—— 31 ——

TO HIS SISTER PAULINE

12th of May, 1807

It may be that the Germans have a very moving poetry. My friend (M. de Struve) of whom I have already spoken to you, has literally translated for me a ballad which in my eyes had the merit of bearing your name: it is entitled *Leonore*, which means *Eléonore*.[3]

The ballad, which I selected for this reason from amongst the works of Bürger, is very moving: in style it is between English and French. The veil that still covers the German genius for me is too thick for me to be able to give greater precision to my ideas. Meanwhile, however, I think I can detect that German is less inflated, closer to nature, truer and simpler than English. In this ballad a horse is described as going " hopp! hopp! hopp!", and there is mention of the " tamtam " of drums.

Leonore awakes from a painful dream: " Wilhelm, are you unfaithful? Are you dead? "

Wilhelm had been with King Frederick's army at the battle of Prague. But the King came to terms with the Empress. There is a tamtam of drums, the army passes through the city, and Leonore goes about asking every soldier to tell her where Wilhelm is: " Where is my promised? " (This is a German idiom: a man is " promised " to his mistress for a year, or often more, before he marries her.) Nobody can tell her. The whole army has gone by. She tears her hair; her mother seeks to console her, but she rejects all consolation. At last, at midnight, she hears " hopp! hopp! hopp! " in the street; she hears a man dismount, she makes out the clink of spurs. He mounts the stairs, knocks sharply: " Hallo! Hallo! Where is my promised? "

---

[1] All the others.
[2] These last twelve words are in English [*sic*] in the original.
[3] Pauline Beyle's baptismal names were Pauline-Éléonore. (Note by M. Martineau.)

"Here I am, dear Wilhelm." And she adds a few more words.

HE: "Make haste: we have yet a hundred leagues before us ere we shall be in our bridal bed: come, mount upon my horse's crupper."

SHE: "How do I mount upon a crupper?"

The chime rings out, it has struck midnight . . .

When Struve and I had reached this point, the clock did, in fact, strike eight. I left Struve to go and be presented to the Governor's wife, who arrived three days ago (a very common woman).

Struve tells me that Leonore sets off with her lover, arrives at the battlefield, and there perceives that her lover is only a ghost. He has been killed in the battle. All the slain are walking at this nocturnal hour.

According to Struve, the English are mad about this ballad: there have been five or six translations.

Send me the eighteen lines by André Chénier[1], and the forty-eight by Lebrun, his translation of the opening of the Iliad. If you haven't them, you will find them at the end of one of my stereotypes[2]. Don't forget to do this, I have promised them to somebody.

I have asked M. Daru for permission to join the Army in the Field. I shall leave Brunswick with much regret, probably in two or three weeks. Ask father for money: I badly need it. We have not received our meagre two-hundred-francs-a-month since January.

Many greetings to Mme Chalvet. How is this kind aunt? Long live Mme Martin.

Farewell: go on loving me, and sometimes tell me so. If I happen to die, I shall have parted from you six months earlier, for it is six months since you wrote to me.

HENRI.

——— 32 ———

TO HIS SISTER PAULINE

Undated

Has your confessor forbidden you to write to me?

. . . .

[1] Cf. letter no. 7.
[2] Editions stéréotypes Didot.

33

TO HIS SISTER PAULINE

The 26th of July 1807

My ears are pricked for the sound of cannon-fire. My hat and sword are on the table, my two horses are stamping on the cobbles of the court-yard and are growing impatient: all this for the prince de Neuchâtel, Minister of War, who is to arrive this evening and will be met this evening, at seven o'clock, by all the general staff. At nine o'clock, the theatre; big reception at the Governor's house, and illuminations. Everybody is running about, everybody is in a state of agitation. As I wait, I read Goldoni. I found a beautiful edition here, and was lent it: sixteen octavo volumes. Each contains four or five comedies, none of them with the force of Molière, but all of them full of naturalness. For me they have yet another charm: they bring back to me the customs and language of my beloved Italy, that fatherland of sensibility. Have you read *Corinne?* People here are enchanted by it: but how remote the portrait is from the original!

The Emperor has appointed me adjutant-commissioner of war, with effect from the 11th of July. Ask grandpapa to give thanks where due.

· ·

34

TO HIS SISTER PAULINE

At the Château de Salzdahlum,
the 2nd of September 1807, 4 *a.m.*

You cannot imagine, sweet Pauline, the pleasure your letter has given me. I had almost forgotten your handwriting. I opened the letter as if it were unimportant. I have never received a letter that was less so. Write to me, I beseech you, and at great length. Nothing must ever induce you to throw what you are writing to me into the fire. Don't you know how much I love you? Must I tell you again?

Write me a lot about the charming V . . .[1] I agree with you: she is a very rare soul. I was much in love with her, once, and I have seen her seven times in my life. All my other passions have been but a reflection of this one. I loved Mélanie because she reminded me of V—— in character. You know how I treasure the least details concerning her. Does she love her brother as much as you say? He is one of the driest personages I know, truly made for the brilliant company of this century. But I should not complain of the illusion that causes sisters to believe that brothers are lovable. I only wish it would go so far as to induce sisters to write to their brothers more often.

The sweet thought of V——, which antedates in my soul almost all the griefs that I now remember, came to me in the middle of a superb forest, still fresh with morning dew, at a moment when I and eight good friends—with whom I take care never to forget for an instant that one must be amiable—were going off to hunt the stag. My superior officer, M——[2] has conceived a passion for hunting, with the result that he views with indulgence, or pretends not to see, the excursions I make from my lair.

I shall think of the pair of you all day long. Try to find out if she is in love with anyone at Paris or Rennes. I almost want to say to you, like the Almighty: " Whenever you are gathered together, I shall be amongst you." What a sweet pleasure it would be if the thousand silly vanities that keep us apart were to allow us, while we are still young, to spend a day in these thick woods, amidst their vast silence. We could find something very like them at the Grande-Chartreuse, but the gossip in the Grande-Rue, the conventions, etc., etc. . . . So seek your pleasure in an embroidered collar, and shun the Grande-Rue.

Farewell, I count upon ten letters from you within a fortnight.

By the way, yesterday I shot a partridge. It was the first in my life, but it did not give me a thousandth part of the pleasure I had from a thrush I shot on the path below Doyatière, on a great ash to the right of the path as one approaches the village.[3]

[1] Victorine Mounier. " I have seen in the *Publiciste* a notice of the death of M. Mounier. . . . Poor Victorine will return to Grenoble. What a come-down! What a misfortune! I must put her in touch with my sister." (*Journal*, February 3rd, 1806.)

[2] Martial Daru.

[3] " I had the delightful pleasure of shooting a thrush. . . . I had been beating the vine-yards of Doyatière . . . The bird fell to the ground with a thud that I can still hear. I went down the path, drunk with joy." (*Vie de Henri Brulard.*)

35

TO HIS SISTER PAULINE

The 25th of November 1807

My dear Pauline, I have not had a moment since the 2nd of this month. But for that I would have told you about a shooting-party from which I returned on that day to Brunswick. I asked the Quartermaster and the Director for leave to go shooting for five days in the Harz, a chain of mountains twelve leagues from here. I went with M. Réol, an intelligent man who lacks even an elementary education and has received a very large dose of good sense from five or six voyages to Africa, four to America, two in the Northern seas, and the campaigns of Vendée and Lyon. As we set out—or, rather, a moment after setting out—we instructed the coachman to change direction, and took the road to Hamburg. Tell nobody of this imprudent journey, of which no one here has any suspicion. We arrived at Hamburg after wandering for forty-five hours over a vast sandy desert, which is called the Lüneburg Heath— a truly Flemish landscape, with huge fields surrounded by wooden fences and intersected by gloomy pine-woods and little streams that overflow and form lakes. At two o'clock in the morning we were in Hamburg and made an appalling din at the best inn, which is on the port. When we had shivered there for an hour, the door opened; a hideous serving woman said to us: " Everything is occupied ", and shut the door. More din, and she opened again. We rushed into the house, and, after arguing for more than an hour found beds in the straw at the back of a barn—the roof of which was such that even when lying down we saw the comet, which looked magnificent, in the middle of a sky lit by a frost hard enough to crack a stone. We were the first to rise, at five o'clock, and found an entire family of Germans taking coffee in the *stube*, a room with a stove where the air had not been changed since the beginning of cold weather. These people live a purely animal life, and had sorrowful expressions, which were so noticeable that we supposed they were suffering from some misfortune.

We left our carriage with the inn-keeper and went to the boat. There was a cold fog. The boat was cluttered with all sorts of human figures, dominated by a German coxcomb, his pipe and his valet: a chilly caricature, the vulgarity of whose feelings and thoughts very soon provoked in us an indifference mingled with scorn. Your French coxcomb is at least amiable: he values himself only by his ability to entertain others. Amongst foreign coxcombs the most passable are young people who satisfy the inclinations of their age with gaiety and prudence: by prudence I mean care not to offend anybody—for often one of the inclinations of youth is to neglect danger. Hamburg lies on a lock that opens on one of the branches of the Elbe. Opposite Hamburg the Elbe is immense. At this season it inundates a number of small islands, and on the 28th of October, the day of our departure, there was more than half a league of open water opposite the city. The wind was contrary, so we were obliged to tack. Réol, an experienced sailor who has been in two or three shipwrecks, explained everything to me in nautical language, which contains at least four or five hundred words that are French only in their terminations. The sailors were so slow that we were almost on the point of capsizing: these small dangers, which were absolutely new to me, gave me much pleasure.

Réol told me that once when he was in North-American waters a gust of wind set the ship upon its side; it remained for several seconds in this embarrassing position. A second gust set it back upon its keel.

We touched at Altona and finally entered the port of Hamburg, which is full of vessels rotting away because of the impossibility of commerce.

(I break off here: all morning I have been taking remedies against the vexatious fever that recurs to me every winter, and I cannot go on. Mme Daru sets off tomorrow for Paris.)

I resume this letter on the 27th. But I prefer to continue the parenthesis rather than the letter itself. Mme Daru set off yesterday. Today we are having real Northern weather. It is not yet four o'clock, and I can scarcely see through the two big windows looking out on the square. I thought of you twenty times, today and yesterday, whilst reading some novels which have no other merit than that of being written in English. What a false idea of society these books convey! One might suppose they were all written by and for inhabitants of the moon.

I fear that *these damned books*[1] may have been responsible for some of your opinions. It is only beautiful souls who are subject to these illusions; but such souls are almost all unhappy, and I tremble to think that you may be added to their number. You will see from the enclosed letter from Bigillion that several of the gossips of the Grande-Rue have seen through your disguises. Unless you put matters in order, you will not find a husband: do not think that I am exaggerating for the sake of effect. I give you my word of honour that I believe marriage to be as necessary to women's happiness as it is injurious to that of men. I would

[1] In English in the original.

[93]

give everything in the world for you to deserve the friendship of Mlle Victorine. Do your utmost to achieve this, and tell me how you succeed. She has had experience of the world's cruelty to the misfortunate—that false pity which is worse than scorn.

What makes all kinds of folly fatal for beautiful souls lodged in women's bodies is the fact that they are supposed to be caused by a weakness which is generally despised. The most intelligent and most amorous young man would not marry you, if twenty or thirty ladies assured him that they had seen you roaming the streets in the clothes of a man.

Two years ago, when I was given advice similar to that which I now want you to follow, I said to myself: " Chilly soul! ", and took good care not to believe a word of it. But a deal of misfortunes (of which I have not told you because they were of every-day occurrence and would have taken too long to describe) finally opened my eyes. I decided to look around me, to test for myself the facts of which I was informed and to found my opinion only upon those of which I had proof. I would give a year of my life to see you in the same frame of mind.

" But I get too bored! " you will say. " I cannot go on leading this monotonous life! "

But bear in mind that, once a scandal has arisen, it is for ever: you will never be able to find a husband. We shall have an income of perhaps four or five thousand francs: you will lead a life very like that which our Aunt Dupré leads on an income of ten thousand. But she is supported by public opinion; she has circles in which she is received with pleasure; if anybody makes any objections against her, they concern her person, her intelligence, her character. You, on the other hand, are a thousand times superior to her in all these respects; and your very superiority will do you harm.

" But," say you, " I shall make myself a teacher of the English language, of drawing, etc., etc."

You are imagining that this trade will provide you with a livelihood, and that you will be as happy on the four thousand francs earned in this fashion as your shopkeeper neighbour on the four thousand francs he earns by his dealings in filoselle stockings. Not a bit of it: your hosier will despise you, and will make you feel it in a thousand ways. If you had seen something of society, you would know that every person who has not some fortune, and a position that vanity is forced to respect, is overwhelmed with scorns that are respectable in form and scurrilous in effect. Your notion of the matter is formed by those *damned books* of which I was speaking a moment ago. You might as well imagine a plough to be a windmill. The truth is just the opposite of what these books tell you: the matter is as simple as that. If they depicted the world as it is, they would be horrifying and would produce, even upon people who share their opinions, an impression of gloom which anyone would seek to avoid.

A man of sense and wit who writes a novel by which he hopes to make money, as well as some reputation that will help him the better to sell a second, is therefore careful not to tackle this fatal question. He depicts the passions as the abbé Prévost does, and he depicts them in rich people. Yet poor abbé Prévost had no need to go far to find examples of poverty: he ran away from his monastery at the age of twenty-five, and from this age until that of sixty-seven, I think—the age at which he died—he was deluged with all sorts of unpleasantnesses. If, instead of running away and creating a scandal, he had used his wits to intrigue successfully for his secularisation, he would have been, in Paris, an highly esteemed man of letters, a member of the Academy, a reader to some prince, and possessing, like Duclos, an income of thirty-five thousand francs.

I quote you this example because it is the briefest to expound, and because you perhaps know the persons concerned; but the world is full of stories that lead to the same conclusion.

A woman must first of all get married—that is what is required of her. Afterwards, she can do what she likes. I keep on coming back to Mlle Victorine. She is said to be living in retirement near Grenoble, at Bachet. Try to go and see her with Mlle Mallein, and, when you are there, open your heart frankly to her (without making any mention of my name): ask her advice. She has a beautiful soul. Your frankness, and the misfortunes into which you are on the point of hurling yourself, will touch her heart. She will give you advice which perhaps will not be the same as mine, but will certainly be worth more.

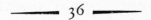

━━ 36 ━━

TO HIS SISTER PAULINE

The 19th of January 1808

Well, you little slut—you deserve it if I resuscitate this elegant and ancient term for you.

Can anybody be lazier than you? For four months you have not written me a word. I get all my news of Grenoble from the public prints.

Give me the family news, which I cannot find in the newspapers. Father will at any moment be receiving a first consignment of seeds. There is one being who, of all others, is purely sublime. Give her all sorts of greetings from me, and, finally, send me three impressions *of father's seal*. At present I am compelled to seal an acceptance of a dinner-invitation with the Imperial Eagle, which is too grand for a small nobody like me. The man[1] who might make something of me has been at Cassel for the last four days, and will be here about the 23rd of January—a date at which I could say that I had loved you for exactly twenty-five years, were it not that I have the honour of being the elder of us. Yet, although I am the elder, I nevertheless give you leave to get married before me. Perform this good stroke of business as soon as you can; but remember that, if ever your husband learns the terrible truth that you are more intelligent than he is, he will hate you for ever—and that, no matter who your husband may be, this truth will always be true.

Farewell, go on loving me, and prove it by writing to me. It is not difficult. Any lover would wish to be in the same case. I wish you knew Mlle Victorine well enough to ask her for some advice concerning the matter of a dear lord and master. Above all, remember to be as humble as Ephestion at the court of Alexander. Let me have an answer, with the seals inside it. Embrace kind Auntie Charvet for me; tell her that I would dearly love to come and eat the cherries at Saint-Egrève. If Barral[2] is at Grenoble, send him the enclosed card.

But *write*. H. B.

. . . .

—— 37 ——

TO FRANÇOIS PÉRIER-LAGRANGE

Brunswick, the 24th of January 1808

My dear Périer, your letter gave me the utmost possible pleasure. You know in advance that it was I who made my sister's choice for her. I

[1] Pierre Daru. (Note by M. Martineau.)

[2] "Louis de Barral, who is at present the oldest and best of my friends, the being who loves me more than anyone else in the world; and it also seems to me that there is no sacrifice which I would not make for him." (*Vie de Henri Brulard.*)

have one more wish, that the matter be completed quickly—you know the proverb concerning long engagements.[1]

What arrangements are you making with father about the settlement? Where will you live? In your own house, I suppose. Which rooms will be your wife's? She is the most reasonable being I know: I am sure that you will be the happiest of husbands.

She was very bored at home, just as we ourselves were bored before we obtained leave to go out by ourselves. It is very natural, when one's present state is not exceedingly gay, to imagine an extreme happiness in a state that one sees only from a distance. This constraint under which she has been for some time may have disposed her to moody moments and wild tastes; but a combination of liberty and reason will soon correct her of it all. Apart from this, I think she is the best woman possible, and you should be happy, if anyone ever will be.

I myself would be happy enough at Brunswick, if only this city lay four or five degrees further to the south. This everlasting humidity is making me ill. I think we shall leave Germany towards April. Perhaps in a few weeks I shall be working at Berlin. It is possible that afterwards we may go to Dalmatia or to Portugal.

I shall do my best to come and embrace you. How pleasant it will be to see my sister your wife at such a time as this. Keep me informed of how everything progresses.

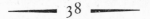

——— 38 ———

TO HIS SISTER PAULINE

The 26th of March 1808

I well realise, my dearest, that you must have a thousand things to do, a thousand duties to fulfil: you will scarcely have time to read my letter. But I enjoy writing to you, and I shall still more enjoy reading and re-reading your answer, if you have time to write me one. It seems to me that in all sensitive souls there are a mass of floating melodies, so to speak: one is suddenly affected by the feelings they express, they come back

---

[1] François Périer-Lagrange was the cousin of the Périer brothers who had the same tutor as Beyle, the abbé Raillanne (" a black rogue "—cf. *Vie de Henri Brulard*). François Périer, born at Grenoble in 1776 and Dr. Gagnon's neighbour in the place Grenette, married Pauline Beyle on May 25th, 1808.

into your mind and you hum them for days at a time, always finding renewed pleasure in them. I am reminded of this notion by what happened to me today: a charming melody came into my mind, set to the little words *cara sorella*[1]. In my memory I went over all the time we have spent together: how in our childhood I did not love you; how I once struck you, at Claix, in the kitchen. I took refuge in the little library. An instant later father entered, in a rage, and said to me: " Wretched child, I could devour you![2] " After that, I remembered all the ills inflicted upon us by poor Auntie Séraphie: our walks along those roads flanked with stagnant water, in the direction of Saint-Joseph. How I used to sigh when I saw the mountains falling away towards Voreppe—especially in the dusk of a summer evening! Their contours were marked out in a gentle orange colour. What a feeling I had for the name, the *Gate of France*! How I loved the word *France* for its own sake, without a notion of what it expressed! Alas for all that delightful imaginary happiness! I had a glimpse of it once at Frascati, and a few other times at Milan. Since then there has been no more trace of it: I am amazed that I was ever able to experience it. The mere memory of it is stronger than all the happinesses that I may procure for myself nowadays.

Such are my daydreams, dearest. I am almost ashamed of them. But, after all, you are the only person in the world to whom I dare relate them. I notice one sad thing: when one loses a passion, one gradually loses the memory of the pleasures it gave. I have told you how, when I was at Frascati, watching some pretty fireworks, at the moment of the explosion Adèle[3] leant for an instant upon my shoulder. I cannot tell you how happy I was.[4] For two years, whenever I was overwhelmed with grief this picture gave me renewed courage and made me forget all my woes. For some time now I had forgotten it, but today I chose to recall it. Despite myself, I see Adèle as she is: but, myself being as I am, I no longer have the slightest happiness from this memory. Mme Pietra Grua[5] is a different case: the memory of her is bound up with that of the Italian language. Whenever I read in a book something that pleases me, spoken by a female character, I involuntarily put it into her mouth. I can hear her—all the sentiment I possess today began with that. I was reading an author whom I scarcely knew or appreciated: the works of

[1] Dear sister.

[2] " ' Unworthy child, I could devour you! ' my father once said, advancing upon me in a rage; but he did not hit me, or only twice or thrice at most. These words: 'unworthy child', etc., were addressed to me one day when I had struck Pauline, who wept and bawled until the house resounded." (*Vie de Henri Brulard.*)

[3] Adèle Rebuffel. (Cf. letter no. 1.)

[4] Cf. letter no. 43.

[5] Cf. letters nos. 13, 82, 83 *et passim*.

Count Gasparro Gozzi. I had come to the *punizione nel precipizio*[1]. Queen Elvira, reduced to hiding herself in immense forests, meets her son, a charming young man who does not know that she is his mother. If the tyrant Don Sancho suspected him of being the son of his predecessor, he would have him killed. Elvira has had no news of him since his birth: prudence dictates that she should forbid him to see her again. She tries to go away, but she cannot: she returns to him and says:

> *Pastore vedi se tamo,*
> *Tu ristora . . . etc.*[2]

I could see Angelina, that noble figure, saying this to her son. At the passage which follows after the description of the grotto, I found myself weeping like a child: for several minutes I read over and over again the word *sepuoi*[3], weeping ever harder. In the last eighteen months I have only thrice experienced so sweet a moment: twice when reading of the death of Clorinda, *o vista! o conoscenza*[4], and again this morning. Since then I have verified an account of 9,007,661 francs and 07 centimes, scattered over a hundred and forty pages of a ledger in folio. I have written out a report of eight pages—nothing could efface that sweet impression. Moreover, this piece is the only delightful work of art that I have seen for eighteen months. My good and frigid companions call it a farce: but what work is to be compared with one which, in a few words and without your being prepared for it, can move you to such a point?

Farewell. Go on loving me, and give me news of Grenoble.

. . . .

39

TO HIS SISTER PAULINE

The 26th of May 1808

I never get accustomed to doing without your letters. I well realise that when one marries one goes into bankruptcy as regards half one's

---

[1] The punishment on the precipice.
[2] Shepherd, see how I love you.
[3] " And if ", or possibly a mistake for seppuoi, " I buried ".
[4] O vision, o understanding.

friendship with all one's friends. Since the misfortune[1] that has befallen us, I have known nothing of Grenoble. It has become a strange town, and, although I do not like living there, nevertheless it is the dwelling-place of a dozen people who ceaselessly come back into my memory.

So give me all details, and never be afraid of giving me too many. Above all, give me an account of your marriage. I almost hope that, by the time you receive these lines, it will all be over: tell me about it.[2] To encourage you to relate sweet nothings, I shall begin myself.

A few days ago I found myself thirteen hundred feet below ground— at the bottom of a mine in the Harz called Dorothea. It's an odd thing, but, as is customary with me, the spectacle that gave me most pleasure was that which I presented to myself. I have such an aversion to evil smells that they suddenly change my very nature: I was afraid of the odour of burnt sulphur which one notices at smelting works. This was my first repugnance; the second was against falling. One descends into the mine by perpendicular ladders: if you miss your hold, you become a lump of clinker. The greasy ladders are so thick with running mud that your hand continually slips. It gave me, in miniature, the impression of fighting on horseback in a swamp. From a distance, the situation seems undignified; but, when one is in it, one is busy with successively surmounting a great number of small difficulties: your first small successes give you infinite joy. The fact is that you are entertained because you are acquiring reasons to think highly of yourself, and are so happy to have reasons for so unreasonable a thought.

After that the King arrived; I was presented to him. I went everywhere, and found my companions vastly entertaining. I attached myself to one of the noblemen of his court, who proved to be a most likeable man. Women, Italy, music, war, ambition occupy the same positions in his heart as in mine. Our minds, however, have less in common. If we were working side by side, we should soon become close friends. At present we find each other agreeable acquaintances.

Four years ago I was in Paris with a single pair of boots with holes in them, without a fire in the heart of winter, and often without a candle. Here I am a personage: I receive a great number of letters from Germans who address me as *Monseigneur*; French notabilities call me *Monsieur l'intendant*; visiting generals come to see me; I receive petitions, I write

[1] Their great-aunt Élisabeth Gagnon, their " kind Auntie ", had died at Grenoble on April 6th, 1808, in her eighty-seventh year. (Note by M. Martineau.) " Élisabeth Gagnon, a tall, thin, dry woman with an handsome Italian face and a character that was completely noble—noble with all the Spanish delicacies and scruples of conscience. In this respect she formed my character, and it is to my Aunt Élisabeth that I owe these abominable illusions of nobility in the Spanish style to which I have fallen a victim." (*Vie de Henri Brulard.*)

[2] The marriage had been celebrated the previous day.

letters, I scold my secretaries, I go to ceremonial dinners, I ride on horseback and read Shakespeare. But I was happier in Paris. If one could arrange one's life as one desires, like moving a piece on a draughts-board, I would still be going to lessons in rhetoric at Dugazon's, visiting Mélanie, with whom I was in love, and wearing a shabby frock-coat that pierced my very soul. When she would not receive me, I used to go and read at a library; and finally, in the evening, I would walk to the Tuileries, where from time to time I gazed in envy at people who were happy. But how many delightful moments I had in that poverty-stricken life! I was in a desert where occasionally I found an oasis. Here I am at a table laden with dishes, but I have not the slightest appetite.

This monotony may be about to change: people think that we are going to punish Austria for all her insolences. For my part, I am not one of these " people ". I have no desire at all for war, and I would prevent it a thousand times if I could. But, once the matter is decided, I shall be delighted that it should be so, and that I should be involved in it. Concerning such matters one can almost always say: " what one has seen once, one never sees again ", and I am beginning to realise that it is only on this condition that one can endure three-quarters of men and things.

Farewell; write to me. Enter into all the same little details. Insist that the orchard at Claix be turned into an English garden. That is the pleasant thing about the region where I am now vegetating: every nook is trans-formed into an English garden, despite unsuitable conditions of water, sun, air and soil; and sometimes I come alive for a moment amidst these attractive imitations of a nature from which I am too far removed.

DUBOIS.

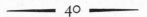

40

TO HIS SISTER PAULINE

June 1808

Well, my dearest, what do you say about it? Was it worth while to be so scared? Yet I confess that the moment when M. Stupi sang the epithal-amium must have been somewhat scabrous, especially for a woman. But if the day caused you some embarrassment, to me it gave a lively pleasure, thanks to the charming description I received from our good grandfather.

. . . Well, one of the great concerns of my life has come to a successful conclusion . . . So you are travelling already, that's excellent. Be economical as regards jewels and such silly gauds, so that you may visit Milan or Paris; but fix in advance a sum of from two to three thousand francs, and resolve not to exceed it.

I quiver with joy like a child when I think of the address which I shall shortly write upon this letter.

One thing I advise you: plant an English garden. Select one of your pieces of ground, and plant it this winter. " But I shall bungle it," say you? No matter! Acacias, chestnuts and poplars cost four francs to plant and give more pleasure than walls costing five francs a yard. My brother-in-law has a very picturesque property at a league from Vizille. It is close to Claix, it would be charming. Select a spot where nature has already done much, and plant in the first year of your marriage: in fifteen years you will be walking beneath those trees with your children. At fifteen minutes' distance from Brunswick there used to be ten journals of horrible heath. The Duchess has spent three thousand francs on trees for it, and now it is a charming spot that everybody goes to look at. Even I do, and I keep a room there.

By the way, lavish ten thousand compliments upon the delightful madame Tivollier, with whom I am always madly in love. Offer ten thousand greetings from me to her excellent husband. How is little Séraphin? Is he still a mischief?

Do not fail to pay our respects to all our new relatives and old friends, especially to Mme Périer. When you see Alphonse tell him that *I am filled with indignation with him*[1].

Farewell, dear madame! Be careful how you comport yourself in this grand condition. It is like a stage to which one ascends from the pit: it seems imposing as long as one does not see the decorations at the back.

How did you support it?

Did you prove bold or cowardly? Well, after the shock given you by an event so agreeable in itself, imagine what Frederick must have felt after losing the battle of Kunersdorf!

Hitherto you were bound to a strong pillar, you could not judge of your own character. Now you are in the open air. Act in accordance with your own counsel. I think that, above all, you will bring some gaiety and childishness into your home-life; and, above all, don't give it a cold, gloomy atmosphere, or I'll desert you. But, alas! before deserting, one must first of all be present, and I am very far away. Embrace Périer for me.

[1] In English in the original.

Just as I was closing this letter, I learnt, from a sure and secret source, that Martial was exposed in Spain to the very greatest dangers. Inform the family of this, but prescribe absolute silence. It was in a revolt, I think, but he came off without harm.

I suppose you know that Joseph is now ruler in Spain, and the Prince of Wales in England. That is where one should go, if only for three weeks, like madame Roland. For my part, I feel I have the courage to go there in a boat six feet long. Farewell. Tell me the name of your confessor. I hope you are entirely reconciled with our Mallein cousins.

You see that I am always somewhat pedantic towards you: that's because I love you, and you don't write to me!

—— 41 ——

TO HIS SISTER PAULINE

The 23rd of June 1808

I am very fond of collections of moralisings, even mediocre ones: they cause me to make a sort of examination of conscience.

When I read in Vauvenargues a not particularly profound thought concerning our tendency to cling to opinions that encourage us to be idle, I begin to wonder which of my opinions I have not lately scrutinised. But what is the use, you will say, of trying to acquire wit? Certainly not in order to shine, but to give oneself a pleasure that nobody can take away from you.

I am writing this from Richemond, where I have been living happily since the eighth of this month, in the deepest solitude.[1] Is that not an achievement? And do you suppose that Gil Blas, in the tower of Segovia, did not have moments of great intellectual pleasure? An excellent work in three octavo volumes, the *Letters* of H. St. John, Viscount Boling-broke, is about to give me five or six days of contentment. This is a small plea on behalf of the intellect, which marriage might cause you to leave in the lurch: on behalf of the intellect, I repeat—it is a fire that goes out if it does not increase.

There is nothing so serious and so boring as the home life of the

---

[1] " In 1808, at the small palace of Richemont (at ten minutes' distance from Brunswick), where he lived by reason of his rank of quartermaster, he began a history of *La Guerre de la succession en Espagne*." (*Obituary*).

couples I have seen here and at Marseilles: they always talk seriously. If one of the couple—some intimate friend with whom one is entirely at ease—permits himself a jest, he is thought to be *seeking to be witty*: provincial pride is up in arms, and all intimacy is lost. At Paris it is very different: when a person ventures a jest, even if it be dragged in by the hair, nobody sees in it anything but a love of gaiety. Everybody indulges in jest, each vying with his neighbour, and people laugh. And when one has laughed all through a dinner, what does it matter whether one has laughed at stupidities or at wit?

"But in a household," you will say, "there are certain matters requiring decision that call for serious discussion." Certainly, but business should be treated as business. Go and find your husband in the morning in his study, and in four sentences you will go further than by sacrificing all the time of a dinner. Perhaps you have already told yourself this long ago, and expressed it much better than I have written it; but, at any rate, my words will afford you an opportunity of making a small examination of conscience concerning the main conversation at dinner on the day after the arrival of this homily of mine.

This is part of the domain of the lady of the house: it is she who governs the conversation. I count upon it that when I come to see you I shall be rewarded for the three or four hundred leagues I shall have covered, *for our grand father*[1] and for the pleasure of your company, by finding that you associate with the most intelligent people in Grenoble. Remember the life that madame Helvétius led at Auteuil with the amiable Cabanis, who has recently died, and so many others. No pedantry, no officialdom of mind. They were people who got on well together, made conversation together, and found happiness at small cost.

I read yesterday in the *Moniteur* that there is to be an edition of the works of Beaumarchais, that gay and courageous man: I love him with all my heart. I took the occasion to re-read a volume of that pedant, La Harpe. Nevertheless, pedant though he be, I found this sentence:

"Whoever is happy, or appears to be so, should be continually on his knees to beg forgiveness, and sometimes does not gain it even at this price."

This evening I shall go to Brunswick to find some engraving that I can send you as a visual reminder of this maxim, which ought to be the foundation of your day-to-day manner of life.

Be assured that every young woman in Grenoble—unless she has a great soul, a thing not altogether common—would be delighted if some mortification befell you, and you would soon be overwhelmed from all

[1] In English in the original.

sides with perfidious pity. That is what kept me on the grill ever since I learnt of certain *walks with dresses of man*[1]. You ran a positively devilish risk; I would have been less disquieted to know that you were in battle three times over.

But, happily, we have for the present come to port. We are about to sit in judgment on you, princess. There have been many examples of heirs to the throne who, when they saw it only from below, would make the sagest comments on the faults of their predecessors: but this lasted only until the moment when they became kings themselves, and made equally ridiculous mistakes. To apply the moral, madame, let us consider what style of appearance your house will have. Will you always be dressed with sufficient decorum to make your inferiors respect you? Will you know how to avoid familiarity with those of them whom you wish to have love you? Will you have the constancy to plant a pretty English garden—without bridges, grottoes and other expensive follies— in the first or second year of your marriage? Will you be in a position to state, on the 30th of August, how much, to within twenty centimes, your housekeeping has cost during the month? Will you have the great kindness to have one of your tenant-farmers breed two or three good pointers for me? Will you not say " yes " to all these five questions, and will they not be mere projects left hanging for seven or eight years?

And the art of governing your life—what shall we say about that? Will you know how to profit by the kindness of Madier and Penet, without making your husband jealous? Do you realise that, whilst you are still childless, you should travel in the world a little? You would prefer to spend your three thousand francs amidst the beauty-spots of Switzerland, but you have no need of that: you have enough ideas of that sort already. What you need is a big city: go and stay for three months in Paris, first promising yourself that you will not spend more than three thousand francs there. For this purpose, take on arrival three rooms at the Hotel de Hambourg, rue Jacob, no. 18, or at any other hotel in the faubourg Saint-Germain. It will cost you eighty francs a month, and in the rue de la Loi it would be a hundred and fifty francs. Dine at a private room of Legacque at the Tuileries: you will spend ten francs for the two of you, and at Véry's, next door, it would cost you thirty francs. In the first fortnight of your stay you will have to visit all the Périer, Daru and Petiet ladies. In order to do this, take a very clean livery-carriage which will carry you wherever you wish from nine o'clock in the morning until midnight. For this you will pay fifteen francs a day to the proprietor of the said livery-carriage, and three francs to the coachman. Apply to

---

[1] In English [*sic*] in the original.

[105]

Gerbot, saddler, rue de l'Université, between the rue de Bucy and the rue de Poitiers, mentioning that you are a cousin of madame Martial Daru. Gerbot will show you his best carriage of this sort, he's a good fellow and not expensive. Before showing yourself in society, go with madame Alexandrine Périer (mademoiselle Pascal) to her dressmaker, and clothe yourself from top to toe. Stay a little behind the fashion. As for my dear brother-in-law, have him go to Léger, rue Vivienne, 13— the most conceited of men, but the best tailor—and buy a complete rig-out for five or six hundred francs. When you've done that, you'll have a week of boring visits, but they won't take as much time as you think. I wish I could be with you in that happy city. I would show you everything—or, rather, I would acquaint myself with everything in your company; for I have never visited the Gobelins, for example. You could end up with a visit to the theatre, in which case you would return home exhausted—but with what a lot of new ideas!

At last, one fine day, you will see your three thousand francs reduced to twenty louis: take your post-chaise and return peacefully to economise at Thuélin,[1] for that seems to be your general headquarters. I would have preferred Vizille, which is handsomer and nearer to Claix; but if you save even as little as twelve hundred francs a year by staying at Thuélin, you cannot hesitate to do so.

My dear Pauline, all this is a hundredth part of what I would have found to say to you had Heaven and M. Daru willed it that I should have an opportunity of embracing you this summer. I quite believe that you have all these same ideas, but you postpone their execution, and you ought never to postpone anything, from the extraction of a tooth to a pleasant excursion to the Grande-Chartreuse. By the way, when will you bend your steps in that direction? Give thirty sous to some old brother who can read, so that he may erase my name wherever it is to be seen. I have often felt ashamed of those scribbles, especially when Mallein told me that Victorine had made fun of them—and, in faith, she was quite right.

. . . .

[1] In 1807 François Périer had bought the château Thuélin, or Tullins, near La Tour-du-Pin.

42

TO HIS SISTER PAULINE

The 12th of September 1808

I thought myself for ever quit of the pomposities of love, and on the point of finding salvation, but my pride has had a nasty fall: I have just received a letter which gave me so much pleasure that I surely must be in love with her who wrote it.

Here is my story: eight months ago there was a colonel here with whom I became acquainted in my official capacity. He had a wife of twenty-three, a lady of infinite wit and possessed of that lofty character which I love so much in Italian women. I exchanged pleasantries with her on three or four occasions, once whilst winning a louis or two from her at a game for stakes of six sous. Her husband went off with his regiment, but he died six leagues hence. A few days later she returned, and I went to see her. I found that she received me courteously, in the midst of her deep grief, but as she would receive anyone else. For my part, being thus received, being bored, knowing that she was bored and feeling sure of spending some agreeable moments in her company, I nevertheless spent four long months without going to see her. One evening, on the promenade, chance brought us side by side. She was departing in a week: and from that moment we spent our whole time together. She knows the same towns in Italy as I do, and almost the same people. She departed, and I galloped ten leagues at her carriage-door. All night long we had the most ridiculous conversation: she almost never composed herself for sleep—and this in order to speak of the pleasures of hunting and other interesting matters! But I think our eyes conversed with greater vivacity. At last I left her. As I rode back, ruining my horses, I thought myself too stupid for things to be natural. She had promised to write to me— tush, she had already forgotten me! The day before yesterday I was brought an ill-seeming little letter, on yellow paper. It looked so cheap that I thought it was from Barral. I opened it, and a long quarter of an hour later I found that my cheeks were red to the eyes and that I was pacing about with great strides, the happiest of men, and sighing deeply.

Is it not comical that for four long months in Brunswick it depended only upon me whether I saw or possessed a charming woman, and that

I postponed thinking of her until we were separated by a little matter of three hundred leagues?

What is more, yesterday—that is to say, the 10th—there was a battle! I witnessed a burst of musketry in which an old woman, with her two hands crossed upon her stomach, had them pierced like Our Saviour's, and her stomach to boot, and at once departed to a place where she would benefit by His mercy. Not to speak of several sabre-cuts, of which nobody is proud. Magnificent moonlight; a wide street full of people. *Fer-flou-Ke-ta Françauze*[1], which means " d——ned Frenchman ", raining from all sides on my uniform hat. A shot. Twenty people casting themselves on the ground all about me. The others hurled themselves against the walls; I was the only one left standing upright. A pretty girl of eighteen, her head almost under my boots . . . I thought she was wounded. She was trembling violently, but not at the touch of my hand, which was most innocently caressing a lovely, cool young arm. I dutifully picked her up to see if it was her leg that was broken. Battle was engaged, there were more shots. I carried her up against a wall: I thought of Sganarelle carrying Célie. I set her down. She looked at me, dropped me a pretty curtsy, and fled.

Meanwhile soldiers were running to the spot . . . At this point my style becomes more humble, because our hero faded from sight. He found himself in the midst of the population in revolt against the French, one of whom had slightly killed a civilian. The population was attacking the hospital where the killer lay, and a hundred and fifty brave soldiers were firing upon the said rabble. I remember the adventure by reason of the superb colouring of the scene: the light was as pure as the eyes of mademoiselle de Bé——; but the comparison is worthy of Chateaubriand, who depicts the Roman Campagna by likening it to the countryside of Babylon. Mademoiselle de B—— is a grown-up person of seventeen who has as many attractions as her ancestors have titles. She has great, dark-blue eyes shining out amidst the loveliest whiteness in the world—eyes whose brilliance and purity pierce the depths of the soul. There is something ethereal about those eyes: 'tis a soul laid bare.

Come now, answer this letter. *Has our great father writed to mister Daru?*[2]

M. Duboin, Captain.

---

[1] *Verfluchte franzose*, " accursed Frenchman ".
[2] In English [*sic*] in the original.

43

TO HIS SISTER PAULINE

29th of October 1808

The arts promise more than they perform. This idea—or, rather, this charming sentiment—has just been given to me by a German street-organ which played, as it passed through the street next to mine, a tune of which two passages are new to me—and, what is more, are charming, in my opinion. The tears almost came into my eyes.

The first time I ever took pleasure in music was at Novara[1], a few days before the battle of Marengo. I went to the theatre, where they were playing *Il Matrimonio Segreto*[2]. The music delighted me like an expression of love. I think no woman I have had ever gave me so sweet a moment, or at so light a price, as the moment I owe to a newly heard musical phrase. This pleasure came to me without my in any way expecting it: it filled my whole soul. I have told you of a similar sensation that I once had at Frascati when Adèle[3] leant against me while we were watching fireworks: I think this was the happiest moment of my life. The pleasure must have been truly sublime, for I still remember it although the passion that caused it is entirely extinguished.

. . . .

44

TO FÉLIX FAURE[4]

Strasbourg, the 5th of April 1809

Two o'clock has just struck in the famous clock-tower of Strasbourg, which I climbed the day before yesterday. Since midnight I have been

---

[1] " In the evening I had a sensation that I shall never forget. I went to the theatre ... they were playing Cimarosa's *Matrimonio Segreto*, the actress who played the part of Carolina had a front tooth missing. That is all I can remember of a divine happiness." (*Vie de Henri Brulard.*)

[2] *The Secret Marriage.*

[3] Adèle Rebuffel.

[4] " About the dullest of all my friends is Félix Faure (peer of France), with whom I have lived intimately. . . . He was born with a vulgar soul, that is why he is a peer of France and First President of the Royal Court at Grenoble." (*Vie de Henri Brulard.*)

walking the length and breadth of a fireless drawing-room. I am freezing, but I have the advantage of being in full dress.

. . . Since I did not see you during my last three days in Paris, I must tell you that Mme Daru treated me as usual, not speaking to me except when compelled and preferring to my company that of persons who, I can say without any vanity, are very much inferior to me in courage, in fortune and in quality. Negligence, almost disdain: she looked at me as one looks at a barrel of gunpowder.

We were completely overturned near Blamont. That was the only incident of our journey that was at all enlivening. On Easter Sunday, at nine o'clock in the morning, I found myself sprawling on my back.

. . . .

—— 45 ——

TO FÉLIX FAURE

Landshut, the 26th of April, 1809

I enjoy fairly complete disfavour. People speak to everybody except to me. What's the cause of it? It seems to me scarcely likely that at the beginning of the campaign I shall be any longer a commissioner of war. No doubt I shall have that rank at the end, like everybody else, when theatrical conventions will scarcely permit anything different.

As for our office, it is rather like the court of King Pétaud. It gives an advantage to the talkers *ad hoc* and *ab hac*, and for my part I hardly talk at all. The good thing in all this is that ambition is rather like love, of which it is said:

If love doth live by hope, with hope it is put out.[1]

I would like very well to talk, but one must have at one's command a flood of dull or commonplace remarks.

Farewell, I am hastening to see His Majesty.

[1] Cf. letter no. 28.

TO HIS SISTER PAULINE

Burghausen, the 29th *of April* 1809

Two days ago, on the 27th, we set out from Landshut to find quarters at Neumarkt for M. Daru and our seventeen comrades. The road was filled with a double file of covered waggons, and since at intervals it narrowed so that only one vehicle could pass at a time, we made occasional halts and had leisure to examine the countryside, which is charming. It is covered with woods of fir and pine: as a rule these woods are planted in squares, and the way in which they are dotted over the hills on both sides of the road makes them look, from a distance, like halted regiments of infantry. We were entitled to have such military thoughts, for fighting had taken place two days before on the terrain through which we were passing. I studied the curious disorder that war leaves behind it. The most striking thing was the large quantity of excellent straw, quite fresh and still quite crisp, that was scattered over the fields. Every half hour we came upon a bivouac; but, even apart from these straw huts, the fields were covered with it. There were caps, shoes, a lot of jackets of cheap cloth, wheels, shafts of hand-carts, and many little squares of paper that had been wrapped round packets of cartridges.

From time to time we came to the top of a hill from which we could survey two or three miles of road. We could descry, in a stifling cloud of dust, two files of cuirassiers slipping through the convoys, sometimes at a walk but more often at a trot, and deviating as often as they could onto the fields on either side. In the middle of the road there was an artillery convoy, and at the sides there were hundreds of vehicles carrying regimental baggage, together with officers' carriages, whose occupants found occasion every league or so to dismount, cursing and calling Heaven to witness that they would have everybody thrown in the cells.

It was by the use of such polite methods that we ourselves, having left Landshut at two o'clock, arrived at Neumarkt, which is only six leagues distant, at about ten o'clock in the evening.

As you can suppose, the bacchanalia was still more hellish in a little country town of two thousand souls which at present harbours a population of forty thousand men who have not dined and don't give a d———n for anything in the world. From ten o'clock until two o'clock we roamed in search of quarters. After that I busied myself, with a little knife worth two sous, at cutting slices of beef from a leg I had obtained at Landshut. In the midst of this operation sleep overcame me, and I let myself slide beneath the table. A big black dog had the impertinence to come and lie on my feet. I let it do so, for love of peace. An hour later a deserter, an Austrian soldier but born in France, whom I had the day before taken as a servant, awoke me by bringing me slices of beef that were approximately cooked but were covered with a crystallisation of salt. I was tearing at them, with my eyes shut, when I noticed, through a chink in the shutter, that day was beginning to dawn. I opened the shutter and saw General P——, in a braided hat, astride of a truss of straw fastened to a waggon.

" Where are you going like that, general? "

" To my brigade! I'm told there will be fighting today, and I'm in despair, I don't know how to get there."

"Since you're in despair, come and eat some abominable beef with me."

He came in and ate like a wolf: he considered the beef tender. Then a courier came for M. Daru. A quarter of an hour later came M. Daru himself, and said to me: " By Gemini, you had better go and do our quartering at Altoetting; perhaps that infernal impudence of yours will do the trick again."

So we set off at half past four o'clock. On the road there was the same tumult, even worse than the day before, because less time had passed since the terrain had been a scene of fighting. Nevertheless, as on the day before, the dead had been removed.

When we arrived in Altoetting, we found there the Imperial Guard, two generals and fifty grenadiers besieging the poor devil of a municipal official in charge of quartering. He did not understand a word of the intolerable jabber that was being shouted into his ears. When we spoke to him in German, he replied: " No understand French, monsieur."

What with the generals forbidding that anybody should be quartered before themselves, and myself stubbornly defending my master's right to the best quarters in the town, everybody threatened, cursed, shouted, all in this execrable little room. Finally the combatants were driven out by the stench. I went seeking quarters in a torrent of rain, and found a little farm out in the fields, surrounded by bivouacs. I dried myself at a splendid fire that some grenadiers had lit, and went to see what fortune had to offer me in this Augean stable. I had set everything topsy-turvy in a huge inn, the quarters of M. Daru. I found a comrade of mine who had done the quartering for the whole general staff. I stole a quartering-order from him, and finally arrived at quarters no. 36. Here I found a countess surrounded by her children. The eldest, a girl of seventeen, not very pretty but fresh and, above all, very well made, spoke French, as also did her mother. The younger children had splendid eyes. I assumed an air of gentleness and brought out my best German phrases; as a result of which I was adored within half an hour. I found myself peacefully installed in my room, which was magnificent but had no fire or bed, turning the pages of *Moore's Travels in Germany*. I was seeking to find in it some different ideas from those with which I had been forcibly preoccupied for the past twenty-six hours, when the mother and six children entered the room.

" Monsieur! The Austrians! They're here. One of my farmers, who has just come in, has told me of it, and I thought it my duty to warn you."

" Madame, has your town any fosses? "

" None at all, monsieur. In any case, my house is outside the town. If you care to go upstairs, you will see the Austrians."

During this colloquy, which was longer than as I have described it, Mlle Rosine displayed great interest in the fate in store for me. " The battalion that's here will be driven out, and you will be made prisoner! That's quite certain."

I was much more interested in the amiable figure thus appearing before me in the midst of all my grim reflections, than in the approach of the redoubtable Kaiserlichen. Finally we climbed into a turret whose windows had no balcony. I had all the trouble in the world to prevent the younger children from hurling themselves out of the window. I nearly did so myself. Mlle Rosine held me back by the arm. At last we raised our eyes, and in the outlets of the surrounding wood we actually saw the spear-points of five or six regiments of cavalry, clad in grey coats; but I realised that they were our own cuirassiers, who had donned their white coats because of the rain, which had turned them grey. We all went downstairs laughing at our mighty danger. For my part, I was wrapt in thoughts of Mlle Rosine, and forgot everything else until seven o'clock, when M. Daru arrived. A great number of people had been quartered on my countess, and I made several speeches to them, urging them not to make a din. They laughed at me somewhat, but finally there was no noise. When I left the house, Rosine did not accompany me to the door; but her mother came to make me promise that I would spend the night in the house, in order to prevent noise. I promised, and went to sup with M. Daru, who said to me, at about eleven o'clock: " It would be no bad idea if you went at once to ask the Prince, who is at Burghausen," etc., etc.

I had had some requisitioned horses, but they had escaped. My servant was in bed—nobody knew where. Whilst I was at the home of Mme la Comtesse, sixty men of the Imperial Guard, and all the employees of the Army transport depôt, had broken into my house. Lastly, it was eleven o'clock, it was raining in torrents, there was not as much as a cat in the streets, which were unknown to me. The only light was that from distant bivouacs, round which shadows could be seen passing to and fro. The comicality of my situation prevented me from growing impatient.

Since I had boasted to my comrades of Rosine, they had begun by assuring me that at No. 37, next to my 36, there was a much prettier young lady. This was appalling news. M. Cuny, my travelling-companion, assured me that I was a sybarite, and that it was my duty to go and search for horses—in this town where I knew nobody, where everybody distrusted us, where nobody would open his door to us, even if he heard it being broken down. He especially advised me not to forget that we were to depart in an hour.

At this I began cursing at everybody and everything, even at the big black clouds that were drenching me with horrible deluges. At every door I said that I had a mission of the highest importance. My eloquence had no effect. The answer was always: *Kein Pferd*[1]. Finally it occurred to me to give details of my mission. I said that if I did not carry to Burghausen the orders with which I was entrusted, next day all the troops would be without bread. This stroke succeeded. Some twenty soldiers— who, not having obtained quartering-orders, had decided to quarter themselves in the very office from which these orders were issued— began to reason amongst themselves. I overheard them, and besought them to let me in. One of them came and debarricaded the door. Once I was inside and under shelter, my eloquence was redoubled; and at last, an hour later, I presented myself at No. 36 with four huge horses and three peasants to lead them—the whole cortège soaked to the marrow.

I found M. Cuny laughing with Mlle Rosine and her mother. He had proceeded to remember that he had left behind at Neumarkt a wretched sabre that hadn't even an edge, and had sent a courier in search of this precious weapon. He therefore informed me that he would wait until two o'clock for the return of his courier.

During our absence a second colonel had arrived, and had taken the very bed of Mme la Comtesse herself. For my part, I had handed over my quarters in her house to M. Joinville, my old friend with the Army

---

[1] No horse.

of Italy.[1] We began dancing, singing and telling stories. From time to time I went out with a glass of branntwein for our peasants.

Mlle Rosine was greatly entertained. She was always attentive to me, but she also seemed to be getting along very well with M. Cuny. The ice had been sharply broken. Finally, after much laughter, the clock struck half past two: the sabre did not choose to make its appearance. The worthy German who carried the despatch, not suspecting that there was to be a reply, had met half-way on the road another courier coming from Neumarkt to Altoetting, and had exchanged his despatch for that of his comrade. Furthermore, the countess wished to serve us with coffee: she had put the yolk of an egg into the cream. At last we set out, crammed with good cheer, at about three o'clock.

Our horses were somewhat restive, but Cuny and I fell into a deep slumber. We woke up, at about five o'clock this morning, to find our horses in full gallop downhill. We screeched like eagles, pulled them to a halt and put on the brake.

The Salzach, a river that is swifter and somewhat wider than the Isère, plunges here into a bed of sandstone. Its banks are nearly three hundred feet high, and so steep that at the point where the river reaches Burghausen, there is scarcely foothold for a few trees, which are beginning to put forth pretty little leaves. At one point the Salzach has worn away the eastern bank, forming a little plain on which the town is built. But the approach to the town is an infernally steep descent—which was what awoke us—and on the other side is a perpendicular rise. All we can do is to look at it.

I am writing to you from a monastery where I am quartered. Beside it is the bridge over the Salzach, but the Austrians have had the good sense to burn this. It has nine arches, the river is very swift, and from time to time I interrupt my letter to go and look at this picturesque structure. The whole Army is held up here because of the bridge. This is the extreme edge of Bavaria: on the other side is Austria. Yesterday M. Daru wagered that by the 13th we would be in Vienna.

On our arrival this morning we carried our despatch to the Prince. His reply made it necessary for one of us to return at full gallop to Altoetting. The rain had become even heavier. On this occasion I succeeded in proving to M. Cuny that it was *his* duty to set off and leave me to do the quartering.

I have never cursed so much in my life, my throat is quite sore. Finally I found my monastery, where I was given an egg-nog, very well

[1] Louis Joinville, Commissioner of War at Milan in 1800, had introduced Beyle to Mme Pietagrua, who at that time was his mistress.

made, with two slices of beautiful white bread. The egg-nog made me want to laugh, but I'm utterly spent. Five o'clock has struck, and I am waiting for my master, who still does not come. M. Cuny has gone to bed; sleep is gaining upon me. I wished to give you a sample of a day in which I thought more than twenty times of you. Anything that awakes tenderness in me brings me back to this feeling.

Today all thoughts of Mlle Rosine have vanished. I sit opposite an ill-made copy of a beautiful madonna by Guido. I spend my time contemplating it and seeking to discover the painter's central idea, and then going to look at the bridge and the swiftness of the Salzach, which now and then carries off to the devil the handsome timbers over which we hope to pass.

Farewell: friendly greetings to everybody, and especial compliments to those who do not want them.[1]

———— 47 ————

TO FÉLIX FAURE

Wels, the 3rd of May, 1809

I have not time to write to you at length: our friend Pacé is here.

Read, if you care to do so, the enclosed letter to my sister[2], and then pass it on.

I need stimulus for my imagination. Pray buy me M. de Chateaubriand's *Martyrs*, a work in three volumes, and send it to me via the offices of the Civil List.

As we went through Ebersberg[3], I truly wanted to vomit when I saw the wheels of my carriage spilling out the entrails of poor little light infantrymen whose bodies were half burnt. To distract my attention from this horrible spectacle, I started talking—with the result that I am now thought to have a heart of stone.

[1] " I described my feelings and adventures prior to Burghausen in an eight-page letter to my sister. The thing lacks depth and is too much prettified." (*Journal*, Enns, May 5th, 1809.)
[2] Probably the letter immediately preceding.
[3] " The whole town of Ebersberg caught fire, the street through which we passed was full of corpses, most of them French and almost all of them burnt.

" . . . In several places the corpses were heaped together. I studied their faces. On the bridge was a sturdy German who had died with his eyes open. Courage, loyalty and German good nature were depicted in his face, which expressed nothing but a tinge of melancholy.

" The street gradually became narrower, and finally, under the gate and in front of it, our carriage had to pass over corpses disfigured by the flames." (*Journal*, May 5th, 1809.)

I am respected, but not liked. This arises from the fact that to talk puerilities for a dozen hours of each day bores me stiff, so I hold my tongue.

—— 48 ——

TO HIS SISTER PAULINE

Vienna, the 14th of July 1809[1]

For me your charming letter is like a beaker full of the coolest water suddenly offered to a traveller painfully crossing the sands of Africa.

For some days I have experienced an access of ambition, which gives me no rest day or night. I am not greatly disquieted by this feverish passion, for soon everything will be decided, and in the event of non-success I shall soon have forgotten my burning desires. I am capable of laughing at myself. When I am tranquil, all that gives pleasure to the others seems to me dull and unworthy of attention. When I am swallowed up by an access of furious desires, which seize hold of me twice or thrice a year, I sigh for the tranquillity which I see withering at my feet. Take it all in all, ever since my arrival in Paris last December I have been pleased with my happiness, which for anyone else would be an intolerable disquiet.

The assurance you give me that my letters will not be seen by others causes me to tell you everything. At Paris I was in love with Elvire: because of the immense difference between us in rank, this species of passion was expressed only in our eyes, as they say in novels. It kept me entertained, especially during the last moments of my stay. Elvire is not overburdened with sensibility—or, at least, her sensibility has never been exercised. I believe that in my company she was astonished to learn that she was capable of feeling. Two or three times we had those moments of rapture at which everything disappears except the object of one's desire. We were prevented, by obstacles that were insurmountable and of the greatest danger for both of us, from speaking otherwise than in expressive glances. But who is this Elvire[2]? I shall tell you as soon as

[1] Beyle had written to Félix Faure from Sankt-Pölten on May 11th: " We are leaving for Vienna, or rather for Schoenbrunn, on the 12th at five o'clock in the morning." And, from Vienna, on May 18th: From the first days of my stay at Vienna I had that feeling of inner contentment and perfect well-being which, ever since Italy, I had experienced only at Geneva. . . . My stay in Vienna delights me, and at the same time awakens a strange feeling of sadness. One is too much inclined to fall in love: at every step one meets a pretty woman."

[2] The Comtesse Daru.

I see you. As for all the details of our conduct, imagine a courtier in love with a queen, and you will realize the nature of their dangers and pleasures.

Since leaving Paris I have seen much that was new: I have had many sufferings, but only physical ones. I finally succumbed to some bouts of fever, which prevented me from going to the battle of the 6th of this month[1], a spectacle which I shall always regret having missed. Five hundred thousand men fought for fifty hours. Martial was there: I would have gone with him, but I was stretched upon a chaise longue, over-whelmed with headache and impatience. From Vienna one could hear every cannon-shot. An armistice has been declared, and people believe there will be peace. If peace is made, I shall probably go to Spain, and will come and embrace you on my way.

If I have the time, I shall leave here and go with a friend to Warsaw, where he has work to do: thence we shall go to Naples, Rome, Genoa and Grenoble. Do not say anything of this project, which would appear extravagant. I am economising in order to carry it out. I have good servants and excellent horses, and I have learnt that I can endure the most extreme fatigue. But I have never yet encountered that perfect happiness after which I chase. I would need a woman with a great soul: and such women are just like novels—interesting until the dénouement, and two days later one is astonished at having taken an interest in things so commonplace.

. . . If you find any poor German prisoners to whom I can be of service, write to me quickly. In this campaign I have saved the lives of two German prisoners and of two hundred-odd merino sheep. A gallant deed, I do believe.

. . . .

————— 49 —————

TO HIS SISTER PAULINE

Vienna, the 25th of July 1809

I have written a long letter to father, in which I describe at length my political position.

I continue to suffer from the fever of which I spoke to you, but it has not much influence upon the condition of my soul. I am happy, although

[1] Wagram.

[118]

still shaken by the passion of which I told you. I pay heed to nothing else. We have been at Vienna for more than two months, and for me this period is as if it had not been. I was recently entrusted with a mission to Hungary, and when I left Vienna I promised myself that for twenty-four hours I would cease thinking of what the city contained. Perhaps I shall never again in my life have an opportunity of seeing the famous Hungary. I found there a superb landscape; magnificent vines, a narrow and superb road fringed on both sides with young chestnuts: the road stood out whitely amidst the greenery of the meadows and crops, and the view changed every half an hour. First of all, on the left, the imposing Schneeberg (which means " snow-mountain "), and after that, as the road recedes from that white summit, the landscape becomes both gentle and majestic: instead of little mountain-peaks, long, rolling hills, and, on the horizon, a big lake called . . . On leaving Vienna I went to Laxenburg, with its lovely gardens and amazing fifteenth-century castle. Even you would tremble at the sight of those poor enchained Templars painfully raising their heads at the sight of strangers descending upon their tomb.

From Laxenburg I went to Eisenstadt, and thence to the edge of the lake which you will see on the map[1]. Here I found the Croat costume in all its purity: it is exactly that of our hussars, the moustache, the little boots edged with silver, etc., etc.

I think I told you that before returning to France I was to go to Warsaw and Naples. I shall have need of it. Leaving Vienna will rend my heart; but a fortnight afterwards I shall think of the city all the more agreeably, especially while I am travelling.

Haydn died here about a month ago. He was the son of a simple peasant, who raised himself to a creator of immortal works by means of a sensitive soul and studies that enabled him to convey his own feelings to others. A week after his death all the musicians in the city assembled at the Schottenkirche to perform Mozart's *Requiem* in his honour. I was there, in uniform, in the second row: the first was filled with the great man's family—three or four poor little women in black, with pinched faces. The *Requiem* seemed to me too blaring, and did not interest me; but I am beginning to understand *Don Juan*, which is performed in German almost every week, at the Theater an der Wien[2].

I do not know whether you have received the score I sent you—from Brunswick, I think. At the end, Don Juan sings an aria beneath the windows of I-forget-whom, accompanied by a single violin. But it is the aria that follows this one that makes the greatest impression on me:

[1] The salt lake of Neusiedl.
[2] In the original, " Théâtre de Widen." Presumably this theatre is meant.

we always arrive in breathless haste to hear it. Yesterday we arrived just as it was coming to an end: we didn't think it worth while to enter the theatre, and went to the ballet of *Paul et Virginie*.

Farewell. This has been a very rambling letter; but even as I write to you I am thinking of something else. Give me news of Victorine's state of soul. I am still in love with that which she seemed to have five years ago.

Farewell. Write to me often.

—— 50 ——

TO HIS SISTER PAULINE

Vienna, the 29th of November 1809

Yesterday I received a mission which enabled me to absent myself from general headquarters at Sankt-Pölten. At the moment of leaving, one of my comrades whom I had invited to share my dinner, which consisted of a few potatoes and a little morsel of tough meat, suggested that when I returned from my trip we should go to Vienna. " Why not at once? " " But shall we be allowed to pass, without an order or passports? " " We'll see." " Let's begin by sending somebody to look for post-horses." I sent somebody. The livery of my coachman had its effect: we were given horses without an order. We left at half-past nine. All along the road we were stopped by our posts. Half asleep, we replied in German: we were pursued and sworn at, and had some difficulty in getting rid of them. A little later, and already asleep, we were asked who we were, in German: we replied in French. We were given fresh post-horses, but the stable-master ordered the postillion to carry to the Vienna police a little note in which our names are mentioned. Our plan was to dismount at two hundred paces from the barrier, enter as if we had been out for a walk, and have our carriage fetched by horses belonging to friends. We stayed awake for an hour or two, then we dozed off and were awoken at the very gate itself, by the sergeant of the Austrian post, who asked who we were. On leaving Sankt-Pölten we had doffed our uniforms, but so carelessly that my comrade had retained his uniform waistcoat, and I my hat. So there was no way of passing ourselves off as anything but French officers. We boldly gave the names of two of our comrades who are still in Vienna. There was some difficulty, but we seemed so sure of ourselves that finally we were allowed to pass. We awoke three of our comrades who were quartered together, and they told us that Emperor Francis II was to go to St. Stephen's to be present at a *Te Deum*. He had arrived in Vienna two days before in a shabby post-barouche, but drawn by six white horses. As he approached the centre of the city he was recognised, and at once loud huzzas burst out on all sides. People tried to unharness his carriage in order to draw it themselves to the palace. He ordered that his horses should be urged forward, saying several times: "I thank you, my children." Scarcely had he arrived at the Hofburg[1] when he emerged on horseback, and for two hours he showed himself to the people, whose enthusiasm is said to have been extreme.

On our arrival this morning at our comrades' house, there was the question of where to find round hats. We were told we could not wear uniform: some Frenchman had been maltreated two days before, in the moment of enthusiasm. But no hat would fit my big head. At last they dug up an old opera-hat, I rigged myself out in it, and all five of us set out for the castle, in the most grotesque equipage imaginable. It was snowing dreadfully; the guard and the populace barred our path. Finally we heard huzzas and, behind a cavalry-picket of forty or fifty noblemen, or flunkeys covered with braid, we descried a thin little man with an insignificant, worn-out-face, saluting comically. Francis II wears a three-cornered hat which he sets squarely on his head. When he salutes, he inclines his head directly in front of him, like someone who is nodding assent from a distance.

We went to St. Stephen's, a magnificent Gothic church which has not been refurbished, like the cathedral of Rheims, but has been left in its venerable greyness, like that of Strasbourg. From the middle of the crowd I five or six times heard the words: " There's another Frenchman " —usually spoken in a tone of curiosity, but two or three times in one of hatred. We could see from a distance that nobody was being admitted to the church.

I said, in a carefree manner and with the greatest politeness, to the two German sentries: " Is one permitted to enter, gentlemen? " We went into the church, where there were forty or fifty members of the clergy in great albs, and thirty or forty burgesses and flunkeys. At once the exclamation: " There are more of those Frenchmen! " could be heard on all sides. I placed myself beside the entrance to the choir. A silence in which one could have heard a fly beating its wings prevailed amongst these people who had come together in honour of an emperor whom they dearly loved. From all directions we heard: " *Franzose, Franzose* ".

[1] Vienna residence of the Austrian royal family since the thirteenth century.

Looking around at all the stars and ribbons gathered by the entrance to the choir, I descried Frau Salmi, who is said to be the most beautiful woman in the city (face of a Raphael madonna who has reached the age of thirty, eyes lacking in expression, but features in all other respects divine). She smiled, and I said to her quite loudly: " It is fortunate for me to behold, on the last day of my stay in Vienna, the most beautiful of women and the most impressive of ceremonies." Everybody turned round, and on all faces I saw nothing but smiles. Francis II entered, with an even more fatuous air—insignificant, worn-out, weary: a man who has to be wrapped in cotton-wool to give him the strength to breathe. He was surrounded, cheek by jowl, by four tall officials of his household, all drenched to the marrow like himself. As I had this in common with them, and for my part was not obliged to listen to the *Te Deum*— although its first bars proclaimed that it was going to be very good— I came home to get warm. I found nobody in, and I am sitting snugly and writing this account for you whilst the *Te Deum* is still being sung and volleys of musketry are being fired under my windows.

Farewell. Write me an account of a day in your life: it would give me much delight.

———— 51 ————

TO HIS SISTER PAULINE

Paris, May 1810

At about eleven o'clock we arrived at the Sèvres factory, which at present is surrounded by fresh green leaves. I would describe it as situated in the midst of an agreeably varied countryside, were it not for the excessive number of houses in the vicinity. Nevertheless, for the outskirts of Paris, whose distinctive characteristic in our eyes is their lack of grandeur, its situation is well enough. We saw there the most beautiful living creature I ever set eyes on—Adolphe Brongniart, the son of the scientist who runs the factory. We also saw the handsomest manufactured object I ever saw—the round table, two foot eleven inches in diameter, which displays the portraits of most of the marshals and, in the middle, that of the Emperor. Isabey (a person without the least vestige of greatness and with the face of an actor, attached by self-interest and forced politeness to a powerful man whom he fears and does not like) did the honours of this table, which truly gave one the idea of perfection, especially in the portraits of Marshals Soult and Ponte-Corvo. The Princes Davout and Berthier are less good. One of these days this charming work will have to be fired, and this may break it. All the rest is well enough, a painted panel which admits the daylight through a pretty figure of a seated woman. I suggested to M. Brongniart that he should make night-scenes for panes in a boudoir. He agreed with me, but said that experiments in this style had never yet been successful.

The sculpture is mediocre: they should ask Canova and Thorwaldsen for models. In general, in their depictions of the Emperor's face, which they are ceaselessly reproducing, they miss its grandeur. We saw a figure of the Emperor that was being set on horseback—a paltry, pretty piece.

As we went out we met Signor de Mareschalchi, with the whole of Italy. M. Z——[1] wished to do them the honours of his factory. We left them and set out for Versailles. A handsome road, very fresh greenery. We quickly arrived at the house of M. de Clédat, cour de Dragon. The streets of Versailles are those of a capital, the shops are those of a country town—as also are M. de Clédat's rooms and society, especially a M. Daguesseau, who is something of an Escarbagnas, and his wife, a tall, chubby-cheeked woman with a blond peruke, whom he calls Pauline.

After a glass of excellent Malaga, we set out for Trianon. M. Clédat, although something of a Versaillomaniac, is not without intelligence, and proves it by having excellent wines—but without ice, which is a great pity.

The Trianons are handsome: nothing sad, nothing majestic. The furnishings are not beautiful enough for a sovereign who wishes to play this rôle. They are sometimes lacking in comfort, especially the beds. Whenever we paused to look at something, we encountered Signor de Marescalchi and his troop. We were cheerful, amused and alert. Handsome pieces in mahogany, a handsome picture of the battle of Arcola, ugly busts of the family with inscriptions in good taste—the names only, Louis, Joseph, Elisa, Pauline. The Emperor's room, on the same floor, is small and not very comfortable or quiet. It has four fine engravings— of *the Virgin in the Garden, Belisarius, the Education of Achilles* and *the Rape of Deianeira*, if I remember rightly. The Trianons' English garden is very handsome: it has tall trees, a great advantage in an English garden, as well as precious trees—a royal pleasure which means nothing to me, but is a great thing for souls who do not rise to the love of the beautiful.

I am constantly in attendance upon Mme Elliot, an agreeable woman although scarcely at all pretty, and thirty-one years of age. I was astonished, a week ago, to meet a woman from the provinces without

[1] The comte Daru, at this time Quartermaster-General of the Emperor's household.

[123]

any affectation or shyness. But I have learnt that she is not a provincial: she was brought up in Paris. The pleasure I experienced at Sèvres remained with me, and at every instant I felt it more closely, until ten o'clock in the evening, when I took leave of Mme. Nardot[1].

I do not know, my dearest, whether you will be able to decipher this descriptive fragment, or whether it will give you pleasure. I have just finished a volume which I began at Marseilles four years ago. (I was very young at that time.) I perceived that I did not sufficiently remember the fifteenth octet of the sixteenth song of the *Jerusalem*, which I invite you to re-read.

Let us rejoice in the day and never count on the morrow. That's what Horace said in Latin 1900 years ago, and what one must do nowadays, or else no longer dream *to the happiness which I shall find with you*[2].

LT. SORBON.

—— 52 ——

TO FRANÇOIS PÉRIER-LAGRANGE

Paris, the 24th of May 1810

My dear fellow, your letter moves me to tears. I promise you that I fully reciprocate your tender affection. I shall never forget the token of it that you have given me; but the sacrifice has been made. For some days I have been suffering a violent grief. It was even so strong that I found no other resource but to travel a hundred leagues. Fortunately, whilst so doing, I had a service to render. At Orleans I spent a night, from one o'clock to four, on the public square—a night that I shall long remember. The conclusion is that one must never enter the house of a family where one is not welcomed with pleasure. Pride has unfortunately become such a habit with me that I could not promise not to send all relatives to the devil—even the most powerful of them—if they in the least depart from an attitude of perfect equality. This would have put the dear girl in a most embarrassing position. In any case, I have not a sou—and there is some difference between being the wife of a Receiver-General and that of a poor devil of a commissioner at 5,000 francs a year: another comparison that would spell unhappiness for me, even if I merely suspected my wife of making it. I shall tell you, between ourselves, that two years ago I refused a very considerable fortune, and a wife so lovable

---

[1] Mother of the comtesse Daru.   [2] In English [*sic*] in the original.

that I have since paid court to her, simply in order to avoid this comparison. She loved me, and she has the sweetest nature; yet, if I still had to refuse and she had by chance not married, I would not now ask for her hand any more than I did then. There now, my very dear friend, I have laid bare my whole soul. Say nothing of this to ——, who might suspect me of an intention that I have *plucked from my soul for ever.*

—— 53 ——

TO HIS SISTER PAULINE

Monday, the 2nd of July 1810

Our little family party[1] was delightful. The couplets composed by Picard, who made merry with us clad in livery, were delightful. Their first effect was a slight emotion—after which we all laughed a great deal. Two hundred people turned up: Fitzjames made us laugh, after which we danced. I was the last to leave, at break of dawn. I tell you all this as if it had happened a thousand years ago. Yesterday, the day of St. Martial, we all dined en famille at Martial's. At half past eight Mme Daru tranquilly set off for a party given by the Austrian Ambassador, Prince von Schwarzenberg. Since the mansion was far too small to contain a thousand guests, they had followed the practice of all recent receptions and had constructed, of deal, an immense reception-room in the garden. The flooring was raised three feet above the ground. To remove the odour of deal—the weather was very hot—the interior of the room had been painted with turpentine, or so they say. Just when the party was at its peak, and His Majesty was making a tour of the room, a candle was overturned and set fire to a curtain. People thought it a matter of no consequence; but the blazing curtain set fire to the wall of planks on which it hung and in a single moment, " as if in drill tempo "—the expression that M. Daru used when telling me of the accident—the whole room was in flames, both sides and top. The fire in the ceiling burnt the ropes of the chandeliers, which fell on the guests' heads; the floor gave way in several places. You can imagine the cries, the tumult, the terror, and also the situation of those who, on emerging from this funeral-pyre, could not find their wives, husbands and children. The unhappy Princess von Schwarzenberg, the Ambassador's sister, fell victim to her maternal love.

---

[1] The saint's-day festival of the comte Daru, June 29th (St. Peter's).

What made this accident unique was the terrible contrast between
the height of gaiety and the greatest imaginable horror, and, above all,
the additional horror of frightful claps of thunder and a dreadful storm.
Luckily our dear relatives were uninjured. A Mme de Boissière from
Grenoble was slightly wounded. M. Mounier was not there.

Farewell, etc., etc.

— 54 —

INSTRUCTIONS TO MM. FÉLIX FAURE AND
LOUIS CROIZET OR LAMBERT (OF LYON)

Paris, the 1st of September 1810

My dear friends, I have appointed you my testamentary executors. I
request you to keep the following instructions secret, to prevent fools
from in any way hindering the execution. I have a few small investments
in Paris: they can be found in the keeping of MM. Oberkampf and
Duchesne. M. Félix Faure owes me from ten to fifteen thousand francs;
M. Joseph-Chérubin Beyle, or M. Duchesne, owes me twenty thousand
francs.

Realise the whole without delay.

These realisations will form a fund from which you will first of all
settle the legacies contained in the Will, and some that are at the end of
this document.

M. Faure knows whether I have a child. If I have none at the time of
my decease, or if M. Faure himself is deceased, I request you, my dear
friends, to invest the moneys provening from the sums mentioned above
in a safe manner and so that the accruing revenue may, as far as possible
be perpetual. I leave the choice entirely to you. An investment in land
near Philadelphia or Edinburgh would correspond to my intentions.

From the annual revenue of the aforesaid fund you will endow in
England, and in accordance with the most firmly established forms of law,
an annual prize. This prize (which shall be administered in England,
provided that this estimable island shall not have been conquered—or,
in this unfortunate event, in America), this prize, I say, shall be awarded:

On the first year, in London;
On the second, in Paris;
On the third, in Göttingen or Berlin;

On the fourth, in Naples;
On the fifth, in Philadelphia;
On the sixth, in London;
And so on, preserving this order.

The prize shall be adjudicated by a society or assembly of more than five members and less than twenty. You will select impartial judges. If such an assembly cannot be held in any of the aforesaid towns on the Continent, each in its yearly turn, without compromising the judges, and upon the judges refusing to act, the prize shall be adjudicated by a society of Englishmen. I am confident that this nation will always furnish more than twenty enlightened and courageous men who will not disdain to be of service to mankind by supporting my project.

It is for you, my dear friends, to ensure the execution of my project by wise measures calculated in accordance with your knowledge of men and governments. In this connection, I advise you to re-read Delolme.

The work that gains the prize must be written in French, English, Italian, Spanish, Latin or German: in this last case, accompanied by a translation in one of the five other languages.

This work must be written in a simple, clear and exact style, in the tone of an anatomical description and not of a speech, and must be divided into three parts: firstly, examples drawn from history, secondly, examples drawn from imitations of nature (poems, novels, etc.); thirdly and lastly, exact and unemotional description.

All candidates, who shall be admitted without restriction, shall be set, by way of the newspapers of the aforesaid capitals, the following questions:

What is ambition, love, revenge, hatred, laughter, weeping, smiling, friendship, terror, hilarity?
Which is the greatest comedian?

To gain the prize, the work must be of sixty pages in octavo, in Cicero[1] face. The judges are invited to prefer the simple style to the so-called rhetorical style, and especially to prefer the thought to the style. When the questions indicated above shall have been exhausted, they shall be set anew, beginning with ambition, etc., provided that revolutions shall permit the legacy to continue. I have no doubt that some friend of mankind will make good any reductions that may occur in the sum destined to be awarded as the prize.

[1] 12-point.

The prize shall be:

Firstly, a gold medal, on one side of which shall be struck the following words: *Nosce te ipsum*[1], and these further words: *Bonheur dans la monarchie tempérée*[2].

Secondly, a complete edition of Shakespeare, in English, to cost ten napoleons (two hundred francs).

I invite you, my dear friends, to refrain from offering the prize until its foundation shall be assured, by the purchase, for example, of a farm in America or Scotland.

55

TO HIS SISTER PAULINE

Paris, the 9th of October 1810

What a beautiful autumn! It appears that you are greatly enjoying it—at least, grandfather always tells me that you are at Thuélin. My new post[3] entirely deprives me of the enjoyment of these fine days, which are so rare here. Fortunately my office, from which I am writing to you, is superbly situated, overlooking the quincunx of the Invalides and, beyond the woods of Meudon, the western extremity of Paris. The official work entailed by the post can be done in forty hours a month; but M——, who is just the man I need, entrusts me with interesting tasks unrelated to my business. I had counted on making my official occupations this winter serve as the mere embroidery of my life, and on using the stuff of it for certain deep studies concerning the knowledge of mankind. I furthermore planned to give myself up entirely to what are here called pleasures, so that if in the next years I am three or four hundred leagues from Paris, I shall be quite free of regrets.

My business leaves me time of my own; I have only from eight to ten hours of work a day. Nevertheless I cannot pursue any particular task. The labour of meditating—for me, at least—cannot be put on and put off like a coat. I must always have an hour of solitary reflection, and I only have moments.

So there, my dearest, you have an exact depiction of a heart that loves you, but which you scarcely requite, for you never write to me. I

[1] Know thyself.
[2] Happiness lies in constitutional monarchy.
[3] " In 1810, on the 3rd of August, commissioner on the Council of State, Quartermaster-General of the Crown Chattels a few days later." (*Vie de Henri Brulard*).

[128]

am reduced to speaking to you only of myself; I do not know any of your thoughts and feelings. I deluge Barral with questions: I dine almost daily with that charming person. Yesterday we enjoyed ourselves so much at the *Nozze di Figaro* that this morning we are quite overcome. Throughout the evening we chattered with a very pretty Italian girl who is burdened with the weight of eighteen years and speaks with a very pure accent. We had never seen her before. She was there with her father, we had sentiments in common, we quickly made acquaintance. You know that I have two affairs to settle at Grenoble: the first is that of the six thousand francs, which uncle told me was progressing; the second is that of the barony.[1] According to what father writes to me, he will send me what is required for that. Nevertheless, speak to him on this head, if occasion presents itself. It must be done soon.

My great father speaks much with me of matrimony with a very sensible girl of your knowledge but he will not understand that I could never jouir *in this family of the* égards *without which I never shall*[2] enter into any household, and, in short, that I have decided to think no more of the matter.

I lack nothing that can contribute to my happiness: my position is most agreeable. People whom I used not to know now pay me visits. Every evening I receive sixty more smiles than a month ago. I can say, into the bargain, that the change is my own doing. Nevertheless I am still troubled a little by the image of the solid happiness that I hoped to find with Victorine. I have a need to love and be loved. I do what I can to love Mme Palfy[3], but she has not *the understanding soul*[4], she does not understand all the subtleties that constitute the happiness or unhappiness of those to whom they are visible. She attaches more value than is right to all those stupid ambitions which, once one has satisfied them, no longer mean anything. Do not mock too much at all these little foibles of the heart; not another soul in the world but you has any suspicion of their existence. I shall move heaven and earth to go to Italy in 1811: what are your plans for that year? Obtain opportunities for Faure to speak to *our father*[5]. They have no notion of Paris, or of my position here: he will try to make them more aware of it. I am keeping house with the handsomest young fellow I know, and also the best and most likeable, apart from a slight melancholy and aloofness: his name is M. Louis de Bélisle[6].

---

[1] Beyle was trying to persuade his father to purchase a barony. (Cf. the letter immediately following.)

[2] The original is in this mixture of English and French words. " Jouir des égards " means " to enjoy the respect ".

[3] The contesse Daru.

[4] In English in the original.

[5] In English in the original.

[6] Louis Pépin de Bélisle, a colleague of Beyle's on the Council of State.

56

TO HIS SISTER PAULINE

Paris, the 10th *of December* 1810

I'll wager that, after all my letters about the barony, you'll think I have turned into an ambitious knave with hollow and wrinkled cheeks, envious eye, etc. . . . Not a bit of it. . . . I am chubbier-cheeked than ever, and two days ago I acted the part of a young man of sensibility, which I would like to describe to you in order to raise myself in your esteem. Well, I was dining at the home of M. le comte Joubert. I found beside me M. Amedée P.[1]. He is one of my colleagues. I therefore immediately gave myself up to the pleasures of re-acquaintance, and we talked Grenoble all through the dinner. I found that this dinner went on too long, for I had three evening parties before me: two for pleasure and one in duty. When M. Amedée had spoken much of Grenoble, he told me how he had recently returned thence, and told me that he had done the journey very slowly, because he was with his mother *and the miss*[2] —— who had actually spoken most enthusiastically of Thuélin and the mistress of the house. *At the name of this once so beloved girl, all my sentiment were awakened*[3]. I therefore was adroit enough to learn from him that this very evening he was going with *this miss to a box*[3] which he had rented at the Variétés, to see the *Chatte Merveilleuse*, which is drawing all Paris. I had no more urgent task than to hasten to get rid of my costume and betake myself, as fast as my horse could go, to the theatre where I hoped to see her. On my arrival, " no more tickets ", except in the fourth gallery (which is the equivalent of a sort of sixth-class boxes, occupied by messieurs the flunkeys). I climbed up, and with the help of opera-glasses discovered *the brother*[4] at the back of a box, in the front of which were six women. I could never clearly make out which of them was she. Sometimes an attractive gesture made me think it was a woman in a black spencer: an instant afterwards a blue hat made me feel sure that *this* was she. I was completely blinded. I succeeded, by dint of using my fists, in extracting myself from this lofty chasm, and went down to the firsts, meanwhile successively bribing three box-openers.

[1] Amedée de Pastoret, appointed to the Council of State in 1809.
[2] In English in the original. (This refers to Victorine Mounier.)
[3] In English [*sic*] in the original.
[4] In English in the original: Édouard Mounier.

[130]

Here I was offered a place at twenty paces from her. I dared not take it. Here, I hope, is an example of the timidity of true feeling. She has not seen me for four years, and has never, I think, seen me in full mourning! My reason told me all this; but, as love is not governed by reason, I refused the seat in the firsts. It was the only one: I had to climb up again to the seconds, whence I turned my glasses in her direction, through the fanlights of a box, enough to ruin my eyesight. It was impossible: I could never once recognise her. Nevertheless I stayed in my seat until she went. I rode off very sadly to one of my evening parties, and was obliged to tell lie upon lie in order to excuse myself from the two others. My rushing-around in the theatre is all the more meritorious inasmuch as all the openers, inspectors, etc. have redoubled their severity—the reason being that Cinderella's big rat and two mice, converted into a coachman and two little mouse-grey flunkeys, have thrown all Paris into a swoon, and truly it is a charming piece of nonsense. (One could say as much, I suppose, of the manner in which I spent that evening.) Nevertheless I want to see it.

. . . .

——— 57 ———

TO HIS SISTER PAULINE

The 25th of December 1810

My dear Pauline, I have been very happy recently: the holy day of Noël granted me a breathing-space. My old itch induced me to read, and to take a book that conformed with the studies that awoke my ardour during my years of poverty in Paris. So I read with pleasure, twenty times setting the book aside, the first twenty-four pages of Burke's *Studies in the Sublime*. At every instant I was distracted by my present ideas concerning ambition, and then I regretted that I no longer live amidst those noble, strong and tender ideas that ceaselessly preoccupied me when I lodged on the rue d'Angiviller, opposite the beautiful colonnade of the Louvre, and, being often without six sous in my pocket, would pass whole evenings in watching brilliant stars setting behind the Museum's façade. For six months I have had no time to ponder over anything I have read, and my reading has been confined to the novels of La Fontaine, because one can pick them up and put them down at any moment. Whilst reading my Burke I would break off to reproach myself for not having gone to see somebody or other. Some powerful friends have made me a loan. I have a handsome apartment, simple, noble and airy, decorated with charming engravings. I sought to enjoy them in the spirit that possessed me in 1804. It is scarcely any longer possible. I have a superb view from the window of my little study: I watched the sun setting behind rain and big clouds torn by a tempestuous wind.[1] I missed the company of Bélisle, who is posting along the road to La Rochelle, where he has a mission. He left yesterday, and I am alone for two or three months. I mechanically opened the drawer in my desk in which I keep papers of interest.

I opened a small letter: it was from you. Never have I experienced with so much delight the pleasure of my love for you. This charming letter bears the date of Wednesday, the 15th of March. But in which year? I don't know. The date-stamp is on the edge, so that all that can be read is "the 20th of March, 18 . . ." Everything you say exactly corresponds to what I feel. I am reading the words of a second self. This charming illusion is enhanced by the likeness of your handwriting to mine. I keenly feel the grief of being deprived of your letters. I am sending you your charming letter of the 20th of March. Read it and send it back to me. If you read it, you will not be able to resist the desire to write to me. For my part, I weep hot tears as I write to you: so let us speak of other matters.

I have in front of me a delightful engraving by Porporati, entitled: *il Bagno di Leda*. At the sight of it loafers would have recourse to their big word: "indecent!" I none the less advise you to buy it (it costs fourteen francs): it is a third of the picture by divine Correggio which is in the Museum; it depicts three women, two swans and an eagle[2]. Next to it, I have the portrait of divine Mozart which I bought in Vienna from Artaria[3], who knew Mozart well and assured me that it was very like him. Tomorrow there is a performance of the *Nozze di Figaro*, but I shall be compelled to miss the first half in order to go to a house[4] where

[1] The apartment that Beyle had taken with Louis Pépin de Bélisle was in the rue Neuve-du-Luxembourg.

[2] "My heir shall buy three copies of the engraving of the Swans (by Porporati, from Correggio), and shall send them to the above-named ladies, without saying from whom they come. . . ." (Will made at Rome on February 8th, 1835.)

[3] The music publisher.

[4] ". . . Fairisland *presentes me to mistress Gay.* (Italicised words in English [*sic*] in the original.) It resembles the society described by Collé and Marmontel. We were there for an hour, and saw Mme Récamier, a charming figure: she has an air of asking forgiveness for being pretty. She still is, very much so. Mme de Caraman (Mme Tallien) came in, and Mme Récamier disappeared. Mme Tallien has the remains of a pretty face, which evinces merely an imperious, sad and commonplace soul. I would willingly go ten leagues on foot to avoid spending a fortnight with her, and I would go twenty to spend some time with Mme Récamier." (*Journal*, December 19th, 1810.)

I was presented last Wednesday: I stayed there a quarter of an hour and saw Mme Récamier, who is charming, and Mme Tallien, who is very uncharming, but remarkable. What a pity you didn't come to Paris! Try to return here in 1811. All the same, I do not conceal from you that I shall certainly come and embrace you, even if in order to do so I have to turn deserter! My wish to see you is overpowering. Farewell, to her whom I love more than anyone else in the world! I am overcome with tears. Burn this letter.

— 58 —

TO HIS SISTER PAULINE

Milan, the 10th of September 1811[1]

M.Z.[2] was so kind as to give me leave of absence, and I am come to embrace my old friends and to see Rome and Naples. Milan holds very tender memories for me. I spent here the sweet years of adolescence. It is here that I fell most deeply in love. It is here, too, that my character was formed. I daily perceive that at heart I am Italian, saving any bent for murder—a bent of which, in any case, they are accused unjustly.

But the mad love of gaiety, music and the freest conduct, the art of tranquilly enjoying life, etc. . . . all these constitute the Milanese character. You will laugh at my nonsense, but it is meant for you only. I am having this letter despatched via Paris, so that the stamp will not reveal where I am.

Burn this letter, and speak to nobody of its contents.

. . . .

[1] "Yesterday, the 25th of August, 1811, I took my seat on the diligence for Milan, 168 francs. I have the second seat for the departure on the 29th of August, at eight o'clock in the morning. I shall be in Milan in ten days." (*Journal.*)
[2] The comte Daru.

59

TO HIS SISTER PAULINE

Rome, the 2nd of October 1811

I am well, and full of admiration. I have seen Raphael's loggias, and have come to the conclusion that a man must sell his shirt to see them for the first time, or to see them again when he has already done so.

The thing that has moved me most in my journey to Italy is the song of the birds in the Coliseo. Farewell; keep this journey a secret, but give news of me to grandfather and *tutti quanti*[1].

The appointment of M. le duc de Feltre will perhaps prolong my stay at Milan. I shall be there on the 25th of October, and remain there two or three weeks.

I love you.   HENRY.

P.S.—A thousand greetings to your husband.

60

TO HIS SISTER PAULINE

Paris, the 6th of December 1821

A word is better than nothing: I wish you would often remember that. Picture to yourself a man at a delightful ball, where all the women are are attired with the utmost grace. The fire of pleasure gleams in their eyes, one descries the glances that they cast upon their lovers. This beautiful spot is decorated with a taste full of voluptuosity and grandeur; a thousand candles give out a celestial brightness; a gentle perfume drives one out of one's mind. Suddenly the perceptive soul who finds himself in the midst of these delights, lucky man, is obliged to leave the ball-room: he goes out into a thick fog, a rainy night and mud; he stumbles three or four times, and finally falls into a hole full of manure.

Such, in brief, is the story of my return from Italy. To console myself

---

[1] Anyone else.

for the physical and moral banalities that I endured en route, I made a mental picture of sweet little Angelina[1] waiting for me, with all her love, in my apartment, beside a good fire. I arrived: madame had left a long time ago. I spent a lover's evening; I felt that my despair was senseless, but despair I did. The sweet little one will return on the 18th of December.

At about the same date I shall perhaps leave for Holland, on a mission lasting a fortnight. Come despite this, do not postpone your journey.

I have found here something that is perpetually divine and has touched my soul in its most tender spot—the acting of Mademoiselle Mars at the Français. That by itself is worth a thousand leagues, and I would travel that distance willingly if I knew that such a pleasure was to be found in Algiers.

I caught a glimpse of Mlle V——[2]. At the moment when my eyes fell upon her, I was looking pompous and insolent. I was gorgeously arrayed, especially by reason of my plumed hat, and I was whipping my horse with the greatest possible majesty. I thought she looked very pale, and perhaps she thought I looked very conceited. I was so taken by surprise that I did not salute her: I count on doing so on the first fine day for a promenade at the Tuileries.

· ·

──── 61 ────

TO HIS SISTER PAULINE

Saint-Cloud, the 23rd of July 1812

My dearest, chance has procured me an excellent opportunity of writing to you. I am leaving this evening, at seven o'clock, for the banks of the Dvina. I have come here to receive orders from Her Majesty the Empress. She has honoured me with several minutes' conversation concerning the

[1] Angelina Bereyter, *seconda donna* at the Théâtre Italien.

" The Minister of Love, who was on the point of being removed from office, and who often diminished the happiness procured by the good behaviour of the other ministers, finally took his revenge. I had written several letters, at intervals of some months, to the lovable and gentle Bereyter. Finally she permitted me to do my homage in person. . . . I tenderly embraced her on the first day I had her in my house, on the second (the 29th of January, 1811)." (*Journal.*) From this date onwards, " . . . living with an actress singer, who came every evening, at half past eleven, to establish herself in my bed. I used to come home at one o'clock, and we would sup on a cold partridge and Champagne wine. This liaison lasted two or three years." (*Souvenirs d'Égotisme.*)

[2] Victorine Mounier.

road I should take, the duration of the journey, etc. On taking leave of Her Majesty I went to visit His Majesty the Prince of Rome; but he was asleep, and Mme la comtesse de Montesquiou told me that it was impossible to see him before three o'clock; so I have two hours to wait. Waiting is not comfortable in full-dress uniform and lace. Luckily I remembered that my post of inspector might perhaps entitle me to some consideration at the palace. I presented myself, and have been shown into a room which at the moment is empty.

Nothing is greener or more peaceful than this lovely town of Saint-Cloud.

My itinerary to Vilna is as follows: I shall travel fast, with a courier in advance, as far as Königsberg. But at this point the sweet effects of pillage begin to make themselves evident, and are doubly so at Kovno: it is said that in the region of this town one can go fifty leagues without finding a living creature. (I regard all this as much exaggerated—a typical Paris rumour, which is as much as to say, utterly absurd.) The Prince Arch-Chancellor told me yesterday to try to have more luck than one of my colleagues, who took twenty-eight days to go from Paris to Vilna. In these ravaged wildernesses travel is very difficult, especially with a poor little Viennese calash that will be crushed beneath a thousand packages: every single person I know has had the idea of entrusting me with one.

By the way, Gaëtan wanted to come with me. I told him that it was physically impossible for my calash to hold more than myself and my servant. Thereupon he wrote me an impertinent letter accusing me of having offered to take him. In this case I am like the honest man mentioned by la Bruyère: my character gives testimony for me. Everyone knows that I dislike the company of bores—especially for twenty days on end! Gaëtan's letter is the sequel to the letter in which his father called me a charlatan. No accusation could be less true, for I shall give them to understand at the first opportunity that they may in future regard me as non-existent as far as they are concerned.

I'm delighted that you have bought Shakespeare: he is still the truest painter I know.

Farewell. If you do not come to Paris, go to Milan by the Simplon and the Borromaean islands, and return by the mont Cenis.

TO FÉLIX FAURE AND THE COMTESSE DARU

Smolensk, the 19th of August 1812

The conflagration seemed to us so fine a spectacle that, although it was seven o'clock, and despite the fear of missing dinner (an unprecedented thing in a city like this) and also of the shells that the Russians were firing through the flames at any Frenchman who might be on the bank of the Borysthenes (the Dnieper), we went down through the gate by the handsome chapel. A shell had just burst, and smoke still hung all around. We courageously ran some twenty paces, and crossed the river on a bridge that General Kirgener was having hastily constructed. We went right up to the edge of the conflagration, where we found a great number of dogs and some horses that had been driven from the city by the general blaze.

As we were steeping ourselves in so rare a spectacle, Marigner[1] was accosted by a battalion-commander whom he knew only by reason of having been his successor in quarters at Rostock. The worthy fellow told us at length of his battles of that morning and the previous day, and went on to lavish infinite praise upon a dozen ladies of Rostock, whom he named: but he praised one of them much more than the others. Fear of interrupting a man so full of his subject, combined with a desire to laugh, kept us at his side until ten o'clock, when the bullets began again in their best style.

We were bemoaning the loss of our dinner, and I was arranging with Marigner that he should be the first to enter our quarters and receive our well-deserved reprimand from M. Daru, when we suddenly perceived an extraordinary brightness in the high part of the city.

As we approached, we discovered that all our calashes were in the middle of the street, that eight large houses adjacent to ours were shooting out flames to a height of sixty feet, and that the house which for the last few hours had been our dwelling was being covered with lumps of blazing charcoal as big as your fist. We ordered holes to be pierced in the roof at six or seven points, and there we stationed, as if in pulpits,

---

[1]Auguste-André Marigner de la Creuzatière had been a commissioner of war and had already served under Petiet and Daru. In the campaign of 1812 he was Inspector of Stores. Beyle had already lived with him in 1800-1801 and in 1809. (Note by M. Martineau.)

half a dozen grenadiers of the guard armed with long poles with which to strike at the sparks and sweep them off the roof. They performed their task very well. M. Daru took every precaution. Bustle, weariness, hubbub until midnight.

Our house caught fire thrice, and each time we put it out. Our headquarters was in the courtyard, from which, sitting on straw, we watched the roof of the house and its outbuildings, shouting to our grenadiers to indicate the points where sparks were falling thickest.

All of us were there, the MM. Daru, the Comte Dumas, Besnard, Jacqueminot, General Kirgener. We were so overstrained that we were falling asleep as we talked. Only the master of the house, M. Daru, held out against sleep.

At last appeared our longed-for dinner. But, hungry though we were, having eaten nothing since ten o'clock in the morning, it was most amusing to see each man fall asleep in his chair, with fork in hand. I am much afraid that this enormous tale of mine may produce the same effect. Deign to forgive me, madame, and burn this letter, since we have agreed that news of the Army should be given only in the bulletin.

Mlle de Camelin will recognise my taste for scribbling. But since we are entirely without ink, and one has to make it every time one dips one's pen, this is the first letter I have written; and long though it be, I could have plenty more to tell. Deign to see in it, madame, at least a token of my respectful devotion, and to pay my respects to Mme Nardot, to mademoiselle de Camelin and to that grown-up young lady Pauline[1].

Tonight the Army has driven the Russians back another four leagues. So here we are, eighty-six leagues from Moscow.

----- 63 -----

TO FÉLIX FAURE

Smolensk, eighty leagues from Moscow,
the 24th of August 1812

I received your letter within twelve days, although it has come eight hundred leagues, like everything else that arrives here from Paris. I see that you are happy, and am very pleased. I no longer have any idea what can have been that piece of advice of mine which you think so good.

[1] The eldest daughter of the Comte Daru, who in 1826 married the marquis d'Oraison.

Would it be my advice to start working soon on the edition of Montesquieu and marrying the theme of this work with that of your happiness?

My own happiness at being here is not great. How a man changes! My old thirst for new sights has been entirely quenched. Ever since I saw Milan and Italy, everything I see repels me with its crudity. Would you believe it that, without any vexation that affects me more than anybody else, and without any personal sorrow, I am sometimes on the point of bursting with tears? In this ocean of barbarity there is not a sound that finds an echo in my soul! Everything is coarse, dirty, both physically and morally stinking.[1] I have found some small pleasure only in having a little music played to me on an untuned piano by an individual whose feeling for music is on a level with my feeling for mass. Ambition no longer has any influence over me: the most handsome ribbon would seem to me no compensation for the mire in which I am sunk. I imagine the heights that my soul inhabits—that soul which composes works, listens to Cimarosa and is in love with Angela[2], amidst a beautiful climate— I imagine these heights as delicious hills. Far from these hills, down in the plain, are fetid marshes—and here I am plunged, and nothing in the world except the sight of a map can remind me of my hills.

Would you believe it that I take a keen pleasure in official business that has to do with Italy? I have had three or four pieces of such business, and, even when they were finished, they stayed in my imagination like a novel.

In the Vilna region, where I rejoined the Army at Boyardoviscoma (near Krasnoya), at a time when the country had not yet been organised, I was plagued by a perversity of detail. I underwent extreme physical hardships. In order to arrive, I left my calash behind, and it has never caught up with me. Possibly it has been pillaged. For me personally this would be only half a misfortune—about 4,000 francs' worth of effects lost, and the inconvenience—but I was carrying packages to everybody! That's a foolish way of making my bow to the people here!

All this, however, has no influence upon the manner of existence that I have described to you. I am growing old. It is my duty to be more active than any of the people in the office from which I am writing to you, with my ears besieged by platitudes—but I find no pleasure in it. Where now is the office I had in Brunswick, or in Vienna? . . . All this is furiously urging me to ask for the sub-prefecture at Rome. I would not hesitate, if I were sure of dying at the age of forty. This is a sin against

---

[1] " Those coarse-grained heroes who were the Emperor's tools at Jéna and Wagram. Posterity will never know the coarseness and stupidity of those men once they were off the field of battle. And even on the field, what prudence they showed! " (*Vie de Henri Brulard.*)

[2] Signora Pietragrua.

Beylism. It is a result of the execrable moral education we received. We are orange-trees that have sprouted up, by the strength of their seed, in the middle of a pool of ice, in Iceland.

Write to me at greater length: I found your letter very short for eight hundred leagues. Make Angela promise to write to me. I am no more in love with Paris than when I was there: I am as satiated with that city as you are, I think; but I love the sensations that *Painting and Opera-Buffa* gave me for six months.

Farewell, I think we are leaving.

 64

TO FÉLIX FAURE

> *Moscow, the 4th of October* 1812,
> *Essendo di servizio presso l'intendente
> generale*[1]
> (*Journal, entry for the* 14*th or* 15*th of
> September,* 1812.)

I left my General[2] supping at the Apraxin palace. As I went out and was taking leave of M. Z——[3] in the courtyard, we noticed that in addition to the conflagration in the Chinese town, which had been in progress for several hours, we had another one quite close at hand: we went to look at it. The blaze was terrific. I caught a toothache on this excursion. We were so good-natured as to arrest a soldier who had just administered two stabs with his bayonet to a man who had drunk some beer. I went so far as to draw my sword, and was actually on the point of running the rascal through. Bourgeois took him before the Governor, who had him set at liberty.

We retired at one o'clock, after having discharged a mighty volley of commonplaces against the conflagration—which did not make much difference, at least as far as we could see. On our return to the Apraxin cottage, we had a pump tried out. I went to bed tormented by a toothache. It appears that several of the gentlemen were so good as to take alarm and run away at about two o'clock and about five. For my part,

[1] In the service of the Quartermaster-General.
[2] Quartermaster-General comte Mathieu-Dumas.
[3] The comte Daru.

I awoke at seven and had my carriage loaded and stationed in the queue of carriages belonging to M. Daru.

They passed along the boulevard, in front of the club. There I found Mme B——, who sought to cast herself at my feet. It was a highly ridiculous meeting. I noticed that there was not a trace of naturalness in anything she said—with the natural result that I was frozen stiff. Nevertheless I did a great deal for her, by giving her fat sister-in-law a place in my calash and inviting her to station her *droschkes* behind my carriage. She told me that madame Saint-Albe[1] had told her a lot about me.

The conflagration was rapidly approaching the house we had quitted. Our carriages remained on the boulevard for five or six hours. Bored by this inaction, I went to see the fire and spent an hour or two with Joinville[2]. I admired the voluptuosity of his house's furnishings: we drank there with Gillet[3] and Busche[4], consuming three bottles of wine, which gave us new life.

Whilst I was there I read a few lines of an English translation of *Virginie*, which, amidst all the general coarseness of existence here, turned me back, to some slight extent, into a moral being.

I went with Louis to look at the conflagration. We saw one Savoye, a mounted artilleryman, drunk, flogging a Guards officer with the flat of his sword and hurling silly abuse at him. He was in the wrong, and finally had to apologise. One of his comrades in pillage plunged down a blazing street, where he was probably roasted. I found a new proof of the lack of character of the French in general. Louis amused himself by pacifying the man, for the benefit of a Guards officer who at the first clash would have had far the better of him. Instead of contemplating all this unruliness with deserved contempt, Louis made himself in turn the target for silly abuse. For my part, I was admiring the patience of the Guards officer: in his place, I would have dashed my sword in Savoye's face—which might have resulted in an awkward interview with his colonel. The officer behaved more prudently.

At three o'clock I returned to our column of carriages and my gloomy colleagues. The adjacent wooden houses were discovered to contain a store of flour and a store of oats: I told my servants to take some. They pretended to be very active, as if they were taking a great deal, and in the end it proved to be very little. This is how people behave in the Army,

[1] Mélanie Guilbert had made her début at the Théâtre Français in 1806 under the name of Mme Sainte-Albe.
[2] Louis Joinville (Cf. letter no. 46).
[3] Commissioner for War.
[4] A colleague of Beyle's on the Council of State. Beyle later called him "the Muscovite Busche".

everywhere and in all matters: it is most irritating. There is no use in trying not to care a damn: they keep on coming to one and whining about their hardships, and one ends by losing patience. The result is that I lead an unhappy life. As a matter of fact, I become less impatient than other people, but I have the misfortune to fly into rages. I envy some of my colleagues, whom one could call useless ——, I do believe, without making them really angry: they raise their voices, and that's all. " They merely shake their ears ", as the comtesse Palfy used to say. " They would be very unhappy if they did anything else," she used to add. She is right: but how can one display similar resignation, when one has a sensitive soul?

At about half-past three, Gillet and I went to visit the house of Count Peter Soltykoff: we thought it might suit H.E. We went to the Kremlin to tell him of it, and stopped at the house of General Dumas, which is on the cross-roads.

General Kirgener had said to Louis, in my hearing: " If I am given four thousand men, I undertake to overcome the fire within six hours, and it will be stopped." This remark surprised me. I doubt whether he would have been successful. Rostopchin was continually renewing the fire: if it had been halted in one quarter, it would have broken out in another, in twenty places.

We met M. Daru and the agreeable Marigner coming from the Kremlin, and took them to the Soltykoff mansion, which we inspected from top to bottom. M. Daru had faults to find with the house, so we induced him to go and inspect others in the direction of the club. We inspected the club, which is decorated in French style and is majestic and black with smoke. Of its kind, there is nothing in Paris to equal it. After the club, we inspected the house next to it. It was a huge, haughty building; and since it was of handsome appearance, white and square, we resolved to occupy it.

We were very fatigued, myself more than most. Ever since Smolensk I have felt entirely devoid of energy; and now I had been so foolish as to follow all this house-inspection with interest and activity—or perhaps it is too much to say, with interest, but certainly with a great deal of activity.

We finally settled ourselves in this house, which appeared to have been inhabited by a wealthy lover of the arts. It was comfortably arranged, full of pictures and little statues. There were some fine books, notably the works of Buffon and of Voltaire, who is to be found everywhere in this city, and the *Galerie du Palais Royal*.

The violent diarrhoea from which we suffered made everybody fear the consequences of our lack of wine. We received the excellent news that wine could be obtained from the cellar of the handsome club that I have just mentioned. I persuaded father Gillet to go there with me. We made our way into it through superb stables and a garden which would have been beautiful were it not that the trees in this country always have for me an ineffaceable stamp of poverty.

We sent our servants charging into the cellar. They sent us out a great deal of bad white wine, some damask table-cloths and some napkins *ditto*, but very much worn. We pillaged these in order to make sheets of them.

A little M. J—— from the house of the Quartermaster-General, who had come to " gather honey " with us, began gratuitously making us gifts of all that we were taking. He informed us that he was requisitioning the building for the Quartermaster-General, and proceeded to moralise: I called him to order slightly.

My servant was completely drunk: he heaped the carriage with table-cloths, wine, a violin that he had pillaged for himself, and a thousand other objects. We made a small repast of wine with two or three colleagues.

The servants put the house in order. The fire was at some distance from us and filled the whole atmosphere, to a great height, with coppery smoke. We settled ourselves in, and were at last about to have a breathing-space, when M. Daru returned and announced that we must leave. I bore the news bravely, but I felt as if my knees had turned to water.

My carriage was crammed, but I gave a place in it to poor, beshitten and tedious de B——, out of pity for him and to pay back to another the favour that Biliotti had done me. De B—— is the stupidest and most boring spoilt child I know.

In the house, before leaving, I pillaged a volume of Voltaire, the one entitled *Facéties*.

My carriages under the charge of François kept us waiting, and by about seven o'clock we were scarcely en route. We met M. Daru, raging. We were proceeding directly towards the fire, along a section of the boulevard. Gradually we advanced into the smoke, and breathing became difficult: finally we were amongst blazing houses. None of our enterprises have ever been dangerous except through an absolute lack of order and prudence. Here was a very considerable column of carriages seeking to escape the flames by plunging into the midst of them! The manoeuvre would have been sensible only if a central section of the town had been surrounded by a ring of fire. This was not at all the case: the fire had taken hold of one side of the city, so we had to escape from it. But it was not necessary to pass through the fire: what we should have done was to outflank it.

The impossibility of our situation brought us sharply to a halt, and we turned back. Since I was preoccupied with the mighty spectacle before my eyes, I forgot for an instant that I had turned my carriage round before the others. I was exhausted, and I had to go on foot because my carriage was crammed with my servants' pillage and because the squalid fellow I have mentioned was perched on it. At one moment I thought my carriage would get lost in the fire. François, at the head of the procession, started up at a gallop. The carriage would have been in no danger, but my men, like everyone else's, were drunk and capable of falling asleep in the middle of a burning street.

On our way back we met General Kirgener on the boulevard. On this particular day I gained an high opinion of him. He restored our audacity—which is to say, our good sense—and pointed out to us that there were three or four roads by which we could leave the city.

At about eleven o'clock we were following one of these roads, when we cut across a file and found ourselves quarrelling with some carriers in the service of the King of Naples. I then realised that we were on the *Tverskoi*, the road to Tver. We emerged from the city, which was lit by the finest conflagration the world has ever seen: it formed a huge pyramid which, like the prayers of the faithful, had its base on the earth and its peak in heaven. Above this atmosphere of flame and smoke there was bright moonlight. It was an imposing spectacle; but in order to enjoy it one would have had to be alone, or with intelligent people. What has spoilt the Russian campaign for me is the fact that I have taken part in it in the company of people who would have caused the Coliseo and the sea of Naples to dwindle.

We were proceeding along a superb road, towards a château called *Petrovsky*, where His Majesty had taken his quarters, when crash! From my position in the middle of the road, looking out from my carriage, in which, by God's grace, I had found a perch, I saw M. Daru's calash lean over and finally fall into a ditch. The road was only eighty feet wide! Oaths, fury: it was very difficult to put the carriage back on its wheels.

Finally we arrived at a bivouac, which faced towards the city. We could clearly descry the huge pyramid formed by the pianos and sofas of Moscow—luxuries we would so much have enjoyed but for this mania of incendiarism. Rostopchin will go down in history either as a criminal or as a Roman; it remains to be seen how his action will be judged. Today a placard was discovered on one of Rostopchin's châteaux He announced that the château contained furniture worth one million

(I think the sum was), etc., etc., but that he was burning it so as not to leave it for the enjoyment of the brigands. The fact is that his beautiful palace in Moscow was not burnt.

On reaching the bivouac, we supped on raw fish, figs and wine. Such was the end of this arduous day, in which we were in a turmoil from seven .o'clock in the morning until eleven at night. What was worse, at this latter hour, when I entered my calash to sleep in it at the side of the tedious de B—— (sitting on bottles covered with equipment and blankets), I found I was drunk with the bad wine we had pillaged from the club. Preserve this gossipy scribble: I must at least derive from these dull woes of mine the advantage of remembering how they came about. I am still very annoyed with my companions in combat. Farewell, write to me and take care to amuse yourself: life is short.

—— 65 ——

TO THE CHEVALIER DE NOUE, COMMISSIONER ON THE COUNCIL OF STATE, QUARTERMASTER AT KOVNO

Moscow, the 10th of October 1812

My dear neighbour,

You are very lucky to have a nice, quiet little quartermastership. The quantities of abominable food we have consumed from Orcha to here are incredible, and unfortunately these provisions are not yet exhausted. Our master[1] was absolutely determined to send me to Smolensk to form a reserve of provisions in this Government and in that of Mohilev and Vitebsk. I resisted like the devil, saying that this was the duty of the quartermaster: I received an answer which my pen refuses to write. At last, after having refused for a week and done everything that discipline permitted, I have been rigged with the aforesaid mission to Smolensk[2].

All this has not cured me of a toothache worse than all the devils, resulting in a fever which I have had for a week—and tomorrow I set forth in wind and melting snow. What a treat!

[1] Mathieu-Dumas.
[2] " He entered Moscow on the 17th of September, with Napoleon, and left the city on the 16th of October, on a mission." (*Obituary*.)

I have some sort of authority over the quartermaster at Smolensk, Mohilev and Vitebsk. I don't know how it will work. It seems to me a mistaken measure. I would much rather have been in charge of some hole of two thousand five hundred souls, where I would, in the normal way, have had no bone to pick with anybody but my general. Well, such is my situation. Send me details of yours, by the first colleague who passes this way. For the present I am going to Smolensk: I shall have no communication with the world except through my colleagues. The couriers will pass under my nose without leaving the least little letter for me. My letters will arrive under the cover of M. Dumas. So my backside will be kept warm in every possible fashion. A fact that will become conspicuous unless I can have one or two pairs of breeches made for myself. Accordingly, and having entire confidence in your obliging kindness, I pray you to have bought for me at Kovno or Vilna, by the first colleague who passes that way, four or five ells of blue cloth or six or seven ells of kerseymere, also blue.

If nothing of that sort exists in your government, have the commissioner buy it in Vilna. I will pay him back when I receive the cloth at Smolensk, where I shall be quartered with Willeblanche or . . . I should much prefer it if you would see to the thing yourself, or would write to M. de Nicolaï to buy the cloth or kerseymere in advance and send it to the commissioner. I shall request you to reimburse M. de Nicolaï; or it would be better if the travelling commissioner reimbursed him. In this case I will settle directly with the commissioner when he passes through Smolensk.

There has been an immense deal of promotion in the Army. If I knew the names of your friends, I would give you news of them. M. de Nansouty, who I think will be going as far as Vilna, will tell you all about it. Eight captains of the Imperial Guard have received their majorities, although they have never fired a shot—like the commissioners who have never done anything, but are nonetheless great suffering heroes.

Saint-Didier[1] has received the Ordre de la Réunion. I am well satisfied: firstly, from natural pleasure; secondly, because it opens the road.

If the commissioners who come here want to buy or exchange furs at a cheap rate, tell them to bring some blue cloth or kerseymere.

Farewell, my dear neighbour, I am entirely at your service. Remind me to M. de Nicolaï and M. de Courtin[2].

Do you keep the provisioning of Séguin. I am keeping mine.

Entirely at your service,

M. SOUCHEVORT.

[1] Secretary-General of the Commissariat of the Grande Armée.
[2] Registrar of the hospitals of the Grande Armée.

TO M. ROUSSE, HEAD-CLERK
TO MAÎTRE DELOCHE, NOTARY IN PARIS

Moscow, the 15th of October 1812

Would you by chance have news, Monsieur, of Madame de Barcoff[1]? On the day of our entry here, I left my post—what could be more natural?—to search for Mme de B. amongst all the conflagrations. I found nothing. At last, three or four days ago I discovered a M. Auguste Fécel, a harpist, who told me that a few days before our entry she had left for St. Petersburg; that this departure had resulted in an almost complete rupture between her and her husband; that she was pregnant; that she nearly always wore a green eye-shade; that her husband was an ugly little man—very jealous and very loving, according to M. Fécel. He added that he believed Mme de Barcoff had just enough money for the journey to France, and that de Barcoff was neither handsome nor rich. Not all of these reports are favourable: perhaps M. Fécel bore some grudge against M. de Barcoff.

I felt, Monsieur, that I owed it to our common friendship for Mme de Barcoff to give you this sad information. At this moment no two cities are more widely apart than Petersburg and Moscow. I think she will find it difficult to get from Petersburg to Paris. Probably she will remain in Petersburg. But what will she do with her husband? And what is become of this husband, amidst all these disorders? Probably you will know the answers before I do. Would you have the extreme kindness, in the event of your learning something, to inform me of it? If she arrived in Paris, she could take my apartment: rue Neuve-du-Luxembourg, no. 3. I should be delighted if she did so. Would you have the kindness to inform her of this, and to settle her in? As regards letters, you would have to be so kind as to forward them to M. Maréchal, confidential secretary to H. E. Monsieur le comte Daru, hôtel d'Elbeuf, place du Carrousel.

Pray forgive this scrawl, Monsieur. I write to you in the middle of the night, under terrible pressure of work, whilst simultaneously dictating to five or six people. Please accept my very best regards.

H. Beyle.

[1] Mélanie Guilbert had married a Russian general.

I request Madame Maurice, caretaker at rue Neuve-du-Luxembourg no. 3, to open my apartment to Madame de Barcoff, who will lodge there if she finds it convenient to do so.

H. BEYLE.

Moscow, the 16th of October 1812.

—————— 67 ——————

TO THE COMTESSE DARU

Moscow, the 16th of October 1812

Madame, I owe a compliment to Aline and Napoléon[1] on their magnificent guinea-pigs: everyone in Moscow is talking about them. I would much rather be able to pay them this compliment *viva voce*: firstly because, in that case, I would be at beloved Bécheville[2], and secondly because, by the time my tardy letter arrives, you may already be mourning for the death of the charming creatures. The people with whom I I have the honour to live are of another species. With the exception of one person, our conversations are the most tedious in the world; we never speak but of serious matters, and with these serious matters we mix an enormous dose of self-importance, and spend an everlasting hour in explaining what could have been said in ten minutes. Apart from this, everything goes well: we have not seen a woman since the postmistresses of Poland, but by way of compensation we are great connoisseurs of fires. Our hasty changes of abode during our first nights in Moscow were truly most entertaining. For you, madame, these things must be a commonplace—you have heard such long accounts of them that you know more of them than we do. You know that Moscow had four hundred or five hundred palaces, decorated with a delightful sensual luxury such as is not known in Paris and is seen only in fortunate Italy. The explanation is simple: the government was despotic, and the city contained from eight hundred to a thousand persons with incomes of from five thousand to one million five hundred thousand livres. What were they to do with this money? Go to Court? A sergeant of the Guards who was in favour with the Emperor would subject them to humiliation, and furthermore would exile them to Siberia in order to take possession of their handsome teams. These unfortunate people had no resources except pleasure, and it seems—to judge by their houses, of which we enjoyed the use for a

[1] Her children.
[2] The château de Bécheville, near Meulan, summer residence of the Daru family.

[148]

period of thirty-six hours—that they made good use of this pis-aller. Their sensuality stood them in good stead: Catherine alone made fourteen of them great nobles; and Count Soltykoff, upon whom the Marshal is quartered, is the true cousin of Emperor Alexander, who is only a Soltykoff. For these amiable people we have substituted the most appalling barbarism. Madame, you would no longer recognise your charming acquaintances. Do you remember, for example, a handsome Apollo amongst whose set you danced last winter? I was myself almost an eye-witness to a most base and unworthy action—this Apollo walking amidst two weeping women and three children, of whom the eldest girl was seven years old! When shall I be in Vienna, in the drawing-room of Duchess Louise, far from all these barbarians and bores? The nearest I can come to this happy state is to leave tomorrow for Smolensk, where I am Director-General of reserve supplies. May God soon hear my prayer and bring me back to the rue Neuve-du-Luxembourg, where I am only three and a half hours from Bécheville. Are you still there, madame, at beloved Bécheville? I seem to remember that you proposed to leave it only in the last extremity. You have eaten grapes there, and so have I. This evening General Van Dedem, who is very amiable, has sent M. Daru a poor little vine-stock in a small vase. It actually bore three little grapes, two leaves and five or six leaf-sockets. It was the very emblem of poverty. M. Daru, with his usual kindliness, wanted all of us to taste the grapes: the poor little things had the taste of vinegar, nothing could have been sadder. I have travelled in search of distractions; I have found none; and I continually think of France.

. . . .

───── 68 ─────

TO FÉLIX FAURE

Smolensk, the 9th of November 1812

Here I am again in this picturesque town, which in this respect always seems to me unique. The snow enhances the effect of the ravines full of trees amidst which the town is built. There is only a light frost, of two or three degrees, but since we are in Russia everybody thinks himself frozen: to have or not to have boots and a pelisse, that is a great matter. For twenty days it has been impossible for me to write to you. There have been moments when I would have wished to preserve the memory of what I beheld in my soul or around me; but it was impossible to write. At present all that is sublime in my soul is neutralised by the enforced company, I shall not say of such-an-one or such-an-one, but of men. Deprived as I am of a shield, all the perversities of life fall flat on my soul, which is duly flattened. Such is the state in which I have the honour to find myself, after having slept with two jolly lads on the floorboards of a little study adjoining a room' where eight or ten colleagues were sleeping in the same fashion—and all this without any gaiety, with people who lay only a thin veneer over the rancour inspired by discomfort. I have noticed that soldiers who take pride in discomfort accept it with a continual gaiety. This gaiety, which in the main is probably only apparent —in young people and, after some really striking mishap, at all ages— is facilitated by an absolute lack of sensibility for others and for themselves. They fall sick of a rotting fever in a forsaken village, for twelve days or a fortnight they are in extreme distress—and a month later they speak of it with light-hearted reminiscence. I feel that this is partly because they are sure that their listeners don't care a damn; but the truth is that they no longer remember what happened. I confirmed this in the case of a battalion-commander of the 46th with whom I journeyed here from Moscow. My colleagues, on the other hand, seek to make capital of their hardships, and go about with long faces and with rancour in their hearts.

I would like to tell you about this journey from Moscow. I wrote some notes on it, but have lost them. Once a thought has occurred to me, I cannot hark back to it—it fills me with distaste. This journey alone has recompensed me for my departure from Paris by presenting me with so many new sights and experiences—things that a sedentary man of letters would not guess at in a thousand years. The most interesting days were the 25th and 26th of October . . .

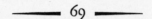

TO THE COMTESSE DARU

Smolensk, the 9th of November 1812

Here I am again, Madame, in pretty Smolensk, which this time is a little spoilt by the snow. I have just performed a sentimental journey from

Moscow, and I beg your leave to give you an account of it. I find nothing so dull as to make a journey of which one foresees all the circumstances in advance. When you go from Paris to Strasbourg, you almost know the names of each post; you know that you will scold certain postillions and tell certain inn-keepers that they are rogues. It all proves to be true, but what could be more boring? You are almost too happy when a wheel breaks in order to provide some sensation.

Instead of all that, I have had a delightful journey: three or four times a day I passed from extreme annoyance to extreme pleasure. I must admit that the pleasures were by no means exquisite: one of the keenest, for example, was that of finding one evening a few potatoes to eat, without salt, with some damp army bread. You see what hardship we endured. This state of affairs lasted eighteen days: leaving Moscow on the 16th of October, I arrived on the 2nd of November. M. le comte Dumas had ordered me to set off with a convoy of one thousand five hundred wounded, escorted by two or three hundred men. You can imagine the huge number of small vehicles, the oaths, the continual disputes—all these vehicles cutting across each other's path and falling into chasms of mud. Regularly every day we spent two or three hours in a muddy stream, without any supplies whatsoever. At such moments I condemned to the devil the silly idea of coming to Russia. On arriving in the evening, after having travelled all day and covered three or four leagues, we bivouacked and slept a little, with chattering teeth.

On the 24th of October, as we were making our fires, we were surrounded by a mob of men who started firing at us. Complete disorder, oaths from the wounded: we had all the trouble in the world to make them take up their muskets. We repulsed the enemy, but we thought ourselves destined for great adventures. We had with us a wounded general, a fine man named Mourier, who explained our situation to us. Having been attacked at that hour of the evening by a great horde of infantry, we probably had in front of us four or five thousand Russians, partly troops of the line and partly insurgent peasants. We were surrounded, there was no more safety in retreating than in advancing. We decided to spend the night on our feet, and on the morrow, at first break of dawn, to form a battalion-square, set our wounded in the middle of it and try to break through the Russians; if we were driven back, to abandon our vehicles, to reform into another, smaller battalion-square, and to be killed to the last man rather than let ourselves be taken by peasants who would kill us slowly with knives or in any other amiable fashion.

After this bold resolution, we made an arrangement. Each of us could be seen making a package of his least necessary effects, which were to be thrown away at the first attack in order to lighten the vehicles. I kept house with five or six wounded colonels, whom a week before I had not known and who on the journey had become my intimate friends. Indeed, there is one of them whom I promised to introduce to Mme Micoud.[1] This was indeed a piece of audacity on my part, but the man in question is worthy of introduction—M. de Collaert, colonel of the 2nd battalion of Hussars, who will be stationed at Liège.

All these people agreed that our goose was cooked. We distributed our napoleons amongst the servants, to try to safeguard some of them. We had all become close friends. We drank the little wine we had left. On the morrow, which was to be so great a day, we all set off on foot beside our calashes, hung with pistols from head to feet. There was such a fog that one could not see at four paces. We kept continually stopping. I had a volume by Mme du Deffand, which I read almost in its entirety. The enemy did not consider us worthy of his fury: we were attacked only in the evening, by a few cossacks who lanced fifteen or twenty of our wounded.

So that, madame, was the most glorious incident of our journey. It is fitting that I should give you an account of it. Although I always retained a great deal of hope, during the night I cast up the balance-sheet of my life—as did everyone else, I think—and bitterly reproached myself for not having had the spirit to tell you the full extent of my devotion to you.

. . . .

——— 70 ———

TO HIS SISTER PAULINE

Vilna, the 7th of December 1812

I am in good health, my dearest. I often thought of you on the long march from Moscow, which took fifty days. I have lost everything, and have only the clothes I am wearing. What is much better is that I am thin. I have had much physical hardship, and no spiritual pleasure: but all that is done with, and I am ready to start again in the service of His Majesty.

[1] Mme Micoud d'Umons, wife of the Prefect of Liège, a close friend of the comtesse Daru.

71

TO HIS SISTER PAULINE

Berlin, the 23rd of January 1813

My dearest, I leave Berlin on my thirtieth birthday. Nevertheless, I enjoyed the day like a child. My first idea this morning was that Victorine was also thirty years of age. Let us make haste to rejoice: time flies. You are twenty-seven, are you not? Write to me at rue Neuve-du-Luxembourg. I have not had a letter from the family since I left Paris on the 23rd of July.

Farewell. A thousand greetings to François, whom I love with all my heart.

TO FÉLIX FAURE

Mainz, January 1813[1]

My dear cousin, at last I write to you! Try to picture the physical condition of my brothers-in-arms and myself. We are appalling, revoltingly dirty, and we go down on our knees at the sight of a potato. When I endure such things by myself, I fall under the sway of their romantic quality, and can take an interest in them. But the presence of my brothers-in-arms makes my knees turn to water. On the whole, it was a detestable life, worse than what I suffered in Spain.[2]

Farewell; write to me: a letter from France holds me in rapture for two days.

CHAPELAIN.

---

[1] " During this retreat M. B. never supposed that there was any cause for tears. . . . Since it had not even been admitted that this Imperial Army was in retreat, he broke off his journey at Slangaud, and then at Berlin, whose default from France he personally witnessed.
" The further he was removed from danger, the greater became his horror of it, and he arrived in Paris harrowed with grief." (*Obituary.*)

[2] Beyle was never in Spain.

TO HIS SISTER PAULINE

13*th of April* 1813

. . . .

Do come. I keenly long to embrace you, whether in male or in female garb. Put a package of woman's clothes on the diligence, for Heaven has blessed you with an handsome sweep of the loins: you would at once be recognised as a woman, and for the past two or three years this highly convenient form of disguise has been out of fashionable favour. But come soon. I have a thousand things to tell you, and perhaps a long time will pass before we have another opportunity like this: I am in Paris, and you are not pregnant. I congratulate you on the stand which you not only took but *maintained*, that you would spend little time at Cularo[1]. Poor grand-father is almost never there nowadays, uncle hates us, father does not love us: I see nothing to recall us to that part of the world. Heaven be thanked, I am daily becoming more accustomed to being happy, what-ever pranks my travelling-companions may play on me. For example, I greatly distinguished myself in Russia: everybody predicted that I would receive great promotion, and people differed only as to its nature. Some friends told me secretly: you have been appointed Master of Appeals —others said, Prefect. Nothing of the sort has occurred. I have not even received any of the usual small signs of favour. I am left in the lurch as usual. This in no way diminishes my zeal in the service of H.M., or my cheerfulness. Father is holding up the matter of the barony, for lack of a scrap of paper of eight lines, to be signed by eight friends whom Faure is procuring for me at a cheap rate. I don't care a damn, and I entertain myself by asking young women to marry me and then marrying them off to my friends. If you come soon, I'll tell you about that episode.

I am more resolved than ever to preserve *cara libertà*. Farewell; enjoy yourself; travel; go on loving me, and bear in mind that a woman of twenty-seven is no longer a child and can run about without provoking gossip. Keep me informed of your doings. You are dearly loved by Mélanie[2], who is married to a Russian general and has come to France to cure a malady of the eyes.

[1] Grenoble.   [2] Mme de Barcoff.

TO HIS SISTER PAULINE

Saint-Avold, the 21st of April 1813
Noon

My dear child, never have I felt so sad[1]. I am going to see again those men and things with which I am more than sated. Everybody thought my departure somewhat extraordinary. Everybody sympathised with me; but they will forget it within a fortnight. My absence in Russia having lasted seven months, I was already rather forgotten. This new absence, after a stay of two and a half months in Paris, will further increase my estrangement from my acquaintances. I wrote to Z. that I wished to be employed at Rome or Florence. I am travelling with the silliest and coarsest of men. I read, whilst he ceaselessly interrogates me in deafening tones, wishing to know the names of all the hovels we pass. At Saint-Menehould, for example, he asked me: " To whom does that house belong? " pointing to a building in the townlet. That's the sort of brute to whose company I am delivered up for six or eight months. The road is full of troops. Farewell. Embrace Périer for me.

75

TO THE BARON VON STROMBECK[2]

Erfurt, the 20th of April, 1813

Here I am in Germany for the fourth time, my dear fellow; but none of my campaigns was worth the first of them; I made no other friend, and you are the only friend I have in the *langue d'ya*[3]. How have you spent your time during the past two months? I believe your home is

---

[1] " His patron compelled him to take part in the campaign of 1813." (*Obituary.*)
[2] Beyle had struck up a friendship with the Baron von Strombeck at Brunswick, and had been his host in Paris in 1811.
[3] A joke not translatable into English. The name of the French Languedoc means " the speech of *oc* " (the local word for " yes "); hence Beyle coins " the speech of *ja* " as a name for Germany.

now the headquarters of Prince von Eckmühl's general staff. Give me detailed news of yourself, addressed to *Imperial Headquarters*. I think these headquarters will soon be in Berlin. The enemy is withdrawing as if the devil were carrying him off. As a patriot I am pleased, but as a man I am quite sorry. It is only seven days since I left Paris, and already the campaign makes me feel sick at heart. I have not yet had time to rest myself after the steeplechase from Moscow. Write to me, my dear fellow, to enable me to endure being with the Army, and above all tell the delightful φιλλιπιδιον[1] that not all the armies in the world will ever cause me to forget the happy time I spent at Brunswick. That charming creature daily becomes more present in my thoughts—do not quote this remark to her in so many words. I fear that Fräulein φιλλιπιδιον would find it too strong; but when one is sad one cannot veil one's feelings.

LUNENBOURG.

. . . .

―― 76 ――

TO HIS SISTER PAULINE

Venice, the 8th of October 1813[2]

My dear one,

The early years of a distinguished man are like a frightful thicket. In all directions one sees only thorns and disagreeable and dangerous branches—nothing amiable, nothing graceful, at an age when mediocrities have these qualities despite themselves, so to speak, and by sheer compulsion of nature. After a time the frightful thicket falls to the ground, and one beholds a majestic tree, which in due course bears delightful flowers.

I myself was a frightful thicket in 1801, at the time when I was received with extreme kindness by Signora Borone, a Milanese lady and the wife of a merchant. Her two daughters were the attraction of her household. Today these two girls are married, but their sweet mother is still alive:

---

[1] Philippina von Bülow.

[2] "He was quartermaster at Sagan under the most honourable and most limited of generals, M. le marquis, then comte, de Latour-Maubourg. Here he fell ill of a sort of pernicious fever. In a week he was reduced to extreme weakness, and it was only for this reason that he was permitted to return to France. He at once left Paris and regained health on Lake Como." (*Obituary.*)

one finds in this circle a perfect naturalness, and an intelligence far superior to anything I have encountered on my travels.

What is more, I have been beloved in that circle for twelve years. It occurred to me that it was here I ought to end my days—or else find healing if, as seemed most likely, strength and youth were gaining ascendancy over the disorganisation produced by extreme fatigue.

At Milan I installed myself in a good inn, at which I paid the waiters handsomely, sent for the best physician in the city, and prepared to stand fast against death. The happiness of seeing my dearly loved friends again was more effective than the drugs I took. I am now out of all danger, and can make sport of my fever. It will not let go of me until after the heat of next summer, and it will leave my nerves extremely irritated. But the fact is that I owe my health to the following manoeuvre: when I have fever, I go and nestle in a corner of the drawing-room, and somebody plays to me. Nobody speaks to me; and soon my pleasure gains ascendancy over the sickness, and I join in the circle[1].

. . . .

I am very pleased with Venice, but my weakness makes me wish I were back at home—that is to say, in Milan. I shall certainly have to return to France towards the end of November: unless it is too inconvenient for you, come to meet me at Chambéry or Geneva.

C. SIMONETTA[2].

━━━ 77 ━━━

At the Imperial Palace of . . . .
the . . . . . of December, 1813
NAPOLEON

. . . .

. . . . .Switzerland

On the recommendation of our Quartermaster-General, we have decreed and do decree as follows:

[1] " At the moment when, at six o'clock this morning, we beheld the dome of Milan cathedral, it occurred to me that my travels in Italy are making me more original, more *myself*. I am learning to seek for happiness with more intelligence." (*Journal*, September 7th, 1818.)

[2] " Simonetta " is the name that Beyle often uses for his mistress, Signora Pietragrua. (Note by M. Martineau.)

ARTICLE 1

We grant exemption from military service to the Sr Henry de Beyle, commissioner of the first class on our Council of State, Quartermaster of our Crown chattels, born on the 23rd of January, 1783.

ARTICLE 2

Our Minister of War is charged with the execution of this decree.

N[1].

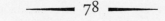

78

TO THE DUC DE FELTRE

Grenoble, the 17th of January 1814[2]

Monsieur le duc, my colleague M. le comte Chaptal having written to me from Lyons on the 15th that the enemy was probably about to occupy that unhappy city, and that no more troops should be sent there, I gave M. le comte Marchand command of the troops of the 7th division. This measure, of which I had the honour of informing Your Excellency in my letters of the 12th and 14th inst., appeared to be necessary to the service of His Majesty. I next called a council of war, of which I have the honour to send Your Excellency the minutes. Opinions were unanimous on all matters, even upon the manner of defending Grenoble. It was agreed that this place should be defended at the positions of the Barraux fort and the château Bayard to the north, and, in the direction of Lyons, at Voreppe, if a sufficient quantity of troops are available—or, if only a small quantity of troops are available, at the bridge of Piquepierre (near Buisserate), at a quarter of a league from the town; but that it was impossible for the walls of Grenoble to hold the enemy back for an hour. Nevertheless, in deference to Your Excellency's orders, measures are being taken to arm this position.

We have no muskets, and it is clearly desirable that all artillery which is not necessary to the armament should be evacuated. We hope to

---

[1] This draft for a decree is in Beyle's handwriting, and Beyle has written over it: " (copy exactly the formula of the decree of the 23rd of August, 1810. Write very carefully. This document is to be signed by H. M.)." (Note by M. Martineau.)

[2] " On the 26th of December 1813, on returning from dinner with Annette, I received a letter from the Minister of the Interior, who informed me that I was to go to Cularo with M. le comte de Saint-Vallier. I was keenly affected at having to leave Paris and absent myself from the Opera-Buffa and Angelina: contending with this feeling was the joyous impulse that I have always had whenever there was any question of setting forth and seeing something new." (*Journal*, March 2nd, 1814.)

complete this operation, thanks to the zeal which the Prefect, M. le baron Fourier, brings to all that pertains to the service of His Majesty. This excellent Prefect is all the more meritorious inasmuch as the nearness of the enemy makes requisitioning very difficult, and the two most populous districts of his Department, those of Vienne and la Tour-du-Pin, on the banks of the Rhône, are in daily fear of the arrival of enemy patrols. The two sub-prefects are behaving very well, and the mayor of Pont-de-Beauvoisin (Isère), the sieur Flandin, has proved himself to be animated with the keenest zeal.

Your Excellency is aware of the appalling situation of the positions in the Hautes-Alpes, where we have almost nothing but the two companies of artillery sent from Turin. General Marchand and I have decided to send a courier to the Prince-Viceroy and to Prince Camille, to ask them for garrisons for Briançon and Montlyon. My uneasiness concerning these positions is increased by the fact that they have no muskets, and that therefore there is no means of profiting by the good morale of the local people, who would like to hurl themselves into these positions. The prefectory adviser who is acting-Prefect at Gap is rendering excellent service.

Such, Monsieur le duc, are the precautions we have been called upon to take. Nevertheless I do not think that the enemy is in force before Lyons, and my private opinion is that he will not come to Grenoble and will not commit himself in our mountains. I must inform you, however, that public opinion differs from mine on this point.

Whatever may happen, I beg you to lay before the eyes of His Majesty the assurance that I shall hold out here to the last moment, and that if anyone is capable of defending this region, it is General Marchand.

At present all we have in our coffers is 6,700 fr. 54. I have given orders that no payments shall be made without my counter-signature[1].

[1] " On the 16th of January, I think it was, when we thought Lyons taken, I decided to spare the Senator the vexation of being awoken by despatch-riders by quartering myself in the Prefecture, in a huge, bright, cold and humid room. Annoyance gave me a fever." (*Journal*, March 2nd, 1814.)

79

TO HIS SISTER PAULINE

Paris, the 1st of April 1814[1]

I am very well: two days ago there was a very fine battle at Pantin and at Montmartre. I witnessed the taking of this mountain.

Everybody behaved well, there was not the least disorder. The Marshals performed prodigies. I seek news of you and your household, and of M. de Saint-Vallier. All the family is well. I am living at home

Gal TERRÉ.

80

TO HIS SISTER PAULINE

Paris, No. 3, the 10th of April 1814

Yesterday I witnessed a very great spectacle. It all passed off with the utmost simplicity. Great and small pursued their own interests without a thought for " what people will say ".

I expect that M. le comte d'Artois is finding it most embarrassing to reconcile all conflicting claims. Thirty thousand noblemen with nothing better to do are flooding into the city in all the diligences to demand everything. Luckily there is here a man of great intelligence and spirit, M. de Talleyrand, who would make a worthy Prime Minister.

I think your brother will lose his emoluments. His office will become an honorary one, without salary. Write to our worthy father and ask him to settle on the poor devil enough land to bring in a net income of two thousand four hundred francs. He must have that to live. (He left two days ago for Versailles.) He makes this request only in the case of a total cessation of his emoluments.

---

[1] " Grenoble, the 22nd of February 1814 . . . M. Beyle's sickness continues. He works as much as he can, but, despite his eagerness, he is of but little service to the extraordinary commission. Since I have reason to be satisfied with him, I gladly accede to his request that he may return to M. le duc de Cadorne, at Paris. . . . The comte de Saint-Vallier."

If he is refused, the poor devil will be in the greatest embarrassment, with debts as his only property.

FLORISE.

Cordial greetings to Mme Derville[1]. What is she doing?

——— 81 ———

WITHOUT ADDRESSEE[2]

Paris, the 26th of May 1814

I notice with pleasure that I am still susceptible of passion. I was leaving the Français, where I had seen *the Barber of Seville* played by Mademoiselle Mars. I was beside a young Russian officer, an aide-de-camp to General Vaissikoff (or some such name). His general is the son of a famous favourite of Paul I. This charming officer would have inspired me, had I been a woman, with a most violent passion, a love *à l'Hermione*. I could feel it burgeoning within me. Already I was shy; I dared not look at him as much as I would have wished. If I had been a woman I would have followed him to the ends of the earth. How different this officer was from a Frenchman! What naturalness, what an affectionate disposition he displayed!

Polite manners and civilisation serve to raise all men to the level of mediocrity, but they spoil and debase all who would otherwise be outstanding. Nothing is coarser or more disagreeable than a foreign officer who is an uncultivated fool. But, likewise, what officer in France could be compared with mine for naturalness combined with greatness! If a woman had made a like impression upon me, I would have spent the night in seeking for her dwelling. Alas, even the comtesse Simonetta[3] made such an impression upon me only sometimes. I suppose that the uncertainty of my future is enhancing my sensibility.

[1] " Mme Derville, of Vizille, whom I had never seen and who is a close friend of my sister. She arrived, and I went with the ladies to Claix and Vizille, and I took some pleasure in inculcating into these pure-minded beings some truths concerning the arts and also some detailed truths concerning human nature." (*Journal*, March 2nd, 1814.)

[2] This letter, which was published by Colomb in the collected correspondence, is perhaps merely a fragment of the *Journal*.

[3] Signora Pietragrua.

TO HIS SISTER PAULINE AND THE
COMTESSE BEUGNOT[1]

Milan, the 28th of August 1814[2]

My dear Pauline,

I have not the patience to copy out again the enclosed account of my doings. It consists of fragments of a letter that I finished, but afterwards thought too heavy in style. I shall be in Genoa at noon tomorrow.

My commissions follow.

" Madame,

" It may well be that so many things have happened at Paris during the past month that you will have little attention to spare for a traveller's tales. Will my letter find you at Mme Curial's[3] château, which I suppose must be charming, or will it have the misfortune to arrive on a Wednesday, like a bill for bread in a poor household? If I were writing for the countryside and for the sweet serenity that such amiable society is bound to inspire, I would devote more space to the interesting part of my journey. If it is for Paris, I would tell you of all the political demonstrations I have encountered.

" After a very keen heartache at leaving Paris and the spots that reminded me of so many illusions that were delightful, but were not only illusions, I came to spend a week in the midst of green, solitary woods, with people upon whose affection I can entirely count. In the morning I set out on horseback, all by myself, and rode two or three leagues through the silent woods—an excellent opportunity for reflection. I realised anew that I had been in love only with illusions, and I shall not tell you the name of the only person whom I sincerely missed. I am bored by the company of men and by serious reasoning. You will perhaps have noticed, madame, that such fine arguments always end by arriving at

---

[1] " Second to her lover, M. Pépin de Bellisle, my close friend, I was perhaps the person whom she loved most," Stendhal wrote of the comtesse Beugnot in his *Vie de Henri Brulard*. In 1814 he dedicated to her his first published work: " *Letters written from Vienna in Austria concerning the famous composer Haydn, followed by a Life of Mozart and thoughts on Metastasio.*"

[2] " I fell with Napoleon in April, 1814. I came to Italy to live as I had lived in the rue d'Angiviller." (*Vie de Henri Brulard.*)

[3] The comtesse Beugnot was the comtesse Curial's mother. (Cf. letters nos. 115 et seq.)

some sad conclusion. I am speaking of those who reason best: three-quarters of reasoners merely make one shrug one's shoulders at the ignorance or banality of their utterances. The sole advantage that can be obtained from conversations that affect importance is that, if the person with whom you have chattered is called Mme Doligny[1], the chatterers who see you leaving the company will treat you with respect. All that remains, therefore, for a man who is at all sensitive, or at all weary of the vanity of uniforms, is the society of women. Well, now, such society is worth infinitely more in Italy, since, in France, women for twenty-three and a half hours of the day are merely men. In Turin I saw a petty king who has some personal courage: almost daily he goes for a walk alone and on foot. In any case, as he was told by the Lord Bentinck who drove on Paris, he is thirty years behind-hand in the art of ruling, and if he stays on the throne it will not be his fault. He is unpopular with the twenty thousand soldiers whom he has allowed to return to Piedmont. Milan is full of all the great families of his country, whom he has banned from favour for having served ' that other ' (this is the name he gives to Bonaparte).

" I take a great liking to the friends one makes whilst travelling. It must be that they find something agreeable about you, since they like you without knowing who you are.

" At Turin I made the acquaintance of an Italian general whose name I shall probably never know. He took me to see the King, and, what was better, a charming actress of eighteen years who has the loveliest eyes in the world, sees the cheerful side of life, mocks at everything both on the stage and in her home, and has the deep wisdom to refuse to marry the rich men who offer her a coach, a livery and the tedium of their gloomy society. Her character, which is extremely frank, causes her to sing and perform in a most unusual style—that is to say, with perfect naturalness. I have seen a whole auditorium laughing for ten minutes until the tears came, so that they all had to wipe their eyes, and everybody going out chanting the comic duet which she had sung with a ridiculous suitor.

" Such are the pleasures of Italy, which are not to be found on the other side of the Alps, where everybody would have been disgusted by the duet's impropriety.

" . . . That's why my conversations with a certain Milanese lady[2]

---

[1] The comtesse Beugnot.

[2] Signora Pietragrua. (Cf. letters nos. 13, 38, 63, 76.)
" Just as one cannot see that part of the sky which is too close to the sun, so I would find it very difficult to give a reasonable account of my love for Angela Pietragrua.
" . . . This celestial, passionate love, which had completely snatched me up from the earth and transported me to the land of chimeras—but of the most celestial, most delicious, most

[163]

are never-ending. The result is that all her circle are jealous of 'the Frenchman'; and, since there are many matters in which she must be circumspect, the result is that she has banished me to Genoa. I shall be there on the 30th of August—for how long I do not know. I cannot judge of the strength of feeling against ' the Frenchman ', since he is very civilly received and it is only to her that people have dared to express this feeling. I am therefore entitled to have my suspicions and to suppose that she is fickle. Indeed, I took the liberty of telling her so: hence tears and a scene; and, since I finally consented to depart, I leave Milan in torments of jealousy. I offered to go and live in Venice, or any other town, large or small, that she cared to name. She is to send her decision to me at Genoa. She made me ask for her portrait, and whilst I was writing this letter it has arrived in a book.

" Farewell, madame, I must end this letter abruptly or I shall never do so. Command my ambassador *Fairisland*[1] never to cease loving me and to ask constantly for some small diplomatic title in this country. One absolutely must have something official to protect one from the machinations of the Jesuits.

" Deign to present my respects to madame Curial and M. Beugnot; and if ever, after a week of constant application, you reach this fourth page, quickly throw my letter into the fire and remember that you have a faithful slave at Genoa."

DOMINIQUE.

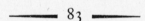

83

TO HIS SISTER PAULINE

Turin, the 14th of January 1815

If ever, my dear one, you assume the airs of having a lover, you will know that one never betrays oneself so much as when there is a quarrel. I was the object of a positively leech-like jealousy—something completely

---

utterly-to-be-wished-for chimeras—did not culminate in what is called ' happiness ' until September 1811.

" . . . The woman I loved, and by whom I supposed myself to be in some sort loved in turn, had other lovers, but she preferred me *ceteris paribus*, I used to tell myself!"

In another passage:

" My self-pride, my own interests, my very personality, had disappeared in the presence of the person beloved; I was transformed into her. What, then, could happen when this person was a villainess like Signora Pietragrua?

" . . . Angela P. was a sublime strumpet in the Italian style, in the style of Lucrezia Borgia." (*Vie de Henri Brulard.*)

[1] Louis de Bélisle.

[164]

unhinged—and Signora Simonetta[1] represented to me that it was necessary for me to absent myself. She added that a conqueror of Moscow
had no fear of the cold; that since Italy was not advancing upon Cularo,
I ought to take a trip there; and that this would spare us a separation
when once we were established in Venice. I tried to plead, but in vain.
So I have come to Turin. But the experience of leaving a charming,
brightly-lit ballroom where one was dancing with one's mistress, and of
coming out into the street in wet weather and finally falling into a manure-
heap—all that would have been a pale reflection of what my heart would
have felt had I left sweet Italy for dull Cularo, where you and I moaned
together a year ago, if you remember.

So I stopped at Turin.

On the 23rd I shall write to the contessa Simonetta that I am back,
and have not been swallowed up in the snows of the Mont Cenis.

Post the enclosed letter from a young Spanish officer who has a charming mistress in Milan—a circumstance that gives him great prestige in
my eyes. Cultivate the Allard family in my name, so that they may not
suppose me to be a monster simply because, at the age of thirty-two and
ruined, I have taken a patrimonial portion of twenty-five thousand francs.

Ah, dearest one, what terrible news I learn from the newspaper that has
just been brought to me! The death of madame Daru[2]. After you, she was
the best friend I had in the world. I cannot go on writing. Farewell.

Achille est mort, grands dieux, et Thersite respire[3]!

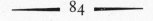

84

TO M. DUPIN SENIOR,
SOLICITOR IN PARIS[4]

Near Nantes, the 1st of September 1816[5]

Monsieur,

I wish to ask you to propose the following law before the Chambers.

[1] Signora Pietragrua.

[2] It was at this time that Beyle headed one of the green volumes in which he was writing
the rough drafts for his *Histoire de la Peinture en Italie*, the inscription: " *To the everlasting
memory of Milady Alexandra Z. Even in our aches love* " (in English in the original). He
forgot the dedication to Signora Pietragrua which he had prepared three years before. (Note
by M. Martineau.)

[3] Achilles is dead, great gods, and Thersites breathes!

[4] M. Dupin senior appears to have been the person to whom this letter was addressed.
Beyle's hatred of duels is all the more remarkable since he himself had had two or three and
was a man of considerable bravery. (Note by Colomb.)

[5] At this time Beyle was at Milan.

If there is anything irregular about this letter, you will forgive me when I confess to you that the person who has the honour of addressing you has recently lost his only mainstay, a nephew of eighteen years, a young man of the purest morals, slain by a duellist, a very skilful fencer, for whom this was at least his fifth duel.

François DURAND.

LAW

Article the first: the Royal Courts shall enquire into a duel as into other offences.

Art. 2: The duellist shall be tried before a jury[1].

Art. 3: The duellist shall be punished by imprisonment. The prisoner shall be detained in complete solitude[2], without paper or inkstand. At night the prisoner shall have no light. During the day, he shall be kept in deep darkness. Every day he shall have one hour of exercise in the morning and one hour in the evening. He shall be deprived of all conversation. He shall likewise be deprived of all fermented liquor and kept on a vegetarian regime. He shall have no book but Livy[3].

Art. 4: The first duel shall be punished with eight days' imprisonment: if death results, with three months' imprisonment.

The second, with three months' imprisonment: if death results, with ten months' imprisonment.

The third, with a year's imprisonment: if death results, with two years' imprisonment.

The fourth, with four years' imprisonment: if death results, with eight years' imprisonment.

The fifth, with eight years' imprisonment; if death results, with sixteen years' imprisonment.

Art. 5: Members of the two Chambers who have been the two principals in a duel shall likewise be tried before a jury. If the duel has had no political motives, they shall suffer the penalties laid down in Article 4. If the duel has had political motives, the aggressor shall be sentenced to a fine of not less than fifteen thousand francs and not more than sixty thousand.

Art. 6: Any person who, as a result of political differences, shall fight a duel with a mayor or a member of either of the two Chambers, shall

---

[1] Indispensable on grounds of moral effect. The object is to correct the jurymen themselves—a consideration extraneous to other crimes. (Note by the author.)

[2] Necessary, since the object is to punish with *boredom*. Cf. the *Panopticon* by Messrs. Jeremy Bentham and Dumont. (Note by the author.)

[3] To teach young minds that it is possible to be brave without fighting duels. The boredom of the first detention will prevent a second duel. (Note by the author.)

be punished as is laid down in Article 4, and shall furthermore be sentenced to a fine of not less than ten thousand francs and not more than forty thousand francs[1].

Art. 7: Any person who is convicted of having fought for financial reward, or from any venal motive, in a quarrel which did not concern him, shall be sentenced to imprisonment for not less than six years and not more than twenty years. If he has killed his adversary, he shall be sentenced to ten years in irons and to branding. If he has killed his adversary in a duel arising from a political dispute, he shall be sentenced to death.

Art. 8: Any person convicted of having hired another person to fight in his place shall be sentenced to two years in irons and to branding. If the duel was fought against a member of one of the two Chambers, he shall be sentenced to twenty years of penal servitude.

Art. 9: If a duel results in death, each of the seconds shall be punished with a month's imprisonment. If a second has duels on his own conscience, the period of imprisonment shall be augmented by not less than ten days and not more than six months for each duel.

Art. 10: If a fencing-master, of whom it shall be proved that he has given lessons in fencing, or in the use of pistols, for payment, fights with a citizen who is not in the same case, and kills him, the period of imprisonment shall be doubled. If he fights a second duel, which results in the death of his adversary, he shall be sentenced to death.

Art. 11: If it is established that the duellists have gone from one Department to another in order to fight, or if, at Paris, they have fought outside the boundaries of the bois de Boulogne, each of them shall, in addition to the ordinary penalties, pay a fine of not less than two thousand francs and not more than forty thousand francs.

Art. 12: In times of peace the present law is applicable to the military, with this difference, that the first duel between military persons shall not be followed by any penalty; the second shall be punished with eight days' imprisonment, or, if death results, with three months' imprisonment; and so on, as laid down in Article 4. Any officer convicted of having fought six duels shall not be entitled to promotion beyond the rank which he then occupies, until he has held this rank for ten further years. He shall not be entitled to receive any military decorations, unless by reason of having been wounded. Any general who fights a duel shall pay, in addition to the ordinary penalties, a fine of not less than ten thousand francs and not more than a hundred thousand francs. If the duel was

---

[1] There must not be too easy a method of getting rid of a Deputy who might give trouble by reason of his talents or character. Example, Mirabeau. (Note by the author.)

fought with a mayor or a member of either of the two Chambers, this fine shall be doubled.

————— 85 —————

TO THE EDITOR-IN-CHIEF
OF THE *CONSTITUTIONNEL*

Rouen[1], *the 26th of September* 1816

Monsieur,

M. Louis-Alexandre-César Bombet[2], my brother, being in London, and being very old, very gouty, very little occupied with music, and still less so with signor Carpani, permit me to answer on his behalf the letter from signor Carpani which you published in your issue of the 20th of this month.

I read last winter the two Italian letters addressed by Signor Carpani to M. Bombet, letters which were noticed in your journal. They led me to read what Signor Carpani calls his *Haydine*, a great, interminable volume on the composer Haydn. I extricated, from amidst many words and details of no interest, the suggestion that several facts concerning Hadyn's life, and given in the book in question, had been " filched " by M. Bombet. How to get out of this awkward situation? I found consolation, and believed on my conscience that my brother's honour was safe, when it occurred to me that Hume was not a plagiarist from Rapin-Thoiras for having said, after the latter, that Elizabeth was a daughter of Henry VIII; and that M. Lacretelle was not a plagiarist from M. Anquetil for having treated, after the latter, the subject of the War of the League.

I was still more consoled, and indeed almost joyful, when I had told myself that Hume and M. Lacretelle had envisaged their subject in a manner different from, and often opposite to, that of their predecessors; that these two historians had drawn from the same facts conclusions that had hitherto not been perceived; and that, finally, they had caused their predecessors to be forgotten. I much fear that this may happen in the case of poor Signor Carpani, who last winter was so proud of his ability to produce some jests upon M. Bombet's surname and Christian names, and who today proclaims himself a Hercules because, so he says, nobody

---

[1] At this time Beyle was at Milan.
[2] The pseudonym under which Beyle had published his *Lettres sur Haydn*, etc.

has been able to answer him. Signor Carpani states that he has assembled terrible proofs against M. Bombet, and he desires a formal reply. (This combat might perhaps call a little attention to the *Haydine* of our *champion* which are at present mouldering at Milan in Buccinelli's bookshop.) Now, there is a simple manner in which M. Bombet and Signor Carpani can publish their evidence jointly and harmoniously. The method is simple. Let Signor Carpani have thirty pages of his *Haydine* translated— let him choose the pages himself—and let him have printed, on opposite pages, thirty of M. Bombet's *Letters on Haydn*, these again to be chosen by Signor Carpani himself.

The public will be the judge.

If other proofs were needed, I would mention that M. Bombet's work, printed by Didot, contains only two hundred and fifty small pages on Haydn, whereas that of Signor Carpani consists of almost five hundred and fifty pages. I would ask Signor Carpani whether he similarly claims the credit for the *Vie de Mozart*, or the excellent literary digression on Metastasio, or the *Lettre sur l'état actuel de la mosque en France et en Italie*, or Montmorency's *Lettre sur le beau idéal*. I would beg him to acquaint us with his rights as regards those questions, which M. Bombet has been the first to plumb, concerning the true causes of the pleasures given by the arts and especially by music; and with his rights as regards the exquisite judgments that M. Bombet pronounces upon the great composers. I would furthermore beg Signor Carpani to tell us whether he would make the delightful claim to have served as model *for the graceful style, full of sensibility without affectation, and not without pungency, which is perhaps the principal merit of M. Bombet's work.*

But I perceive that I, in turn, am becoming a Hercules, that I am stealing Signor Carpani's thunder, that I am falling into the serious and tedious. M. Bombet, who does not like this modern style and, above all, is the last man to filch his own style from Signor Carpani—I feel sure that M. Bombet, who is my elder brother, will greatly reproach me for the liberty I take of boring the public in his name. I shall therefore end this letter by reiterating to Signor Carpani my challenge concerning the thirty pages. It is only by accepting it that he will prove his good faith.

I have the honour, etc.

H. C. C. BOMBET.

86

TO LOUIS CROZET[1]

Rouen, 28th of September 1816[2]

. . . .

The happiest chance in the world has procured for me the acquaintance of four or five *Englishmen of the first rank and understanding*.[3] They brought me enlightenment, and the day when they provided me with the means of reading *The Edinburgh Review* will mark a turning-point in my mind's history—but a most discouraging turning-point, I must add. Imagine it, almost all the good ideas in the *H.*[4] are the consequences of general and loftier ideas expounded in this accursed review! *In England if ever the H.*[3] arrives there, the work will be taken for that of an educated man, and not for that of a man who writes at the immediate dictation of his heart.

The note on romanticism in temperaments is very silly. These dull Germans, always so stupid and emphatic, have laid hands on the romantic system, have given it a name, and have spoilt it. This system, as practised by Lord Ba-ï-ronne (Lord Byron, a young madman, a Lovelace of thirty-six), and as taught by the *Ed. Review*, is sure to have a vast effect upon the human race. Schlegel remains a mere ridiculous pedant. He says that he wishes French literature had but one head, that he might cut it off; that perfection in all styles is anterior to the Greeks; that we are continually diminishing it; that only the Germans still preserve the sacred fire; that Italian is merely corrupt German. For the rest, he is the very original of the three lawyers from the *Cid*, in Helvétius. He hurls all French literature into the nether void. " I think I have proved to the English that they have no literature," he said one day. " There is nothing but Germany. Schiller is only a pupil of Shakespeare. Goethe is immoral, and has squandered his genius in small fragments. There are left only

---

[1] " My childhood's friend, the excellent Crozet." (*Souvenirs d'égotisme.*) "I had the good fortune to meet Louis Crozet often again, at Paris, in 1800. . . . Indeed, we once slept in the same room (hôtel de Hambourg, rue de L'Université), on the evening of the capture of Paris in 1814. His grief gave him a night's indigestion; whereas I, who was losing everything, considered the thing rather as a spectacle." (*Vie de Henri Brulard.*) In 1816, Louis Crozet was living at Plancy dans l'Aube, where he was an Engineer of Bridges and Roads. Beyle bequeathed to him all his manuscripts, which Mme Crozet presented to Grenoble Library in 1860.

[2] At this date Beyle was at Milan.

[3] In English in the original.

[4] *L'Histoire de la Peinture en Italie.*

my brother and I, and it seems that the *Lessons of Dramatic Literature* are the book of the century."

If you can do so, bring the fool into ridicule; otherwise M.B.A.A.[1] will seem to be making common cause with this monster of vanity, who one of these days will certainly be dragged in the mud. Byron, Byron is the name that one must ring out loud and clear. The *Ed. R.* ranks him immediately after Shakespeare for the depiction of strong passions. His works are stories of tragic loves: *The Corsair*, a poem in three cantos; *The Giaour* (a Christian who elopes with a Turkish woman—his lover is killed, he avenges her and dies of grief), a poem in three cantos; *The Bride of Abydos*, in three cantos, more tender and less tragic. Three or four of the leading men of England regard these works as sure to live until the year 2,500. Half of what we French admire has in England been overthrown. We know nothing of their progress since 1790; and they, for their part, without troubling themselves with the Continent, have boldly followed their reason. For them, Plato, Cicero, Aristotle, etc., are in the mud as far as " present utility " is concerned, but are to be admired as having been great in their day. The imitators of these authors are fools who do not know how to question their own hearts on matters of pleasure.

. . . In short, during the past two months my ideas have been revolutionised. I have made the acquaintance of seven or eight persons who are of the first rank both in ribbons and in intellect. I have achieved successes that were gratifying to my vanity. They appreciated my gift of the gab. This has removed the shyness I feel towards people whom I consider great. In one of my next letters I shall give the names of these acquaintances.

To return to our business—

I insist on M.B.A.A.

. . . On the page following the title print the following words, in lapidary style and characters:

TO

THE HAPPY FEW[2]

I have had this project for two years. It is the explanation of the whole book. I dedicate it to sensitive souls. People like Mgr. Z will not understand a word of it, and will think it " odious ".

. . . .

[1] *Monsieur Beyle, Ancien Auditeur* (former Commissioner). The History of Painting appeared in 1817 under these initials.

[2] In English in the original.

87

TO LOUIS CROZET

Paris, the 30th of September 1816[1]

Reasons for not producing the third, fourth, fifth and sixth volumes of the Histoire de la peinture en Italie.

Since I read Destouches, at the age of twelve, I have destined myself *to make co*[2]. I have been constantly preoccupied with the depiction of characters and the adoration I feel for all that is comic.

By chance, in 1811, I fell in love with the contessa Simonetta and with Italy. I made my declaration of love to this lovely country when I prepared the great draft, in twelve volumes, which I lost at Molodetchno. On my return to Paris I had the aforesaid draft copied out from the original manuscript; but I cannot recover the corrections made in the twelve handsome green volumes, small folio, which were eaten by the Cossacks.

In 1814, beaten upon by the storms of a keen passion from the 22nd of December to the 6th of January 1815, I was on the point of saying good night to everyone. Having had the misfortune to allow myself to become irritated by the bastard's[3] Jesuitism, I found myself in no condition to do anything reasonable, far less anything light-hearted. I therefore worked four to six hours a day, and, in two years of sickness and passion, I wrote two volumes. It is true that I thus formed my style, and that a great part of the time which I spent in listening to music *alla Scala* was employed in effecting a harmony between Fénelon and Montesquieu, who share my heart between them.

These two volumes may have a hundred and fifty years in their belly. If my Will[4] is carried out, and if the study of mankind is treated as an exact science, this study will make such progress that one will be able to see, as clearly as if through a crystal, just how sculpture, music and painting touch the heart. Thus what Lord Byron is doing will be done for all the arts. And what will become of the conjectures of l'abbé Dubos,

---

[1] Beyle was probably still in Milan at this date. (Note by M. Martineau.)

[2] [*Sic*] in the original. It means " to write comedies ".

[3] Chérubin Beyle, his father. In Beyle's private idiom the " bastards " were those disinherited of naturalness and intelligence, the enemies of the *happy few*, of sensitive souls.

[4] Cf. letter no. 54 (instructions to MM. Félix Faure, Louis Crozet and Lambert, of Lyon).

when we have people like Lord Byron, passionate enough to be artists and at the same time thoroughly understanding mankind?

Apart from this unanswerable argument, it is a paltry thing to spend one's life in *saying how great others have been. Optumus quisque benefacere*, etc.[1]

It is in the whirl of passion that the soul's fire becomes strong enough to perform that smelting of substances which creates genius. I regret all too much that I spent two years in studying just how Raphael touches the human heart. I am striving to forget these ideas, and also the ideas I have concerning other painters of whom I have not written. Correggio, Raphael, Il Domenichino, Il Guido—they're all done, in my head.

But I none the less think it wise, at thirty-four years less three months, to return to *Letellier*[2] and to try to write some twenty comedies between the ages of thirty-four and fifty-four. By then, or even before then, I shall be able to finish the *Painting* and give myself a rest from the art of the *komiker*. When I am older, I shall write about my campaigns, or moral and military memoirs. In these, some fifty striking characters will make their appearance.

At the jesuit's death[2], *if I can, I will go in England*[3], for 4,000 fr., and to Greece for a like sum; after which I shall try Paris, but I think I shall end my days in the " land of beauty ". If at forty-five I find a widow of thirty who is willing to regard a small amount of fame as valid coin of the realm, and who, moreover, has an income equal to two-thirds of mine, we shall spend life's evening together. If fame is lacking, I shall remain a bachelor.

Those, you see, are my entire plans for my future.

. . . .

―――― 88 ――――

TO LOUIS CROZET

Lyon, 20th of October 1816[4]

I have dined with a handsome and charming young man—a face of eighteen years, although his age is twenty-eight, the profile of an angel,

---

[1] The Latin words are thus in the original.
[2] A play that remained unfinished.
[3] In English in the original. (The " jesuit " is the same as the "bastard ".)
[4] Beyle was still at Milan. (Note by M. Martineau.)

the gentlest of manners. 'Tis the original of Lovelace—or, rather, a thousand times better than that babbler. When this young man enters an English drawing-room, all the women immediately depart. He is the greatest poet living, Lord Byron. The *Edinburgh Review*, his chief enemy, against which he has written an atrocious satire[1], says that not since Shakespeare has England had anyone so great at depicting the passions. *This I actually read.* He has spent three years in Greece. Greece is to him what Italy is to Dominique[2]. Apart from that, he has written some verses which, now that he is back from Greece, he finds dull. He is returning there.

. . . .

━━━ 89 ━━━

NOTE FOR THE PUBLISHERS
(*Addresses for the despatch of the Histoire de la Peinture en Italie*)

The 15th of September 1817

N.B.—Do not advertise or send to the newspapers until copies have been despatched to the persons listed below.

Do not send a copy to the *Quotidienne*, the *Débats*, the *Bon Français* or the *Quinzaine*.

Send to:

M. le duc de la Rochefoucault-Liancourt, rue Royale-Saint-Honoré, 9;

M. le duc de Choiseul-Praslin, rue Matignon, 1;

M. le comte de Tracy, rue d'Anjou-Saint-Honoré, 42;

M. le comte de Volney, peer of France, member of the Académie française, rue de La Rochefoucault, 11;

M. le comte Garat, rue Notre-Dame-des-Champs;

M. le lieutenant-général, comte, peer of France Dessoles, rue d'Enfer-Saint-Michel, 4;

M. le lieutenant-général Andreossy, rue de la Ville-l'Évêque, 22;

M. de Cazes, minister;

M. le duc de Broglie, peer of France, rue Lepelletier, 20. Also le duc de Broglie, of the Chamber of Deputies, rue Saint-Dominique, 19;

M. de Staël junior;

[1] *English Bards and Scotch Reviewers* (1809).
[2] This was Beyle's name for himself at times when he thought of himself with indulgence.

M. Benjamin Constant (*Mercure*);

Sir Francis Eggerton;

M. le duc de Brancas-Lauraguais, peer of France, rue Traversière-Saint-Honoré, 45;

M. Terrier de Monciel;

Mme la comtesse de Saint-Aulaire;

M. le comte Boissy-d'Anglas, peer, rue de Choiseul, 13;

M. le comte Chaptal, member of the Institut, president of the Société d'encouragement, rue Saint-Dominique-Saint-Germain, 70;

M. Thénard, member of the Académie des Sciences, rue de Grenelle-Saint-Germain, 42;

M. Biot, member of the Institut, at the Collège de France, place Cambrai. Abroad;

M. le chevalier Poisson, member of the Institut, rue d'Enfer-Saint-Michel, 20;

M. le comte La Place, peer of France and member of the Institut, rue de Vaugirard, 31;

The Freiherr von Humboldt;

M. Maine-Biran, rue d'Aguesseau, 22;

M. Manuel, lawyer;

M. Dupin, lawyer, rue Pavée-Saint-André-des Arcs, 18;

M. Berryer, lawyer, rue Neuve-Saint-Augustin, 40;

M. Mauguin, lawyer of the Royal Court, rue Sainte-Anne, 53;

M. de Jouy, of the Institut, rue des Trois-Frères, 11;

M. Say, of the *Constitutionnel*;

M. Villemain, Divisional Chief of Police;

M. le comte de Ségur, Grand Master of Ceremonies, rue Duphot, 10;

M. de Lally-Tollendal, peer, member of the Institut, Grande-Rue-Verte, 8;

M. Laffite, banker, Deputy, rue de la Chaussée-d'antin, 11;

M. le maréchal duc d'Albufera, rue de la Nille-l'Évêque, 18;

M. le prince d'Eckmühl, rue Saint-Dominique-Saint-Germain, 107;

M. Béranger, author of the *Recueil de Chansons*;

Mme Récamier;

M. Récamier (Jacques), banker, rue Basse-du-Rempart, 48;

M. Dupuytren, Chief Surgeon, opposite the colonnade of the Louvre;

M. Talma, rue de Seine-Saint-Germain, 6;

Mlle Mars, rue Neuve-du-Luxembourg, 2 *bis*;

M. Prud'hon, historical painter, rue de Sorbonne, 11;

Herr Goethe, Minister of State, at Frankfort on Main;

M. Sismonde-Sismondi, at Geneva;

Sir Walter Scott, poet, at Edinburgh.

TO THE BARON DE MARESTE[1]

Milan, the 1st of December, 1817

. . . *Psami re d'Egitto*, a rather entertaining ballet by Vigano, has been
performed here for the last time. We arrived on the 1st. *Psami* was
preceded by the second act of the *Matrimonio Segreto*. Galli, in the rôle
of the count, is for me the only perfect performer. The frigid Festa
played Carolina, and the tenor Monelli, who is good in a small auditorium,
lacked colour in this enormous gulf. After the main ballet, the second act
of Rossini's *Cenerentola*. Like *Psami*, this is a lesser work by a great artist.

    Le tre Melarancie are three princesses who are carried off by genii
whilst they are asleep in their bed, which the genii carry into a forest
where a Witches' Sabbath is being held; here they cast the bed on the
ground, all in the manner of the *Thousand and One Nights*. At once an
enchanted fairy turns them into three lovely oranges and carries them off
in a sack. In comes the genius *el Mourab*, mounted on a gigantic ram. In
a twinkling of an eye he sends for a knight, who happens to be only
two thousand leagues away, and makes him a present of a sack which
contains: firstly, a handsome Army loaf; secondly, a three-sou broom; and,
lastly, a ball of twine. At the sight of these handsome gifts, the knight
(the young and haughty Molinari) jumps upon the ram, which sets out at
a gentle trot and brings him before a courtyard with an iron gate. He
pushes the gate open; an enormous dog leaps upon him; he welcomes it
amiably and gives it the Army loaf, which the dog quickly goes off to
eat in a corner. A prodigious giant, who is seen drawing water in a pail
which he has fastened to a huge plait of his own hair, bears down upon
the knight, who offers him a respectful greeting culminating in the gift
of the ball of twine. The giant, delighted, sits down on the lip of the well
and goes to sleep.

    There remains a devilish old hag who is stoking a huge furnace with
a shovel. She is pacified with the little broom. Then the knight rushes into
the château and steals the bag containing the three oranges. On his way he
rescues a band of knights; they carry the three oranges to their father.

---

[1] Adolphe de Mareste was born at the château de Montfleury (Savoie) on September 1st,
1784. The family of his mother, née Vaulserre des Adrets, had dealings with the Gagnon
family. In 1817 he had recently been appointed Chief of the Passports Office at the Police
Prefecture in Paris.

The oranges are set on a table, where they grow enormous, and one sees the three princesses hatch out of them; wedding-ceremonies, *balabile*, etc. Final act in the interior of the château, where the three princesses, restored to their natural shapes—for some, no doubt excellent, reason they have been turned into maidservants—appear in a hall where the fairy, on leaving, has struck the captive knights motionless. This act I find very funny. The beginning of the ballet is magnificent, the middle part is still good, the end falls flat. The whole is only third-rate Vigano.

Since the 21st of November my heart and vision have been filled with contemplation of these wonders . . . I have sought and found an apartment for my sister[1], and have given her introductions; she already has three close women friends . . . I have heard a deal of politics in the boxes that I visit: you know the effect that vague rumours have on an expert who has benefited by conversation with Maisonette[2] and Besançon[3]. I hastened to shut my ears.

I still find this country much superior to yours: I leave you to judge. General Prince von Starhemberg is perhaps the only man in the Austrian Army who possesses French courage: he is a very Lannes, a Lassalle. Moreover, he is a great prince; moreover, he is the Emperor's natural brother. For these reasons he is one of the greatest personages imaginable. In this quality, he two years ago thought fit to rob a dog of an Israelite of a hundred thousand francs' worth of musty hay. The Aulic Council brought an action, which the young prince and his friends found highly amusing. Three months ago all the officers, himself included—they are in Milan—received orders to appear in full-dress uniform at the Ministry of War. When they arrived, the Secretary to the Council of War read out a twenty-page judgment, by which, it is said, the young prince was sentenced to " pull at the boats " for six months on I know not which river of the Austrian States; he was to be deprived of his rank, declared unfit to serve, and, into the bargain, sentenced to make restitution, with costs—the total amounting to a trifle of twelve hundred thousand francs. The prince began to weep. The clerk produced a new document: the Emperor commuted the six months in the galleys to six months in

[1] On January 13th, 1817, Beyle wrote to Crozet: " Poor P. has gone to a better world at a bad moment. . . . What will become of *the good sister*?" (In English in the original.) " I shall scrupulously leave her to do as she chooses, but I think that at thirty-one she ought to live with Dominique. Their two little lamps could together give out an honest brightness." Périer-Lagrange had died on December 14th, 1816. In 1817 Beyle went to Grenoble to look after his sister's affairs, which were in great confusion. After a stay in Paris and his first voyage to England, he returned in November to Milan, accompanied by his sister.

[2] Joseph Lingay, at this time collaborator of the duc Decazes, whom Beyle used to call " Maison ".

[3] Mareste himself, who had been Secretary-General to the Prefecture of the Doubs.

prison, and confirmed the rest of the sentence. The prince drew his sword, handed it to the clerk, and, without returning home, set off, in the same town carriage as had taken him to the Ministry, to serve his sentence in a fortress in Bohemia. His wife, an ugly woman who adores him, learnt this an hour later, took the stage-coach and chased after him. She is rich and will pay his debt; but he is left, at thirty-three, disgraced and penniless. All this must seem ridiculous to some of those brilliant people who do not know how to exact obedience from a Prefect. The story is a counterpart to that of the lieutenant, a son of the Marshal, who was shot at Vienna: but you know of that.

I was afraid I would not find enough to fill four pages. You will perhaps find them very empty, but I can furnish nothing better.

I read daily until two o'clock, walk until four, and dine at five. At seven I pay one or two visits. At eight I visit my sister's box; one or two friends come there to fetch me, and I begin one of my little tours of the Scala, until at midnight *le tre Melarancie* begin to swell up on the table of their royal father and become pregnant with the princesses. Since the rest of the performance is worthless, I then return home, where I read in bed until one o'clock. I am reading the letters of d'Alembert, Montesquieu and other authors to Mme du Deffant, 2 vols., published by Léopold Collin. D'Alembert's letters have made a great impression on me, especially in view of the fact that for us, my dear fellow, they are arguments *ad hominem*. In 1764 he was content with an income of seventeen hundred francs—so well content that he refused a great position at Berlin. And you have the effrontery—you who are capable of a c-ckst-nd, what's more—to complain of ten *thousands*[1]!

My *six thousands*[1] are not so clear. I have a certain 4,250 francs a year, and 6,000 that I can lay my hands on. Furthermore, if two people, one of them aged fifty-nine (le Salvaing[2]) and the other seventy-one[3], quit the stage, I gain eighty or a hundred thousand francs.

Down there, I was suffocated with contempt: my digestion was spoilt by the sight of all that I had seen so fair, on Berlin's Unter den Linden or at Schoenbrünn, being dragged in the cow-dung. It is very certain that I shall nowhere else find the conversation of men of wit like Besançon, Maisonette, etc. For this reason your letters are a prime necessity to me.

I had already suspected that van Bross had guessed who Bombet is. But I have at least served my purpose, which has been *not to speak as*

---

[1] In English in the original.
[2] M. de Salvaing had the use for life of a floor of the house that Chérubin Beyle had had built in the rue de Bonne, and of which Beyle was the proprietor. He sold the Salvaing apartment on April 16th, 1819, to Joseph Robert. (Note by M. Martineau.)
[3] His father.

the author. After my fall from the heights, I found myself crammed with pride—a tenacious pride which neither prayers nor fasting could drive out. This pride is convinced that I am made to be a Prefect or Deputy. The trade of author seems to it degrading—or, more accurately, degraded. In the mornings I write to dispel boredom: I write what I—*I*—think, and not what *people* think—all this whilst waiting to learn from the *Moniteur* that I have been appointed to the prefecture of Nantes—a post that I would refuse with horror, inasmuch as I would see myself as a colleague of M. Montlivaut, etc., etc., etc. All this is what I have learnt from the examination of my " interior ", as the late Tartufe used to say. You are as familiar as I am with all my affectations of mystery, and you will please me greatly by continually thickening the veil.

. . . .

———— 91 ————

TO THE EDITOR OF THE *EDINBURGH REVIEW*

Sienna[1], *the* 10*th of April* 1818

Sir,

I did not suppose that such a trifle as *Rome et Naples en 1817* deserved to attract the attention of such serious people[2].

It seems to me that your critic was to some extent duped by this seriousness. He " sees courage only beneath a moustache "—an Army saying which, translated into terms of the present case, means that he thinks nobody is educated unless he is a pedant.

My object was to compress as many things as possible into the fewest words. Probably, if I had employed phrases as heavy as those of M. Millin, the critic would not have thought me so flippant[3].

How many pages would a serious Englishman have needed to present his portrait to the reader? Stendhal's portrait is presented in the first ten lines; and the reader who dislikes this character can shut the book. A great advantage in the midst of the modern deluge of print, which will soon stifle all knowledge.

For the rest, old Colonel Forsyte is none other than the *Edinburgh*

---

[1] Beyle had first written " Naples ". He was actually at Grenoble at this date.
[2] *Rome, Naples et Florence*, the first book published under the name of Stendhal, had appeared in 1817, and the *Edinburgh Review* had reviewed it in its issue no. XXIX, in November.
[3] The *Edinburgh Review's* critic had accused Stendhal of flippancy.

Review. It is also the real name of the Conte Neri who speaks of Alfieri. It is the *Edinburgh Review*, too, that has supplied me with the epigraph.

The piece concerning the poor, moribund Italian language is by me. It is a new and original subject, which I invite you to investigate.

Fear of the police has caused my book to be truncated by a quarter. You conclude from " Herculanum " that I do not know Latin. Must I conclude from " Cardinal Gonsalez " that you cannot read the Almanack?

Surely the essential thing in 1817, on the eve of great events, was to study what effect the apparition of Napoleon had left upon Italian hearts; for a people never has more liberty than it achieves by force.

Well, then, the state of minds and hearts in Italy—the " strength of resilience " and the direction in which it is guided—are not these things better indicated in Stendhal than in Millin?

I have never read this scholar, and I shall never read him, for he is generally regarded as too much of a bore. Just as, on the Continent, people are duped by Mr. Calquhanus, so, in England, they are duped by the insipid writings of M. Millin. Since they are incapable of beholding nature, their " second-hand " knowledge is acquired only from the dead letter of books.

Of Eustace I have read only the first volume; I consider that he in no way depicts the *contemporary* inhabitants of the country through which he travels. Time and again his priest-riddenness makes him a dupe of the crudest follies. For example, he believes the story of an archbishop who boasted of his native country: has he never heard of " Antechamber Patriotism ", that great characteristic of modern Italy? He has no knowledge of the Arts, not even of current popular taste: he goes into ecstasies over the statues of Plaisance! But he is serious, and for you that is enough. I undertake to point out ten gross errors in Eustace's first volume, each of them the result of his total ignorance of the men and customs that for five centuries have been changing the surface of the country of which he writes. The explanation is simple: travelling Englishmen never see any-one but a few noble families; they never enter amongst the *ceto di mezzo*[1]. Or, when I have seen them do so, they displayed an insolent coldness and haughtiness. To write of their travels, such people can do nothing but copy from books. In 1817 the English at Rome saw nobody but each other. If they visited the banker Torlonia, it was to quarrel with him about his Jewishness. I never saw any of them at the house of Signor Nota, the lawyer, or in other circles where one can study humanity.

I admit that, in view of the general execration in which the English are held, an English traveller who wanted to see something other than

[1] Middle class.

servants and bankers would require a certain sort of *responsiveness*, and this would be the antipode of the national character. Of the three great men of Italy—Canova, Rossini and Vigano—two are invisible as far as the English are concerned. But they will quote you lines written on Roscius and Pilades.

If I ever became a writer, I would hatch out twenty pages of learned and heavy phrases; and then, perhaps, the critics would deprive me of the handsome title of being " flippant ", and perhaps their " seriousness " would come to realise that it is more difficult to make a single observation on contemporary customs than to quote Silius Italicus and Statius twenty times over!

Sir, I must make the painful admission: the English are abhorred in Italy; a *sigh of hatred* breathes out upon them from all Continental hearts. No distinction is drawn between you and your government, which paid the people who struck down Napoleon. With Napoleon, life itself departed from Italy. (In addition, people consider your policy extremely darkling and perfidious: they are afraid of the dark.)

You should know that Napoleon is mourned as much at Milan as at Florence. His most appalling act of tyranny was less harmful to the people than the present inertia. You would shudder if I told you of Piedmont. The government of the Bey of Algiers is better, perhaps, than that of the *Diletti Reggi*[1]. A *Diletto reggio* interferes in the private affairs of a family in order to settle a dispute between a father-in-law and son-in-law, or between a mother and son! (Compare the case of M. de Prié, younger son and favourite, 1818.) How could anyone print that? You, sir, who say whatever you like, you cannot understand hints, you cannot read between the lines of what is printed on the Continent. For example, an English author in my place would not have failed to boast heavily of having lived in Italy for sixty months. To avoid pedantry, to avoid shocking the French *reader*, one avoids such manners—and the serious English think you frivolous!

Read the legal opinions of Signor Dalpozzo, the lawyer, which nearly put him in Fenestrella (they are printed in Milan).

I have often broken a lance for the English. Yet I continue to find in all the English I have met a secret *principle of unhappiness*. I believe that in a given situation an Englishman is more unhappy than an Italian or a German. And, above all, the English are made unhappy by small misfortunes such as people more luckily born forget within a quarter of an hour. What is the reason for this? A great problem. Religion, perhaps.

I would add, sir, that the best publication I know, the one which for

[1] Beloved kings.

[181]

six years has given me the greatest pleasure, is the *Edinburgh Review*. But, ye gods! do not require a moustache to believe in courage! I was forgetting the lovely story of Ayturyd.

For . . .[1] ridicule cannot be encouraged by men of wit whose first interest is to display all the details of their own. The debates in our Chamber of Commons are superior to yours because the Deputies dare to laugh.

For the rest—

I have the honour . . .

―――――― 92 ――――――

TO THE BARON DE MARESTE

Milan, Saturday the 25th of May 1818

JUMP for joy, I am sending you the most amiable, gayest and most natural woman Venice has ever produced. She has never cost her lovers a sou, and I do not doubt that with your Italian you will succeed in being . . .[2] In short, I am sending you two months of bliss and folly, a happy episode in your life.

Yesterday morning she formed the project of departing tomorrow: her father has given his permission. The pretext is that of giving three or four piano concerts: she is Italy's leading amateur, a pupil and friend of Rossini and Michele Caraffa. Her real object is to see Paris; her dream would be to be engaged for the new company that is being formed at Louvois. Heaven forfend! Italy would be deprived of one of its flowers; but you Parisians are so obtuse that I do not wish to say anything to you concerning this divine talent. Moreover, I am falling asleep: I was with her until three o'clock, and at nine o'clock I woke up to write. Do not suppose that, if I am her lover, the place is taken; in any case, I like her better as a friend.

I shall give her letters for you, for the accommodating Smidt, who can take her around in default of you, and even for the father of seven children[3], although I count little upon him. But kind Annette[4] would do her a great service by helping her with the first purchases, which are

---

[1] A page is missing.
[2] Illegible.
[3] The comte de Barral.
[4] Annette Questienne, of the Opera Buffa, a colleague of Angelina Bereyer and Barral's mistress.

so essential, of a hat and gown. If the seven children keep the house too busy, the amiable van Brossy will fill the gap. Notify these two personages.

At heart she is a little frightened of casting herself upon Paris in the company of a valet de chambre, who has gone to Lyons, and an old banker who arrived yesterday from Leghorn and is going to spend fifty days at Paris in the matter of a bankruptcy. So, on the first day, supply a double measure of reassuring pleasantries. Paer is the friend of the family.

Of whose family? What, do you not realise? Of the lovable, crazy, divine Elena Vigano[1]. If you sent me such a gift, I would embrace you for a fortnight on end at our first encounter. I have puffed up Your Excellency to her in suitable terms.

. . . .

------ 93 ------

TO MADAME DEMBOWSKI[2]

Varese, the 16th of November 1818

Madame,

I would like to write you a tolerably entertaining letter; but I spend my life amongst worthy citizens whose whole day is taken up with the price of wheat, the condition of their horses, their mistresses and their brothels. Their fat enjoyment and easy happiness inspire me with envy. How can a heart that is content with such coarse pleasures fail to achieve happiness? Yet they run at random amongst the reefs that seem so easy to avoid, and they, too, are almost always unhappy. They scarcely heed the world that interests us: for them it is like a foreign country. One thing has made a great impression on them: they claim to know for certain that Signora Annoni has taken a lover. So it is again a Russian who has possession of this pretty woman; for it seems to be agreed that M. de Pahlen has little L——, the Genoese. So it must be a certain M. de Berg, whom I know—a very handsome youth, but perhaps the most desiccated individual one could hope to meet, the most garrulous and egoistical,

---

[1] Daughter of the famous choreographer, Salvatore Vignano.

[2] Mathilde Viscontini had married Jean Dembowski, of Polish extraction, who became an Italian citizen and a general in the service of France. At the beginning of 1818, when Beyle was introduced to her, probably by their common friend Vismara, she had already for some time been separated from her husband. Beyle dates his love from March 4th, 1818. " Métilde absolutely occupied my life from 1818 to 1824. And I am not yet cured," he wrote in 1835 in the *Vie de Henri Brulard*.

the most removed by a hundred leagues from sentiment—who succeeded in persuading Signora Annoni that he adored her, and, what is more, that she adored him. They spent their days in reading "sentimental" novels together. When she was here, she never listened to a word in the theatre, because she was always talking to him. So much is certain, but I doubt the rest.

The keenest pleasure I have had today was that of putting the date on this letter: I hope in a month to have the happiness of seeing you. But what to do during these thirty days? I hope they will pass like the nine long days that have just elapsed. Every time an amusement or a walk in company comes to an end, I fall back upon myself, and find a terrifying void. A thousand times I have pondered upon, and a thousand times I have given myself the pleasure of still seeming to hear, the least remarks you let fall during the last days in which I had the happiness of seeing you. My exhausted imagination begins to boggle at mental images that henceforth are too closely united with the frightful idea of your absence, and I feel that every day my heart becomes more sombre.

I found a little consolation at the church of the Madonna del Monte. I recalled the divine music that I once heard there. One of these days I shall go to Milan to meet one of your letters—for I rely enough upon your humanity to believe that you will not have refused me a few lines which for you are so easy to pen and are so precious and consoling for a heart in despair. You must be too well assured of your absolute power over me to be impeded even for a moment by the empty fear of appearing to encourage my passion by answering me. I know myself: I shall love you for the rest of my life, and nothing you may do will ever change the notion that has imprinted itself upon my soul—the notion I have conceived of the bliss of being loved by you—or the contempt it has given me for all other forms of happiness! Indeed, aye! I need, I thirst to see you. I believe I would give all the rest of my life to converse with you for a quarter of an hour on the most indifferent matters.

Farewell, I leave you in order to be the more with you, to dare to speak to you with all the abandon, all the energy of the passion that devours me.

HENRI.

94

TO THE BARON DE MARESTE

Milan, the 20th of November 1818

Books[1].

It is easier for Henri to nave *Books*[1] translated into English than to have them reviewed in Paris. Here we have the " voyage "[2] translated, with ten pages of the greatest praises. (*Esthetic Review* for May, 1818.)

Egron promised payment for 158 copies, at three francs, in October. 158 x 3 = 474. Here is his receipt. In a moment of leisure and friendship, see if he will consent to disburse the whole or a part, and then pray send the money to M. Flory against a letter of exchange on the house of M. Robert. If he or Chanson wishes to *print again*[1], gratis or nearly so, *I can send matter for four hundred or five hundred pages.*[1]

The additions are in a more serious style, solider and less deserving the accusation of "*flippancy* "[1].

It was you who told me the anecdote about Grécourt. I was suffering from nerves that day, and I added it, as best I could, *to a sheet*[1] that I was correcting. Revise this story for me, also that of *la Bisteka; gran francesi grandi in tutto*[3], and add it to the manuscript when it is laid before you. I have suppressed the last thirty pages. I have so much material that I can suppress extensively: just show me the blemishes. You well know that I am not an author in the style of *Villehand*[4]. I pay these follies the attention they deserve: it amuses me to do so, and I especially love to follow their fate in society, just as children set paper boats on a stream. Did I tell you that Stendhal was a wild success here four months ago. For example, the copy for the Vice-King[5] was read in the café by four people who intended only to glance through it, and found themselves at one o'clock in the morning thinking it was still only ten o'clock in the evening, and having forgotten to go and bring back their ladies from the theatre, etc. They discovered three errors.

But all this is futile. The essential thing is to pay that devil Didot. At Cularo, for one thousand four hundred francs I am asked for a note for one thousand eight hundred, with interest at five per cent.

[1] In English in the original.
[2] *Rome, Naples et Florence en 1817.*
[3] La Bistecca (beefsteak): great Frenchmen, great in everything,
[4] Villemain.
[5] [*Sic*].

Could not this article be placed with the *Journal des Savants*? Daunou seems to me an excellent judge of the historical part. M. Cousin, who visits Maisonette, places boring articles with this journal, favouring Scotch philosophy or against Helvétius's " personal interest ". But even a stupid man can be useful. Did *Le Commerce* notice *Painting*[1], as they promised *to my friend Rey*[1]?

When you have the time, ask Didot how many of the *Haydn* he has sold. I would take steps to send Didot enough to cover the one thousand four hundred francs, and I shall punish my ungrateful country by not producing the last three volumes for another twenty years.

To finish with all that, have you the courage to write an article on the subject of *Haydn*?

I see there is going to be a *Revue encyclopédique*. Indeed, since there are no more literary journals, there must be a demand for such a thing. I sincerely think that all we need wish for in politics is that matters should proceed at the present pace for ten consecutive years. There are no new alarms that we can undergo. This means that interest in politics must give ground a little to interest in literature. In any case, political discussions are beginning to be so good—that is to say, so profound—that they are boring. Who, for example, can follow the Budget? So see if you can gain access to the *Revue encyclopédique*: it has a section entitled *Painting*. Is there an Exhibition this year? In that case, a new advertisement is needed. So much is *essential*. A luxury—to please my vanity—would be a genuine appreciation, conscientiously written, by Dussault, Feletz or Daunou. Lastly, have the book announced by its title every six months. I shall write to Didot that when next he reprints he must suppress some twenty drawings that were demanded in 1817 by timidity and memories of Ri. Ch[2]. Furthermore, I shall ask him for eight sub-titles of the Haydn for eight copies which I have here and shall send as gifts. I shall ask him for fifty copies of the *Peinture* for gifts here.

Here in Milan there are eight or ten excellent judges of " sensations of beauty " who have an extreme contempt for *M. Quartremère de Quincy* and for French connoisseurs. M. Quatremère's *Jupiter Olympien* for example, is ridiculously exaggerated. . . . Which people are regarded in Paris as (1) connoisseurs, (2) great painters, (3) good sculptors? Don't allow me to become a stranger in Paris. I have had nothing *from you*[1] for six weeks.

Ch. Durif.

7th of December 1818

---

[1] In English in the original.   [2] Rioust and Chevalier.

95

TO MADAME DEMBOWSKI

May 1819

Madame,

Ah! how heavily time seems to pass since you went away![1] And it has been only five and a half hours! What shall I do during these forty mortal days? Must I abandon all hope, go off and fling myself into public affairs? I fear I have not the courage to traverse the Mont-Cenis. No, and I shall never consent to let mountains separate you and me. Can I hope, by dint of love, to reanimate a heart that cannot be dead to this passion? But perhaps I am ridiculous in your eyes, my shyness and silence have bored you, and you regarded my arrival at your dwelling as a calamity. I detest myself: if I were not the most abject of men, should I not have had a decisive explanation yesterday, before your departure, and now clearly know what I have to hope for?

When you said, in that tone of a truth so profoundly felt: " Ah, 'tis well that it be midnight!" should I not have understood that you were pleased at being delivered from my importunities, and have sworn to myself on my honour that I would never see you again? But I am courageous only when I am far away from you. In your presence I am as bashful as a child, speech dies upon my lips and I can do nothing but gaze at you and admire you. Must I be so much inferior to myself, and so dull?

96

TO MADAME DEMBOWSKI

Varese[2], *the 7th of June* 1819

Madame,

You throw me into despair. You repeatedly accuse me of failing in delicacy—as if, on your lips, this accusation were nothing. Who would

---

[1] The undated rough draft of this letter is in Grenoble Library, headed by the following note in Beyle's writing: " Observe the naturalness *of this man* " (these words in English in the original). (Note by M. Martineau.)

[2] This letter dated from Varese was in fact written at Volterra, where Beyle had followed Métilde, who had gone to see her son at the college in this town. (Note by M. Martineau.)

have thought, when I parted from you at Milan, that the first letter you wrote to me would begin with " monsieur ", or that you would accuse me of failing in delicacy ?

Ah, madame, it is easy for a man who has no passion to conduct himself always with moderation and prudence. I, too, when I can hearken to my own counsel, I believe that I am not lacking in discretion. But I am dominated by a fatal passion that leaves me no longer master of my actions. I had sworn to myself to take coach, or at least not to see you, and not to write to you until you returned: a force more powerful than all my resolutions dragged me to the places where you were. I perceive all too well that henceforth this passion is to be the great concern of my life. All interests, all considerations have paled before it. This fatal need I have of seeing you carries me away, dominates me, transports me. There are moments, in the long, solitary evenings, when, if it were necessary to commit a murder that I might see you, I would become a murderer. In all my life I have had only three passions: ambition, from 1800 to 1811; love of a woman who deceived me[1], from 1811 to 1818; and, during the past year, this passion that dominates me and ceaselessly grows. At all seasons and amidst all distractions, anything unrelated to my passion has meant nothing to me: whether happy or unhappy, it has occupied every moment. And do you suppose that the sacrifice I have made to your conventions, of not seeing you this evening, is a little thing? Assuredly, I do not wish to make a merit of it: I present it to you only as an expiation of the wrongs of which I may have been guilty two days go. This expiation means nothing to you, madame: but for me, who have spent so many frightful evenings deprived of you and without seeing you, it is a sacrifice more difficult to endure than the most horrible tortures; it is a sacrifice which, in the extreme pain of the victim, is worthy of the sublime woman to whom it is offered.

In the midst of the confusion of my whole being, into which I am thrown by the imperious necessity of seeing you, there is nevertheless one quality which I have preserved, and which I pray that destiny will continue to preserve for me, unless it seeks to plunge me, in my own esteem, into the underworld of abjection—the quality of perfect truthfulness. You tell me, madame, that I so greatly " compromised " matters on Saturday morning, that in the evening it was necessary for you to act as you did. It is the word " compromised " that wounds me to the bottom of my soul; and, if I had the good fortune to be able to pluck out the fatal affection that pierces my heart, it would be this word " compromised " that gave me the strength do do so.

[1] Signora Pietragrua. Cf. letter no. 82.

[188]

But no, madame, your soul has too much nobility not to have understood mine. You were offended, and you used the first word that came to the end of your pen. I shall accept as judge, between your accusation and myself, a person whose evidence you will not reject. If Madame Dembowski, if the noble and sublime Métilde, *believes* that my conduct of Saturday morning was the least in the world *calculated* to force her, out of a just care for her reputation in this country, to take some further step, then I confess that this infamous conduct was mine, that there is a being in the world who can say that I fail in delicacy. I shall go further: I have never had any talent for seduction except in respect of women whom I did not love at all. As soon as I am in love I become timid— as you can judge from the manner in which I am always out of countenance in your presence. If I had not started prattling on Saturday evening, everybody, even including the good padre Rettore[1], would have perceived that I was in love. But even if I had had a talent for seduction, I would not have employed it upon you. If success depended only upon the making of vows, I would still wish to win you for myself, and not for another being whom I had set up in my place. I would blush, I would have no more happiness, I think, even though you loved me, if I could suspect that you loved a being who was not myself. If you had faults, I could not say that I did not see them: I would say, and say in truth, that I adored them: and, indeed, I can say I adore that extreme susceptibility which causes me to spend such horrible nights. It is thus that I would wish to be loved, it is thus that true love is created: it rejects in horror the idea of seduction, as a means unworthy of it, and, together with seduction, it rejects every calculation, every stratagem—including the least thought of " compromising " the beloved object in order to force her to certain further steps to its own advantage.

Had I the talent to seduce you—and I do not believe that such a talent exists—I would not use it. Sooner or later you would perceive that you had been deceived; and to lose you after having possessed you would be still more frightful, I think, than if heaven had condemned me to die without ever having been loved by you.

When a being is dominated by an extreme passion, all that he says or does in a particular situation proves nothing concerning him: what bears witness for him is the entirety of his life. Thus, madame, were I to vow all day long at your feet that I loved you, or that I hated you, this should have no influence upon the degree of credence that you decided to grant me. It is the entirety of my life that should speak. Now, although I am very little known, and still less interesting to the people who know me,

[1] The Rector of the College.

[189]

yet you might enquire—for lack of another topic of conversation—whether I am known to lack either pride or constancy.

I have now been in Milan for five years. Let us assume that all that is said about my previous life is false. Five years—from the age of thirty-one to the age of thirty-six—are a fairly important interval in a man's life, especially when during these five years he has been tested by difficult circumstances. If ever you deign, madame—for lack of a better occupation—to think about my character, then deign to compare these five years of my life with five years taken from the life of any other individual. You will find lives much more brilliantly talented, lives much more fortunate: but that you will find a life more full of honour and constancy than mine, this I do not believe. How many mistresses had I in Milan, in five years? How many times have I weakened on a point of honour? Well, I would have disgracefully failed in honour if, in my relations with a being who cannot make me draw my sword, I had in the least sought to " compromise " her.

Love me if you will, divine Métilde, but in God's name do not despise me. Such torment is beyond my strength to endure. In your manner of thinking, which is very just, if you despised me it would be impossible for you ever to love me.

With a soul as lofty as yours, what surer way could there be of earning your displeasure than that which you accuse me of having taken? I so much fear to displease you that the moment when I first saw you, on the evening of the 3rd—the moment which should have been the sweetest of my life—was, on the contrary, one of my most wretched, by reason of the fear I had of displeasing you[1].

—— 97 ——

TO MADAME DEMBOWSKI

Florence, the 11*th of June* 1819

Madame,

Since leaving you this evening, I have felt a need to implore your forgiveness for the failures in delicacy and respect to which I have been

[1] " *Reflections—Thursday evening,*
8th of June 1819.
"Notions of throwing the whole thing over.
"This evening, chilliness to the point of resolving not to set foot in the College again; jealousy of the Cavaliere Giorgi, who came to make conversation from the other end of the

driven during the past week by a fatal passion. My repentance is sincere: I wish, since my arrival displeased you, that I had never gone to Volterra. I would have expressed this feeling of deep regret already yesterday, when you deigned to admit me to your presence; but permit me to say that you have not accustomed me to indulgence, quite on the contrary. Consequently I was afraid that by asking forgiveness for my follies I might seem to you to be speaking of my love and breaking the oath I made to you.

But I should be lacking in that perfect truthfulness which, in the abyss in which I am plunged, is my only rule of conduct, if I told you that I was capable of condoning a failure in delicacy. I fear that you will see in this confession an indication of a soul that is coarse and little likely to understand you. You have felt these failures in delicacy: therefore, for you, they existed.

Do not suppose, madame, that I formed all in a moment the project of coming to Volterra. Truly, I have not such audacity in my dealings with you. Every time I am overcome by tenderness and fly to your side, I am sure to be brought down to earth by a most mortifying harshness. Seeing from the map that Leghorn was quite close to Volterra, I enquired and was told that from Pisa one could see the walls of this fortunate city where you were. During the crossing it occurred to me that by wearing green spectacles and changing my coat I could quite well spend two or three days at Volterra, going out only at night and without being recognised by you. I arrived on the 3rd, and the first person I saw in Volterra, madame, was yourself. It was one o'clock, and I think you had left the college and were going home to dine: you did not recognise me at all. In the evening, at a quarter past eight, when it was entirely dark, I removed my spectacles in order that Schneider should not think me odd. Just as I was removing them, you came by, and my plan, which hitherto had been so successful, was overturned.

At once I had an idea: "If I accost Madame Dembowski, she will say something harsh to me." (At that moment I loved you so much that a harsh word would have killed me.) "If I accost her as her friend from Milan, everybody in this little town will say that I am her lover. Therefore I shall show her far more respect by remaining incognito." All this reasoning occurred in the wink of an eye, and it governed my conduct for the entire day of Friday the 4th. I can swear to you that I did not know the Giorgi garden belonged to your house. I thought I had seen

sofa, and when she went out she leaned heavily on his arm, with an air of intimacy. Respectable women are as hussy-like as hussies." (Note by the author on the margin of the rough draft of this letter.)

you turn off to the right of the street, as you walked along it, and not to the left.

On the night of the 4th to the 5th, it occurred to me that I was the oldest of madame Dembowski's friends. I was quite proud of this idea. " She may have something to tell me," I said to myself, "of her children, her journey, a thousand matters extraneous to my love. I shall write two letters to her, of such a nature that she will be able to explain my arrival to her friends here, and to receive me. If she does not wish to do so, she will answer ' no ', and all will be over." As I was sealing my letter, I kept on thinking that its contents might be discovered: therefore, since I understand the nature of vulgar souls and the envy that possesses them, I rejected the notion of adding a private note to the two official letters—so that if your host inadvertently opened them, nothing incorrect would be discovered.

I confess to you, madame—and in confessing it I risk your displeasure —that up to this point I see no failure in delicacy.

You wrote to me most severely; you believed especially that I was seeking to force an entrance, which hardly seems to be in my character. I went to ponder on these matters outside the "a Selci "[1] gate. On leaving the gate it was a pure chance that I did not turn to the right: I saw that I would have to descend and climb up again, and I wished to be in peace and entirely given up to my reflections. Thus it was that I came to the Meadow, to which you yourself came later. I leaned on the parapet and remained there for two hours, gazing at the sea which had carried me near to you, and in which I would have done better to end my destiny.

Observe, madame, that I was entirely unaware that this Meadow was the scene of your usual walk. Who could have told me so? You appreciate that with Schneider I was discretion itself. I saw you approach, and at once I struck up a conversation with a young man who happened to be there, and I went off with him to look at the sea from the other side of the town: at this point I was accosted by Signor Giorgi.

I confess I thought you no longer believed that I was seeking to force an entrance: I was very happy, but at the same time very shy. Had I not had the resource of speaking to the children, it is certainly true that I would have compromised myself. It was much worse when we entered the college: I was about to find myself face to face with you and to have a clear sight of you—to enjoy, in a word, that happiness which had kept me alive for the past fortnight and which I dared not even hope for. At the gate of the college I was on the point of refusing this happiness. I did not feel I had the strength to support it. As I mounted the stairs I

[1] A gate of Volterra.

could hardly hold myself erect: if I had had clever people to deal with, I would certainly have given myself away. At last I saw you: of events from that moment to the moment when I left you, I have retained only confused impressions: I know that I talked a lot, that I gazed at you, that I played the antiquarian. If it was at this time that I committed failures in delicacy, this is very possible. I have no idea. All I can remember is that I would have given anything in the world to be able to stare at the green tablecloth. I suppose that this was one of the happiest moments in my life, but it has entirely escaped me. Such is the sad destiny of tender souls: they remember their woes in the smallest detail, whereas moments of happiness throw them into such an ecstasy that they cannot remember them.

When I spoke to you on the evening of the following day, I saw clearly that I had displeased you. " Could it be possible," I asked myself, " that she is in love with Signor Giorgi? " You handed me the letter that began with the word " monsieur ". While I was in the college I had time to read almost nothing but this fatal word, and I was in the depths of misery on the same spot where the day before I had been mad with joy. You wrote to me that I had sought to deceive you by pretending to be sick, and that a man who could go for a walk could not have a fever. Yet on Friday, before I wrote to you, I had had the honour of meeting you twice while walking, and in my letter I did not pretend that my fever had come over me all of a sudden, on the night of Friday to Saturday. My thoughts were so sad that to be shut up in a room increased my discomfort.

On the morrow of that fatal day I punished myself by not coming to see you. In the evening I saw that Signor Giorgi was jealous: I saw you leaning on his arm as you left the college. Full of astonishment, consternation and misery, I thought that there was nothing for it but to take my departure. I proposed to pay you only a courtesy visit on the eve of my departure—a visit that you would not have received. At that moment the chambermaid ran after me in the garden, where I already was, with Signor Giorgi, and called out: " The Signora says that she will see you this evening in the college." It was solely for this reason that I went there. I thought that, after all, you were free to love whom you chose: I had asked for an interview with you in order to express my regrets at having importuned you, and perhaps also to see you without interruption, and to hear the sound of that delightful voice which always finds an echo in my heart whatever may be the meaning of the words it utters. You demanded of me a promise that I would say nothing to you concerning my love: I kept this promise, no matter how great the violence I had to do to myself. Finally I left, longing to hate you and finding no hatred in my heart.

Do you believe, madame, that I seek to displease you, or to play the hypocrite with you? No, impossible. You will say: " What a coarse soul, and how unworthy of me! " Well, in this faithful account of my conduct and feelings, point out to me the moment at which I failed in delicacy, and by what conduct mine should have been replaced. A chilly soul would at once exclaim: " Never return to Volterra! "

But I do not fear this interdict from you.

It is all too plain that a prosaic being would not have appeared at Volterra: firstly, because there was no money to be earned there; secondly, because the inns there are bad. But, since I have the misfortune to be truly in love and to have been recognised by you on the evening of Thursday the 3rd of June, what should I have done? It is superfluous to point out to you, madame, that I am not so impertinent as to seek to wage a war of words with you. I do not claim that you should answer my disquisition at length: but perhaps your pure and noble soul will do me a little more justice, and, whatever may be the nature of the relations that destiny will allow to exist between us, you will not disagree, madame, that the esteem of one tenderly beloved is the first of possessions[1].

---

[1] " I consider the reply in fourteen pages to be the key of keys: a procacio brought it to me yesterday evening, demanding a gratuity.

" This reply, dated the 26th at the end of the letter, either (1) did not come to Florence by post-chaise; or (2) she despatched it with a request that it should be brought back to Volterra, if I could not be found in Florence; or (3), which is unlikely, she consulted Lenina (Signora Bignani, a friend of Madame Dembowski) concerning the reply—which would thus arrive from Bologna: there is no mark on the envelope. M(étilde) did not receive my letter of the 11th until the 15th or 16th; her reply was not sent off until ten days later; she did not begin to answer until the 22nd—that is to say, six days after having received the letter.

" I was wise not to write a second.

" It is singular that M(étilde) did not reply by post. Why choose another route? There must be a motive.

TACTIQUE
29th of June 1819

" What made me tremble at not receiving, within due time, an answer to my letter of the 11th, was that I thought the contessina was at last truly on the defensive. She might have sent back my letter of the 11th, unopened, with the words:

" 'Monsieur,

" 'I do not wish to receive any further letter from you, or to write to you. I am your obedient servant ', etc.

" Or she might have written the same three lines to me at Florence, and have adhered to this attitude. Instead of which, the same attitude as on the 10th and a reply of fourteen pages. Even if she had written as above, love finds its reasons: I would have persisted. Perhaps even if I saw her in bed with Greek *IX* (?), I would find an excuse for her.

" Usefulness of what Cain said to me, although at present unpalatable. I do not persist, like Blücher, from reasoning and obstinacy, but the heart wills it so." (Note by the author at the end of the rough draft of this letter.)

TO MADAME DEMBOWSKI

Florence, the 30th of June 1819

Madame[1],

It is my misfortune, the greatest possible for one in my position, that my most respectful—I might say, most timid—actions seem to you the height of audacity. For example: to have refrained from pouring out my heart at your feet on my two first days at Volterra, and to have confined myself to acts of respect which perhaps cost me more than anything else in my life. Continually I was tempted to break the rule that duty imposed upon me. Ten times, full of things to say to you, I took up my pen. But I said to myself: " If I begin, I shall succumb." I felt that the happiness of daring to write ten lines to you was worth more to me than anything else. But, even if ten lines could win your forgiveness, it seemed to me that in writing them I was departing from the sort of incognito that I must sedulously preserve in order not to wound you. To have been seen by you was a matter of chance: to dare to write to you would have been an act of my full and free will.

It is plain that, as " foreigners "—and permit me to believe that it is only in nationality that we are foreign to one another—as "foreigners ", I say, we do not understand each other: our attitudes speak a different language.

I shudder at the past: how many failures in delicacy I must have revealed to you, whilst telling you quite the contrary! We simply don't understand each other. When I wrote: " Schneider, in the course of his chatter, will assure you that I am sick ", I meant that he would assure *you*, the mistress of my life. What do I care for the opinions of the population of Volterra?

Another thing: I never assumed that it was proper to go to the house of the Rettore. Indeed, with the cruellest of sacrifices, I promised myself that I would never go there again; and I thought I was doing wonders when I did not appear there on Tuesday. I thought that to do so would be to pursue you, to vex you with my love; for in visiting the Rettore I was

---

[1] " With a slight fever, on coming away from a performance of *Il Inganno Felice*, which for the first time gave me great pleasure, and during which I composed this letter. I wrote what follows on the 29th, between half-past ten and midnight." (Note by the author at the head of the rough draft of this letter.)

visiting your home, and you had received me coldly. And, if you remember, madame, when I spoke to you, trembling, on Wednesday, I felt a need to excuse my presence there by mentioning the invitation I had received from the chambermaid.

How much my simplest actions in Milan must have caused you displeasure! Heaven knows what they mean in Italian.

Out of respect for truth, and in order not to have to mention the fact again, I assure you that when I saw you go by on the 3rd, at one o'clock, an instant after you had looked at me without recognising me, Schneider told me, in a few words, who this lady was, and that she lived in the casa Guidi. I dared not ask him to repeat the name of the house. Whenever anyone speaks to me of you, I feel that I am transparent. On the 3rd I explored the town, from the Arco gate to the gate of Florence, finding my bearings by the map drawn by your brother. Beside the porta Florentina I noticed Signor Giorgi's English garden. I entered it and saw some young ladies on the wall. The sight pleased me, and I decided to return on the morrow, not knowing whom I was destined to meet there. Similarly, there was not the slightest preparation behind my excuse to Signor Giorgi, for I had not addressed the smallest enquiry to Schneider, I had not even pronounced your name.

Be assured, madame, that my letter of Saturday was not handed to you at the moment when I brought it. I went for a fairly long walk. When I again passed the casa Giorgi, it was certainly more than one o'clock by my watch, and I clearly remember that I was very hesitant: I did not consider the interval long enough. Finally, I said to myself: " Accursed timidity! " and knocked. It was Signor Giorgi himself who suggested that I was seeking to see you; and precisely the same thing happened when I visited his gallery in order to send you a letter. He insisted on my entering your room, although it was only half past nine.

I have badly failed to make myself understood, madame, if you think me a man " so difficult to discourage from hoping ". No, I no longer hope, nor have done for a long time. I had hopes, I admit, in January, especially on the 4th: a friend who visited you on the 5th said to me as we went out (forgive this plain speaking): " She is yours: will you behave like a gentleman? " But on the 13th of February I lost all hope. On that day you said things to me that I have often repeated to myself. You must not suppose that these harsh things—which I do not in any way blame you for saying to me, quite on the contrary—have been wasted. They have sunk deeply into my heart, and it is only considerably later that they have begun to take effect, to impinge upon my daydreams and disenchant my image of you.

For four months I have often wondered what I should do. Make love to an ordinary woman? The very idea revolts me, and I am incapable of it. Make it impossible for me to see you again, by means of some well-calculated piece of insolence? Firstly, I would not have the courage. Secondly—forgive my apparent incivility—it would mean putting myself in the situation of exaggerating the happiness of being with you. Thinking of madame Dembowski at a hundred leagues' distance from her, I would forget her harshness; I would set beside it those other, brief moments when I deceived myself into thinking that she was treating me less badly. Everything would become sacred to me, even to the country where she lives, and at Paris the mere name of Milan would bring the tears to my eyes. For example, for the past month, whilst thinking of you from Milan, I would have imagined the happiness of walking with you in Volterra, around those superb Etruscan walls: and it would never have occurred to me to tell myself the bitter truths which I have since had to swallow. This state of affairs is so genuine that whenever I have spent some time without seeing you, as on my return from Sannazaro, I visit you with ever greater devotion. So I can truthfully tell you, madame, that I do not hope. But the place on all the earth where I am least unhappy is at your side. If, despite myself, I reveal my love when I am with you, it is because I am in love; but it does not mean that I hope to make you share this feeling. I shall now permit myself a long philosophical explanation, at the end of which I shall be able to say:

Trop d'espace sépare Andromaque et Pyrrhus.[1]

The governing principle of Italian conduct is a sort of emphasis. Remember how Vismara knocks at your door, how he sits down, how he asks you for your news.

The governing principle of French conduct is to lend simplicity to everything. In Russia I saw five or six great deeds performed by Frenchmen, and, although accustomed to the simple tone of Parisian good society, I was still touched by the simplicity of the behaviour of those who performed them. Well, I suppose, madame, that to you, who adorn another climate, these simple manners must have seemed " frivolous " and lacking in passion. Bear in mind that, in these fine actions in Russia, life itself was at stake—and life is a thing, that as a rule, one loves well enough when one is in cold blood.

The manners of M. Lampato and Pecchio may give you some idea of the simple tone of us Frenchmen. Observe that Vismara's face has an

---

[1] Too great a space divides Andromache and Pyrrhus.

entirely French cast: it is his manners that form a contrast with ours—and I would give half my life to be able to acquire them. It follows from this that my attitude—so it suddenly occurred to me yesterday while I was reading your letter—that my attitude, I say, must often depict in your eyes a feeling very remote from that which inspires it. This is probably the reason why you consider me " presumptuous ".

You know that, in novels, unsuccessful lovers have a resource: they tell themselves that the object of their love is incapable of loving. I find that during the past few days this resource has been presenting itself to me. The fact that I thus confide in you, madame, shows you that I am taking the liberty of disclosing my most intimate thoughts to you—in short, that I no longer hope.

You have received a letter, madame, informing you that " it is thought in Milan that I have come to be with you, or that I wished people to think this." This is the first time, madame, that I have spent a year at Milan without travelling. I speak to very few people, and these people are accustomed to seeing me come and go. You left on the 12th and I on the 24th: I said that I was going to Grenoble. Here in Florence I met Vaini and Trivulzi: I told them that I was back from Grenoble; that, as I passed through Genoa, the Pisan *Luminara*, which was announced for the 10th of June, had brought me to Leghorn, and that the delay in the arrival of the Emperor had brought me to Florence.

As for the notion of my " wanting people to think " that I came here to be with you, if ever in the world there was a malignant supposition of which I could easily clear myself, not by words but by good, reliable facts, it is this one.

In all the five years I have been in Milan, the few people who know me can certify that I have never once mentioned a woman's name. I am not speaking of a person who wished, against my will, that I should lodge with her. Another woman called attention to herself at a Carnival masked ball; but she did this of set purpose, and I had not the least part in it—and what gives me a completely clean slate in this respect is the fact that my most intimate friends were very astonished at this relationship, which was already old and long since broken off. It is true that those women I had, I treated as mere wenches. But, far from my indulging in the small vanity of boasting of it, my silence on the subject served only to give it a veneer of better tone. I defy your correspondent to mention two other women whose names have been associated with mine. À propos of which, madame, would I have selected you as the target of an infamy—you, especially, whom public esteem renders it so difficult to attack on this point? I may add that in my youth I always had too great a love of true fame—and, thanks to a deal of pride, too much hope of achieving it—to have any love of a reputation built on lies.

Madame, if I am calumniated in a matter in which Cagnola, Vismara and the others can justify me with mathematical proof, what will be said of me on other subjects on which, by their nature, I cannot receive so clear a justification? But I shall say no more, out of respect for the friendship with which you honour the person who wrote to you.[1]

I think, madame, that the best thing for me to do on arriving at Milan is to tell the same story as I told Vaini. If you think otherwise, madame, deign to give me your orders. Should I say that I have been at Volterra? It seems to me that I should not.

I hope, madame, that I have removed from this letter anything too overtly reminiscent of love.[2]

——— 99 ———

TO THE BARON DE MARESTE[3]

Florence, the 18th of July 1819

How delightful! I was returning from a walk to the *Uffizzi*—to which, as you know, everybody goes on Sunday—and was actually thinking of you. " What a pleasure it would be to walk arm in arm with him! " I was saying to myself. " But the rascal has forsaken me, like a vile Jacobin." Then I arrived home and found your letter. I am very sorry to learn that you are ill, and urge you to be very careful. Old Moscati once said to me that it took thirty years of temperance to comfort the urethra after a stab of the syringe. Give me details.

On the 23rd of May I had the luck to lay hands on seven hundred francs: great celebration in the manor-house of Hell! What to do with so huge a sum? On the 24th I took the diligence for Genoa—fifty francs. A week in Genoa—delightful crossing in twenty-seven hours, supping

---

[1] Perhaps one may detect here an allusion to Métilde's cousin, Signora Traversi, who always armed Mme Dembowski against Beyle's inclination towards her. (Note by M. Martineau.)

[2] " She answered me with a rupture apparently founded on my employment of the line:
Trop d'espace sépare Andromaque et Pyrrhus.
" Letter of despair from Dominique, of which no copy has been kept. The following letter was addressed to her on the 6th of July. She must have received it on the 9th. This letter, which is well written, occupies only a page." (Note by the author.)

[3] " To what friend have I ever spoken a word of my lover's grief? " (*Vie de Henri Brulard.*)

at Porto Venere, from Genoa to Leghorn—a week at Leghorn and Pisa, for those dull festivals—and finally back here in Florence for the past forty days, and I still have a hundred francs. I'm at Hembort's in the via Lambertesca, living in great style, five paoli for dinner and three for the room. Dinner of thirty covers, at which I had a dogfight of an argument concerning Marshal Ney. His widow has no dignity. She has brought grief into disrepute in this country. At present she is at Rome.

When the Vicomte[1] sees this letter he will say: " Why, that's exactly the opening of *I sow my wild oats*! "

I am carrying a chip on my shoulder. I may tell you that I dislike the Florentines intensely. There is something dry and correct about them which reminds me of France. Lombardy and my heart are made for one another: what a great heart, I hope that means! You will say something insulting to me when I tell you that in the space of forty days, and being out in the streets all day long looking at the Corpus Domini and San Giovanni processions, I have not found a single Florentine woman who was really beautiful. My beauties here are two young Englishwomen whom I see every evening at the Cascine and on the ponte della Trinità, at about eleven o'clock. Even these are merely fish-like beauties: I mean to say, without expression. The ponte della Trinità is where we go in search of a remedy against the infamous heat in which we have been baking for the past ten days. Imagine it, in Florence they never water the streets! The paving-stones in the piazza of the Great Duke were still literally scorching at midnight. The Bottegone was scorching; but it must have made a fortune—one had to take a gramolata every hour, under pain of perishing of heat. They say we have had only twenty-eight and a half degrees. At this moment I have just finished *The Black Durward* and *Old Mortality* by W. Scott. The last half-volume of *Old Mortality* isn't worth a d——mn, the rest ranks with *Tom Jones*—it's up in the clouds. Admittedly, Scott's work is more serious, and the depiction of love is sacrificed. This is the new fashion: love, that poor passion, is out of favour with our modern novelists, madame de Genlis, miss[2] Edgeworth, W. Scott. Do you know why? Because they are intelligent enough to know that in order to depict passion one must have felt it.

What do they say about M. Daru's *Histoire de Venise*? He used to say that in 1790 there was a Venetian ambassador at Versailles who sent most original despatches to his Republic. What an infamous tyranny that aristocracy was! I have been over the ground, and have twenty anecdotes to tell: not a shadow of liberty; a hundred powerful families feeding some thousands of impoverished noblemen—all the rest ground

[1] Barral. [2] [*Sic*.]

down. Apart from these two last circumstances, it is like in Vienna. By the way, the Emperor has been incredibly generous: he gives away three or four thousand sequins as one might give twenty-five louis—the opposite of three years ago. He makes up for this by economising on his togs. He wears a hat with a time-battered crown, such as your servant's servant would throw away. His whole rig-out is worth all of thirty francs. Of course, the Count of St. Helena has ruined the profession: these sovereigns go about like monstrances, more or less pleasing to the eye, but they do not issue decrees intimidating the public, they are not centres of action. The result is complete indifference, and worse. By Jove, where shall I post this letter? If I were an Irishman, I would say to you: "Don't fail to let me know if you don't receive it." I depend upon you to write to me.

My circle here is composed of goldsmiths, with whom I go on picnics, at which we drink the health of Benvenuto Cellini. To our last dinner— by Dante's tower, near the *Acienda del Ghiaccio*—serves execrable dinners, which these people consider very good and which cost five paoli—to our last dinner, I was saying, the goldsmiths brought two Americans who have no doubt that the English loan is a *para bellum* as far as they are concerned. But they believe the English ministers want war in order to keep themselves in power. The English aristocracy is dying of fear and closing its ranks against the Cabinet. I hope to have the joy of beholding a revolution in that country. The hulks and St. Helena will be avenged . . . Farewell, I am going to la Mombelli's *Cenerentola*: it is very well sung; but eternally Rossini, he is their staple dish.

Arrange a performance of Rossini's *Sigillara*, or the *Pietra del Paragone*. The principal part, which was written for Gallini, should suit Pellegrini. Forgive me for sending letters carriage-forward: I treat you as an opulent Departmental chief. I want to pay my debts to Didot.

———— 100 ————

TO MADAME DEMBOWSKI

Florence, the 20th of July 1819

Madame,

Perhaps, in my position of disgrace, you may think it improper of me to dare to write to you. If I have become so hateful to you, I shall try, at least, not to do more to deserve my misfortune, and I beg you to tear up my letter without reading further.

If, on the contrary, your sensitive but over-haughty soul has the kindness to treat me as a friend in misfortune, and you deign to give me news of yourself, then I beg you to write to me at Bologna, where I am compelled to go: "Al signor Beyle, nella locanda dell' Aquila Nera." I am truly disquieted concerning your health. If you were ill, would you be so cruel as not to inform me in a few words? But I must expect anything. Happy the heart warmed by the tranquil, prudent and unvarying light of a feeble lamp! Of such a heart, it is said to love, and it commits no improprieties hurtful to itself or to others. But the heart which blazes with the flames of a volcano cannot please the object of its adoration; it commits follies, fails in delicacy and burns itself away. I am very miserable.

HENRI.

───── IOI ─────

TO MADAME DEMBOWSKI

Grenoble, the 25th of August 1819

Madame,

I received your letter three days ago. Upon again seeing your handwriting I was so deeply moved that I could not immediately undertake to reply to you in a proper fashion. Your letter is a fine day in the midst of a fetid desert, and, severe though you are towards me, yet I owe you the only moments of happiness I have had since Bologna. Ceaselessly I think of that happy town where you must have been since the 10th. My soul strays beneath a portico, through which I have often passed, to the right on leaving the Porta Maggiore. Ceaselessly I behold those lovely hills, crowned with palaces, which provide the view from the garden where you walk. Bologna, where I received no harshness at your hands, is sacred to me: it is there that I learnt of the event that drove me into exile in France, and cruel though this exile be, it has made me feel all the more the power of the link that binds me to a country where you are[1]. Every single one of these views is engraved on my heart, especially that of the road to the bridge and the first meadows one meets on the right after leaving the portico. It is there that, in fear of being recognised, I used to go in order to think of the person who lived in that fortunate

[1] On July 24th Beyle wrote from Bologna to Mareste: " Did you know that on my arrival on the 22nd I found nine letters informing me that I had lost my father on the 20th of June, and scolding me for having been so long absent from Grenoble? One of these letters contains a copy of the Will, which is a sort of manifesto against poor Henri . . . I must go and suffer boredom at Cularo."

house which I scarcely dared to look at as I passed it. I write to you after having transcribed with my own hand two long documents destined to safeguard me, if possible, against the rogues by whom I am surrounded. All this is veiled beneath the finest hypocrisy: I am the heir, and to all appearance I have no grounds for complaint. This is precisely what in times gone by would have made me fly up in a rage; and I do not doubt that it was intended to make me do so.

The Will is dated the 29th of September 1818; but nobody could foresee that on the morrow of that day a small event would occur which would make me absolutely insensitive to the outrages of fortune. Whilst I admire the efforts and resources of hatred, the only feeling which all this gives me is that I am apparently destined to feel and inspire strong passions. The Will is an object of curiosity and wonder amongst the local men of affairs. Yet I think, after having read and pondered over the Civil Code, that I have found the means of parrying the blow which it seeks to inflict. To do so would involve a long law-suit with my sisters, one of whom is dear to me. Consequently, although I am the heir, I this morning proposed to my sisters that I should give each of them a third of my father's estate. But I foresee that I shall receive, as my share, properties encumbered with debts, and that the result of two months of vexations, which are making me take so gloomy a view of human nature, will be that I shall be left with very little fortune and the prospect of being a little less poor in my extreme old age. I had set aside until the present period my plans for several long journeys, and I would have been cruelly disappointed had not all my liking for travels and horses long since disappeared before a deathly passion. Today I deplore this passion only because it drove me in its madness to displease her whom I love and respect more than anyone else on earth. Besides, all that the world contains has become entirely indifferent to me; and I owe to my obsession the perfect and amazing insensibility with which I see myself changed from a rich man into a poor one. The only thing of which I am afraid is to seem a miser to my friends at Milan, who know that I have inherited.

In Milan I met the amiable L——, to whom I said that I had arrived from Grenoble and would go back there. As far as I know, nobody, madame, has had any such idea as you were told of in that letter. Unless one has fine horses, it is easier than one might suppose to be very quickly forgotten. I discovered that L—— had an idea which caused me much pain, and which I shall endeavour to destroy on my return to Milan. I beg you to give me news of yourself in the greatest detail. Have you absolutely no pain in your chest? You did not answer me on this point, and you are so indifferent to all that preoccupies lesser souls that, as long as you do not expressly say no, I shall fear yes.

After having deeply hated Porretta[1], I shall passionately love it if the waters have rid you of your stomach-trouble, and especially of your eye-trouble. By dint of longing for it, I almost find hope that you will consent to give me news of yourself: this hope is the only thing that makes me endure the detestable life I lead.

I have the prospect of finding my liberty curtailed at Milan, and I cannot escape the obligation to take my sister there. She has been seduced by *Otello*, and in this country she becomes continually worse.

I must end this letter: it is impossible to go on feigning indifference. Here in Grenoble my only happiness is the idea of love. I do not know what would become of me if I did not spend the hours of long discussions with lawyers in thinking of her whom I love.

Farewell, madame, be happy. I do not believe that you can be, except if you love. Be happy, even if in loving another than myself.

I can truthfully write to you what I continually say:

> La mort et les enfers s'ouvriraient devant moi,
> Phédime, avec plaisir j'y descendrais pour toi[2].

HENRI.

──── 102 ────

TO THE BARON DE MARESTE

Cularo (Grenoble), the 1st of September 1819

I am most grateful for your splendid eight-page letter. I have also received the Vicomte's[3]. I intend to leave on the 14th of September, after the elections[4], and to lodge, if necessary, with M. Petit, hôtel de Bruxelles.

Please do me the favour of taking a room for me on the fourth storey —that is to say, as cheap as possible. I am sure to leave after the elections. The matter is certain, for I have in my table six thousand francs in gold. But the bastard has left *dei debiti infiniti*[5]: I shall have from thirty to

---

[1] Bagni di Porretta, a watering-place in the Apennines.
[2] Death and hell might open before me, Phédime, with pleasure I would enter there for thee.
[3] Barral.
[4] " He went to Grenoble, where he gave his vote to the most honest man in France— M. Henri Grégoire." (*Obituary*.)
[5] Infinite debts.

[204]

fifty thousand francs, that is all. I have discovered a hundred and twenty thousand francs' worth of debts, plus two thousand five hundred francs' worth of annuities to be paid yearly: all the estimates that I had been sent were exaggerated; and, as you see, it is only after twenty days of errands and sustained attention that I have a clear view of the situation.

Nevertheless, tell people who know me that I shall have better than a hundred thousand francs.

I already have my half-pay, about eight hundred francs, plus an annuity of one thousand eight hundred francs. If I find any way of scraping together a yearly income of four thousand francs, I shall not take a post; if I don't, I shall seek for one.

I have to deal with a brother-in-law who is the most " niggling " of men. He is advised by some Grenoble money-grubbers, and is trying to wear out my patience and exploit my longing to get the thing over. To frustrate this subtle stratagem, I propose to go and wait in Paris until the creditors compel him to finish the business.

I would be with you now but for the elections. Although my contempt for *our dear countrymen*[1] is already at its peak, I nevertheless intend to sacrifice ten days to this spectacle. After all, I am an elector, for I pay four hundred and eighty francs.

The Prefect is supporting the comte Bérenger instead of Grégoire; but the present probabilities are as follows: Rollin, Grégoire, Sappey, Français[2].

The Government is putting forward: Bérenger (the comte and Councillor of State), Pinelli-Lavalette, General du Bouchage.

The best organised party is that of the ultras: they will not waste a vote. The country priests will rob Grégoire of a hundred and fifty votes by the faithful.

The Prefect is despised, although a man of great intelligence. His trouble is that he is a miser: he did not buy drinks lavishly enough on the day of the Saint-Louis. There has been a semi-duel over a dancer— what I mean is, a pretty and respectable young lady—against whom an officer stumbled whilst waltzing: the Prefect intervened in a clumsy fashion. To crown it all, he sent a written invitation to one Comeirau, who is a vulgar pork-butcher but pays more than three hundred francs in taxes: the said pork-butcher is gloating over it with his friends the hemp-corders.

· ·

[1] In English in the original.
[2] Beyle's prophecy was a good one. The candidates elected at the first ballot, on September 12th, were the baron Savoye-Rollin, Français de Nantes and Charles Sappey. Grégoire was elected next day. (Note by M. Martineau.)

TO THE BARON DE MARESTE

Milan, the 21st of December 1819

A host of bayonets or guillotines can no more stop an opinion than a host of louis can stop gout.

This, my dear ultra, is the notion that occurred to me as I read the second part of your letter of the 8th. I laughed heartily at your political ignorance—or, rather, at the veil which pride in your title and the doctrine of " individual superiority ", inoculated into you once upon a time at the Académie d'Alfieri, have thrown over your eyes. You laugh at me in just the same way when I speak of Vigano; and we are both right, for no moral question is involved and our physical natures are different. A proof of this is that, of all Paris, I miss only Nina. All the rest seem to me like an aged coquette, and your pictures and books make me think of Mme de Saint-Aubin: isn't that the name of Mme Lambert's friend? All it comes down to is that Correggio would have painted black madonnas if he had painted in Senegal.

The summum bonum, between friends, is to be frank. In this way one gives oneself the pleasure of being original. That is why, apart from his age, I would like to be Grégoire. My only weakness is that I do not love *the blood*[1]; but since one must rely upon nothing, not even upon the Charter, I rejoice at Grégoire's election, even more than I did when we accomplished it. The reason is that his exclusion, after the Fouché cabinet, is a *palpable* fact, and that even the dullest peasant, who has acquired national land, will understand it when we have explained it to him in every possible fashion for a year. Even from the point of view of your king, I would have admitted it: what would such a token of respect for the Charter have cost? Anyway, the present session is certainly not soporific. You think me the height of absurdity, so *basta cosi*[2]. Only, now that we no longer have the *Débats* and the *Courrier, after Karlsbad*[3], do tell me who was the serious young fellow who threatened to interrupt the gaiety of the session of the 6th?

I give you my word of honour, that if I had been a Deputy, I would

---

[1] In English in the original. The blood royal?
[2] Let us leave it so.
[3] In English in the original.

have given some expression to the ideas I have been expounding to you—which would have brought me fame in 1830. I find the liberals watery: even M. d'Argenson was watery in 1815, for not speaking more *trenchantly* on the subject of Nîmes. So, once again, you are in error when you tell me that at the session of the session of the 6th I would have beheld two hundred and fifty great men.

In your answer, write any "ultra" phrase you use in very legible characters. For the rest, the style of French that you and I employ is unintelligible here, and your handwriting is arch-unintelligible: so you need feel no embarrassment. I thank you for your letter, which I received through Domenico[1]: both methods are good.

We are no less divided in our views on tragedy than as regards politics and ballets. A physician saves your life by giving you an emetic: does that diminish the reputation of a physician who saves *my* life, three hundred leagues from you by giving *me* an emetic?

This is the principle of "romanticism", of which you are not sufficiently aware. Its merit consists in administering to the public the very drug that will give it pleasure. The merit of Signor Manzoni—*if merit he has, for I have read nothing by him*—is to have captured the savour of the draught for which the Italian public is a-thirst. Perhaps this liquid would upset the stomachs of the public of the rue Richelieu; but what difference does that make to me in Milan? Do appreciate this principle of "romanticism". It admits of no Academy of Turin between you and me.

At Paris a melodrama is something that any of two thousand men of letters could compose: at Milan a *Death of Carmagnola* is something that could be composed only by two or three. I assure you that, if Signor Manzoni succeeds, he will be immensely famous, and that all the young poets in Italy have been racking their brains for twelve years to write a tragedy unlike any of Alfieri's, and have found nothing. Therefore, even if *Carmagnola* were a translated melodrama, nevertheless, if it sends a whole nation into raptures, it has great merits: quote this sentence to those Saint-Aubins of yours.

I spend my evenings with Rossini and Monti: all in all, I prefer extraordinary men to ordinary ones . . . I must now leave you, to go and dine with Rossini—I'm regarded here as an "ultra-anti-Rossinian." People here are very much taken up with music and with Grégoire. I shall read Rossini your letter: he is very comical and witty—on the exact level of Bombet's letters; he creates *without knowing how*. Schiller has written two or three excellent tragedies like

[1] Vismara.

Wallenstein, which contain some ideas of the sublime that are worthy of M. Cousin. If Rossini saw the *how* of his works he would be a thousand-leagues ahead of M. Bombet's theories. I myself am far ahead of them today, after five years' experience.

—————— 104 ——————

TO THOMAS MOORE

Bologna, the 25th of March 1820

Sir,

Friends of the charming author of *Lalla-Rookh* must have a feeling for the arts. They are certainly a part of those " Happy Few "[1] for whom alone I have written: I am greatly vexed that the rest of the human rabble should read my daydreams.

I beg you, sir, to present the enclosed three copies[2] to your friends.

I have just read *Lalla-Rookh* for the fifth time, and am ever more astonished that such a book should have come to birth in England, a country which, in my opinion, is corrupted by a tinge of Hebraic ferocity.

I have the honour to be, Sir, your very humble and obedient servant,

H. BEYLE.

—————— 105 ——————

TO THE BARON DE MARESTE

Milan, the 12th of June 1820

IMPRESSIONS OF LOVE[1]

Do you know that for three years Crozet has been scolding me for not being clear in my ideas and commissions? This has caused me to fall into the contrary vice.

You shall immediately receive *Love*[1] in two volumes. It contains

---

[1] In English in the original.
[2] Of the *Histoire de la Peinture en italie*.

erasures. Another copy would have cost me forty francs and a month's time. If the compositor says he cannot read it, enlighten his vision with twenty or thirty francs. Print three hundred copies in decimo-octavo. Make them supply very good paper, and tell M. Chanson that you must have a new, bold fount, so that the book may be easy to read.

The only complication is as follows: it will be necessary to print one hundred and fifty copies of the complete manuscript, and after that to spend fifteen or twenty francs on suppressing seven or eight passages which describe the life of a friend of mine who recently died here of love, and would give away my identity. Of the manuscript thus gelded, one hundred and fifty copies are to be printed, and only these one hundred and fifty copies are to be sold.

You have despotic authority over everything. The passages to be suppressed in the second edition are marked in red.

Since I have only this manuscript, tell me when you have received it. If it is lost, *Love* itself is lost[1].

Send the galley-proofs to me at Novara, in a letter, as you receive them. I shall enjoy that: I don't care a damn about proof-reading. Nevertheless, if you are so patient and obliging, read the proofs yourself. All I ask for are a handsome new face and handsome paper. For ten or fifteen francs more we can have very good paper. It is only a matter of ten or fifteen thousand sheets. Since the book will not be sold, I would as soon have two hundred copies as three hundred. Have *Love*[2] noticed in both your journals, *Paris* and *Moniteur*. That will make an interesting contrast: they say every second day that you are at daggers drawn. In 1819 the wasps' nest was asleep: who awoke it? What harm would Grégoire do you in the Chamber?

I was counting upon having two readers in Paris: Volney and Tracy. I see that I have lost half my audience[3].

I shall send you a short list of people to whom I beg you to send copies of the gelded edition. The list will include MM. de Tracy, de Ségur, de Chauvelin, and the literary offices of Galignani, Rosa, le Vicomte, etc., and seven or eight of the most thriving.

The essential thing is carefully to preserve the one hundred and fifty ungelded copies: in four or five years the anecdotes will have been forgotten, and we shall sell them in a trickle.

I should have corrected the style, but I would have needed a second copy, and it would have taken a month. It is for this purpose that I ask

---

[1] Cf. letters nos. 107, 108.
[2] In English in the original.
[3] Volney died in April, 1820.

you to send me the galley-proofs as they come: they will serve as a manuscript.

LIST.

Employ an intelligent agent and send, gratis, copies of the gelded edition to MM.:

De Tracy, rue d'Anjou-Saint-Honoré, 42;
De Salvandy, Master of Appeals;
Thierry, of the *Censeur*, if he hasn't shaved;
Teste, the lawyer;
Picard, the clown of the Institut;
Jouy, of the *Minerve*, if he has not been hanged;
De Pradt, ditto;
Manuel, the Deputy, ditto;
De Ségur, peer of France;
Anatole de Montesquiou;
Thomas Moore;
to M. Garat, of the Institut;
Talma;
Delavigne;
Prudhon, the painter;
Guérin, ditto;
Pariset, censor and physician;
Chateaubriand;
the young Prince de Beauvau;
and to two or three distinguished Englishmen, if you have any.

Cut out with scissors the chapter on *Fiascos*, and send two copies to Mlles Mars, Bigotini, Bourgoing, Levert, Perrin, of the *Vaudeville*, Minette, ditto, Bourgeois, Noblet, Mme la duchesse de Duras—in short, to all the fashionable strumpets. Send them twenty or thirty copies: the young men who bed with them gratis will read *l'Amour*. Also to all the ambassadors, MM. de Vincent, Galotin, Stuart, and to your friends and acquaintances, without naming the author.

TO THE BARON DE MARESTE

Milan, the 23rd of July 1820

My dear fellow, I have suffered the greatest misfortune that could possibly come down upon my head.

Certain jealous enemies—for who has none such?—have circulated the rumour that I was an agent here of the French government.

The rumour has been going around for six months. I noticed that several people were seeking not to greet me: I did not care a d—mn, until the good Plana wrote me the letter which I enclose. I bear him no grudge for this: but what a terrible blow! For, after all, what *is* this Frenchman doing here? The cheerful, good-natured Milanese will never understand my philosophic life, or that I live here better on five thousand francs than at Paris for twelve thousand.

I beg you to send this letter, together with Plana's letter, to Crozet, to Troyes. I beg Crozet to write a few sentences to Plana. Give me your advice: how am I to undeceive my acquaintances here?

I am too much upset to speak of anything else. I assure you that I am not exaggerating. For the past three months I have not been admitted into a certain circle because an impartial person said: " If he comes, several people " (admittedly, these are people who hate me) " will withdraw."

I learnt this only two hours ago.

This is the most shattering blow I have had in my life.

For three months I have received none of your letters.

A thousand good wishes to the Vicomte and to Lambert. Tell them what has happened to me.

H.

TO THE BARON DE MARESTE

13th of November 1820

My dear father,

I am beginning to be uneasy about the two red volumes[1] that were at Strasbourg on the 7th of October, and which you should have received on the 15th. Give me news of them, especially in the case of your not having received anything. You will receive two note-books of *thoughts*[2] to add to the seventy-two or seventy-three that are already to be found at the end of the volume. If these thoughts arrive when everything is finished, have them printed on a page to be inserted at the end of the *pensées*, or after the poem, as a supplement.

Preserve the baroque, the false, the sentimental: excise any thoughts that are ridiculous. As soon as you have a sheet printed, send it to Dominique at Novara.

As soon as the *book*[2] is finished, send it by post, at five centimes a sheet, to Dominique at Novara, and a copy by post also to Signor Angostini, merchant, at Chiasso in Switzerland. I should have sent you a more correct form of this address. At present, dear papa, I give it you from memory . . .

Add the enclosed pensée to the seventy-three you have already. I am well, and you? I am happy, and you? *I dare not say more*[2]. Would it be prudent to invest six thousand francs in the Tontine at the rue de Richelieu, no. 89? Ask Lambert: It would be better than simply buying an annuity. I would go so far as to invest twelve thousand. I would like a receipt for colouring hair that is greying on the temples, to a dark chestnut.

Farewell, dear Father.

[1] *De l'Amour.*
[2] In English in the original.

TO THE BARON DE MARESTE

Milan, the 22nd of December 1820

Dear Annette, a thousand greetings, and also to that great banker the Vicomte. I shall see you in 1821. Send this letter to Besançon, who will pay you for the carriage. Read it all, if you can, it is all *music.*

I have received your letter of the 7th, which, despite its faults, has given me the greatest pleasure, for I have been in bed for eighteen days, with three cuppings and an inflammatory rheum which attacked a spot which you know very well—the fatal prostate gland. I expect to go out one of these days.

The Scala theatre has been banality itself since the men of genius have left it. You know that they are performing almost nothing but new pieces: this is beneficial to the art, but less so to our pleasures. This custom, being contrary to French taste—which is to admire the established *vieux-beau*—lends Italian taste a particular cachet. You are a great booby for not *giving to me letter to molest*[1].

The Jacobins will be the undoing of the theatre at Naples. The games have already been suppressed, and it has one foot in the grave. To finish last year's season, Levasseur had a great success in the *Calumny* from the *Barber* and in Meyerbeer's opera, the name of which I have already forgotten, although it ended only on the 30th of November. Meyerbeer is a man like Marmontel or Lacretelle—some slight talent, but no more genius than you could put in your pipe. When he wants to put in some singing, he borrows the vulgarest street-ballads. The only remarkable thing about this composer is his private income of eighty thousand francs, not an obol less: he leads the life of a recluse, working fifteen hours a day at his music. He refuses to play the piano any more, and he is said to be the best pianist in Europe.

On the 26th of December we have, as you know, two new ballets and a new opera—*Phèdre*, by Mayer the elder, an outrageous thief . . . Signorina Tosi, daughter of a highly respected lawyer—the equivalent of Tripier at Paris—and with a superb voice, is making her first bow in the hope of winning two hundred thousand francs. She has a figure and face that will be magnificent in the theatre, and she has a lovely voice,

[1] In English [*sic*], in the original.

but she cannot sing. What do I mean by that? She cannot steep all her arias, sad or gay, in the same piquant sauce (which, it may be mentioned, is also Rossini's merit and fault). *Write no more to me my name pernicious*[1].

. . . Nowadays Rossini merely repeats himself: he is huge, eats twenty beefsteaks a day, has himself ——d by la Chomel, ——s la Coldbrand, and in a word is a disgusting *pig*. Young Mercadanti, a twenty-year-old Neapolitan, who has played *Ercole*, is said to have talent. I have never perceived this talent, although la Schiassetti ceaselessly sang his praises during the twenty-five days I spent with her in the country. Caraffa you know: one could make a single good opera out of extracts from all his operas. Pacini junior, a handsome young man of eighteen, has written or stolen a sublime duet, of Frederick the Great refusing clemency to the mistress of one of his officers who is about to be shot. Have Remorini sing you it, and you will be compelled to weep. There is no tenor like the younger Davide.

It is even more difficult for me to write than for you to read me: my body is positively deserting me, my dear fellow. I am still expecting my *sister*[1]. I do not know *if I will have five or six*[2] . . . *Pay the post of this letter to the fair Annette, and write every fortnight*[1], I shall earn two hundred francs. If you do not receive *Love*[1], go to the rue J.-J. Rousseau and ask at the agent's office for the courier from Strasbourg. *My friend the*[1] comte put the package on the mail-coach, addressed to you. *I write to the said friend*[1], he is staying with M. le directeur Fischer. Post this letter, if you are still *orbi* when you receive it; *'tis for my pleasure, that I ask you*[1] for the galley-proofs, and not in order to make any corrections. I most *altamente*[3] don't give a d—mn for *corrections. I ask only fair paper and good characters. I want a manuscript, and I will find some pleasure in seeing*[1] as soon as possible this insufficiently corrected draft. For example, I would have corrected it in bed. There are pages that I have not re-read. How can an innocent of this sort go astray between Strasbourg and Paris? There must be a mistake in the address. See the courier[4].

If Lambert has any money of mine, use it to make a handsome decimo-octavo. Print up to four hundred of the edition with the suppressions, and up to one hundred and fifty or one hundred of the complete edition. *It is the envoy for Painting*[1] that has lent wings *to the spy rumour*[1]. You will shrug your shoulders, just as people blamed Voltaire for taking communion at Easter. Infamous injustice. I must suppress these ten pages.

. . . As soon as Lord Byron's tragedy on the doge Faliero—who

---

[1] In English in the original.
[2] (Thousand francs.)
[3] Deeply.
[4] The manuscript of *L'Amour* was not found until 1821, when Beyle had already left Milan.

[214]

cut his throat in 1208, I think—has been reprinted, send it to me by the post, but only if it costs three francs. The said lord has no dramatic genius. At the ball in Venice he addressed some words to a Miss Montgomery: next day Colonel Montgomery sent him a challenge. The affair was settled by negotiation. The expression Byron used was insignificant, short and entirely proper: but the breath of this monster has defiled a pale, chilly beauty. He is always with his fat-titted blonde, the contessa de Pesaro, whose husband has an income of fifty thousand francs and is quite capable of murdering the noble lord, or, if he can do no better, of fighting a duel with him. The wife displays a vast, twenty-two-year-old throat, to be seen on the piazza San Marco, on which she promenades in red silk slippers. I must have told you that already: I had it from the apothecary Ancillo, who is the second-best poet in Venice: the best is the satirist Buratti. He has real genius, but is a little prolix. Do you understand Venetian? You will say " yes "—but is it true?

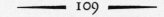

109

TO MADAME DEMBOWSKI[1]

To send the[2] 3rd of January 1821

Madame, would you find it improper if I were to dare to ask your permission to see you for a quarter of an hour, one of these evenings? I feel overwhelmed with melancholy, and my friendship would fully

---

[1] " At last I took leave of Métilde.

" ' When will you return ? ' she said.

" ' Never, I hope."

" We had a final hour of tergiversations and vain words. A single word could have changed my future life—but, alas! not for very long. That angelic soul, hidden in so fair a body, quitted life in 1825.

" She became for me like a tender phantom, deeply sad, that, by appearing before me, gave me a sovereign inclination to tender, good, just and tolerant ideas." (*Souvenirs d'Égotisme.*)

" . . . To worship Mme Dembowski . . . I can mention the name of that charming woman: who thinks of her today? Am I not perhaps the only one who does so, eleven years after she departed from this earth? The same thing is true, I believe, of the comtesse Alexandrine Petit." (*Note*: the comtesse Daru. Cf. letters nos. 48, 83.) " Today, after twenty-two years, am I not her best friend? And when this book appears (if ever a publisher is not afraid to waste his time and paper!), when this book appears after my own death, who will any longer think of Métilde or Alexandrine? And, despite their womanly modesty and the horror of attracting public attention that I observed in both of them, I ask myself whether, on learning, wherever they may be, of the publication of this book, they will not be truly content." (*Vie de Henri Brulard.*)

[2] In English in the original.

appreciate the worth of a token of kindness in which the public will certainly take no interest. You can yield to my request without danger to the generosity of your lovely soul. I shall not be indiscreet: I do not claim that I have anything especial to say to you. I shall be agreeable. I am, with respect,

D.

═══ 110 ═══

TO SIR WALTER SCOTT

At la Porretta, the 18th *of February* 1821

Sir,

If you care to have obtained for you in Paris the books named on the enclosed list, I shall have found a feeble means of showing my gratitude for the extreme pleasure that I got from *the Abbot*.

What a pity that the author has never chosen to depict the Middle Ages as they were in this wonderful Italy! He would have found here the human soul's first steps towards liberty. Instead of the egoistical heroics of absurd feudalism, he would have discovered on his path the depiction of all that the human soul could *at that time* do for the happiness of all. Ideas were still obscure and uncertain, but in Italy, in 1400, human souls nevertheless had a degree of energy which since then has been found nowhere.

Unfortunately, in order to obtain a clear picture of the Middle Ages in this country, one must busy oneself with piles of dusty parchments, which as recently as about 1650 were deliberately confused and spoilt by the Jesuits. No writer has sought to give a sincere collection of tales depicting the life of this period. What would be the raptures of Europe if a man like the author of *Waverley* revealed to it the life of Cola di Rienzi, or the exile of the first Cosimo di Medici!

. . . .

TO LORD BYRON[1]

Paris, the 23rd of June 1823

My lord,

It is most kind of you to attach some importance to individual opinions. The poems of the author of *Parisina* will live many centuries after such pamphlets as *Rome, Naples et Florence en* 1817 have been forgotten.

My publisher yesterday put in the post for Genoa the *Histoire de la Peinture en Italie* and *de l'Amour*.

I wish, my lord, I could share your opinion of the author of *Old Mortality*. "*With his politics I have nothing to do*[2]"—by saying this you refuse to take into consideration precisely the thing that makes me regard the character of the illustrious Scotsman as *little worthy of enthusiasm*. Private virtues are not very difficult in a man who has the pleasure of enriching himself, nor very rare or worthy of truly high esteem. When Sir Walter Scott solicits, with the passion of a lover for his mistress, the glass from which *an old King*[3], a somewhat contemptible character, had drunk; when he is one of the secret supporters of the *Beacon*[4], I see a man who desires to be made a baronet or a Scottish peer. Out of a thousand people who do such things in all the antechambers of Europe, there is perhaps one who does them because he naïvely believes that absolute power is beneficial to mankind. Sir Walter would be such an exception if he had refused the title of baronet and other personal advantages. If he were sincere, his horror of being despised— a sentiment that holds so much sway over generous hearts—would have caused him long ago to regard such a simple step as his duty. He had no such idea: consequently, the odds are nine hundred and ninety-nine to one that my heart does right to refuse him any passionate interest. What I refuse Sir Walter is not my legitimate esteem, but my enthusiasm. Human nature is such that one can no longer have this feeling towards characters who have lost a certain " flower of honesty ", if I may use such an expression. 'Tis a misfortune: but any man who is reduced to finding

---

[1] Answer to a letter from Lord Byron (of May 29th, 1823) in which Byron strove to defend Sir Walter Scott against some criticisms by Beyle. It is not known whether the following letter was actually sent to Lord Byron. (Note by Colomb.)

[2] In English in the original.

[3] Do. (George IV).

[4] A Tory newspaper,

explanations for an action such as that of the *Beacon* has forever lost this flower, which is as easily tarnished as that which is the pride of a young maiden.

My opinion of Sir Walter Scott's morality is held almost unanimously in France: " A clever man who knows how to feather his nest. He's not crazy like other men of genius." Such is the approbation of the vulgar, which in my eyes is a deadly criticism.

Actions such as those of Sir Walter are all the more deserving of severity in that nowadays there is everything to lose in joining the opposite party to his. The *Kings*[1] and aristocracy, awakened to their dangers, have ever more magnificent rewards for great men who prostitute themselves.

If the author of *Ivanhoe* were as poor as Otway, my heart would be inclined to forgive him for a few base acts committed in order to have bread. Contempt would be, as it were, drowned in my pity for the fatality of human nature which causes a great artist to be born without an income of sixpence a day. But it is Sir Walter the millionaire who supports the *Beacon*!

If this newspaper seems to him to be beneficial to the happiness of the majority of Englishmen, how is it that, knowing that he might be taken for a vile flatterer, he does not refuse the title of baronet?

It is quite against my inclination, my lord, that I persist in saying that, until Sir Walter has explained his action in a *probable* manner, I, as judge, would not declare from the heights of a tribunal that Sir Walter has failed in honour; but I would say that he has lost all right to the enthusiasm of a man who has seen something of courts.

I am vexed, my lord, that my letter is already so long. But, since I have the misfortune to hold an opinion contrary to yours, my respect for you has forbidden me to curtail my argument. I regret sincerely that I am not of your opinion—and there are not ten men in the world to whom I could sincerely say the same.

Poor Pellico has not Sir Walter Scott's talents: but there you have a soul worthy of the most tender and passionate interest. I doubt whether he can work in his prison: his body is weak, it has for long been sapped by poverty and the dependence that results from it. Reduced almost to Otway's position, he has several times said to me: " The finest day of my life will be the day when I feel I am dying." He has a brother at Genoa and a father at Turin. Besides *Francesca* and *Eufemio di Messina*, he has written, so he told me, ten other tragedies: his father could get hold of the manuscripts. If sold in England, that nation which contains so many lofty natures, these tragedies might win a patron for the unhappy poet.

[1] In English in the original.

During the ten years for which Pellico has still to inhabit the *Spielberg*, death might bring about rapid changes in the monarchy. One of the ministers of one of these kings might calculate that it would be profitable to his vanity to obtain Pellico's release from prison, on his giving his word that he would live in America.

It has been extremely agreeable to me, my lord, to have enjoyed some personal relation with one of the two or three men who, since the death of my worshipped hero, have done something to break the dull uniformity into which our poor Europe has been moulded by the affections of high society. A long time ago, when I read *Parisina* for the first time, my soul was agitated by it for a week. I am happy to have an occasion to thank you for this keen pleasure. *Old Mortality* made a still keener first impression on me, but one that I have found neither so deep nor so lasting.

I have the honour to be, my lord, your very humble and obedient servant.

H. BEYLE.

—— 112 ——

TO ALBERT STAPFER[1]

No. 4, rue des Jeûneurs, Paris.
8th of August 1823

Alas, Monsieur, I would very much like to send you the *Elective Affinities*, but to do so I would need to be two hundred leagues from these desiccated Parisians. The sweet and simple Othilie is with my books in Milan, and you may have seen in the newspapers how they have treated a certain M. Andryane. He was condemned by an Economic Tribunal to ten years' imprisonment, and he was perhaps as innocent as I am. What Goethe has depicted, with a mathematical exactitude, in the *Affinities* is the *involuntary*, all-powerful, and therefore not criminal, effect of love. But he has put all this into some d-mn-d German hearts, which are too much lacking in *logic* to interest us greatly in the long run. They are poor, sweet, amiable madmen. We should be *lazy* madmen if we abandoned ourselves to despair because the crop we had expected for March was not going to be ripe until August. In every century there is

---

[1] The Albert Stapfer whose translation of *Faust* into French appeared in 1828, illustrated by Delacroix.

this sort of sense of waiting, which can be clearly felt: is it a reason for doing nothing?

I enjoin you to write to me often: your letters interest me greatly. Gray used to say that every man was capable of writing one good book—the mere story of his life. For lack of anything better, depict for me what happened to you yesterday. The genius of the inhabitants of la Beauce[1]—and by "genius", as you know, I do not mean intelligence—is as unknown to me as that of the peasants of Bosnia.

La Guiditta[2] is going to sing *les Horaces* on the 14th of August; she is already in the pangs of childbirth and in terror of failure. Yesterday at the Pharaon she was unable to gamble, she remained on her sofa, right against the table, without punting! " I would not know what card to play," she said, " I have no inspiration !"

I am mad about the naturalness of these Italian hearts. By the way, she remembers you as if you were a white butterfly whom she saw last year. If I go to Switzerland, it will be the same with me. Why remember a man who has not been one's lover? 'Tis one of the accursed errors of our civilisation. I am very pleased with the letters of M. Lécluze[3]. One feels their sincerity. I do not think they have enough boldness of style for good description.

Do not forget that Herr von Gagern, Germany's first jurist and a man of intelligence, believes in ghosts. Do not forget that everybody aged eighteen has set about making *balles fées* on the pattern of Jean Paul's *Freischütz*. Schiller is unpopular at Frankfort, where he is thought too classical, too French, insufficiently involved. Goethe is more involved: the main verb occurs on the second page—that's what wins a German heart. They believe in everything, and we in nothing.

Be assured of my cordial friendship.

La Borde.

I hope much *of Spain*[4].

[1] Albert Stapfer used frequently to reside at the château de Talcy, which belonged to his family.

[2] Signora Pasta. She sang Cimarosa's *les Horaces* at the théâtre Louvois on August 14th, 1823.

[3] Étienne Delécluze.

[4] In English in the original.

TO MME ———[1]

Rome, the 5th of December 1823

I could die of longing, madame, to arrive in a town whose name would enable me to use the permission you gave me to send you news of what is happening in society. High society here presents itself at M. de Montmorency's[2] and M. Demidoff's. M. de Montmorency does the honours of his house with a charm that is truly perfect, for it is never embarrassing. As a rule it is fatiguing to see a master of the house coming towards one in an assembly of two or three hundred people: in the Duke's house, it is merely one more agreeable person joining the group. There are three or four Roman women of the greatest beauty: the Dodwell ladies, Princesa Bonacorsi, etc. These ladies have completely caught the assured, decisive, trenchant tone which once upon a time, 'tis said, was the tone of the French court. They wear extremely décolletées gowns, and one would be very hard to please if one did not feel most grateful to their dressmakers. Depict to yourself, madame, a throng of forty women dressed in this fashion, fourteen cardinals and a host of prelates, abbés, etc. The bearing of the French abbés would really make you die of laughter: amidst so many charms, they do not know what to do with their eyes. I have seen some of them actually turn away to avoid seeing them. The Roman abbés gaze fixedly at these charms, with a most praiseworthy intrepidity.

Amongst the minor pleasures one can obtain from high society, one of the greatest is to see a cardinal, in full red, giving his hand to a young woman in order to present her in a drawing-room—a young woman with keen, sparkling, bedazzled eyes, sensual and clad as I have described. Three hours on end are spent in exchanging glances, moving about the room, consuming excellent ices: after which the company breaks up, to meet again next day.

At M. Demidoff's one is seated, for he spends a hundred thousand francs on performances of French light comedies, by a company of actors who are his own people, and are not too bad. There is one gifted man whom M. B—— will certainly know, a valet named Frogers.

---

[1] M. Martineau thinks that this letter was addressed to the comtesse Curial.
[2] The duc de Laval, French ambassador.

Despite the pretty gowns, and despite the agreeable masterpieces which one sees in the mornings, Rome does not at all carry me off my feet. I feel too much isolated.

It is not worth while to spend a month paying court to all the bores of a great household in order to angle for the post of fourth aide-de-camp to one of these lovely women. I know not if it be a sign of old age, but I feel a need for intimacy which, since it is possible nowhere else, makes me almost long for the fogs of Paris.

Here one sees at every street-corner handsome yellow oranges standing out against magnificent greenery appearing over a garden wall. The great obstacle to walks in the morning is the heat of a pitiless sun blazing in a clear sky. Today, however, it is raining for the first time in ten days. This is not the reason why I have the honour to be writing to you. But with a fine French lady one must mind one's P's and Q's: your permission extends only to news of high society, and I must have had a glimpse of it in order to speak of it. If you have the goodness to write me a line in answer, that will be a sign that you are not offended by my extending to Rome a permission you gave me for Paris. Do you still intend to return there in February?

114

TO THE BARON DE MARESTE

Paris (midnight), Saturday, the 26th of April 1824

. . . .

The Académie française has just issued a manifesto against " romanticism ". I could have wished it were less stupid. However, such as it is, all the newspapers quote it. This fact interests me. For a publisher like Ladvocat, this is a question " palpitating with topical interest ": the more so as the said Ladvocat has made a sort of fortune out of Schiller and Shakespeare. Fortified by these weighty arguments, and a thousand others that your skill in dealing with such people will suggest to you, I would like you to visit the said Ladvocat, with the serious yet carefree air of a man of means, and pronounce a discourse somewhat as follows:

" Monsieur, I have come to propose to you a reply to M. Auger's manifesto against ' romanticism '. All Paris is talking of the attack published by the Académie française. My friend M. de Stendhal, author of the *Vie de Rossini* and of *Racine et Shakespeare*, which you know well, is writing a reply to M. Auger. This reply can be delivered to you in three days: it will be three or four pages long. The price I ask for it is three hundred francs—for a first edition, of course, which will not exceed five hundred copies."

You can come down to two hundred francs for a thousand, or to a hundred francs, or to nothing.

. . . .

─── 115 ───

TO THE COMTESSE CURIAL[1]

Paris, Tuesday evening, 18th of May 1824

What a sad thing prudence is—or, at least, how sad it makes *me*! I was the happiest of men—or, at least, my heart was beating with extreme emotion—as I went to visit you this morning; and the emotion was a sweet one. I spent the evening, and almost the day, in your company, but with such an appearance of indifference that I must make an effort to persuade myself that things might be otherwise. I regret, for the first time in ten years, that I have forgotten French manners.

When shall I be able to see you? When will it be proper for me to visit you again? I did not come yesterday because, on the day before, a man-servant had heard me asking the janitress if you were at home. Are you pleased with my circumspection? Did I have a sufficient air of indifference? I am furious with myself. I implore you to tell me, by letter, when I shall be able to find you alone. By now I am far from avoiding such moments, and I despair of hitting on one, since you receive so many visits.

A little sign at the window of the boudoir where you were this morning—a shutter half closed, for example, or the sun-blind half drawn down—would tell me that I could come up.

[1] The rough draft of this letter was scribbled on the reverse side of the page containing the draft for the preface to the second part of *Racine et Shakespeare*. (Note by Colomb.)

The comtesse Curial, née Clémentine Beugnot (cf. letter no. 82), for whom Beyle conceived a violent passion. "The honour of having inspired me with the greatest passion is to be debated between Mélanie, Alexandrine, Métilde and Clémentine.

". . . In point of intelligence, Clémentine was superior to all the others.

" The pleasure I took in the amazing victory of Menti is not comparable to a hundredth part of the pain she gave me by leaving me for M. de Bospier." (*Vie de Henri Brulard*.)

If I do not see this sign of solitude, I shall not knock at your door, and I shall come by again a quarter of an hour later.

Must you depart without my seeing you?

―――― 116 ――――

TO THE COMTESSE CURIAL

Paris, the ―― 1824

My dear one, so that you may suffer as little as possible from my extravagances, I am about to play the fool—that is, to speak to you of myself.

My good qualities, if I have any, depend upon other qualities which, if not extremely bad, are at least very disagreeable, but even more displeasing to myself than to others. I compare myself to a conscript who arrives in a regiment of dragoons. He is given a horse: if he has a grain of sense, he quickly acquaints himself with the qualities of this horse. The virtue of a horse depends upon its character: but mere awareness that the horse one rides is restive does not take away that horse's quality of restiveness[1]. Now, the same is true of my character: especially in the last two years, I have begun to understand it. Its faults were scarcely evident in Italy, where everyone is an original and does only what pleases him, without " bothering about his neighbour ". In France one always asks oneself: " What will the neighbours think? "

Do not have the least uneasiness on my account. I love you to the point of passion: this perhaps means that my love does not resemble that which you have seen in society or in novels. I could wish that, in order to spare you disquiet, it might resemble whatever is the most tender thing you have ever experienced. I am sad when I think that *you* must have been sad on Thursday, Friday and Saturday. Ought we to add to the contrarieties that pursue us? If you had done such a thing, I would have been beside myself. Is it inevitable that my accursed originality should have given you a false idea of my devotion?

[1] " I realise that I was like a restive horse, and indeed I learnt this from something said to me by M. de Tracy (the illustrious comte Destutt de Tracy, peer of France, member of the Académie Française and, what is more, author of the law of the 3rd of Prairial (May 22nd) concerning the Technical Colleges). I owe this discovery to something said to me by M. de Tracy." (*Vie de Henri Brulard.*)

TO THE COMTESSE CURIAL

Paris, the 24th of June 1824, *at noon*

You can have no notion of the black thoughts into which your silence has plunged me. I was thinking that yesterday night, when you were packing, you might have found the time to write me three lines, which you could have put into the box at Laon. When no letter came yesterday, I hoped for one this morning. " Whilst changing horses at S——," I said to myself, " she will have asked for a sheet of paper." But no: occupied solely with her daughter, she forgets the being who can no longer think of anything but her!

As I pondered at my desk, with the shutters closed, my black grief found entertainment in composing the following letter which you will perhaps write to me before long—for, after all, what would it cost you to write me a few words? Here, then, is the letter which I shall have the sorrow to read:

" My dear Henri, you exacted from me a promise to be sincere. This opening to my letter already enables you to foretell what remains to be said. Do not take it too greatly to heart, my dear friend. Bear in mind that, in default of keener sentiments, I shall always be bound to you by the sincerest friendship, and shall always take the tenderest interest in whatever may befall you. You realise, my dear friend, from the tone of this letter that a very sincere trust in you has taken that place in my heart which was formerly occupied by feelings of another sort. I like to believe that this trust will be justified, and that I shall never have to repent what I have been to you.

" Farewell, my dear friend, let us both be reasonable. Accept the friendship, the tender friendship, that I offer you, and do not fail to come and see me when I return to Paris.

" Farewell, my friend . . ."[1]

---

[1] This stormy liaison was not broken off until two years later, in September, 1826. (Cf. letter no. 132, note 1.)

TO THE BARON DE MARESTE

Paris, July 1824

My dear fellow, I was not able to take advantage this evening of your obliging kindness in keeping a place for me in the stalls: our picnic ended only at eight o'clock. The purpose of these few lines is to ask you to leave word for me with your porter, in answer to the following question: "Are you going to Maisonette's this evening, and at what time will you be there?" I would not care to go there without you. If you are going, I would like to be there.

Crozet is of the opinion that, since nobody reads the newspapers any more, an honest man is permitted to write for a newspaper[1]. This suits me well, for, by means of my dear colleagues who toil at literature, I shall be able to tap four thousand francs for books of my own.

I would willingly take charge of:

1. Opera buffa;
2. Notices of prints and pictures that appear in the course of the year.
3. Monthly, if required, I would contribute an article on the best works appearing in England.

This would keep our loafers abreast of both literatures. Since I read the English *Reviews* at Galignani's, and Stritch explains the pen-names to me, I can keep up-to-date.

4. If there is nobody to review the Exhibition at the Louvre, I would do so—telling a few lies in order to husband our national fame.

What degree of absurdity and falsehood does the chief editor demand? *That is the question*[2]. Since one always ends by being known, I cannot do the work if one has to be ridiculous and lie too crassly. On

---

[1] Cf. some articles in the *Journal de Paris* of 1824, signed M. or sometimes A. (Note by Romain Colomb.)

[2] In English in the original.

the other hand, if honour is safe, I promise punctuality, and I shall allow the chief editor—a great judge of the conventions and personal vanities that have to be appeased—to mutilate my articles as much as he likes.

If there were a vacant post of dramatic critic, I would gladly take it. But up to what point would I be allowed to preach the doctrine of my pamphlet *Racine et Shakespeare?*

In a word, be my ambassador. I am indifferent to honoraria, but not to honour.

I would wish to be entirely and absolutely known under the name of
ROGER.

------ 119 ------

ADVICE TO GAY GADABOUTS GOING TO ITALY[1]

10th of October 1824

1. Read Lalande, de Brosses;
2. Valandi's Itinerary;

Or you won't understand anything at all.

Read, if you can, an history of Italian Painting, and something on Italian Music, or you will be bored.

Try not to quarrel before you reach Geneva.

When your travelling-companion bores you, pretend to be asleep.

In every Italian town as big as Bologna or Florence, buy the local guide, *La Guida*: otherwise you will be bored and will understand nothing at all.

Before arriving in a city, read the article on it in Lalande, de Brosses, the notes by Childe Harold, Valandi, etc., etc., or truly you will understand nothing at all. Always travel by the *veturini*, ordering them by letter. Pollastri in Florence is honest. Whenever you can, take a Florentine *veturino*. Minchioni is also honest.

A single person pays, at most, from ten to twelve francs a day. These twelve francs pay for the journey, the room and supper in the evening.

Since you are two, you should have carriage and *spesate*[2] for eight or nine francs. Make your offer and go away. An hour later an unknown *veturino* will come and say " yes ". 'Tis always the same.

Never conclude a bargain at the first *Parlata*[3].

[1] To his sister Pauline and her full cousin, Mme Bazire de Langueville, who were about to leave for Italy.
[2] Meals.
[3] Parley.

[227]

By the way, there is now a diligence from Milan to Rome. The prices were published in the Milan *Gazette* early in April, 1824.

If you have been *spezzate*[1], give tips of twenty-five centimes each when you leave in the morning.

I went from Florence to Rome for ten crowns cash down. My *veturino* was Minchioni of Florence. It is better to travel by *veturino*. The diligence costs double, and when you travel by night and at fixed hours, you have less view of the country and more fear of highwaymen.

Dress badly when you travel; endeavour to make avarice and prudence have it over vanity.

If you travel by the *veturini* you will be able to study Italian manners in the persons of your three or four travelling-companions.

Of course, since I recommend the *veturini* to you, you will not fail to take the diligence.

Stay three days at Varese and three at Como and Tremezzina. Do not go to Milan until after Tr. It takes six days to Bologna, and as many to Florence if the weather is already foggy. If it is fine, stay for a while in Florence. I am giving you a letter to M. Vieusseux, a publisher and man of intelligence who looks like a sparrow-hawk.

Corso Buondelmonte, I think, opposite the colonna and the Church of the Holy Trinity in Florence.

Daily, or every second day, let each of you write down how much money you have left. Whoever fails to do this becomes involved in all sorts of expenses.

Do you, Pauline, make me a cravat on the 23rd of each month. It is the day on which I was born in 1783. May the total number of my cravats arrive at one thousand seven hundred and eighty-three!

What are the pleasures of a journey in Italy?

1. To breathe sweet, pure air;
2. To see superb landscapes;
3. " *To have a bit of a lover* "[2];
4. To see fine pictures;
5. To hear fine music;
6. To see fine churches;
7. To see fine statues.

A Frenchwoman is an expert on shawls, stuffs, ribbons, on good packs of cards for piquet or for any other game, but for the rest has not the smallest idea of pictures, music, statues or architecture. Each one of you,

[1] Fed.   [2] In English in the original.

mesdames, believes that the architecture of your parish is the most beautiful thing in the world. You ought to refine your spirit a little and read some good book—for example, *Erasme* or the education of youth.

I have made it clear to you that:

1. It is better to take the *veturini* than the diligence;
2. You should pay from eight to ten francs a day, with dinner and room. One pays half on the first day, a quarter at the middle of the journey, the last quarter on arrival. Always prefer the *veturini* of Florence. Always distrust those of Rome, Ancona and Rimini. Go from Baveno to Laveno, from Laveno to Varese, for twelve lire. (The Milan lira is worth seventy-six centimes.)

The post will carry you from Laveno to Varese.

At Milan, go to the *Bella Venezia*, piazza San Fidele, beside the theatre, two francs for a handsome room and three francs for dinner.

At Genoa, the Pensione Suiza, fifty centimes for dinner, two francs for a room.

At Bologna things are bad: go to the Frenchman Dupuis, at the Pensione Suiza.

At Florence, go to Mme Imbert's, a former chambermaid to Mme. de Bourcit, very honest.

At Rome, go to Franz's.

Franz, via Condotti . . . Visit M. Agostino Manni, the apothecary, Piazza San Lorenzo in Lucina, near the Corso. M. Agostino Manni, the most obliging of men, will find you an inexpensive apartment. Take one with a handsome view. I recommend the via Gregoriana, beside Santa Trinità dei Monti, opposite Monsieur the Prussian Consul.

At Rome you must sacrifice eighty francs and have a beautiful view for two months—you will have a memory for life.

Ask His Holiness's Nuncio at Florence to procure an authorisation for the Roman Customs to inspect your possessions *a casa*, where you are staying.

Leave this authorisation at the door of *Il Popolo*, where you will be admitted as Signora Périer.

Otherwise, when you arrive in Rome, you will be taken to the Customs and kept there *three hours*; for you will have to wait in a " queue " whilst the employees visit, each in its turn, all the carriages that arrive through all the gates of Rome.

At Florence, go and read the newspapers at the dwelling of M. Vieusseux, opposite the Santa Trinità.

At Naples, ask for the Pensione Suiza.

Sacrifice forty francs a month in order to have a view of the sea. Lodge on the Chiaja.

From the Simplon to Florence you must have your passports stamped every evening. You pay twenty-five centimes to a little boy who takes them to the police.

The only danger is of the passports becoming confused. Put a red mark on yours.

Buy Valandi's itinerary in French. Read it beforehand in such a manner as to know that there are galleries worth seeing in Bologna—the Museo di Cità, the Ercolani-Tanari-Mareschalchi gallery.

At Parma, the museum in the Farnese palace and the hall of St. Paul's monastery.

All Correggio's masterpieces are at Parma: take a look at the churches with domes, which today are spoilt.

At Saronno, between Como and Milan—take a look at the painting of Bernardino Luini.

At Rome the excellent Agostino Manni will want to lodge you in the Largo dell' Impresa at the Lotteria, in the lodging which I used to occupy. You might as well lodge on the rue Tirebouchon at Paris: the view is disgraceful. Settle yourselves on the via Gregoriana, on the Pincio. You will have eighty steps to climb every day when you return home.

STENDHAL.

——— 120 ———

TO M. DUBOIS, EDITOR OF THE *GLOBE* NEWSPAPER[1]

Paris, the 3rd *of November* 1824

Monsieur,

The praises that you are so kind as to bestow upon me in no. 24 of the *Globe* are highly exaggerated, which is perhaps no reason why they should

[1] Discussing the *Conversations of Lord Byron*, an unpublished work by Captain Medwin, the *Globe*, in its issue of November 2nd, 1824, reproduced a letter contained in this work, a letter from Byron dated from Genoa on May 29th, 1823 (reproduced by R. Colomb in his notes). The *Globe* accompanied this letter with the following introductory note: " This letter is addressed to a witty Frenchman who for a long time has concealed himself under various names and initials, and whose sharp originality, excellent critical tone, ingenious surveys and frank and picturesque style might truly have made the fortune of three or four authors. After such an eulogy, I should add that I have never met M. le baron de Stendhal (M. Beyle) . . ." It is to this caption, which too crudely unveiled his identity, that Beyle was replying in his letter of November 3rd, 1824. (Note by M. Martineau.)

displease an author's vanity. What especially pleases me about them is that they were not solicited, and our profession of men of letters, Monsieur, would be less degraded if everybody behaved as you and I do. It is true that in the Corps of Prefects and the Corps of Colonels there are men who behave like MM. Ancelot, Lacretelle, etc.; but the public knows nothing of these, whereas the vulgarities of men of letters are obvious.

I go to Italy every year, which is what causes me from time to time to use the name of Stendhal. You know how M. Courier was treated: since I am not so celebrated as that eloquent man, I must be more prudent. I would be obliged to you, Monsieur, if you no longer spoke of me again except under the name of Stendhal.

It appears that the *Globe* somewhat exaggerates the talent of the people it likes, but for the rest seeks to be impartial. The first journal that has the courage to do this for three years will make its fortune. The public is thirsty for truth; many people in the provinces wish to buy books, and are amazed when they have sent for a work pompously reviewed by MM. Jouy or Casimir Delavigne, and receive some piece of utter silliness. I do not know how French literature will extract itself from this unpleasant situation: *the bad faith of literary journals*. Some provincial academy that has suffered from this misfortune should make it the subject of a prize essay.

Poor Pellico—perhaps the first tragic poet of the Continent—will be released from the Spielberg in a few months[1]. This great poet is the poorest man in the world. He will probably publish ten tragedies of which I saw the manuscripts in 1818. The public should be informed that *Francesca da Rimini* is the nearest thing to Racine that the Italian language has produced. At my first moment of leisure I shall take the liberty, Monsieur, of sending you a page on Pellico[2]. I urge you to confirm the truth of the praise that Pellico seems to me to deserve, and to give it publicity. Signor Ugoni of Brescia, an excellent judge of Italian literature, is in Paris and can perhaps be consulted on the poetic worth of the author of *Francesca* and *Eufemio di Messina*.

I have the honour to be, Monsieur, you very humble and obedient servant,

STENDHAL.

---

[1] Pellico was not released until 1830.
[2] *Le Globe* published an article by Stendhal on Pellico on November 30th, 1824.

TO LOUISE SW. BELLOC[1]

Paris, the ——— 1824

I should be happy, madame, to be able to give you some information for the work you are preparing on Lord Byron. It is true that I spent some months in the society of that great poet: nevertheless, it is not an easy thing to speak of him. I never saw Lord Byron at any of those decisive movements that reveal a whole character: all that I know of that singular man is my memory of what I have felt in his presence[2]. How am I to give an account of this without speaking of myself, and how to speak of myself after having mentioned Lord Byron?

It was during the autumn of 1816 that I first met him, at the la Scala theatre in Milan, in the box of M. Louis de Brême[3]. I was especially struck by Lord Byron's eyes at a moment when he was listening to a sestet of an opera by Mayer entitled *Elena*. I never in my life saw anything finer or more expressive. (Even today, if I happen to ask myself what expression a great painter should give to genius, this splendid countenance suddenly enters my mind.) I had a moment of enthusiasm, and, forgetting the proper repugnance that any man who is at all proud ought to feel against asking for an introduction to an English peer, I begged M. Breme to introduce me to Lord Byron.

Next day I was dining at M. de Brême's, with Byron and the celebrated Monti, the immortal author of the *Basvigliana*. We talked of poetry, and somebody asked which were the twelve most beautiful lines written during the past century in French, Italian and English. The Italians present agreed in designating the twelve first lines of Monti's *Mascheroniana*[4] as the most beautiful thing that had been written in their language for a hundred years. Monti was so kind as to recite them. I looked at Lord Byron—he was enraptured. The shade of haughtiness— or rather the air of a man *who has to ward off an importunity*—which used

---

[1] Author of the work entitled *Lord Byron*. (Note by Colomb.)
[2] Cf. letter no. 88.
[3]   " The 23rd of October, 1816
" At the Opera, in Brême's box, met M. de Beyle, one of the intendants de la mobilière de la couronne, and former secretary to Napoleon's private office. He told us several extraordinary stories." (Hobhouse: *Recollections of a long life*) (Cf. pp. 234–7.)
[4] A poem on Buonaparte, composed in 1801, on the occasion of the death of the geometrician Lorenzo Mascheroni.

slightly to mar his handsome face, suddenly disappeared and gave way to an expression of happiness. The first canto of the *Mascheroniana*, which Monti, yielding to the acclamations of his hearers, recited almost in its entirety, awoke a most keen sensation in the heart of the author of *Childe Harold*. I shall never forget the divine expression on his features—the serene air of power and genius: and, in my opinion, Lord Byron was at this moment guilty of no affectation.

We compared the tragic methods of Alfieri and Schiller. The English poet said that it was very ridiculous that, in Alfieri's *Philip II*, Don Carlos should find himself, without difficulty and from the very first scene, *en tête-à-tête* with the spouse of the suspicious Philip: Monti, who is so successful in the practice of poetry, put forward such singular arguments concerning poetical theory that Lord Byron, leaning towards his neighbour, remarked: " *He knows not how he is a poet.*"[1]

After this I spent almost every evening with Lord Byron. Whenever this singular man was in the vein, and was speaking with enthusiasm, his sentiments were noble, great and generous—in short, on a level with his genius. But in the prosaic moments of life, his sentiments seemed to me most commonplace. They contained much petty vanity, a continual and puerile fear of appearing ridiculous, and sometimes, if I dare say so, some of that hypocrisy which the English call " cant ". It seemed to me that Lord Byron was always ready to make a compromise with prejudice in order to win praise.

One thing which especially struck the Italians was that it could easily be seen that this great poet was much more proud of being descended from the Byrons of Normandy who followed William during the conquest of England than of being the author of *Parisina* and *Lara*. I was so fortunate as to awaken his curiosity by giving him personal details concerning Napoleon and the retreat from Moscow, details that in 1816 were not yet generally known. This sort of feather in my cap earned me several *tête-à-tête* walks in the huge and empty foyer of the Scala. The great man made his appearance for half an hour every evening, and on these occasions I enjoyed the finest conversation I have ever encountered: a volcano of new ideas and generous feelings, so mixed together that one seemed to be learning his sentiments for the first time. For the rest of the evening the great man was so much an " Englishman and lord " that I could never resolve to accept the invitation to dinner with him which he had from time to time repeated. At this time he was composing *Childe Harold*: every morning he wrote a hundred lines, which in the evening he reduced to twenty or thirty. Between these two tasks he

---

[1] In English in the original.

needed rest, and he found this necessary distraction in chatting after dinner, with his elbows on the table and, it is said, with the most agreeable naturalness.

I noticed that, in his moments of genius, Lord Byron admired Napoleon, just as Napoleon himself admired Corneille. At ordinary times, when Lord Byron was thinking of himself as a great nobleman, he sought to cast ridicule upon the exile of St. Helena. He had a certain envy of the brilliant aspects of Napoleon's character: Napoleon's sublime sayings irritated him. We used to put him out of humour by reminding him of the famous words addressed to the Army of Egypt: " Soldiers, remember that from the top of these pyramids forty centuries are looking down upon you! " Lord Byron would have found it easier to forgive Napoleon if he had had the slightly dull look of Washington. The amusing thing was that it was not at all the despotic side of Napoleon's character that offended the English peer.

One evening, as Lord Byron was doing me the honour of walking with me in the foyer of the Scala, he was informed that the Austrian officer of the guard at the theatre had just arrested his secretary, Mr. Polidori, a physician who attended upon him. Lord Byron's face at once took on a striking resemblance to that of Napoleon when he was angry. Seven or eight people accompanied him to the guard-room, where he was magnificent in his restrained indignation and energy, for the hour's duration of the vulgar anger of the officer of the guard. When we were back in M. de Brême's box, we began praising the aristocratic principle, which as a rule was much to my lord's taste. He was aware of the jest, and left the box in fury, but without ever departing from a tone of perfect politeness. Next day the secretary was compelled to leave Milan.

Shortly after this, M. de Brême persuaded me to take Lord Byron to the museum at Brera. I admired the depth of feeling with which this great poet understood the most opposite sorts of painter: Raphael, Guercino, Luini, Titian, etc. Guercino's *Agar dismissed by Abraham* electrified him. From this moment we were all struck dumb with admiration: he improvised for an hour—and better, in my opinion, than madame de Staël.

What struck me most in this singular man, especially when he spoke ill of Napoleon, was that, in my opinion at least, he had no real experience of men. His pride, his rank, his fame had prevented him from ever dealing with them on equal terms. His haughtiness and distrust had always kept them at too great a distance for him to be able to observe them; he was too much accustomed to refuse to undertake anything that he could not carry off with a high hand. On the other hand, one admired his host of subtle and accurate ideas if one happened to converse with him concerning the women whom he knew—whom he knew, it may be added, because he had felt a need to charm and deceive them. He felt sorry for the Englishwomen in Geneva, Neuchâtel, etc. One weakness in Lord Byron's genius was that he had never been obliged to negotiate and argue with equals. I am convinced that, if he had returned from Greece, his talents would have seemed to be suddenly increased by a half. In his endeavour to make peace between Mavrocordato and Colocotroni he would have acquired positive knowledge of the human heart. Perhaps, in that case, Lord Byron would have been able to rise to the heights of real tragedy.

He would have had fewer moments of misanthropy; he would not have continually thought that all around him were concerning themselves with him, and doing so to create envy or to endeavour to deceive him. The great man's fundamental misanthropy had been embittered by English society. His friends used to notice that the more he lived with Italians, the happier and kindlier he became. If one substitutes black ill humour for outbursts of childish bad temper, one finds that Lord Byron's character had strikingly much in common with that of Voltaire.

But I shall now stop, in order not to write a dissertation. I ask your pardon, madame, for these general reflections—I would much rather have been able to replace them with facts. An interval of seven or eight years has banished these from my memory, and all I can find in it, concerning Lord Byron, are the conclusions that I drew at the time from the facts themselves. I shall think myself most happy, madame, if you will be so good as graciously to accept this kind of moral portrait, and to see, in these pages written in haste, a mark of the deep respect with which I have the honour to be, etc.

H. BEYLE.

———— 122 ————

MEMORIES OF LORD BYRON[1]

I can speak freely, for all the friends I shall mention are either dead or in fetters. My words can do the prisoners no harm, and, indeed, nothing that is true could harm these noble and courageous souls.

[1] Here, as an appendix to the preceding letter, is a complementary fragment of a letter published by Colomb as having been sent to him by Beyle and dated August 24th, 1829.

Nor do I any longer fear the reproaches of my friends who are dead. Long oppressed as they are by the harsh oblivion that follows upon death, man's natural desire not to be forgotten by the "world of the living" would make them lend an ear with pleasure to the voice of a friend pronouncing their names. In order to be worthy of them, the voice of this friend will say nothing false, nothing in the least exaggerated.

M. le marquis de Brême, a Piedmontese nobleman, very rich and very noble, who perhaps is still alive, was Minister of the Interior at Milan at the time when Napoleon was King of Italy. After 1814, M. de Brême had found the weathercock's trade unworthy of his birth, and had retired to his estates, leaving his palace in Milan to one of his younger sons, "Monsignore" Ludovic de Brême.

This latter was a very tall, very thin young man, already suffering from the malady of the chest that sent him to his grave a few years later. He was called "monsignore" because he had been almoner to the King of Italy whom his father had served as Minister of the Interior. At the time when his family was in favour, he had refused the bishopric of Mantua. M. Louis de Brême was haughty, learned and polite. His sad, slender figure resembled those statues in white marble that one sees in Italy on tombs of the eleventh century. I still seem to see him ascending the immense stairs of the old, sombre and magnificent palace of which his father had left him the use.

One day Monsignore de Brême hit on the idea of being taken to visit me by Signor Guasco, a young and very intelligent liberal. As I had neither palace nor title, I had refrained from calling upon M. de Brême. I was so pleased with the noble and polite tone prevailing in his circle that in a few days our acquaintance became intimate. M. de Brême was madly devoted to Madame de Staël, and later on we quarrelled because one evening, at the Scala, in his father's box, I claimed that Mme de Staël's *Considerations sur la Revolution Française* teemed with errors. Every evening this box belonging to M. de Brême brought together eight or ten remarkable men: one scarcely listened even to the striking parts of the opera, and conversation never ceased to flow.

One evening in the autumn of 1812, I entered M. de Brême's box on my return from an excursion on Lake Como. I found that the gathering had a sort of solemn and awkward air: everybody was silent. I was listening to the music, when M. de Brême said to me, indicating my neighbour: "Monsieur Beyle, this is Lord Byron." He turned to Lord Byron and repeated the same formula. I beheld a young man with magnificent eyes that had something generous about them: he was quite short. At that time I was mad about *Lara*. From the second glance,

I no longer saw Lord Byron as he really was, but as I thought the author of *Lara* should be. Since the conversation had languished, M. de Brême sought to make me speak. This was impossible for me: I was filled with timidity and affection: if I had dared, I would have burst into tears and kissed Lord Byron's hand. Pursued by M. de Brême's questioning, I tried to speak, and uttered only commonplaces, which were of no help against the silence which this evening prevailed amongst the circle. Finally Lord Byron asked me, as the only one who knew English, to tell him the names of the streets that he would have to pass through on the way back to his inn. It was at the other end of the town, near the fortress. I saw that he would go astray: in that part of Milan, at midnight, all the shops were closed. He would wander amidst empty and ill-lit streets, and without knowing a word of the language! In my devoted affection I was so foolish as to advise him to take a carriage. At once a shade of haughtiness passed over his face: he gave me to understand, with all necessary politeness, that what he wanted of me was the names of the streets, and not advice as to how to use them. He left the box, and I understood why he had reduced it to silence.

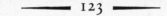

123

TO MESSIEURS THE MEMBERS OF THE ACADÉMIE FRANÇAISE

Paris, the ——— 1824

Monsieur,

It is my intention, perhaps a bold one, to solicit your vote for my admission to the Académie française. I propose to take this liberty in approximately the year 1843. By that time I shall be sixty years of age, and the Académie will probably no longer number amongst its members several gentlemen who are very honest, very estimable and very amiable, but seem to me, perhaps wrongly, not to be judges of literature.

A physician of experience writes a monograph on fever. Nearing the end of a troubled youth, an idler has endeavoured to write a monograph on that malady from which everybody claims to have suffered, and which is called Love. The early pages are said to be obscure. The author would be happy if a superior man, whom perhaps it might scandalise, could reach the final pages of "L'Amour" and say to himself: "After the admission of MM. Such-an-one and Such-an-One, I shall give my vote to this man."

He is, with respect,

B ——

author of the *Vie de Rossini*

—— 124 ——

TO HIS SISTER PAULINE

21st of March 1825

. . . *Meta parere meta danaro*[1], say the Italians. Since Dominique could give you only *pareri*, he has not written to you. I am astonished at Joséphine's[2] degree of malevolence. You must have made her jealous. Since you are under obligations to her, I advise you not to speak serious ill of her. I never spoke to her about the trip to Italy, since I desired no responsibility for such an obstinate person. While I'm on the subject of obstinacy, I have something to say to *you*. If I had any fortune, you could fold your arms and forget yourself as you did at M. Lorr—'s. You know that this is not so. In view of the fact that: (1) climate is the treasure of people in ill health and people with little riches; (2) neither you nor Dominique has the necessary spirit of intrigue which is indispensable in Paris; (3) in the country of the blind the one-eyed man is king—in view of all this, I advise you to find a post as teacher at some good convent at Rome or Naples, laying out the sum of eighty louis as a pledge of good conduct. If fortune ever smiles upon me, I shall get you out of it. When one is not rich, one must work, and not bay for the moon. What do you do in Paris? Your true task is to find a task. Endeavour to reflect a little, and to understand the aforesaid three considerations.

Ever thine,

B.

[1] Half-advice is half-money.
[2] Mme Bazire de Longueville, with whom Pauline travelled in Italy. (Cf. letter no. 119.)

TO M. X

Paris, the ——— of April 1825[1]

Monsieur,

I would be obliged to you if you did not print this letter. I thank you heartily for the civil article you published on *Racine et Shakspeare*. I could wish it had contained more criticisms.

I am not the author of the letters from *Classique*. The local post really did carry these letters, at the end of April 1824. I mentioned this in the note on page 50.

I made a point of changing nothing in the letters of the man, of very good society, who was so kind as to write to me. I confess that I would not have expressed myself as he did on the subject of M. de Lamartine. I find genuine talent, not in M. Hugo's prose, but in his verse. My classical correspondent being a man of the Old Régime, I respected his taste regarding anything to do with pleasantry. Today I am vexed that I did so, for I attach great importance to politeness.

I consider, Monsieur, that you are illogical in reproaching me for having quoted the *Pandore* instead of the *Miroir*. First of all, this note was by *Classique*. Even had it been by me, would it not have been a somewhat admirable feat of memory to recall, after a year's interval, a particular issue of a small journal? The essential thing is that the fact recorded is true. I do not think it impolite to call another man's work " detestable ". Every man who publishes is soliciting praise and must expose himself to catcalls. For my part, I desire the whole truth and the most " acid " truth.

I do not know by sight any of the people I have named. I should be in despair at having been impolite. If the pamphlet on Racine and Shakspeare goes into a second edition, I shall suppress any remarks by *Classique* that MM. Hugo and de Lamartine might regard as discourtesies.

. . . It seems to me that French literature is becoming atrophied by articles full of either " obligingness " or " insults ". I wish for the severest criticism and the whole truth. If I am persuaded that I have faults, I will correct them. I often re-read M. de Lamartine's *Méditations*. I have read M. Hugo's *Odes*.

[1] *Racine et Shakspeare II* had just appeared.

I would be in despair at having been impolite towards men of letters of this calibre, or indeed towards anybody. I beg you not to speak of my letters, and to believe me, Monsieur, your very humble and obedient servant,

STENDHAL.

—— 126 ——

TO THE BARON DE MARESTE

Paris, the 21st of August 1825

My dear fellow, la Giuditta[1], as you know, claims to be proof against love-letters: let us test her. Here is a letter that I beseech you to have copied out on handsome vellum. A lover like M. Edmond de Charency does not neglect such accessories.

Do you, too, compose a letter: if this one does not succeed, we will launch the second. But it must carry an address. Give it that of our friend, Porte, under a fictitious name; but she has heard speak of Porte. Seek for a name that is unknown. For example, if you were to put: " M. de Charency, chez M. Dubouchage, rue Neuve-du-Luxembourg, no. —." In any case, if we want to amuse ourselves and have a laugh, we must take steps. What do you think of my discreet restraint? It is only in the second letter that I shall ask her to send me a leaf of jasmine by way of reply. Don't forget that we must have Viago to Rheims, instead of Viaggio.

If the thing took, we would have a good laugh together.

If all went well, we would look for a handsome young man amongst our friends, and say to him: " Would you care to play the rôle of enamoured swain to a celebrated woman? But you will have to be devilish discreet."

PORCHERON.

[1] Signora Pasta.

TO SIGNORA PASTA[1]

Paris, the 21st of August 1825

I am aware, madame, that what I am doing is ridiculous. For more than two months I have been telling myself how ridiculous—nay, how improper—it is for an unknown like myself to dare to write to a woman who is surrounded by fame and is, for a certainty, connected with the most amiable and gayest circles in France. For my part, I am an unknown, simple lieutenant in a cavalry regiment of the Guard. I arrived here recently, with an allowance from my father; I am not handsome, without, however, being ugly. Before I had the happiness of seeing you—before I entered upon that new life which began for me on the day when you played the *Viago à Reims*, I believed myself to be a man well enough made, striking, with an air of nobility. Since then, I can see nothing of that. Everything in my nature is vulgar, except the frenzied passion that you have inspired in me. But what boots it to tell you this? I am aware that what I am doing is ridiculous: you will show my letter to people who will mock at me for it. Ah, what a freak of wretchedness, to hear my passion for Signora Pasta made a mock of! I swear to you, madame, that what I fear is not the ridicule it may bring upon me. For you I would brave far worse perils. But I would die of grief to hear my feeling for you spoken of. This feeling is my life: I am learning music, I am learning Italian, I read newspapers which before seeing you I never looked at, in the hope of finding your name in them. Even if it be at the bottom of a page, as soon as I turn to this page my eye immediately falls on the capital P which begins your name, and which makes me tremble even when it is the beginning of some completely indifferent word.

But what boots it to tell you of all my follies? What shall I gain by it? How am I to be known by you? How to be introduced? I am known a little in a few ancient drawing-rooms—but I suppose they have no connections with you? I visit M. le duc de—, but do *you* visit there? Ah, madame, I am very wretched! You cannot conceive of my exceeding wretchedness! For twenty years I longed to come to Paris, I was fond of horses, I adored the Army. Today all that is my torture.

How to become known to you? When you were in Paris, I used to

[1] Letter enclosed with the preceding.

station myself in a carriage, as if I were waiting for a friend, and would gaze at your windows. You are in the country, I am told, but the porter would not tell me whereabouts in the country. I fear I frightened the man. Ah, I shrink from myself in abhorrence! Nay, for a certainty, if I gained the happiness of being presented to you, I would terrify you.

I was obliged to interrupt this letter, I was too miserable . . . I am twenty-six years old, brown-haired, fairly tall, and am said to have a very military air: but, after what happened to me with your porter, I have clipped my moustaches as short as possible. But for regimental orders I would have cut them off entirely. Ah, if ever I have the happiness to be introduced to you, I pray that at least you will not be frightened by my distraught manner. Do not fear that I shall importune you, madame. I shall never speak to you of my unhappy passion: it would be enough for me to see you. I should only say to you: " I am Charency " —idiot that I am! You would have heard my name when I was intro- duced to you. But I want to go on telling you of myself. I am of a good family in Lorraine; one day I am due to have a competence; I have had an excellent education. Ah, Heaven! if they had had the idea of sending me to Italy, I would know Italian, and, above all, I would know music. Perhaps—but I think it impossible—if I had a scholar's understanding of the divine arias you sing, I would love you still more: but no, that seems impossible.

Farewell, madame, this letter is certainly too long: besides, what boots it to write to you?

I am, with the deepest respect, madame, your very humble and obedient servant,

Edmond de CHARENCY.

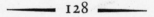

128

TO PROSPER MÉRIMÉE

Paris, the 23rd of December 1826

There are many more impotent men than is generally supposed. A woman whom you will see on Monday has an Olivier[1]. In the charming little fragment of the *Mémoires de la Duchesse de Brancas*, published by

[1] The duchesse de Duras was supposed to have written a novel bearing this title. She did not publish it, as the theme was scabrous. Thereupon La Touche played the hoax of publish- ing a novel under the same title, and this novel was attributed to Mme de Duras. This prob- ably gave Stendhal the idea of writing *Armance*. (Note by M. Martineau.)

the late duc de Lauraguais, which de Mareste will lend you, there are two impotents, *viz.*: M. de Maurepas, the Minister, and M. le marquis de la Tournelle, the first husband of the duchesse de Chateauroux. I have also studied Swift in Sir Walter Scott's *Lives of the Novelists*.

I chose the name Olivier, without thinking what I was doing, because of the challenge. I retain it because this is the only name that is *explanatory* without being indecent. If I said Edmond or Paul, many people would fail to recognise the fact of *Babilanismo* (an Italian word for M. Maurepas's condition). I want to awaken interest in Olivier, to give a live depiction of him[1]. The dénouement that you suggest, Lord Seymour's surprise, etc., is characteristic of your fine instincts for drama; but, after all, my poor Olivier is odious. Wiseacres will say: " What the devil! When one is a *babilano*, one does not marry. Olivier is about to embarrass his wife and Lord Seymour. Farewell and a pleasant journey to him! "

Babilanismo makes a man timid, else the best thing would be to confess to it. That Monday-night husband, M. de Maurepas, and M. de la Tournelle both did so. M. de la Tournelle died in despair and madly in love with his wife. Olivier, like all *babilani*, is very good at all the auxiliary methods which are the glory of the " Président ". A clever hand, an officious tongue, gave Armance keen pleasures. I am sure that many young women do not know exactly what physical marriage is.

I am equally sure of the second case, which is much more frequent. The consummation of marriage is odious to many young women *for three or four years*, especially when they are tall, pale, slender and blessed with a fashionable figure. It is true that I modelled Armance upon the lady companion of the mistress of M. de Stroganoff, who last year was always at the Bouffes.

I have, like you, the greatest scruples concerning the letter written by the Commandeur. But I must have some small reason for preventing Olivier from confessing. My experience has taught me that a modest young woman much prefers to put her letters in a hiding-place than to hand them directly to her lover. She dares not even look at her lover when she knows that he has just read the letter she wrote.

The name of my village is " Malivert ". " Bonnivet " was the name of François I's favourite admiral. If he had had offspring, Bonnivet would be very like Montmorency, and better than Luynes or Sully.

The novel is too *erudito*, too learned. Is it spicy enough to keep a pretty French marquise awake until two o'clock in the morning? *That is the question*[2]. This is what I felt on receiving your letter. Madame

---

[1] This is the hero of *Armance*, who was finally called Octave.
[2] In English in the original.

d'Aumale is Mme de Castries, whom I have depicted as chaste. But I return to the question of spice, of which you say nothing. Is that a bad sign? If the novel is not of such a nature as to while away a night, what is the use of writing it?

Would a young woman be interested in Olivier?

I have to write a love-scene. Armance will reveal that she is in love. If Olivier killed himself because of this accident, he would be infringing upon the character of " the cuckold ": he would turn into Meinau, from *Misanthropy and Remorse*[1].

The true *babilano* should kill himself to avoid the embarrassment of confessing. For my part (at the age of forty-three years and eleven months), I would make a frank confession: I would simply be told: " What matter ? " I would take my wife to Rome, where, for a sequin, a handsome peasant would pay her three compliments in a night.

But this truth is one of those which painting " in black and white "— painting through the medium of the spectator's imagination—cannot depict. How many true things are beyond the means of art! For example, love inspired by a man without arms or legs, like that infamous caricature that disgraces your desk.

It seems to me, therefore, that the *babilano* should not be cuckolded. The really fine cuckold is *Émile*, who married for love and reputation. Have you read that sequel to *Émile*? Dean Swift was unwilling to marry, because he did not want to confess. He finally did marry, on his mistress's solicitation, but he never saw her *en tête-à-tête*, either afterwards or before.

In the drawing-room of a count, a peer of France, a nobleman in 1500 and very rich, I am cold near the window when the wind is from the north. Your objection is derived from *probable truth*, my contention from *the study of nature*. Your objection would be perfect in England. I have read your letter again.

Even although Armance, going to bed with Olivier every night at Marseilles, might be " astonished ", nevertheless:

1. She adores him, and he gives her two or three ecstasies every night by hand.

2. Out of shyness and feminine modesty, she would not dare say anything.

But love alone suffices to explain all.

The style of depiction I employ, the black-on-white style, does not allow me to adhere to the truth. In 2826, if civilisation continues and I return to the rue Duphot, I shall report that Olivier bought a fine

---

[1] By Kotzebue.

Portuguese *godmiché*, of elastic rubber, which he fastened upon himself by a belt, and that with the said instrument, after giving his wife one complete ecstasy and one " almost complete " ecstasy, he bravely consummated his marriage in the rue de Paradis, Marseilles.

When one is a dreamer, a man of intelligence, a pupil of the Military Academy, like Olivier, this is what one does. " Giving ecstasies by hand "—what a fine periphrasis to avoid the dirty word! The object of Olivier's meditations: to give ecstasies, etc., was the object of Olivier's meditations throughout his youth. You must realise that he spent his boyhood with girls: I have tried modestly to indicate this. Armance tells him of this slander of which he is the victim.

But, in Heaven's name! answer me concerning " spice ". Keep my letter, we will perhaps discuss the matter again in 1828.

Comte de CHADEVELLE.

—— 129 ——

TO SUTTON SHARPE[1]

Versailles, the 7th of February 1827

We spoke of you at length at the Jardin[2]: you are popular, but people are anxious concerning certain *bonbons* sent to friends in London. Write and tell us whether you sent them. I said in your defence that you were in a turmoil of very important business.

The indiscretion committed by M. d'Apponyi[3], who sought to call the duc de Reggio " le duc Oudinot ", has caused the said duc, a person of courage, to go and ask the baron de Damas, the Minister for Foreign Affairs, whether the " king[4] " would be sorry to see a dead ambassador. He proposed to call upon M. d'Apponyi that same day. Before the end of the day the duc de Reggio received a letter from M. d'Apponyi addressed " to M. le duc de Reggio ".

M. d'Apponyi had discovered that the town from which the duke takes his title is Reggio *in Calabria* and not Reggio in Lombardy. M. d'Apponyi continues his approaches to M. Soult, duke of Dalmatia . . .

---

[1] An English lawyer who had numerous acquaintances in Paris and was part of the group of friends consisting of Beyle, Mérimée, Mareste, Delacroix, etc. He was to be encountered as a guest of the baron Gérard, Cuvier, Mme Ancelot or Signora Pasta.

[2] The Jardin du Roi. Sutton Sharpe was supposed at the time to be betrothed to the charming Sophie Duvaucel, Cuvier's stepdaughter.

[3] Austrian Ambassador.

[4] In English in the original.

You knew of that. But the true version is as follows—and I did not get it from any newspaper. The present ministers are openly spat upon in the Chamber of Peers. This Chamber has so thoroughly re-made the law governing juries that it is said the Minister will not present it to the Chamber of Deputies.

I have suffered a misfortune. You will see from the enclosed copy of a letter of the 2nd of February that Mr. Colburn is breaking off relations[1].

That extra source of income was very useful to me. Would you, on your return to Westminster, visit some friend and find out whether it is possible to establish a regular or irregular sale of articles once a month, once a fortnight or once a week? I am ready to start immediately.

I would prefer not to interrupt the series of reviews of which you know. They form a continuous narrative for people who are interested in the progress of Letters. *These articles are translated there and I hear with some applause, etc.*[2]

Tell all this to potential customers, if you succeed in finding any. The affair is a matter of necessity to me. Do not speak to anyone of it.

Ever yours,

OLD HUMMUMS[3].

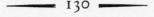 130

TO SUTTON SHARPE

From my château de B——,
the 30th of April 1827

. . . Do you realise that the greatest event that has occurred in France for twelve years was the fireworks of Wednesday the 18th of April[4]?

The people, which was believed to be dead and to have " handed in its papers ", to quote M. de Sémonville, has given signs of life—a thing that has frightened all the " rich liberals ". *I say nothing of the* " peur " *of one august person*[2]. It passes all belief. *I suppose they have sent twenty or thousand* frs. *to the* " Constitutionnel "[2], so that it may command *the*

[1] " An essential part of his means of livelihood consisted in payment for literary articles that he sent to England." (Note by Colomb.)

Henry Colburn was the editor and proprietor of the reviews that published Beyle's articles.

[2] In English in the original. (Certain articles that had first appeared, in English, in London, had been re-translated into French and published in Paris by the *Revue Britannique*.)

[3] In English in the original.

[4] On the occasion of the repeal of the law concerning the press which was nicknamed the " law of love ". (Note by Paupe.)

people to cry only[1]: Vive le *King*[1]. That *said Constitutionnel*[1] has earned its money. *The Débats*[2] *by fear of seeing the people living a second time, has made his utmost. However the third and the seventh*[1] Legions did not behave as well as we could have wished[2]. One man left the ranks of the Third Legion, presented arms *to the King*[1] and shouted: "Down with the Ministers!" Marshal Oudinot, duc de Reggio, pursued him sword in hand, shouting: "I must kill him!" The man fled: the Marshal (who is ceaselessly in need of money) ran after him, and was about to kill him when one of the aides-de-camp said to him: "Monsieur le Maréchal, the King asks for you immediately." The duc de Reggio let the man escape.

In the Seventh Legion a man broke ranks holding his musket in one hand and his white handkerchief in the other. He marched up *to the King*; *the horse of the King*[2] took fright and shied away six paces. The *King*[1] reined in his horse towards the National Guardsman who was shouting: "Down with the Ministers!" The *King*[1] said to him: "I came here to receive homage from my National Guard, not to be given advice. Break that man! I do not wish him to parade before me." ("Break" means "discharge".)

No newspapers reported these two incidents. The two hundred thousand spectators on the slope of the Champs-de-Mars were too far away to notice anything. This day was the sequel to the 18th. The people, which is very mild and very much at its ease, has obeyed its tribunes, the *Constitutionnel* and the *Courrier*.

An astonishing thing was the attire of the one hundred and fifty thousand spectators, who were remarkably well dressed. What a difference from the Federation in 1792! Instead of twenty millions, we are now thirty-two millions—a result of the partition of farmlands.

The people might have shown itself much more hostile. I cannot depict to you *the* "peur" *of the Court*[1]. The Third Legion, while passing beneath the windows of the Hotel-de-Ville, shouted: "Down with Villèle!" loudly enough to be heard from the château. I have spoken to twenty national guardsmen known to myself and my father-in-law: nothing could be more peaceable, timid and kindly than this *people*[1]; but nothing could be more fickle. Four articles in their newspapers can throw them into a rage. *Say all this to the*[1] Dr. Black. I saw Mr. Kean, an intelligent man: did he realise what was happening? That brute of a Mr. Colburn is taking no steps to pay what he owes me.

---

[1] All italicised words are in English in the original.
[2] At the general inspection of the National Guard performed by Charles X on April 29th. (Note by Paupe.)

I have written to[1] Mr. Jeffries, who will receive my letter on the 6th of May. If you have received two copies of a *Voyage to Rome*[1], give one to any *Reviewer*[1] who mentions it either favourably or ill, it is of little consequence: the bad thing is silence. I forgot to praise Mr. Justice Hullock and my expulsion from his country, with the result that I am told that I abhor *Old England*[1], than which nothing could be more false. I feel towards her as the late M. Jesus Christ felt towards mankind.

. . . .

———— 131 ————

TO SUTTON SHARPE

Rue d'Amboise, the 2nd of July 1827

My dear friend[1],

I gathered information concerning the person of whom you speak. About the 12th or 15th of July he will leave for Nyon on the Lake of Geneva, thence to Genoa by the Simplon. He will breathe the sweet air on the seashore at Chiavari, or else will embark for Leghorn and Florence, or else for Naples, Corfu or Palermo. He does not announce his plans, in order not to be tied: so do not speak of them to Mademoiselle Sophie[2] or to anyone else. The only certainty is his departure for the Lake of Geneva.

(I learnt all this from the wife of the person in question.)

I set no less store than you, my dear fellow, by the company I enjoyed at Lancaster. I *passionately* hope that you may be able to join the traveller: two hundred francs and ten days will bring you to Genoa. The steamboat[1] from Marseilles to Naples touches at Leghorn. Two or three feluccas— excellent for drowning oneself like Mr. Shelley—leave Genoa daily for Leghorn, thirty-six hours and twelve francs. From Leghorn to Naples the steamboat takes four days, I think: it costs one hundred and twenty francs. If one is obliged to wait at Leghorn, ten hours and ten francs bring you to Florence or to the baths of Lucca. You return from Lucca or Florence in time for the departure of the steamboat, the date of which is known in advance.

Say nothing to a living soul: I have said nothing to Mareste.

On the 30th of June, Mlle Sophie, her sister, her mother and I went

[1] In English in the original. *Rome, Naples et Florence.*
[2] Sophie Duvaucel.

by the Seine steamboat to *Villeneuve-Saint-George*, to meet La Girafe. Mlle Sophie told me you had written that you were counting the days until your journey to France. In French, to " count the days " means that you are within a fortnight, at most, of a given event. I wish you knew the language perfectly: if so, we could expect you for the 20th of July at latest. The strict sense of your words would mean that you will be here between the 5th and the 10th: I dare not believe it.

By the way, that demi-rogue of a Colburn is not paying up. *If it is not beneath your dignity*, pay him a passing visit. If he paid eight hundred francs for January, and four hundred plus two hundred for the months of March, April, etc., when he used fragments *saved over* from my previous letters (he informed me in October that I was sending too little), I could devour the eight hundred or one thousand two hundred at Palermo or Corfu, to excellent purpose.

Since I am bored by the prospect of having to reply to all *foolish queries*[1] concerning the journey, I have spoken of it to nobody. If I am lucky enough to tempt you, procure letters of introduction. I know nobody at Naples. After that, the Mediterranean might repay a visit in September, in the direction of Corfu. An introduction to some Englishmen attached to the government of the Seven Isles can get you admitted on a vessel going to Athens or Constantinople. In short, never could letters of introduction be more useful.

CORNICHON.

—— 132 ——

TO SUTTON SHARPE

Leghorn, the 14th of August, 1827

My dear brother[1],

I shall write in French in order to show you that I know something of the language.

The last year[2], on this day, I was with you. I can tell you without any exaggeration that I would much rather have been with you this year,

---

[1] In English in the original.
[2] In English in the original. " I shuddered as I thought of the 15th of September 1826, at San Remo,* on my return from England. What a year I spent from the 15th of September 1826 to the 15th of September 1827! On the day of this formidable anniversary I was on the island of Ischia. No woman's departure ever caused me so much grief as Clémentine's." (*Vie de Henri Brulard.*)

* Anagram of Saint-Omer. General the comte Curial commanded the camp at Saint-Omer, where Beyle probably stopped on his way back from London.

too. I have been a guest of honour in the best Genoese society, at the house of the amiable marchese *di Negro*, Genoa's Joseph Bank, but more cheerful. In the great heat—which was, however, only twenty-three degrees Réaumur—on the 4th of August, I dined under a charming grotto, in a garden, with a view of the sea, intelligent people and pretty women. I wished you were there. This evening I leave for Naples. But, in truth, I cannot tell you how long I shall stay there. That depends on the state of exhaustion of my purse. If Colburn consented to pay the one thousand two hundred francs he owes, I would devour them at Naples. But none are so deaf as those who do not wish to hear. If by any chance he pays, I shall devour the money at the foot of Vesuvius, and I would do so with greater enjoyment if I were with you.

In order to bind you to the journey, I shall tell you that the heat is very moderate—twenty-three degrees Réaumur. This means that about the 15th of September it will be endurable, even for an inhabitant of Ultima Thule, unrivalled for its justice, its Navy, etc.

Everybody tells me I am an enemy of the English, so that is why I hasten to apply this poultice. In any case, I don't care a d-mn for the world and what it thinks; I am happy as soon as I am taking coffee within three paces of a pretty Italian woman—even though, between her and me there happened to be three successful suitors, each one a foot thick.

. . . .

ROBERT BEYLE.

──── 133 ────

TO THE BARON DE MARESTE AND TO
ROMAIN COLOMB[1]

Florence, the 19th of November 1827

"Above all, when you write to M. de Mareste, do not fail to tell him how often we think of him. He used often to come and spend the early evening with us at Paris."

[1] " My cousin Colomb (a man of integrity, just and reasonable, my childhood's friend)." (*Souvenirs d'Égotisme.*)
" My friends at this time, MM. de Mareste and Colomb, were friends of a singular sort: they would certainly have taken active measures to save me from any great danger; but, if I went out in a new coat, they would have given twenty francs, especially the former, to have somebody throw a glass of dirty water over me." (*Vie de Henri Brulard.*)

[250]

This is what madame de Lamartine was saying to me yesterday.

The husband[1] desired to see me, and I find him very friendly and as admirable as ever . . .[2]

Nothing could be more magnificent than the balls given by the Principe Borghese: he has thirty-five great rooms on one floor, furnished with unsurpassed freshness and taste. At his last soirée dansante there were quite eighty Englishwomen, also three Italian women, the Signore Ruccellai, always sprightly and charming, and Nencini, who is still well, and . . .

What I have enjoyed best since leaving you was a sea-journey of twelve days, which I underwent without any resulting sea-sickness. I saw Porto Ferraio for two days, Capo d'Anzo, etc. I spent ten days lodging with a peasant of Casamiccia, on the island of Ischia: I owe the idea to 🜍 [3]: thank him on my behalf. The place is delightful.

Every morning I went to Forio or Ischia, by donkey. I spent a month at Naples and three weeks at Rome. M. de Laval used me with the utmost kindness.

Thank M. Delécluze for the pleasure I got from his two articles on Signor Manzoni: I knew this great poet at Genoa.

. . . .

[1] In English in the original.

[2] " I had an intimate association, going back to my early years, a spiritual kinship (which still exists and grows closer) with one of Beyle's most intimate friends, M. de Mareste . . ."

" Mareste, however, had agreed to give Beyle a letter of introduction for me : he came to see me."

" . . . I was lodging in a suburb of the town. Every evening, before or after dinner, Beyle used to come. We would throw a bunch of fragrant myrtle on the fire and would talk with the mutual trust that solitude and truthfulness inspire in men. I inoculated him with a few doubts of his own incredulity, whilst he, for his part, greatly enlightened my ignorance on matters of music, art and poetry." (Lamartine.)

" How could M. de Lamartine be a judge of wit? In the first place, he has none; and, in the second place, he is still devouring two volumes a day of the dullest works. (Seen at Florence.)" (*Vie de Henri Brulard.*)

[3] The amiable and witty Signor di Fiore, of Naples, resident in Paris since 1800. (Note by Colomb.)

TO SUTTON SHARPE

Paris, rue Richelieu, no. 71,
the 23rd of March 1828

My dear fellow, I waited for you at Florence. If ever you go to Italy, you will find some letters, of no consequence, poste restante. My journey occupied six and a half months. I spent a delicious fortnight on the island of Ischia, near Naples. I saw Ferrara, which I had never seen! I was much moved by Tasso's prison. Lord Byron had himself shut up there for two hours: he kept on knocking his forehead, the present custodian told me. But what put it into my head to mention this dungeon? I saw Mr. Roger's name written on the wall to the left. Pay my respects to your uncles and your aunt. Have you received a novel entitled *Armance?* All my friends think it detestable: for my part, I think *them* coarse brutes. It deals with the greatest of the "impossibilities" of love. The hero, Octave, is *impotens*.

. . . Signora Speroni's concerts are divine, and Señora Malibran Garcia, whom you know, will be the world's leading singer, unless she overworks her high notes, which she will wear out. Her forte is in her lower ones.

A thousand greetings to the sublime Giuditta, also to dear Micheroux. Give me news of these pleasant people. Do not forget me with Signor Pasta and Madame ———.

This letter is cursory and superficial. For the ten months I have been in Paris, I have had time for nothing, *auri sacra fames* has kept me still writing for that rascal of a Colburn. My friend M. Stricht, who is in London, has made an arrangement of £150 *per annum* for short articles in a journal called *Athenaeum* and an article in the *New Monthly*. It is all too frequent, I feel harassed. And that rascal says nothing of paying me the one thousand francs owed for February, 1827.

Since there are all kinds of people in the world, even an honest publisher—if chance ever brought you in contact with such a phoenix and you could make an arrangement for me, I would gladly leave Colburn, whose ear has to be tweaked to make him pay once every three months. O that I could tweak both his ears as I would wish!

TO VIOLLET-LE-DUC

Divisional Head in the Royal Household[1]
17th of November 1828[2]

Dear and obliging friend,

. . . Delécluze is invisible this year, but if *you* are visible on Friday, I shall have the honour of paying my court to Mme Leduc. Will you be going to the Académie on Thursday? M. de Barante is bound to say unpleasant things about the late M. de Robespierre, who has no ribbons to hand out.

My devotion to you is as great as if your hands were full of them!

H. BEYLE.

TO PROSPER MÉRIMÉE

*Paris, the 26th of December 1828, at five
o'clock in the evening, without a candle*

This evening, of the 26th, there are new operas at Milan, Naples, Venice, Genoa, etc., and the thought drives me wild.

Jealousy does not kill love except in a chilly, forty-year-old heart that has begun to despair. This jealousy is engraving your name for ever in the heart of de M. Its crystallisation may be slow: you can alter its rate of development by six months (plus or minus), by saying to her: "For three years I have worshipped you, but I have an income of only seventeen hundred francs, and I cannot marry you. I have no wish to die a madman." No more nor less. Leave the development to her heart.

These words happily serve as transition to my next point: have you put too much "development" into your novel[3]?

---

[1] Beyle was an assiduous visitor to Viollet-le-Duc's receptions. The addressee of this letter was Étienne Delécluze's brother-in-law and the father of the architect.

[2] The date of this letter had been determined by the allusion to the speech by M. de Barante. M. de Barante was received into the Académie française on November 20th, 1828: he pronounced the eulogy on his predecessor, the comte de Sèze. (Note by Stryienski.)

[3] *La Chronique du Règne de Charles IX.*

I think you would be *greater*, but a little less known, if you had not published the *Jacquerie* and the *Guzla*, which are much inferior to *Clara Gazul*. But how the devil could you have known that? As for fame, a work is a ticket in a lottery. *Africa* is forgotten and Petrarch is immortal only for his sonnets[1]: the thing for us to do, therefore, is to write a lot. In any case, to judge by the exercise practised by our friend Sand, a poor devil's main pleasure is to write.

What will you do with a thousand francs? Will you go to Naples? Perhaps you will. Will you go to Meudon?

Unless you are pressed for money, forget the novel for a year. After that you will be able to judge of it. For my part, at least, after six months I have forgotten it entirely. Admittedly, there is more than one duke who would be glad to make himself a name for a thousand francs. More than one respectable woman would be glad to be keeping her fourth assignation with you. But where are you to find the broker for such a transaction?

If you intend to devour a thousand francs without delay, read your novel aloud to me—for, like Courier, I cannot judge it by the manuscript. I shall listen to it with pleasure from seven o'clock in the evening until midnight, in two or three sittings.

I would be very severe on your style, which I find somewhat " below stairs ". *J'ai eu du mal à faire*," etc., for: J'ai eu de la peine à faire, etc.

The only literary men I consider as such are you and M. Janin, author of the Dialogue between Don Miguel and Napoleon. (*Figaro* of the 19th or 20th of December.)

If you like, I will bring you together with M. Janin. This will parry the thrust of the *Figaro*. But, in my opinion, the great men of the *Globe* are jealous of you. I often sense in you the same manner of reasoning as in Maisonnette—i.e., a pretty phrase instead of an argument, i.e. the failure to have read Montesquieu and de Tracy plus Helvétius. You are afraid of being " long-winded ".

It all smacks of the " light-comedy " taste of 1829.

You and I, or you alone, will never be able to sink below the level of the piece you mention. What prudence! 'Tis there that you will find payments of a thousand francs, and you will not run a quarter of the risk to which your novel will expose you. If it is not superior to the *Jacquerie*, you will have a fall.

[1] " I always regard my works as tickets in a lottery. I do not expect to be reprinted before 1900. Petrarch relied upon his Latin poem, *Africa*, and scarcely thought about his sonnets." (*Souvenirs d'Égotisme.*)
" I am taking a ticket in a lottery in which the biggest prize comes down to this: to be read in 1935." (*Vie de Henri Brulard.*)

It often seems to me that you do not show sufficient *delicate tenderness*.
And a novel must have this to move me.

CHOPPIN.

—— 137 ——

TO MME GAULTHIER[1]

Paris, Thursday, the 5th of February 1829

. . . M. Victor Hugo is not an ordinary man, but he *seeks* to be extraordinary, and the *Orientales* bore me: do they bore you?

COTTONET.

—— 138 ——

TO THE BARON DE MARESTE

Paris, 5th of March 1829

Since that Firmin Didot does not answer, I must try to come to an
arrangement with M. Delaunay. But at what price? A thousand francs
down, and a note for eight hundred or six hundred.

Since Colburn does not pay, I must sell, even at a loss. So, when your
affairs permit, speak to M. Delaunay.

The paper used for *Rome, Naples, etc.* is uglier than that of any contemporary published work. M. Delaunay was ashamed of it and told me
that he had been cheated. He should be made to promise to use a paper
like that of some particular volume in his shop. If he had spent a hundred
francs on three advertisements of twenty lines each, *Rome, Naples, etc.*
would be sold out. 'Tis a great disadvantage. M. Delaunay is rich enough
to afford to be idle and refrain from advertising, but it spells ruin for the
author. I would prefer to sell a fourth edition of *Rome, Naples, etc.* than
to sell the *Promenades* at a loss[2].

All that is unimportant. The thing is to sell, and to get a thousand
francs down.

. . . .

CHAMPION.

[1] Mme Gaulthier, née Sophie-Jules Rougier de la Bergerie, belonged to a family from the
Dauphiné. Beyle had been introduced to the demoiselles La Bergerie by Crozet, who was in
love with the elder, Blanche. A loving, affectionate and faithful friendship sprang up between
the younger, " the adorable Jules ", and Beyle.

[2] *Promenades dans Rome.*

[255]

TO DAVID D'ANGERS

Paris, 24th of July 1829

Dear and obliging friend—you who will give me life after my death—
if you are putting a name on the medallion, put, in small characters,
Henri Beyle.

A thousand and one friendly greetings.

H. BEYLE.

TO SUTTON SHARPE[1]

Paris, the 18th of December 1829

Monsieur le philosophe,

I was born at la Nouvelle, near Narbonne. It is a small, straggling
village on the seashore, where all the inhabitants live by fishing. My father
was a fisherman and extremely poor: had two brothers. Regularly,
in summer, when our little boats returned fishing, father took off our
jackets and threw us into the sea. I had learnt to swim like a fish when,
during the last days of the Empire, I was carried off by the conscription.
In 1816 I left the Army of the Loire and returned to la Nouvelle, with
empty pockets and rather uneasy about my future. I found that my
father, brothers, mother, everybody was dead. But a week later one of
my great-uncles arrived, a man who for forty years had been believed
dead. He had made millions in the British Indies, and he gave me an
allowance of three thousand francs a year, paid with great regularity.

I lived alone in Paris, not having the talent for making friends. Like
all compelled solitaries, I read a lot.

Two days ago I was walking towards the pont d'Iéna, in the direction
of the champs de Mars. There was a high wind, the Seine was turbulent
and reminded me of the sea. My eyes followed a little boat, laden to the
gunwales with sand, which was trying to pass beneath the end arch on

---

[1] Letter written on the subject of a discussion with Duvergier de Hauranne on the motives
of human actions.

the other side of the Seine, near the quai des Bons-Hommes. Suddenly the boat capsized. I saw the boatman trying to swim, but he was making a poor fist of it. "The clumsy fellow will drown," I said to myself. I had some idea of jumping into the water; but I am forty-seven years old, and I have attacks of rheumatism: it was piercingly cold. "Somebody will jump in from the other side," I reflected. I watched, despite myself. The man came to the surface and shouted. I rapidly made myself scarce. "It would be crazy," I said to myself. "If I were nailed to my bed by an acute rheumatism, who would come to see me? Who would think of me? I should be left alone to die of boredom, like last year. Why did that silly brute become a sailor without knowing how to swim? Besides, his boat was overloaded." By this time I was perhaps already fifty paces from the Seine: I could still hear a shout from the drowning boatman, calling for help. I quickened my steps. "Devil take him!" I said to myself, and set about thinking of other matters. Suddenly I said to myself: "Lieutenant Louaut," (my name is Louaut) "you are a sh-t. In a quarter of an hour this man will be drowned, and all your life long you will hear his cry for help." "Sh-t! Sh-t!" said the side of prudence, "'tis easy to say that. What of the sixty-seven days when rheumatism kept you in your bed last year? Devil take him! A boatman should know how to swim." I walked very quickly towards the École militaire. Suddenly a voice said to me: "*Lieutenant Louaut, you are a coward!*" This word startled me. "Ah, *that* is serious!" I said to myself, and started running towards the Seine. When I reached the bank, it took but one movement to throw off my coat, boots and trousers. I was the happiest of men. "No, Louaut is no coward! Not a bit of it!" I said to myself aloud. The upshot was, I saved the man, who would have drowned but for me. I had him carried to a warm bed, where he soon regained speech. Then I began to be frightened on my own account. I had myself, in turn, installed in a well-heated bed, and had my whole body rubbed with eau-de-vie and flannel. But in vain, it was of no avail, my rheumatism has come back—although, to tell the truth, it is not so acute as last year. I am not too badly ill: the devil of it is that, since nobody comes to see me, I am bored to tears. After thinking of marriage, as I always do when I am bored, I began thinking of the motives that caused me to perform "my heroic action", as the *Constitutionnel*, which reported the incident, was pleased to call it. (No. 350, of the 16th of December, 1829, at the top of the third page.)

What caused me to perform my fine action?—for "heroic" is certainly too strong. Upon my word, it was fear of contempt. It was that voice saying to me: "*Lieutenant Louaut, you are a coward.*" What startled me was that the voice addressed me in the second person plural. "*Vous*" are a coward! As soon as I had realised that I could save the poor clumsy fellow, it became my *duty* to do so. Had I not jumped into the water, I would have despised myself, just as I did at Brienne (in 1814) when my captain said to me: "Forward, Louaut! Mount the embankment!" and I amused myself by staying down below. This, monsieur, is the story—or, rather, the "analysis"—for which you asked me, etc., etc., etc.

JUSTIN LOUAUT.

—— 141 ——

TO SUTTON SHARPE

Versailles, the 10*th of January* 1830

. . . *Hernani*, a tragedy by M. Victor Hugo, a bad imitation of the *two gentlemen of Verona* and other pieces in this style by the divine Shakspeare, will cause a battle royal at the Théâtre Français, about the 6th of February[1].

. . . .

—— 142 ——

TO SOPHIE DUVAUCEL[2]

January, 1830

. . . Here's a story I heard yesterday evening:

The *King of Naples*[2] beats his servants. He is very strong, but he cannot walk and is more than half blind. While at Madrid, he let fall his handkerchief. His servant came up to him. At this the *King*[3] seized the man's ear with his left hand, and with his right hand gave him a drubbing.

"*Faro ricorso*" (I shall make a complaint), said the poor victim.

[1] "I want to ask you for stalls for some people who should be coming with me to the first performance of *Hernani*. 1, Beyle, one stall." (Mérimée to Hugo.)

[2] Daughter of the Taxfarmer-General Louis-Philippe Duvaucel, guillotined in 1794, and of Marie-Anne Coquet de Trayzayle, who later married Cuvier. She was pretty, and her friends considered her to be as witty as she was good-hearted. Beyle used to call her "my friend with a capital F".

[3] In English in the original.

"To whom, insolent fellow?"

"To that Madonna over there," said the servant, pointing to a picture by Velasquez.

"Come, now, here are six ounces (one hundred and sixty francs)," said the King in alarm. "Don't say anything to the Madonna."

Please accept my best regards.

Tombouctou.

—— 143 ——

TO SOPHIE DUVAUCEL

Sunday at 7 o'clock, 7th of March 1830

Mademoiselle,

After two hours of vast research in the ocean of my papers—a thing I would not have done for God the Father, even if he existed—here is Sir T. Lawrence[1]. It is seven o'clock and I am dying of hunger—which much curtails my eloquence. The man with the fish and the Etruscan pitcher—your favourite[2]—has had an article published this morning on Lord Byron. It contains more philosophy and true wit than 1830 issues of the *Globe*. I am forced to agree that this is so, despite the envy with which he inspires me because you think him so handsome. If you have not the *National*, I shall keep today's issue for you. Look for the story of the sublime brigand *Rondino*[3], in the issue that was prosecuted. It is exactly true to life. The man with the fish has, if anything, understated the beauty of Rondino's character. He has deprived him of a little of his dash.

So M. Chevreul has received an appointment. There's another conquest for *me* to attempt. How am I to set about it? Since yesterday evening my rustic tastes have kept me dreaming of the delights of a lodging on the Jardin, with a prospect of green trees even in the middle of winter[4]. But I shall never be dull enough to win favour with seven people out of thirteen. I would have to avoid making their acquaintance until the eve of the great day of the election. The most gentle of men, when they have been subjected to my acquaintance for six months, would give six francs to see me fall into a hole full of mud just as I was

---

[1] The painter Thomas Lawrence, who had recently died. His portrait of Sophie Duvaucel can be seen in the Louvre Museum.

[2] Mérimée.

[3] Mérimée's article.

[4] Beyle was thinking of seeking a post at the Royal Library.

preparing to enter a drawing-room[1]. Nevertheless, I hate nobody, and I adore Rossini, Napoleon, Lord Byron, all the men of intelligence with whom I have spoken.

—— 144 ——

TO SOPHIE DUVAUCEL

Paris, the 10th of March 1830

. . . Why should I not say it? I assure you, without flattery, that since Saturday I have thought several times how happy I would be to live in the neighbourhood of the bear Martin. When I am old I shall make friends with this grave personage, and, unless I come too much to resemble him, I shall appear every evening in your drawing-room, escorted by the likenesses that all my enemies have of me. For example: the Misses Garnett think me hump-backed. Essentially, I am thin, they say, but, since I am obliged to compensate for the hump by covering the rest of me with cushions, I appear elephantine. Signorina Arconati (whose family-name *Trotti* I despise: at Milan it is what Duclon or Irénilly is at Paris) says that I wear rouge. The fact is that all this gives me a headache.

Farewell, forgive my follies and accept my best respects.

H. BEYLE.

—— 145 ——

TO SOPHIE DUVAUCEL

23rd of March 1830

My weakness prostrates itself at your feet, mademoiselle. I am very comfortable there, for they are pretty feet, and, although you are on the side of virtue, you are not gloomy. On Saturday, at six o'clock, I shall appear in the Jardin des Plantes, to eat and not to speak. In other words, I shall not embarrass you, however stuffed with *cant*[2] my fellow-guests may be. It suits me very well to keep silent in future. 'Tis a crazy new

---

[1] Cf. letter no. 133, note 1.   [2] In English in the original.

French fashion. People are wrong, in my opinion, to think your humble servant amusing. But, after all, once the brute has been received under this definition, what could be more ridiculous than to find him likeable when he does not speak?

. . . .

H. BEYLE.

P.S.—Will the " great sneerers "[1] be able to have tickets for the 10th of April[2]? Will M. de Lamartine know how to write prose? A poor diplomat can speak of nothing, not even of the life of M. Daru. 'Tis said that he is being made Minister in Greece. So much the better: we shall go and see him there. Get married and come with the party. I shall dress myself up as Harlequin, with a slap-stick. I shall mock at everything that exists, and at many other things; and, however great your virtue, I shall make you smile. Have you read Hoffmann's " Cremona Violin "?

------ 146 ------

TO SAINTE-BEUVE

After having read the Consolations *for three and a half hours on end, the 26th of March 1830*

If there were a God, I should be very pleased, for he would reward me with his Paradise for having been an honest man, which I am.

Thus I should in no way alter my conduct, and I should be rewarded for doing exactly what I am doing.

One thing, however, would diminish the pleasure I take in pondering on the sweet tears that are shed for a noble deed: this idea of being *rewarded by payment,* by a Paradise.

This, Monsieur, is something that I would say to you in verse, if I could write it as well as you do. I am shocked that you people, who " believe in God ", should imagine that, because you have been in despair for three years at the desertion of a mistress, you ought to believe

[1] " Beyle was certainly the centre of those ironical spirits who awoke Mme Cuvier's distrust and whom Cuvier, in conversation with his stepdaughter, called " tes grands dégoutés ". (Note by M. Martineau.)

[2] Lamartine was elected by the Académie française to the chair of the comte Daru, and was received by Cuvier.

in God. As well might a Montmorency imagine that, in order to be brave on the field of battle, one must be called Montmorency.

I believe that you are destined, Monsieur, for the highest of literary careers, but I still find a certain amount of affectation in your verse. I could wish it were more like La Fontaine's. You speak too much of fame. One loves one's task, but Nelson (read his Life, by the abominable Southey) got himself killed only to become an English peer. Who the devil knows whether fame will accrue? Why, we have Diderot promising immortality to M. Falconnet, sculptor!

La Fontaine used to say to la Champmeslé: " We shall be famous— I for writing my verses, you for reciting them." He guessed aright. But why speak of such matters? Passion has its modesty: why reveal such intimacies? Why should names be mentioned? The whole thing smacks of trickery, of a " puff ".

This, Monsieur, is what I think, and all that I think. I believe that you will be spoken of in 1890. But you will write something better than the *Consolations*, something *stronger* and *purer*[1].

—— 147 ——

TO MME GAULTHIER

Paris, the 16*th of May* 1830 (*Saturday*)

The brute is original: the gods made him so.

. . . .

COTONET.

—— 148 ——

TO SUTTON SHARPE

Paris, 15*th of August* 1830—
71, *rue de Richelieu*

Your letter, my dear fellow, gave me the greatest pleasure. I have not written a line for ten days: this is my excuse for the delay in answering[2].

[1] Cf. letter no. 149.

[2] " I was enraptured by those July days: I saw the bullets striking the pillars of the Théâtre Français—very little danger to me. I shall never forget the lovely sunshine and the first sight of the tricolour." (*Vie de Henri Brulard*.)

Properly to enjoy the spectacle of this great Revolution, one must stroll on the boulevard. (By the way, there are no longer any trees between the rue de Choiseul and that hôtel Saint-Phar where we lodged for a few days on our arrival from London in 1826. They were cut down to make barricades on the road; but the shopkeepers too were glad to get rid of them. Have you in England not yet discovered the secret of transplanting trees as thick as your thigh? If you meet a man who knows in detail how to do this, get exact information. Bring us the means of restoring our boulevard.)

The further one gets from the "great week", as M. de la Fayette called it, the more astonishing it seems. It creates the same effect as colossal statues; or as mont Blanc, which is more sublime when seen from the slope of les Rousses, twenty leagues from Geneva, than when seen from its foot.

All that the newspapers have told you in praise of the people is true. On the 1st August the intriguers came on the scene: they are doing a certain amount of damage to our cause, but very little. The King is excellent: he has chosen two bad advisers, MM. Dupin, lawyer, who on the 27th of July, after having read the decrees of Charles X, declared that he "no longer regarded himself as a Deputy", and . . . After an interruption, I have decided to send you this scrap. Tomorrow I shall write to you again. A hundred thousand men have volunteered for the Paris national guard. That wonderful man La Fayette is the anchor of our liberty. Three hundred thousand men of twenty-five years would go to war with pleasure. Defended by the present enthusiasm, Paris would not yield to two hundred thousand Russians. I am scribbling down the mere superficial facts for you: people are waiting for me . . . We are all well. Unfortunately Mérimée is at Madrid: he has not seen this unique spectacle—on the 28th of July, for every well-dressed man there were a hundred without stockings or jacket. The lowest rabble was heroic, and after the battle was full of the noblest generosity.

P.S.—A second letter follows soon.

TO SAINTE-BEUVE

This 29th of September 1830,
71 rue de Richelieu

Monsieur,

I have this moment been assured that I am appointed consul at Trieste. 'Tis said that the scenery in this region is beautiful. The islands in the Adriatic are picturesque. My first consular act is to invite you to spend six weeks or a year at the consul's house. You would be as free, Monsieur, as at the inn: we should see each other only at table. You would be left entirely to your poetical inspiration.

Pray accept, monsieur, the assurance of my most distinguished sentiments[1].

BEYLE.

————— 150 —————

TO M. LEVAVASSEUR, PUBLISHER

Paris, November 1830

The truth is, monsieur, that I no longer have the strength of mind to correct proofs[2].

Be so kind as to have the insets well corrected.

'Tis with the greatest regret that I must deprive myself of the pleasure of dining with you and M. Janin. What would I give to have a pen that could ease Mathilde's pregnancy!

May this novel be sold, and compensate you for the author's delays. I thought it was going to be printed at the rate of two sheets a week, like *Armance*.

I ask of you, as a proof of friendship, monsieur, to see to it that not a copy is sold without the insets.

[1] "I learnt that he was interested in poetry to the point of worship, and that Sainte-Beuve's *Consolations*, a copy of which had by chance come into his hands, had inspired him with such enthusiasm that he had written : ' I have just spent three whole days in reading you. I am leaving for Italy: come there, you will always find at your service a private room for your work, entire freedom for your leisure, and sincere and passionate admiration for yourself." (Lamartine.)

[2] *Le Rouge et le Noir* was published by Levavasseur in November 1830.

Please send the letters to M. Colomb.

Pray accept all my apologies for not being able to see you again this year, and all my thanks for your kind and amiable treatment of me.

H. BEYLE.

My best compliments to the mighty M. Courtep-n, aristarch of the quai Malaquais.

——— 151 ———

TO THE BARON DE MARESTE

Paris, ——— 1830

I wish to tell you that I have discovered a great and true poet. I discovered him this morning, for six sous, at the *cabinet littéraire.* He is M. de Musset, *Contes d'Espagne et d'Italie.*

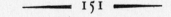

——— 152 ———

TO DANIELE BERLINGHIERI[1]

Paris, the 6th of November 1830

Monsieur,

'Tis perhaps a great temerity on my part, poor and aged as I am, to confess to you that I would consider my life's happiness assured if I could win the hand of Mlle your niece. I required her reassurance before I could nerve myself to do so. Mlle your niece told me that your affection for her and your good nature are so great that, even if you did not accept my proposal, you would not mock at it too severely.

Almost my sole fortune is my post. I am forty-seven years of age. I am too poor to ask whether or no Mademoiselle had any fortune. If I were rich, I should still have no interest in the matter. I regard it as a miracle that at forty-seven I can win a woman's love.

---

[1] " In 1829 he fell in love with G———, and spent the night with her, being still with her on the 29th of July (1830)." (*Obituary*). Berlinghieri, Minister Plenipotentiary of Tuscany, was the uncle and guardian of Giulia Rinieri. (Cf. letter no. 176.)

Mademoiselle your niece would not for anything in the world be separated from you. She would spend six months at Trieste with me and six months with you. I give my word of honour to bring her to Geneva after the first six months, and to come and fetch her six months later. I shall sign the marriage contract without reading it: if Mademoiselle has something, it could be assigned to any children she might have. In this way the husband would be an "unconcerned party". The marriage could take place at Varese, near Lake Maggiore, on the 1st of May, 1831. I have spoken, Monsieur, as honest man to honest man. I shall part for six months every year from a person who would like to spend her life at your side.

I am, with the deepest respect,

H. BEYLE.

———— 153 ————

TO THE BARON DE MARESTE

Trieste, the 24th of December 1830

"*Let George live here, since here George knows how to live!*"

This is what I said to myself on leaving Paris. I cast my nets too high. My nomination has given my friends no pleasure. Have I any friends? *Facta loquantur.*

I have this moment received a letter from M. le marquis Maison, ambassador at Vienna, who tells me that Herr von Metternich has refused the *exequatur*, and has ordered the Austrian ambassador at Paris to protest against my appointment. My first, misanthropic idea was to write to nobody. The letter from M. le Marquis Maison is dated the 19th of December, and it reaches me on the 24th.

Nevertheless I am writing to friends who have truly helped me: *facta loquantur.* I am writing to Mme Victor de Tracy: M. de Tracy, a former aide de camp to M. le comte Sebastiani and always a friend, can be useful to me. I am begging Mme Victor—you know how much I am indebted to her—to "decide" for me.

I make no particular suggestion: I feel that nowadays, at the age of forty-seven and with the mercury falling, *heat* is for me a necessary element of health and good humour. So let it be consul at Palermo, Naples or even Cadiz, but, for Heaven's sake, not in the North! I went into no details with Mme de Tracy, I begged her to "decide".

[266]

M. le comte d'Argout was for ten years my friend; but one day I said that a hereditary "peerage" produced stupid elder sons. What say you to such a want of tact?[1]

I was petrified with amazement to learn that I had been successful. But the port in which I reckoned on finding refuge lies open to the wind from the North. Nevertheless, I have shown complete prudence. I have not seen the woman friend of the friend to whom you introduced me. If Mareste wishes me well—*a matter of which you can be the judge*—he can speak to M. le comte d'Argout.

The task of consul, which is altogether paternal, is infinitely to my liking. So the thing to be wished for is to be consul at Palermo. Perhaps the ill humour of which the letter of the 19th informs me can be conjured away. Mme Victor de Tracy is a friend of the MM. Désages, upright and reliable souls, who will tell her what is to be hoped and feared. But it takes ten days, *at least*, for a letter from Paris to reach Trieste.

Farewell: I am in black gloom. Perhaps our patron can tell you what I must expect and ask. Ah! if Mareste wishes me well, he might say as much to M. le comte d'Argout.

POVERINO.

154

TO MME ANCELOT

Trieste, the 1st of January 1831

Alas, madame, I am dying of boredom and cold. That is my latest news, as of today, the 1st of January 1831. I do not know if I shall remain here. I read nothing but the *Quotidienne* and the *Gazette de France*, and am growing lean on this diet. In order to be "dignified" and avoid ruining myself as I did in Paris, I do not permit myself the slightest pleasantry. I am as moral and truthful as Telemachus. In this way I win respect. Heavens, what a dull century—well worthy of all the boredom that it feels and exhales!

Here I live on the verge of barbarism. I have rented a little house in the country with six rooms that are as large, all six together, as your bedroom. This comparison is the only agreeable thing about them.

---

[1] "The comte d'Argout, my comrade when we were on the Council of State—a brave man and a pitiless worker, but without any intelligence—was a peer of France." (*Souvenirs d'Égotisme*.) In 1830 Apollinaire d'Argout was a minister. Hereditary peerage was abolished in 1831.

Here I am in the midst of peasants who have only one religion, money. Everything that in your country is accomplished by vanity is here accomplished by money. The greatest beauties adore me at the price of a sequin (eleven francs sixty-three centimes).—Why, of course, I am speaking of peasants, not of good society! I add this out of respect for the truth, and for the friends who will open this letter.

If you have the charity to write to me, address your long letter (of your gracious kindness, may it be as long as my deserts) to no. 35, rue Godot-de-Mauroy, to M. R. Colomb, former inspector of Taxes. In the neighbouring house there is a vicomte Colomb, a sick lover of Mme Bucary, who opens my relative's letters unless the number 35 is written as big as that. In my spell-bound sojourn here, I know nothing of anything: you will realise how appalling is my stagnation when I confess to you that I read the advertisements in the *Quotidienne*. If ever I meet the advertisers in the streets of Paris, I shall surely strangle them. If you seek the explanation of this revengeful feeling, which your heart of a dove would never understand, ask the profound and gloomy Mérimée.

I learnt only a week ago that the *Rouge* had come out. Tell me frankly all the faults you have to find with this dull work, which does not conform to the academic rules and—perhaps despite this—is tedious. Write to me once a month. If I stay here, I shall send you a description of my rocks. Everything here is original, even the cooking, I'm sorry to say.

. . . .

CHAMPAGNE.

———— 155 ————

TO THE BARON DE MARESTE

Trieste, the 4th of January 1831

I am like Augustus, I desired empire without knowing what it was. I am perishing of boredom, and nobody treats me badly: this makes matters worse. Nevertheless, having spent the inheritance from my father on the acquisition of experience, I must try to accustom myself to this absolute lack of communication of thought.

Since my arrival on this island I have tried not to crack a single joke. I have not said one thing intended to amuse. I have not seen one man's sister. In short, I have been moderate and prudent, and I am perishing of boredom.

Farewell, the post is leaving. Try to interest Mme —— in my favour. *I date ever a month back*[1]. Many greetings *to lady Azur and to my sister*[2]. Tell her that I am bored.

Recommend me to Apollinaire[3]—provided that he is still there, and has forgiven me for the abolition of hereditary peerage.

—— 156 ——

TO SOPHIE DUVAUCEL

Trieste, the 4th of January 1831

Mademoiselle,

I have not yet been able to pass your letter of introduction on to Signora Albrizzi. She is in Milan. But I read the letter, and was overcome with an attack of giggles. It was not your style, worthy of my colleague, Cicero, that made me laugh, but the serious praise, applied to me! I would be vexed if you had spoken ill of me, but such praise seems to be an unrivalled burlesque. Perhaps the reason for my feeling is too much pride. It is as if I were well received at a certain house because my name began with B: so I would be ill received if it began with a C. While we are on the subject of names, did you see the black malignity of the *Débats* at the beginning of December?[4] They married two names together—and this marriage might well send me off on a fine honeymoon! I have been most civilly received here. I have found what Paris lacks: a rich woman of thirty-eight who has a large drawing-room and receives her friends *every evening*[5]. This social machinery is so convenient that people do their utmost to be presented at her house. I would have had myself introduced even had she lived alone. She is completely without affectation. To me she almost represents Italy. I go there every day. The public here has taken to supposing that I am married. I speak of nothing but the amiability of my elder daughter.

As a result of giving so many details of my elder daughter, and also of the younger, I have begun to regret that I have not a daughter or two. If I retain this uniform, I shall marry. You have no idea how the title of a

[1] In English in the original. (The letter is dated the 4th of December, 1830.)
[2] In English in the original.
[3] The comte d'Argout.
[4] The *Journal des Débats* had reported that Metternich had refused an exequatur to " M. Bayle de Stendhall."
[5] Mme Reyer.

former Cicero ennobles and rejuvenates a man. It fills me with utter disgust and enhances the boredom that crushes me. Would this boredom be so strong if I were in Italy? That is the question which I often ask myself, and which seems absurd to a lover of Paris like yourself. I continue to find that city ridiculous. You have no idea, Mademoiselle, of the effect produced by two months of life amidst people so different. There are a thousand leagues between Corfu[1] and the Palais Royal. I look back on 1830 as if I were in 1840. If I do not leave this place, offer M. Valenciennes my services as a supplier of fish. I am so bored that a commission for fish might plunge me into the study of natural history.

This serves me as a connecting link—such a capital thing for French men of letters: present my homage and gratitude to monsieur your father. I shall never forget the letters which he was so kind as to write to the brutes at the Bibliothèques who preferred a certain M. Paris to myself. Have you seen this M. Paris's translation of Lord Byron's *Don Juan*? À propos, I still have a letter written to you by the aforesaid gloomy egoist. I am grief-stricken to see that I am coming to the end of my paper. I am speaking to you without affectation, which must give my letter a remarkable character of originality. This morning I feel most upset. One of my colleagues had a daughter of sixteen. She died three days ago. She was kept in the house for twenty-four hours. Then she was laid in the chapel for twenty-four. After forty-eight hours she was taken to the cemetery. After the ceremony, the gravedigger was throwing earth on the coffin, when he heard a cry. But—and here you have the advantage of religion—he thought it his duty to go to the town (half a league distant) to fetch a priest. The priest sent him packing—the way was too muddy! Finally, two hours later, the priest arrived and the coffin was opened. The poor girl had torn her cheeks with her nails, and had just that moment expired. Her name was Mlle Viber.

I date ever a month back[2].

Kindly accept, Mademoiselle, my homage and respect.

General PELLET.

Be so gracious as to tell the story to Clara Gazul[3].

[1] The envelope is dated: " Corfu, the 4th of December."
[2] Cf. note to letter no. 155.
[3] Mérimée.

TO THE BARON DE MARESTE

Trieste, the 17th of January 1831

What a good week! On Thursday a letter from the divine Clara, today one from you. This country's rue de Jérusalem[1] has taken a copy of the young woman's letter, and for this purpose kept it three days. Never use proper names: apart from that, tell me absolutely everything, and I shall receive your blessed letters three days earlier. I did not think I was so curious: it is funny to make discoveries concerning oneself at the age of forty-eight, which I shall attain tomorrow. Being reduced to a diet of the *Quotidienne* is turning me into a clod.

I have never felt more keenly the misfortune of having a father who ruined himself. If I had known, in 1814, that the *father*[2] was ruined, I would have become a tooth-puller, lawyer, judge or something of the sort. Think of having to tremble for the retention of a post at which one perishes of boredom! I have no complaint to make of anyone; I have found friends—solely, one might say, because of Lady Morgan (whose Jacobin opinions I do not share). My whole life is reflected in my dinner: my high rank demands that I dine alone—first tedium. Second tedium, my dinner is of seven courses: an enormous capon—impossible to carve with an excellent English knife, which costs *less* here than in London; a superb sole, which they have forgotten to cook—a local custom; a woodcock killed yesterday—they would think it rotten if it were kept waiting two days. My rice soup is defiled by seven or eight sausages full of garlic, which they cook *with the rice*, etc. How am I to protest? It is the custom; I am treated like a nobleman; and certainly the good inn-keeper, who never meets me in his house without halting, uncovering and bowing to the ground, makes no profit on my dinner, which costs me four francs two sous. My lodging costs six francs ten sous. My quality of a bird on a branch (Clara does not understand this slight metaphor) prevents me from employing a cook. I am so poisoned that I have resorted to boiled eggs: I thought of that only a week ago, and I'm quite proud of the happy notion.

---

[1] The police. Mérimée mentioned *Le Rouge et le Noir* in his letter, and described the King of Spain's wedding night.
[2] In English in the original.

Tell Mme Azur[1] how miserable I am, and tell her, if she knows mathematics, to multiply my whole life by the wretchedness of the dinner. The lack of a fireplace is killing me: I freeze as I write to you. In the other room there is a stove that would give the coarsest Auvergnat a headache . . . I prudently avoid seeing Mme ——[2], which I much regret. She has Ancilla's[3] tact, a constant gaiety and a certain haughtiness: she has a fireplace! I could have taken root beside so precious a construction! . . . I have found a true friend in a captain of the same regiment[4]. It is incredible how well we get along together. But, Monsieur, for how long will I have the patience to perform this sentry-go? Two or three years at most.

I am much occupied by my profession. It is a good one, honest, agreeable in itself, altogether paternal. My correspondence deals with the commerce *of corn*[5]. Do not think that Paris is the country most fertile in this crop. 'Tis the Banat, Monsieur. I travelled in the direction of the said Banat in order to study the trade. I went as far as Fiume, which is the very extreme point of civilisation. A foreigner who is also a captain[6] is received like the late Mlle Jeek, the Paris elephant. During the past five days there have been five " Carnivals ". I was so popular that I was told: " You do not incur outrageous debts and bankruptcies, like one of your predecessors; but he had two Croix, and you have none." " I refused it," I replied . . . In this charming city of six thousand souls there is a man with a capital of forty thousand francs who lives in abundance, esteem, etc. He has a dwelling so sunny that a stove is unnecessary; he adores the usurper and reads the history of his love-affairs in a volume with what he calls " enlumined " engravings. He insisted on lending me this " rare " book, which he had procured " at great expense ". Every time I went to see him, he at once had chocolate prepared for me. "How much does this delightful life cost you? " I said on my last day, having surprised him at dinner with his mistress. " I am ruining myself," says he, " but what can one do? Life is short: I spend three thousand six hundred francs a year."

[1] " Mme Azur, a strumpet not in the sublime style, à la Du Barry." (*Vie de Henri Brulard.*) The baronne de Rubempré (who lived in the rue Bleu, hence the name Azur) was related to Eugène Delacroix, who introduced Beyle to her in 1828. Beyle loved her " for six months at most ". When Mérimée fell in love with her, Beyle was in despair for four days. Finally, on his return from Spain in December, 1829, he found her in the arms of Mareste, where he left her: " He whom I so entertainingly inoculated with my own frantic love for Mme Azur, whose faithful lover he has been for two years (and, what is more comic, he has made *her* faithful)." (*Souvenirs d'Égotisme.*)

[2] Mme Reyer.

[3] Mme Ancelot.

[4] Another consul.

[5] In English in the original.

[6] A consul.

On my journey out I came upon Porto Maurizio, near Genoa, which was absolutely like the town I have just been describing: warmth and situation just what one would wish. Because of the coastwise trade the vice-consul pockets, what with one thing and another, nine thousand francs a year. He must be the most comfortably off of all French State employees . . . I also came upon the amiable and amabilissimo M. Masclet, consul at Nice, in the middle of a garden filled with rosebushes in flower, on the 15th of November. At once the serpent of envy hissed in my heart. Because of the " coastwise trade "—blessed word!—Nice is worth twenty-two thousand francs a year. But what a task to get the post . . . Are you not pleased with my handsome handwriting? I am writing carefully in order to please your beautiful eyes and to earn a long reply.

I think that the *great*[1] citizen will be *all in six months*[1], and that the present Chamber, in the course of giving itself the pleasure—a new one, in France—of eating humble-pie, is leading us towards the abominable condition of a republic—a horrible condition anywhere else than in America: 'tis the real cholera-morbus. By the way, this horrible malady will put an end to my days within two years at most. I maintain that it is inevitable here: when next you see the kind and amiable Doctor Edwards, ask him to send me a prophylactic as soon as possible. One captain, my colleague, has seen people die in this frightful fashion: the victim, Monsieur, becomes a corkscrew by reason of his pain: he is dirty both above and below. Furthermore, it is my own special complaint, from which the Doctor has twice saved me—except that I was not dirty, quite the contrary.

The bells are deafening me in honour of the election of the Pope. If it is Cardinal Giustiniani, he is of the same height as Apollinaire and I have several times dined with him at Rome, in the house of that courteous man, M. de Laval. He was returning from Spain and wore diagonally a great white and bright-blue ribbon. He had been an intimate friend of His Sweet Majesty Ferdinand VII. You'll have a rough time of it, and so will Dominique, if he goes to Civitavecchia. The general rumour here is that he will stay where he is.

As for me, I am so stunned by boredom that I no longer desire anything: my wishes extend no further than a fireplace.

It was very stupid of Apollinaire to take offence at the note concerning the Cardinals[2]. When it was written, had they read the Paris newspapers?

---

[1] Italicised words in English in the original. The sentence means: " I think that in six months La Fayette will be everything."

[2] This confirms Colomb's statement that in 1829, after the death of Pope Leo XII, de Pastoret, a former colleague of Beyle on the Council of State, asked the latter for a note, to be sent to King Charles X, on the cardinals who might succeed to the papacy. (Note by M. Martineau.)

It is an abridgement of a note of eight pages that I handed to Pastoret twenty months ago. I think he has a copy of it and is pretending that it is his own work. When one receives a note of no consequence, from a distance of two hundred leagues, one throws it on the fire. Apollinaire will be acting with equal restraint if he refrains from profiting by the two months which he has to spend in that house to send a little gift to each of his friends, whether deserving or not. I could say more.

The first Minister of the Interior with a little intelligence will seek to remedy the state of degradation into which the Croix has fallen by giving it to MM. Béranger, Clara Gazul, Dubois, myself and Artaud[1]: this will raise the status of the Croix. But no government, of whatever sort, can ever sincerely protect any literature which is not *flat*, i.e. elegant and *devoid of ideas*. *Ideas* are the bugaboo of people in power. The ornament I mention would be very agreeable to me, but my views on heredity . . . Let us forget the matter.

It was on the 12th of the month that I received the first letter mentioning the *Rouge*. It was from Clara. She has the same opinion as Mme Azur concerning the second volume, and when I read your letter, which is more incisive than Mérimée's, I found myself almost in agreement with Mme Azur[2].

The present ending seemed to me good when I wrote it: I had in mind the character of Méry, a pretty girl whom I adore[3]. Ask Clara whether Méry would not have acted in the same way. The young Montmorencies and their females have so little " strength of will " that with these elegant and effete beings it is impossible to avoid a flat dénouement.

Remember how, in July (1830), when ten thousand rapscallions were fighting God knows why, there was not a single Montmorency present. If there had been even *one*! And for them all was at stake. Any of them would have fought a duel; but the *bon ton* forbade them, on pain of everlasting infamy, to fight in the street. This opinion of the upper classes' lack of character caused me to *make an exception*: it was a mistake—is it ridiculous? Quite possibly. The reason is that I was thinking of Méry.

---

[1] Professor and journalist. In 1827 Beyle wrote to him, in a letter accompanying a gift of the new edition of *Rome, Naples et Florence:* " I confess to you, monsieur, that I have some contempt for the manœuvres employed by MM. Jouy, Villemain, Delavigne, etc. to have themselves praised in the journals. These are the gentlemen who have done so much harm to the profession of letters.

" Endeavour, therefore, to review me as soon as possible, but treat me as a conceited person, tell me the truth and use the most ' harsh ' words.

" You will see that we shall be none the less good friends."

[2] Mme de Rubempré considered the character of Mathilde de la Môle improbable. This character seems to have been modelled to a great extent upon her own—at least in parts, despite the author's denials.

[3] Mary de Neuville, niece of Charles X's minister, who eloped with Edouard Grasset.

I would not know what to do in a novel with a young Rohan-Chabot who was really *de bon ton*. How would Raphael himself have painted a *complete night*? Exact conventionality consists in the *continual* presence of the conventional, the complete absence of individuality . . . And an author who receives catcalls takes refuge in metaphysics. I do not doubt the hatred of intimate enemies: I can see the faces they are pulling at " Mammouth " 's[1]; but one acquires new friends, like my amiable T—— here. Clara says I am an abominable character in a discussion. Perhaps in a month, after twenty efforts, I shall succeed in reading my own character; and then it will no longer give me any pleasure—there will no longer be anything piquant, novel, *unexpected* about it.

You must be working day and night. I have just read M. Odilon's letter. I would do the same as he, and I am fond of him. But such letters must keep you at your office until six o'clock in the morning. You tell me of M. Apollinaire's[2] colic; but it seems to me that you all have it. My brother[3] was at peace with nothing less than absolute good faith. For my part, I would willingly have slept with the Great Citizen[4]. He mowed down the rabble on the Champs de Mars, in his day. That line should lead to the salvation of my brother[3], and, perhaps, of France. But M. Guizot has no use for men of spirit, as I noted in the second volume of the *Rouge*, on the very same day as you informed me of the fact when I was dining at your home, with excellent wine. It was the 11th of August, I think. My audience numbers three, ten days after my placard[5]. It was an admirable placard. It said what needed to be said, kissing the Great Citizen four times a day. It was necessary to make the author of the placard a Councillor of State. But its message of good sense irritated old Réal, and probably also Apollinaire. But what is to be done? The course indicated by the placard will seem excellent in 1832. After 1831 your malignity will not be able to prevent you from recognising *in petto* that it was a better course than the one which has been taken.

The demand for eighteen thousand, especially, made me laugh a lot. The transfer to Civitavecchia is not as fine as you think. 'Tis an abominable hole. I was cast up there by a storm on my way back from Naples. The place is soaked with fever, and is inferior in rank and emoluments

[1] Cuvier.
[2] The comte d'Argout.
[3] Louis-Philippe.
[4] Lafayette.
[5] " . . . he put up a small placard bearing his signature, with his title of former Councillor of State, and declaring, in substance, that the throne should be offered ' to M. le duc d'Orléans, and after his death to his eldest son, if the nation judged him worthy.' " (Note by Colomb.)

to a modern Prefecture. Lastly, the friend of the amiable 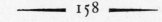 [1] has told me that the post will be abolished.

You say that literature is dead because the cold weather has killed the caterpillars and other noxious insects that live by grace of the *Journal des Débats*. Nothing could be more fortunate or more fertile than this seeming death: does it take away the gifts of people like Clara or Musset? It is true that your friends Lamartine and Co. lose eighty per cent. Try to sweeten Apollinaire towards me. M. Molé, who does not know me, has thrown *fifteen thousand*[2] at my head. Next time there is question of a promotion, may he give me an helping hand!

MÉQUILLET.

158

TO SOPHIE DUVAUCEL

20th of January 1831

Mademoiselle,

A thing that always astonishes me is to find a brute who is grateful. When you have an opportunity, thank M. Cuvier for the letters which he wrote, in days gone by, in order to perch me on a librarian's ladder. The post was worth 1,500 francs a year, and now I have ten times as much. But, alas, I perish! I burn away, like Phaedra—but not of love, please God! This boredom is about to make me as thin as M. Roulin. He is one of the men whose conversation I miss most. Conversation is my game of whist, without which I languish. You scarcely seem to be languishing in Paris. Could anything be more stupid than that Chamber of yours, which is leading you, with drums beating, to a Republic, for fear of a Republic? I hope you will have been sent a rhapsody of my fashioning[3]. It will horrify you, and likewise MM. the members of the Académie. I do not enjoin upon you to read this plea against politeness that exhausts the strength of the will. See in the book only a homage and a token of gratitude for pleasant evenings spent at the Jardin. All your powerful men—or rather, your men " in power "—should be very polite, for their *will* has been furiously exhausted. Whenever an unhappy Frenchman takes his handkerchief from the left-hand pocket of his coat, he is assailed—especially if he is noble and rich—by the " terror " of

---

[1] Eugène Delacroix.
[2] In English in the original. This refers to his consular salary at Trieste.
[3] *Le Rouge et le Noir.*

breaking the nineteen rules for blowing one's nose. What drives him to despair is the fact that several of these rules are, or seem to be, contradictory. The result is that there is nothing *individual*, nothing strong, about the behaviour of these men in power. From a distance, *and without newspapers*, I would be inclined to believe that they have doubled M. de la Fayette's power in an attempt to diminish it. Imagine, Mademoiselle, the excess of my wretchedness; I am reduced to reading and studying the *Quotidienne*!

Augustus said:

> J'ai souhaité l'Empire, et j'y suis parvenu,
> Mais en le souhaitant, je ne l'ai pas connu.[1]

It would be a great charity on your part, Mademoiselle, to write to me. Send the letter by the post to M. Colomb, no. 35, rue Godot-de-Mauroy. He is my ambassador. Be you mine to M. de Mirabel[2], and beseech him to remember me. But be also an ambassador in the complete sense— namely, *be discreet*. Don't go and tell him that I do not admire the masters of our destinies. They can send me to some chilly, obscure and loveless spot. It would be a hell for me, who have the soul of a Saint Teresa. The general rumour at V. is that I am being left where I am. I would prefer Rome, Naples or Florence—which three names are also that of my mortal offence.

Pray accept my respects.

COTONET.

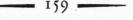

159

TO DI FIORE[3]

Venice, the 25th of January, 1831

I have just heard Velutti[4]: it was in a drawing-room on the piazza San Marco, at noon, on a fine, sunny day. Veluti[2] never sang better. He looks like a young man of thirty-six or thirty-eight who has suffered, and his real age is fifty-two. He has never been better. He was accompanied

---

[1] I wished for Empire, and I attained it. But when I wished for it, I knew not what it was.
[2] Professor at the Museum.
[3] "... A big, very handsome man, resembling *Jupiter Mansuetus*. ... He had been condemned to death at Naples in 1800 or 1799. His name was Di Fiore, and today he is one of my dearest friends." (*Souvenirs d'Égotisime*.)
[4] Name spelt in these two ways in the original.

[277]

by the divine Perucchini. There were twenty-four women, but not one hat in good taste.

Bad news of the progress of the Judith. Carcano is forsaken. They are performing caricatures. The Scala is triumphant: one sees actors from the Scala at table, eating pasta, and the Duca Litta, who pays the excellent Velutti, had a fiasco at la Venice: he was sick and tried to force himself.

Do not tell anybody that I am here, except our patron[1] if he speaks of me to you. By the way, does he think that the *Rouge* has some reality, some *knowledge of little men* possessing a little power? Such knowledge is one of the gifts required for the post at which he placed me. The hubbub of masqueraders on the piazza San Marco prevents me from sending you the usual polite phrases: I am writing from the café Quadri.

You already know that Machi was excluded from election "on information received" from France. Giustiniani already had twenty-two votes. They were continuing to open *le schede*[2] when he received Spain's formal ban. If you already knew that, do not mock at me like Besançon. Albani is still supporting Pacca, who will not win . . . Will your old friend get Civitavecchia, with its fifteen thousand francs? Farewell, I write to you as to a father: do not answer me.

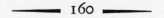

160

TO MME DE RUBEMPRÉ

Trieste, the 6th of February 1831

Do you know anything, madame, of General Bolivar? Well, he is dead. Do you know, of what? Of jealousy at the success of the *Rouge*. There is another pretty woman in Paris besides yourself who thinks me the falsest and most dissembling of men. And even if all this ridicule were true, would you not be all too happy that there is something about me to ridicule?

If you want a perfect man, have Besançon introduce you to M. Rokebert. He was poor and a lawyer's clerk: but by his integrity and rare prudence he deservedly became the lawyer's factotum, friend of a peer of France and a knight of the Légion d'honneur.

---

[1] The comte Molé, Louis Philippe's Minister for Foreign Affairs. Domenico Di Fiore and Mme Victor de Tracy had persuaded him to make Beyle a consul.

[2] The voting-papers. (Beyle is clearly referring to the Conclave.)

I am in the heights of joy: I thought, as if in a frightful nightmare, that the present Chamber, composed of Rokeberts, would sit upon France's neck for a year or two—and now, probably as I write to you, it is being hissed at as much as it deserves. That is a great deal, it has cut the " swivelling " root of the Frenchman's love for the *King*[1]. You remember the novel, *Tom Jones?* Well, this Chamber had plenty of " Bilfils ". Urge some shrewd brain of your acquaintance to give me— from time to time, and as often as possible—the news behind the news. Imagine the fury of an enquiring man (and who would not be so?) who finds himself reduced to the *Quotidienne* and the *Gazette de France*. By the lies they tell about what occurs within fifty leagues of my island I can judge of their veracity concerning Paris.

I spend my time observing human nature: I amuse myself with facts that have no other merit than that of being true. Since they are not at the same time " piquants ", they are worthless to Parisian curiosity— I was about to say, French curiosity, but they would find an audience at Toulouse, Avignon or Béziers, places that have a soul, places where one is not constantly concerned with the " neighbours ".

. . . Dominique has no news of his future destiny: he lives at Trieste, where he is somewhat bored. But it must be admitted he is amused and delighted by his post. He would be happy to have even a quite small one in your heart. There you have a compliment in true Rokebert style: I could pay you a much better one—but at the moment I cannot think of it.

Next time Besançon goes with you to the rue Saint-Guillaume, I would like him to visit the shop of M. Deville—or is it Delville? Sit in one of his armchairs, and once you are in it you will not want to rise. M. Delville makes armchairs to fit posteriors. Unfortunately, I would never be able to rise from an armchair that fitted you, even supposing I could sit down in it. M. Delville has made an armchair for Mme la baronne Apelle[2], Besançon knows it well: it is in the bedroom of the aforesaid baronne, a place that he much frequents—God knows for what delights!

I enjoin upon the said Besançon to order from M. Delville an armchair for a person of somewhat " better port " than himself: this armchair to be covered in some solid material, not easy to begrime. It is at this point in my commission that I throw myself at your feet, which I still love despite your injustice to them. Do you choose the material. If this admirable armchair happened to be spoilt by my accursed perspiration, the sleepy dogs here would be incapable of making a fresh cover for it.

[1] In English in the original. [2] The baronne Gérard.

M. Colomb will hand over a hundred and fifty francs to M. de Mareste for the cost of the piece. If ordered *a posta*, for a fat man, it will be ready in May; whereupon M. Delville will despatch it to Marseilles, whence one of my ships will bring it to me at Trieste or Civitavecchia. I promise, madame, not to involve you in any other commission during 1831.

There is a lack of everything here, except victuals and English piqués. Many friendly greetings to M. La ✠ [1] and to Clara, if you see them.

. . . .

MEYNIER.

────── 161 ──────

TO MME DE RUBEMPRÉ

Trieste, the 19*th of February* 1831

I do not think, dear friend, that I am all you say. I have no such keen desire for the Croix. It will come one day when I would rather not have it: but I do not know whether I shall be in France when you in your wisdom have given us a republic.

Three days ago I received a letter in the same style as yours, and yet worse—for, since the writer regards Julien as a rascal and assumes that he is a portrait of myself, the quarrel is with me. In the days of the Emperor, Julien would have been a very honest man: I lived in the days of the Emperor—therefore . . . But what does it matter? If I had been a handsome, fair-haired young man, with that melancholy air which promises the delights that are now in fashion, my other woman friend would not have thought me such a rascal.

There are twenty of us here. The French consul takes first or second precedence at ceremonies. Ceremony is everything with these peoples, just as a woman is thought " pretty " only if she has a new gown at every ball. But five or six consuls have the Croix; my predecessor and his predecessor had it: so one must ask for it. I deserve it for Berlin, Vienna and Moscow. The Emperor would not have given it for so little; but all the boobies who have since received it never even saw Moscow. But for fear of awakening envy, I could tell you that on the way back from Moscow—at Borisov, I think—M. Daru thanked me in the Emperor's name. M. de Pastoret was present, and M. Labiche, who is now divisional chief under M. de Montalivet. He is an honest man and will confirm what

[1] Eugène Delacroix.

I say—if he still remembers the incident, for at that time everybody was pale and thinking openly of himself. So this, dear friend, is what I think about the Croix, and I shall have it within two years from now—if it has not meanwhile been abolished—from the first Minister of the Interior who has any intelligence. If your vanity is offended by mine, I shall not wear this future decoration in France.

The trick to which the envious resort when an author depicts a character who is energetic and, consequently, somewhat rascally, is to say: "The author has depicted himself." What reply can one make to that? A man sees himself from within, as one sees the Georama in the rue de la Paix.

In me the pleasure of the moment has ascendancy over everything else. If I were Julien, I would have paid four visits a month to the *Globe*, or I would have presented myself, with my suite, at the house of M. le marquis de Pastoret. Find your answer to that, envious woman! I did not once go to the Luxembourg when M. de Pastoret was head of the chancery. Bear in mind that M. Dacier, of the Bibliothèque, had given me clearly to understand that he would allow M. de Pastoret to force his hand.[1]

Julien would have taken advantage of all that, and still more of Mme Aubernon's salon and the friendship of M. Béranger. Supposing that in the reign of Charles X we had had a sensible Minister like the present one, sooner or later M. Béranger would have been in charge of literature. Clara Gazul will tell you that I even neglected the Great Citizen, and quite wrongly; for that family did me Trojan service. The fact is that I owe everything to Di Fiore and Mme de Tracy. And you see how an old friend or acquaintance like Apollinaire is about to leave the shop without having given me a tiny morsel of his own good fortune. You think I suppose the *Rouge* to have been successful, and you are seeking to punish me; but in the violence of the punishment I see the great opinion you have of success.

Look at our painters, Gérard, Gros, etc.: people boast of them. Twenty years after their deaths they will not be thought equal to such men as Bonifacio, Palma Vecchio, Maratta, Pordenone, etc.—all of them third-rate painters in fortunate Italy. I say this to calm you, but, at the same time, nothing is more true. I suppose—I do not know, since I read no newspaper except the *Quotidienne* and the *Gazette de France*, but I suppose—that *le Rouge et le Noir* is having some success: in twenty years the booksellers and public will not esteem it as highly as *la Religieuse portugaise*, *Jacques le fataliste*, *Marianne*, etc., etc. If you are still in a

[1] An allusion to the post at the Royal Library which Beyle had solicited.

rage, you will think I am lying. How in the devil's name do you want me to prove to you that I am not lying? Here I have had, up to the present, three women writing horrible things to me because of Julien, and one of these women has a tender friendship towards me. So do not think me so proud of success. Finally, be assured that I do want the Croix; but if, instead of that, you choose to employ me at Naples or Genoa, I shall be much better pleased. If you seek to increase my joy, arrange for a country of good sense, like New York, to have the spirit and climate of Italy, its arts and its ruins: then send me *there*, and you may think me a boor if ever I ask you for the Croix.

You know that I am being sent to Civitavecchia; but how am I to get there? The insurgents have cut the roads to Spoleto and Perugia. All around the armies of both sides there are bands of robbers who hold the countryside. I shall probably go to Genoa, and there embark for Rome. To the devil with the insurgents! . . . Forget your anger: in six months nobody will be talking of the *Rouge*, and I will make you a confession: I never was in Russia; it was my brother Henri Marc, whose papers I stole—which I was able to do because my name is Marie-Henri, same initials.

A thousand affectionate greetings to MM. Dela ✚ and Schnetz. Ask M. Schnetz to tell me the address of his apartment in Rome. You are quite right. Besançon is the man who can induce Apollinaire to help me. It seems that Apollinaire finds letters a nuisance.

━━━ 162 ━━━

TO THE BARON DE MARESTE

Trieste, the 28th of February 1831

. . . We have *borra* twice weekly, and a gale five times. I call it a gale when one is constantly busy with holding one's hat, and " borra " when one is afraid of breaking one's arm. The other day I was swept up and carried four paces. Last year a wise man who found himself at the other end of the town, which is quite small, *slept at the inn*, not daring, because of the borra, to return home. In 1830 there were twenty cases of broken arms or legs. I would, of course, completely disregard it—think what courage I showed against the robbers of Catalonia! But, Monsieur, the wind gives me rheumatism in the guts. I have not had two absolutely *painless* days since the 26th of November.

I received, at the same time as your interesting letter, a despatch from my master. Not another hint of Civitavecchia. They wanted to have the Pope's *exequatur* first. " Bee "[1] is an abominable place to stay in. It has a big tower built by Pope Barberino, whose crest, as you know, is that winged insect who steals from the flowers their sweetest scents, etc., etc. That is why the air at " Bee " is abominable. But, with leave to dwell for six months in the Eternal City, which *to day*[2] is having a rough time, and with twelve thousand francs instead of ten, I should be quite satisfied.

I shall no longer speak of boredom, but that is not my main trouble. Remember the remark made by the duc de Castries concerning d'Alembert: " They talk only of people who have incomes not even of three thousand francs." So it is that always the man in power will feign to believe that some unknown work contains some indiscretion. M. Lamartine agreed with me about that. I hasten to add, in order to barricade the avenues against criticism, that I am neither d'Alembert nor Lamartine.

. . . .

———— 163 ————

TO MME ANCELOT

Trieste, the 1st of March 1831

Your beauty makes me wretched, in that you do not write to me. " All my friends' wives recognise themselves in my last rhapsody." Heavens! Did I ever climb up to your window on a ladder? Indeed I have often wished to, but, after all, I implore you in Heaven's name, have I ever displayed such audacity? When one pines so far away from you, one fears everything and believes everything. Do, as an act of grace, tell me if you are piqued like Mathilde or Rénal. I hope Saint-Germain-l'Auxerrois[3] has frightened you so much that you have returned to your natural feelings.

[1] Civitavecchia.
[2] In English in the original.
[3] On the 24th of February, 1831, during a service held in the church of Saint-Germain-l'Auxerrois to commemorate the anniversary of the assassination of the duc de Berri in 1820, the people tumultuously entered the church and wrecked it from top to bottom. (Note by Colomb.)

. . . I hear from Paris that I, too, must be a deceiver and must stop saying I am bored, and this on pain of being regarded as a frivolous person, never satisfied with anything, etc., etc. Alas! I should be regarded simply as a poor man. Certainly, if my father had not ruined himself, I should be either at your feet or in the real Italy. If you want me patiently to endure the continual rightness of the good Germans amongst whom I have so kindly been placed, write to me every month. Send your letter to M. Colomb, no. 35, rue Godot-de-Mauroy, and ten days later I shall be happy. Do not lose sight of the fact that I am reduced to reading our friend the *Quotidienne* and the *Gazette de France*. This never seemed to me an amusing task until today: today there is an article, paid for by my publisher, which says that M. de Stendhal is not a fool. But is there still anyone in Paris who bothers to read?

Have you seen *Napoléon* at the Odéon? I prophesied in 1826 that such a drama would be written, and that within ten years the political situation would afford an opportunity for its performance. And people deny me brains! This great misfortune comes from my lack of seriousness.

Imitate me, my kind friend or charming enemy, tell me about yourself in infinite detail. If I had been able, I would have told you about my personal surroundings; but M. Ancelot will explain to you how there is no means of doing that.

Of what party are you, fair enemy, at the present moment? 'Tis said that you ultras are making a thorough show of right-thinking. Is it possible? If so, I would profit by that delightful new disposition: you would read my heart, and would see that I adore you. Were you wholesomely afraid when the enemies of the altar laid their hands upon that of Saint-Roch?

. . . .

GAILLARD.

164

TO THE BARON DE MARESTE

Trieste, the 1st of March 1831

. . . My brother Dominique writes me a long letter. He says: " I was not at all surprised by what happened at Saint-Germain-L'Auxerrois. I had been expecting it ever since the stupid dismissal of M. Pons de l'Hérault. I would condemn the man who suggested it to *copy out twice by his own hand* the life of Cosimo, Duke of Tuscany, the one who conquered Sienna. What! To banish the Great Citizen, dismiss M. Pons de l'Hérault and receive His Greatness the Archbishop of Paris—all in the same month!" Ah me! the people whom Apollinaire sees every day have really no good quality save powerful protectors. Here's something to make your envious soul laugh!

Dominique would be in no way embarrassed at becoming President of the Council of Ministers. Do you know why? He would be sincere, and he has his plan ready made: all he desires is fame. He would take as colleagues MM. Odilon Barrot, de Tracy, Dunoyer, Prefect of the Allier, and Pons, Prefect of Paris, and he would restore the Great Citizen to the National Guard. He would put forward an electoral law in two articles: three days later the Chamber would have refused to pass it, and he would dissolve the Chamber. He would withdraw the armies two leagues from the frontier.

Do you want to know why right-thinking people are uneasy? One is made to pay for a dinner, and then is not given it. With your extraordinary Budget you are made to pay for liberty, and then, *by fear of Europe*[1], you are not given it. Nothing could be more stupid than this bait offered to a sovereignly distrustful people—and rightly distrustful, for ever since 1814 everybody, both liberals and ultras, has been impudently lying from the rostrum.

You impose an extraordinary Budget, and in Belgium you cover yourselves in flour; you arrest MM. Blanqui, Plocque and Co. when the alibi has been proven, as clear as daylight, in twenty-four hours; you allow my friend Félix Faure to insult, for fifteen days on end, all who can think and are twenty-five years old. "But," you will tell me, "he is popular with the sort of people who go home and put on woollen socks when the weather turns cold." Agreed. "These people are the richest." Agreed. "And the most numerous." Perhaps, etc. But they cough instead of speaking. They go home as soon as there is a brawl in the street. I, as President of the Council, would regard these people as minors under tutelage. I would do nothing unjust to them, but I would pay no more attention to their words and moans than I would to the fine speeches made in Charenton under the guidance of our friend Pothey.

People in power hate people whose words get printed. If you prefer to forget this wise maxim, you will learn from the *Commentaire de l'esprit des Lois*, by my friend M. Destutt, that wealth is its own sufficient protection—except when there is a brawl in the street.

[1] In English in the original.

My electoral law—which would prevent me from getting the Croix, if Apollinaire knew of it—states: All Frenchmen paying a tax of a hundred and fifty francs, and being over twenty-five years of age, shall elect seven hundred and fifty deputies, selected from amongst Frenchmen being over twenty-five years of age and paying a tax of a hundred and fifty francs. Peers shall be appointed for life by the *King*[1], being selected from amongst the ten thousand Frenchmen of the greatest wealth: they shall be three hundred in number. Furthermore, each Department shall appoint one peer for ten years. The merchants of Bordeaux, Lyons and Marseilles shall, in addition, appoint twelve special deputies. The intellectuals, whom M. Humblot-Conté so much dislikes, shall similarly appoint twelve deputies. The six oldest captains of infantry, the six oldest lieutenants, the six oldest ensigns, the three oldest colonels, the three oldest battalion-commanders and the oldest Major General shall be *ex officio* members of the Chamber of Deputies. This will prevent dissolutions by force of arms, as practised by the late Cromwell, the late Napoleon, and attempted at the Jeu-de-Paume, etc. . . .

Once my twelve mayors of Paris were freely elected, I would wax insolent, and would take the first opportunity of sending to the guillotine —after sound and quite regular verdicts—any man who had *really* tried to overthrow order. Do you know why I would be so strict? Because hang me if I have an ulterior motive. On entering the Government I would publish my sources of income in a newspaper, and would promise never to wear a Croix.

All the *Kings of England*[1] have always betrayed the Whig ministries. Hence M. Guizot's boast that in England a Whig minister never lasts for more than a year . . . My writing-desk is insufficiently roomy. I am cold. I *don't write*[2] the Journal *of my life*[2]. Keep this scrap of paper for me, or, better, give it to Mme Azur, who has a great sense of order and few documents.

M. Thouvenel has stolen my idea: $2 + 2 = 5$; $2 + 2 = 4$. Along comes the Centre and says: $2 + 2 = 4\frac{1}{2}$, and that under the noses of MM. Blanqui, Plocque and Co., unjustly locked up for three weeks, and under the nose of M. Pons de l'Hérault. Between " yes " and " no " there is no compromise except to sit on your arse. *All this make me thoughtful upon a letter from the Count de* Willcotner[2]. The herring-barrel always smells of herring. It would be sufficient merely to act in good faith. The only impossible thing in France, after—I repeat—sixteen years of hypocrisy on both sides, is to deceive men in the depths of their

[1] In English in the original.
[2] All italicised words in English, *sic*, in the original.

souls. Hence the popularity of Dupont de l'Eure and the *great*[1] citizen[2]. You do not like them—you, M. le baron de Montfleury—and yet you will not say that they are people *a seconda fine*, with secret aims. They desire fame, and an income of six thousand francs so that they may eat. In this respect, Dominique resembles them. To be re-printed in 1900; six thousand francs a year in Lutetia[3]; elsewhere than in Lutetia, fifteen thousand and the ✠. Plus, if people want to be generous, the secret of how to ——, on appointed days, three times a year. I am paying court to a woman; but when I see the moment of happiness approaching, I begin to be afraid of not being ready until the second reception. At the third, I am passable.

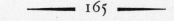

TO THE COMTE D'ARGOUT

Trieste, the 17th of March 1831

Monsieur and dear Friend,

On the 5th of this month I lost the third part of my small fortune, having been appointed consul at Civitavecchia. Could you write to M. de Sainte-Aulaire[4] asking him " to do me no harm "?

You are aware, monsieur, that one day M. Guizot was very much for me, two days later indifferent, and twenty-four hours later hostile.

So I have an " enemy " in doctrinaire society. The consul at Civitavecchia has always been permitted to maintain a pied à terre at Rome. In 1817 a storm drove me ashore at Civitavecchia. It is a town a little bigger than Saint-Cloud, and for two months of the year it is full of fever. The distance between this fine sea-port and Rome is only fourteen leagues. As soon as M. Levasseur, my successor, arrives at Trieste, I shall leave for Rome. M. le comte Sebastiani tells me that he is sending my credentials to His Majesty's ambassador at Rome, with a request that I be sent directly to Civitavecchia as soon as the Pontifical government has equipped him with its *exequatur*.

If we can arrange for M. de Sainte-Aulaire to do me no harm, that will be a great matter. By the end of a few months we may have a chargé d'affaires who is not doctrinaire and not hostile to my puny self. M. de

[1] In English in the original.
[2] Lafayette.
[3] Paris.
[4] French ambassador in Rome.

Latour-Maubourg, for example, would have treated me excellently: he is not a writer, nor a writer in the emphatic style.

I thank you sincerely for what you have done in the matter of the ✠. I request your benevolence towards my successor, who perhaps will not be a partisan of the *Globe*, at which I was so mistaken as to mock.

I read your writings in the *Moniteur* with great pleasure.

I congratulate you on the award of the Croix to that poor fellow Corréard and other castaways[1].

Please accept my thanks and respects.

H. Beyle.

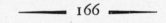

TO SOPHIE DUVAUCEL

Rome, 28th of April 1831

Mademoiselle.

Your letter gives me the greatest pleasure. I have just returned from St. Peter's, where there was a festa. I was so idle as to miss it. I found the church's marble pavement strewn with flowers and laurel leaves. These somewhat bruised leaves gave out the sweetest perfume, not at all strong, a thing that suits my nerves, which are those of a pretty woman. My soul was in a suitably receptive state when your letter appeared, like a sweet daylight destined to dawn upon the most delicate eyes. In my days of ardent patriotism, it would have made me indignant. I have a sincere contempt, untinged with hatred, for most of the people whom you esteem. In order to mix in public affairs one must have experience. Perhaps M. Dejean, or any other young man appointed prefect by M. Guizot, will be a clever man in 1840. But remember that the public eye sees sharply and clearly, within the first six months, all that passes in the heart of any man who receives more than twenty thousand francs a year from the public funds, and that the rôle of Penelope is a dangerous one. *See*[2] Louis XVI. But let us talk of trivialities.

You have seen some very young people make great fortunes. Be assured that, whatever their phrases and outward appearances, for two or three months of their lives they were like Julien. From 1806 to 1813

---

[1] The castaways of the *Méduse*.   [2] In English in the original.

I was virtually aide de camp to M. le comte Daru. He was very influential at Berlin in 1806-8, and at Vienna in 1809. I was, in some sort, in favour at Saint-Cloud in 1811. I assure you that nobody has made a great fortune without being a Julien. The shape of our civilisation precludes great movements, or anything that resembles passion. Hence the pitiful part played by women. Modern society employs them only as intriguers. For example, Mmes Récamier, Pastoret, Rumfort.

To get on in life one must be mild and humble and pay twenty visits in silk stockings every week. A day when your patron is bored, a rainy day at Saint-Cloud in the month of October, or a well-placed act of lick-spittlery, will be worth a prefecture to you. I despise all office. Julien is not so shrewd as you think. Any young man of eighteen is a simpleton in Paris. He is always dreaming of a model to imitate. And sometimes he has four contradictory rules concerning the proper manner of pulling out his pocket-handkerchief in the home of a duchess. The perplexity that arises when one has to choose between contradictory rules—a perplexity enhanced by the necessity of changing one's attire in Paris three times every twenty-four hours—is what makes a man a simpleton. Our young peasants in the Dauphiné know very well how to pursue their own advantage.

I love to discuss the human heart, a difficult thing to do with French-women, who almost always tell lies in order to conform to rule one thousand four hundred and fifty-one or rule eight thousand six hundred governing their conduct. Your letter is infinitely more sincere than any other you have ever written to me. It does not sufficiently blame the novel to which it refers. You have sugared the pill. You should have written to me the day you read it. There was a man at Venice who, to love his wife, had to have her box his ears. I am that man. Nothing bores me like a compliment. If I had had ten thousand such, I reflect, I would be a baron and academician. But of what use are one or two handfuls? They are not enough to light the kitchen stove. I beg you, therefore, Mademoiselle, to be ultra-sincere with me: the harder the box on the ear, the more I shall feel that I am alive. Mme Azur thinks me the original of Julien because, when I was appointed Inspector of Chattels, General Duroc, who liked me (by reason of my sincerity, I may add in parenthesis), seeing the words: " son of the noble knight Beyle " on my certificate of baptism, gave me the " de " Beyle in the draft of the decree signed on the 11th of August, 1810. That was the beginning of my period of greatest happiness.

To return to what I was saying, Mme Azur's letter, which overwhelmed me with the most scornful tauntings, was all my joy during a journey that

I made to Capo d'Istria, and a month later I still think of it. If I had chosen to play the Julien in M. Aubernon's salon, or at the home of M. Pastoret, whom I never went to see at the Luxembourg, or at the home of M. de Lafayette, etc., I should now have at the very least the prefecture of Guéret. But I would be dismissed, for I would certainly have conducted my administration like M. Pons de l'Hérault, Prefect of the Jura. Keep this statement to yourself: it would do me harm in my present retreat. I have fallen from fifteen thousand to ten thousand. If I fell lower, there would be no way of living with the necessary dignity. Here—south of the Apennines, I mean—the public cannot be duped by any affectation. It does not help you to loll with noble carelessness on four chairs on the promenade: the rabble judges you only pro rata of the money you spend. The liberals have been our enemies since Bologna[1], the ultras since 1789. The rôle of a representative of France is difficult, very difficult. There should be fewer of them, and better paid. Otherwise I shall shut myself up in a complete nullity, like my predecessor—who, nevertheless, began dancing in the only café in the town when he heard the news of the decrees of the 25th of July. I spent five days at Florence without finding the time to go to the Gallery or the Palazzo Pitti. I sought to know the truth; I wrote four despatches to my minister. You would be amused by my despatch describing what almost happened in Florence. Since you are a Frenchwoman, I must here interpose a little bastion against ridicule: I therefore hasten to add that you would be amused, not by the gifts of the narrator, but by the entertaining character of the actors. My despatch, being sincere, will have caused displeasure. I told myself this as I wrote it. But, by the greatest of chances, there may be a man of merit, a Mérimée, at headquarters, and I should be very well content if he said: " That one is not so silly as the others." When I was sixteen years old my father gave me one hundred and fifty francs a month to study at the École Polytechnique. That was in 1799. The boobies and half-hypocrites whom you hold in esteem are leading you straight into the Great Wrath of the *Père Duchêne*. The tiger will awake to drive out the foreigner who despises us, and who will give us so many buffets that we shall have to end where we should have begun. The operation would not have taken more than six months. In the patient's present state, it will take three years. I offer you refuge in a forest three leagues from where I am. I mean this seriously. Unless you act in good faith, you are ruined. Do you understand the admirable subtlety of my language? Nothing is more

[1] The Austrians entered Bologna on March 21st, 1831, to suppress the insurrection of the liberals, who afterwards bore a grudge against France for not having supported them. (Note by M. Martineau.)

firmly established than our correspondence. Nothing gets lost. Condescend, therefore, to write to me more often. My respects to M. and Mme Cuvier and to Mme Martial. Tell all the ninnies that I have become very serious, very profound, very worthy of the *docto corpore* to which I belong. The root of the matter was that a few more or less trenchant phrases cost me five thousand francs. That was all the "superfluity" I had—a thing that is so necessary. This misfortune should take away the anger and envy of fools. In any case, I am sorry for them: in a few months they are going to get a fine scare from this part of the world. Do you want to know the remedy?

Receipt: Sincerity and good faith.

F. DE MARTIN.

—— 167 ——

TO THE BARON DE MARESTE

Civitavecchia, the 11*th of May* 1831

I am writing to you merely to give you a sign of life, and an unpleasant life at that. On the 26th of April, as I was leaving the world's finest apartment, in the palazzo Colonna, where I had dined with Horace Vernet, his wife, father and daughter (all this had doubtless overheated me), what did I find in the street? The Tramontana, which gave me an abominable rheum which I still have. Simultaneously the Tramontana stole my purse, with twelve napoleons: what good luck that this did not happen on any of my other trips abroad! All that was nothing. I decided to take hot elder-water, in order to sweat. I forgot that hot water taken in the evening gives me my celebrated neuralgia in the stomach, which makes me curse. It descended upon me, the bitch—not to the point of making me swear, but very painful—and lasted four days.

It was so painful that for some time I was separated only by a small, ill-closed door from the prettiest woman in this country. I heard her screaming every night: her screams were caused by a sort of neuralgia, but the sound of them was agreeable. She emitted little shrieks, at intervals, for three-quarters of an hour at a time . . . She has been married only two months. One thing cut short my imagination: the chair with a chamber-pot in it was beside her bed. On the first day I heard her husband, who was undressing at her side, letting out an abominable succession of farts on this chair. They are very poor. There are also seven orphans in the place. They all laugh so loudly that I am dazed by it, but nevertheless happy.

Despite the fourteen per cent deduction, I am ruined. Tomorrow the national festa will cost me twenty-five francs for lights. A man like me—or, rather, like my coat—must use torches and not lampions. A man like me can lodge only on the piazza grande, in a provisional apartment at six francs fifty centimes a day. In Tuscany one can still economise, but amongst these African barbarians here the only thing that is respected is expenditure of cash, and of cash *on the nail*.

. . . .

——— 168 ———

TO MME CUVIER

Civitavecchia, 25th of December 1831

Madame,

If Europe had had to appoint a peer, she would have appointed M. Cuvier[1]. In my own case, I would have given him my vote not only from admiration but also from gratitude. I remember the letters he was so kind as to sign when it was a question of Libraries. I have spoken much of the " Saturdays " with M. Ampère, whose lively French wit has brought France into our midst. I spend my life in playing the pedant with M. de Jussieu. I do not allow him to admire Rome as the vulgar do, I want him to admire it in exactly the same manner as myself. You will think it indiscreet of me, Madame, to speak so freely of Rome. My serious, mature self has command over thirteen vice-consuls or consular agents who are lending lustre to the name of France at Rimini, Ravenna, Pesaro, Ancona, Terracina, Fermo and many other places, of which Rome is, as it were, the centre. The result is that for a few days every month I present myself at the centre. As soon as it is hot, fear of fever binds me to the shore, where, like Louis XIV, I bemoan my " greatness ". It is not at all amusing, this greatness of mine! Happy are the frequenters of the " Saturdays "[2]! From the bottom of my heart I wish them continuance of the present state of affairs for I know not how many years[3].

---

[1] Cuvier had been appointed a peer of France.

[2] " I adore meeting friends at social gatherings in the evening—on Saturdays at M. Cuvier's, on Sundays at M. de Tracy's, on Tuesdays at Mme Ancelot's, on Wednesdays at the baron Gérard's, etc., etc." (*Souvenirs d'Égotisme*.)

[3] Cuvier was to be carried off by cholera in the following year.

Will you have the kindness, madame, to remind me to monsieur your son and his pretty wife? I have taken the sage advice of Mlle Sophie: I compel myself to be dull, I write little or nothing. I get along very well with my chief. I intend one of these days to send Mlle Sophie a letter describing all my virtues, all my acts of prudence. In this way I hope to cause my friends to forget me. But you, madame, who wish me ill at the bottom of your heart, but do not say so in public, I beg you not to forget me, and to say, if ever my name has the honour to be mentioned in your presence, that I am " becoming heavy and pedantic, as the result of age ". All my aim is to be as moral as an office sub-chief. If Mlle Sophie and you, madame, have the kindness to repeat the above words even as seldom as twice a month, I shall be very grateful. I am engaged on excavations at Corneto, three leagues from my home. I took M. Ampère there. I no longer concern myself with anything but Etruscan vases, and I am becoming as severe and brusque as M. de Caylus. Deign, madame, to present my respects to M. Cuvier, and to accept the homage of my devotion.

H. BEYLE.

———— 169 ————

TO DI FIORE

Naples, the 14th of January 1832

Dear friend, I am writing to you from La Speranzella. Do you know the place I mean? La Speranzella, behind Toledo, above la Trinità degli Spagnuoli. Ever since I came here I have been thinking of you, with the result that I am now writing to you without having anything to say.

The enclosed picture is the cause of my arrival here. Imagine a street of lava eight to ten feet high, flowing from the very edge of what was formerly the crater, but now is full—a thing that heralds a great " eruption ", so the Vesuviologists say. This lava is flowing at the rate of four yards a minute: its course is twelve or fourteen hundred yards wide. If it continued with the same ardour, it would threaten Resina[1], but it is cooling every day. Yesterday, at two o'clock, I arrived at the fountain-head of the lava and stayed there, quite flabbergasted with wonder, until two o'clock at night. Also present—to name them in order of utility—were an urchin selling wine and apples, which he cooked on

[1] The ancient harbour of Herculaneum.

the edge of the lava, a sight that gave me great pleasure; also Prince
Charles, who is said to be the son of an Englishman, because he is less
enormously rotund than the *King*[1] and his other brothers. He was having
pieces of lava stamped in the same way as cornets of pastry, with wooden
moulds, and the moulds repeatedly caught fire. It would have been
possible to make very fine colossal busts of the lava. It would cost the
price of a wooden or plaster mould, and the busts would be everlasting.
The Prince's chamberlains prevented the curious from remaining on any
spot towards which His Royal Highness waddled his imperious way.
Nothing could be more ridiculous than a chamberlain at this height!
Since the Prince was continually moving from one place to another,
I braved the chamberlains, without realising what I was doing, and
the Prince spoke very handsomely of the French. I was there with my
friend M. de Jussieu, of the Institut. He is a man of subtle intelligence,
and as disgusted with everything as Fontenelle. He thinks me a
madman.

On the crater there is a little sugar-loaf which every five minutes hurls
out red-hot stones. M. de Jussieu insisted on approaching it and handsomely scorched his hands and ankles whilst passing over a tract of
filigrees of lava of the kind that breaks beneath the foot. The ascent is
abominable—a thousand feet of cinders, on a slope of exactly forty-five
degrees. Continually the foot on which one is applying one's weight slips
back. In my rage I made five or six plans for making the ascent easy at
a cost of a thousand francs. For example, fir-trunks laid end to end, and a
chair sliding on this inclined plane and towed, as on a scenic railway, by
a small steam-engine[2]. The King of Naples would acquire international
renown with this fine invention.

. . . I had two intentions: to be restrained and to write legibly—but
the truth is that, when I am writing to you, I cannot do this. This letter
will wait for the steamboat. I spent six hours at M. de Latour-Maubourg's[3]
delightful ball, at which the King[4] was present—and I assure you that
he was the least foppish and affected of all the wearers of uniform in the
room. He made a conquest of me. He does not walk, he *waddles*—like
Louis XVI, 'tis said. Withal, and although furnished with enormous
spurs, he elected to dance. But who is without any pretensions? Those
of the *King*[1] did not go beyond dancing, as you will see.

He had taken as his partner Mlle de la Ferronaye, the younger, who
was blushing to her shoulders at dancing with a king. These shoulders

[1] In English in the original.
[2] The Vesuvius railway was built in 1879.
[3] The marquis de Latour-Maubourg, at this time French ambassador at Naples.
[4] Français I.

were within two feet of my eyes. The King said: "Ah, my God, made-moiselle, I asked you for the pleasure of this dance, thinking it was a quad-rille, and 'tis a gallop. I do not know this dance." " I have very seldom danced the gallop," said the damsel, scarcely able to speak. They both looked very embarrassed. Finally the King said: " Look at the first couple that has taken the floor—they are not doing it too well, let us hope that we shall fare no worse "; and the worthy sire began to hop. He is very fat, very tall, very shy: you can imagine how he fared. His spurs, especially, were a horrible embarrassment to him.

This last remark is true in more senses than one: he is ruining himself on his army. He has eight thousand Swiss guards who terrify the army, and the army terrifies the citizens. Just imagine it, a Swiss colonel (who is often a merchant draper or grocer who went bankrupt at Freiburg) receives at Naples six thousand ducats a year, in addition to pickings on the clothing and rations. I have written four pages on the present political situation: they would bore you. What is incredible, incomprehensible, quite contrary to the customs of the nineteenth century, is that people claim that this young man, whose buttocks are so big, is gifted with *firmness*. I am not speaking of physical courage—a thing not necessary to a king: he is strong enough to have a will and to stick to it. If this proves to be true, he is my hero. If he begins thus at the age of twenty-two, he will be King of Europe at fifty. He is said to be somewhat impotent, which does not prevent him from continually conversing with a certain Englishwoman with a pinched expression: the husband, a true aristocrat, is enraptured. To crown his joy, Prince Charles is paying court to his wife's sister. This Prince Charles is a fop without a figure, just as the Crown Prince of Bavaria, who comes to Italy to form his character and mind, is a fop who possesses a figure.

M. de Latour-Maubourg made a conquest of me. He is a sensible man—a very rare thing in our profession, I assure you. Have you read a note by M. Chateaubriand in his *Discours historiques?* Put four sharps at the end of anything he reveals, and you'll still be far short of the truth. These diplomats spend their time entirely with a nation's " ultras "—who, moreover, in order to pay court to them, conceal from them, or refrain from mentioning in their presence, anything that might shock them. Dominique learns more about the situation in two days, by talking to his tradespeople, than these fine gentlemen who have been here for two years. Their ignorance is carried to the point of not being able to distinguish between uniforms: they mistake a chamberlain for a field-marshal.

The Princesa (or is it Duchesa?) Tricasi is regarded at Naples as the prettiest woman in the city. All these ladies are duchese. Signora Tricasi has the pinched look of a French beauty who is not making a sufficient impression (the physiognomy of Mme de Marcellus-Forbin, if you like). I prefer the Duchesa di Fondi. The Princesa Scatella (or is it Catella?) has been married for five years and still has no lover: she is a rare beauty, resembling a figure in wax. For my part, I prefer to all others a Sicilian marchesa, blonde, a truly Norman figure, whose name nobody has been able to tell me. I saw all these ladies at two balls at the noblemen's casino, on the via Toledo, opposite the palace of the Principe Dentice. The Duchesa Corsi is light-footed, lively, as alert as a Frenchwoman: the sublime —— is like Mlle Mars, thirty years ago, in *Araminte*. Mlle de la Ferronays the elder resembles M. de Chateaubriand: she is said to have much wit, indeed genius. Perhaps she is merely " etiquette " disguised as a young lady. When she dances—and she dances a lot—she has the air of performing a diplomatic duty.

Neapolitan society is a *mass*. Things are not as in Rome, where the embroidery seems to carry away the stuff, where foreigners seem to constitute a society in which a few Romans are seen here and there. At Naples there are eighty women whose names I could copy out for you in my journal and who are seen everywhere. Often their lovers do not speak to them in public. Napoleon reformed the morals here as he did at Milan. The only ladies who are quoted as having several lovers at once are those who spent their youth in Sicily, whilst Napoleon was civilising Italy. The Protestant gloom that infects Paris is felt here in the circle around Acton[1], whom I have not seen. Naples is more active and noisy than ever. There is an appalling contrast between Toledo, livelier than the rue Vivienne (for here one does not *walk* in the street, one *lives* there), and sombre Rome.

The mosaic discovered two months ago at Pompeii is truly the most beautiful piece of ancient painting known. It is a work of art almost on the level of the *Apollo*, not for its beauty but for its curiosity. It depicts a battle[2]: a barbarian king on his chariot is about to be captured by warriors bearing helmets and pikes. A barbarian is giving his life to save his king, the which king, on his chariot, looks thoroughly scared. These characters are all of more than life-size. One is forbidden to draw, or even to write, in front of this masterpiece.

. . . A peasant was digging a hole on Cape Miseno. Two days ago he found two heads in marble, which I have bought. I won a prize in

---

[1] Former minister to Queen Caroline.
[2] The battle of Alexandria, discovered in the House of the Faun at Pompeii, now in Naples Museum (no. 10020).

this lottery: I had recognised the beaux yeux of Tiberius. Would you believe that the old rascal is a great rarity! Yet he reigned for twenty-two years, I think, and over a hundred and twenty million " subjects ". In any case, my bust ranks in merit immediately after the masterpieces: it cost me four piastres, and is valued at a hundred at least. One of the best sculptors in Rome, Herr Fogelberg, a close friend of mine (like me, he loves " the beautiful" passionately, madly, foolishly), is busy with adding a nose to my bust. If I am snuffed out, the positively *unrepeatable* circumstance of my death will give me audacity, and I shall ask you to receive this bust *without cost* and send it to M. Dijon[1].

Were you " liberated " on the first of January? 'Tis a great ordeal. We all underwent it in 1814. How are you faring? Are you dictating the true history of your life of a *Paglietta*[2] at Naples to a young chamber-maid? Also your conspiracy to deliver the port of Naples to the English, in collaboration with Signora de Belmonte? Also the sale of buttons bearing the imprint of St. Peter? Also your arrival at Genlis with eighteen sous, and finally the delightful story of the gifts of " conserves "[3]?

I am amusing myself by writing a description of my life's pleasant moments[4]. After that I shall probably do as one does with a dish of cherries, and describe also the unpleasant moments: the wrongs I have suffered and the misfortune I have had of always displeasing the very people whom I sought all too much to please—as happened to me recently at Naples, with Mme des Joberts (born at Brussels). Of course, I had no thought of a love-affair: she had gentle eyes which attracted me, and her profile was like Mme de Castellane's. Alas, it was the same as with Giuditta[5]; a président Pellot robbed me of all special favours. Do not speak of my trip to those dear friends of mine who keep on erasing my name from the lists of recipients of the Croix. I think that by invoking oblivion I can cause petty jealousy to become extinct. Say of me: " He is growing old, he is rusty." Stick to that.

Do you know what is truly troubling me? The question of how you are to read this letter. How many pairs of spectacles will you need? In any case, read a little every Sunday, when you have nothing else to do.

---

[1] The comte Molé, to whom Stendhal in fact bequeathed the bust. It is now at the château de Champlâtreux.

[2] Di Fiore had been a lawyer in Naples.

[3] On September 14th, 1831, Beyle wrote to Di Fiore: " Write the story of what took place in your heart when your mistress was feeding you on conserves at Genlis, pretending she did not know what she was doing. After dictating the story three times, the facts will come surging back to you: you will *live it anew*."

[4] Stendhal wrote his *Souvenirs de l'Égotisme* between January 20th and July 4th, 1832. And the *Vie de Henri Brulard* opens: " This morning, the 16th of October 1832, I was in San-Pietro in Montorio, on the Janiculum in Rome, amidst glorious sunshine."

[5] Signora Pasta.

They are having fine games with me; but *semper benedicere dei Domini Priori*[1].

Rest assured of my affectionate devotion.

A.–L. FÉBURIER.

—— 170 ——

TO THE BARON DE MARESTE

Civitavecchia, the 11*th of June* 1832

I have received your letter of the 28th of April. I wrote several times last year to you, to Lolot, to poor Lambert and to de Barral: no reply. I supposed that, in your case especially, you found our correspondence a nuisance. Nothing could be more natural: two men of fifty have said to each other all they have to say on every topic. Their political aspirations differ. Hence, writing is a nuisance. Nothing could be more reasonable and less liable to give offence. 'Tis the approach of old age: sensibility takes its leave.

In reply to your letter of the 28th of April I wrote a page that I have just now torn up . . . To confine myself to personal matters: I am beginning to build my nest here—Paris seems as remote to me as Babylon . . . Colomb wrote to me on the 23rd of May that my nephew will be sent, not to Jack the Dreamer, but to Dulcinea de Toboso: he will take that very reasonably[2]. But if they do the thing in style and consult their chief, the trip can scarcely take place before the winter. What joy for my nephew's friends in Paris! Not only has he not received the Croix, but also he is to be sent travelling. If the young man really has any goodness of nature, he will try to take the thing reasonably. The country will be new to him; he will follow the advice of the great Mérimée and study Spanish literature.

. . . When I am not here, I have my quarters at Riccia, three leagues from Rome, on the road to Naples. Here an innkeeper provides bed and board for twenty or thirty sight-seers, at six paoli, or three francs twenty centimes, per diem, breakfast not included. It is half an hour's walk to Albano[3] . . . They have just completed four charming promenades,

---

[1] *Sic* in the original.
[2] Beyle is speaking of himself and his transfer, planned by the Ministry, to England or Spain.
[3] A spot that Beyle was fond of and described in *L'Abbesse de Castro* and *Une Position sociale.*

[298]

which are called the Galerie—I do not quite know why: His Holiness often goes there.

The town of Albano furnishes me with two households where I spend the evenings and with whom I go on picnics . . . At Rome I find the sirocco unendurable from the 10th of June until the first rains. Today, the 11th, for example, I can feel in my bones the first sirocco of the year; but, since I am at Civitavecchia, the sea enables me to endure it.

At Rome I lodge with the excellent Constantin[1], in an apartment of eight rooms, three of which have been furnished in French style by the late Signora Candellori, mistress of the late Cardinal Lante. This apartment is within a few paces of the Palazzo Caetani: the three princes of that name are my best friends. Their mother, a former friend of Paul-Louis Courier, used to afford me opportunities for a delightful evening's gossip. But for the past three months she had been suffering from a woman's malady: she is scarcely yet out of danger . . . There is a ball or a great dinner three times a month at the residence of our ambassador—an admirably civil and ingenious man[2]. There is also an evening reception four times a month at M. Horace Vernet's, in the Villa Medici: 'tis Paris in Rome, and I go there seldom[3].

My love for the aristocracy has led me to make the acquaintance of a Neapolitan princesa and a Roman marchesa, whom I visit four times a week. Every second day I go and settle my business *viva voce* with the chief . . . If chance had made me aide de camp to such a man at the age of eighteen, instead of to General Michaud, my manners would be much better. My chemical elements did not fuse with those of the rest of that French chevalier's family . . . My mission to Ancona interested me greatly, I have just torn up a whole page on the subject.

I continually play the cicerone to several French people, amongst whom I get along very well with M. Adrien de Jussieu, also with M. Giraud (of Chaillot). And now you know all about my life. Write and tell me what people are saying, thinking and doing in Paris.

. . . .

SIMON.

[1] The celebrated painter on porcelain who copied Raphael so admirably. (Note by Colomb.)

[2] The comte de Sainte-Aulaire, at that time French ambassador in Rome.

[3] On August 6th, 1831, Mareste wrote to Sutton Sharpe: "The other day I saw Horace Vernet, director of the Academy of Painting at Rome. He told me that the great man was outrageously bored in the Eternal City."

TO DI FIORE

Civitavecchia, the 12th of June 1832

" Boring as the plague! " I hope, my dear fellow, that the cholera is nothing worse than " boring ", as the everlasting platitude of fools has it . . . My heart bled when I learnt of the immense loss that has befallen our common benefactor[1]. For me it is the sole tragic memory of that affair, which humanity at large found so vexatious. But why, at the first certainty of *real* danger—I am not speaking of society gossip—did he not send that being whom we loved to Marseilles?

I suppose that throughout the month of April you, for your part, were no more bored than one is bored in a battle. 'Tis said that you were transformed into a walking apothecary's shop. Here in Civitavecchia we never believed the newspapers. When the mind is busy examining degrees of probability, the heart feels less. We had no notion of the danger until the arrival of private letters. Here, in this little hole of seven thousand five hundred inhabitants, the influenza was killing seven persons daily. But it occurred to nobody to be afraid: the press had not yet stimulated people's imaginations. I realised for the first time that freedom of the press can be harmful. Napoleon would have forbidden the word " cholera " to be printed. What did Mme de Curial do? You perceive that I love those who love me: let the reader take note.

I have had an attack of gout in the right foot: the approach of the fifties. But my heart is stronger than ever.

I have become a friend of the princesa Torella (Caraccioli), who is lodging at Chiaja. You know my liking for the aristocracy: I love it when it is not enfeebled by an education of excessively *bon ton*. 'Tis said that an emissary has been acting against your son Dominique. The chief here is very well disposed, or appears to be so. What thrilling joy for Dominique's friends in Paris! Not to give him something that is given to the meanest spoiler of paper, and to make him run from country to country like a dismasted ship before a gale. He would not give his friends the pleasure of seeing him reduced to despair—but that does not

---

[1] This refers to the death of Mme de Champlâtreux, daughter of the comte Molé. (Note by Colomb.)

stop him from manoeuvring. How much matter have we here for an ironical smile!

During my exile here I am writing the story of my last visit to Paris, from June 1821 to November 1830[1]. I find entertainment in describing all the brute's foibles: I in no way spare myself. It will be funny when it is displayed in the show cases of the Palais-Royal (by that time Palais——) in 1860.

. . . The uncertainty of duration is spoiling the haven into which you cast my vessel. If there were any certainty, I would plant a few trees. Everything here falls like manna. Twelve hundred artichokes cost twenty-one sous, twenty-five figs cost a sou. . . . The inhabitants are much better off than the English: they eat very white bread, they have excellent meat, wine *ad libitum*, they make love and yell like Neapolitans (four thousand of the seven thousand five hundred are natives of Torre del Greco).

DURAND.

—— 172 ——

TO M. HENRI DUPUY, PRINTER AND PUBLISHER

Civitavecchia, the 23rd of June 1832

I am extremely grateful, Monsieur, for your obliging offer. I have resolved to publish nothing as long as I am employed by the Government. My style is unfortunately so designed as to puncture the twaddle that several coteries seek to pass off as truths.

In days gone by I had the misfortune to offend the coterie of the *Globe*. The present coteries, of which I know not even the names, but who undoubtedly want to make their fortunes, as the *Globe* did before them, would write articles injurious to that small portion of peaceful esteem that should surround a Government agent.

If we were to enter into an arrangement, I would not conceal from you one terrible obstacle: I am not a charlatan; I cannot promise any editor *one single* newspaper article.

If ever I alter my intention, I shall have the honour, monsieur, to inform you in advance. The setting of the novel is Dresden in 1813.

---

[1] " To employ my hours of leisure in this foreign land, I want to write a brief memoir of what happened to me during my last trip to Paris, from the 21st of June 1821 to the —— of November 1830." (*Souvenirs d'Égotisme.*)

Before negotiating with anybody else, I shall have the honour to inform you in advance; but I expect to remain silent for eight or ten years.

Pray accept, Monsieur, my assurance of the high respect with which I have the honour to be

Your very humble and obedient servant,

H. BEYLE.

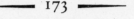

173

TO DI FIORE

Rome, the 20th of January 1833

My dear fellow, I am growing stupider every day. I find nobody with whom to play those games of shuttlecock and battledore which are known as " displaying wit ". Consequently, no more indiscretions. I hope, with time, to be as stupid as my predecessor. So you clearly see that I shall not compromise your sage protection. Love is a fire that goes out if it does not increase. You think that I am speaking of my brains, but not a bit of it: I am speaking of my post. Even if there is no thought of rewarding me, others will think of seeking to replace me.

I used sometimes to play a game or so of shuttlecock and battledore with M. de Sainte-Aulaire[1]. After him, I had to lay the racquet aside— no more ideas expressed in half-utterances.

" If you had a daughter, which would you like her to be: Mme la duchesse de Lavallière, or Ninon de l'Enclos? " I bravely replied: " Ninon."

How is M. Dijon taking life? Is he still *ammareggiato*[2] by the memory of the woeful cholera?

I wanted to open my letter with the enquiry: " How do you find this freedom? " But I feared your Macchiavellism: " The rascal is going to talk to me about his post." Such is the result of your high wisdom: it makes people dry and egoistical against their will. This is serious, and applies, in my opinion, to the whole of Parisian society.

When do you expect to return to Naples? Once at Nice, you take a vetturino for the delicious Corniche route. It is like travelling on your

[1] The comte de Sainte-Aulaire had been replaced by the marquis de Latour-Maubourg.
[2] Embittered.

mantelpiece: the sea is like a polished floor, the mirror is the crest of the Apennines. There are very passable inns, and not a shadow of a brigand.

—— 174 ——

TO COUNT ALEXANDER TURGENEV[1]

January 1833

This is to present to you, Monsieur, a Frenchman named Michelet, who has shed light, or almost, on the daydreams of the Germans concerning Rome. Once these daydreams, or theorisings, are clearly exposed, one can easily see all their emptiness.

M. de Beaufort, in 1738, was the first to " doubt ". Niebuhr and the Germans have set " truth " on stilts, and believe that they stand higher than M. de Beaufort.

I have been keenly preoccupied with the idea that the Germans have altered the history of the first centuries of Rome. Perhaps the same idea has sometimes occurred to you. In this case, monsieur, you will find some pleasure in falling asleep over M. Michelet's volumes.

. . . .

—— 175 ——

TO ROMAIN COLOMB

25th February 1833

Dear and kind friend,

. . . The pension of seven hundred francs to Mme P. L.[2] continues, and will continue as long as I am a comrade of Cicero. The three hundred francs were a small gift.

[1] " . . . I explored Rome and its vicinity in the company of Beyle (Stendhal) . . . whom I had formerly known at Paris and had again met at Spoleto and Florence. This witty Frenchman is the best of ciceroni.

" . . . He is unpopular here because of the truths he expresses and the witticisms with which he seasons them; but, in my humble opinion, it is he who, fundamentally, is in the right." (Turgenev.)

[2] Mme Périer-Lagrange, his sister.

Friendship sinks and does not rise again: I dearly love Clara, his talent enchants me. He is almost the only man to rank with Béranger. What does Flowers[1] say to Dominique's trip? Thirty or forty days in Paris cost fourteen francs a day, since one is on half pay. On the other hand, the poor boy is being stifled by boredom: he was a hundred times happier at no. 71. He should have had fifty louis more income, and not just ten thousand francs to be squandered on stupidities—on carriages, for example, which one must have here on certain days. Lastly, he is dying of boredom: but he gets on well with everybody, barring petty social envy, which, however, is little in evidence in a non-literary country. Will Flowers come and see Rome? Try to let me know in advance; I shall chance to be there, and will greatly enjoy it. But I have little hope. All the same, what could be more interesting than Naples after twenty-three years of change? Probably, if my new chief is as admirably accommodating as his predecessor, I shall be able to accompany Flowers, I do not say to Naples, where he will have no need of me, but to Florence, Viterbo, Sienna, Corneto, Tarquinie, which is admirable for the Cavaliere Manzi's tombs[2]. The painted male figures are three feet in height, one can make out the expressions on their features for six months, but after that they become a little spoiled by exposure to the air. They look as if they were painted by a pupil of Il Domenichino—and that after at least three thousand years, three thousand and five perhaps. I'm becoming the deuce of an antiquarian.

. . . .

———— 176 ————

TO GIULIA RINIERI[3]

My sweet angel, I have received your letter written at Pietra-Santa on the 1st of April. It seems to me that you write me very little. Ah well, then, we shall be no more than friends. In that case I return to you,

[1] Di Fiore.

[2] A lawyer and archaeologist friend of Beyle's at Civitavecchia.

[3] In 1830 Beyle had proposed marriage to Giulia, with whom he was in love (cf. letter no. 152, to Berlinghieri). In the *Vie de Henri Brulard* he wrote that, of all the women in his life, "Giulia, it seems to me, [was first in] strength of character, what though at the first moment she seemed to me the weakest".

On the margin of the rough draft of this letter he noted: "My letter will arrive next Tuesday or Wednesday, about the 24th. I have sweetened this draft and made the letter more friendly." Giulia had just informed him of her marriage.

enclosed, a document that no longer means anything . . . To console me, give me a thousand details. To start with, when Signor Berlinghieri was paying court to Sofia[1], how far did his happiness extend?

Was he aware of the birth of Sofia's inclination towards the marchese Greppi[2]?

Do I know this marchese? Is he handsomer than I am—I find it hard to believe?

When did you first see him? Does he come every day, and at what time? Which region does he come from?

Why do you say you will be unhappy? The only unhappiness is a life of boredom. Without wishing to offend you—for you know how deeply I am attached to you—it seems to me that the life you have been leading for the last two years must often be boring. Supposing the very best, it is the life of a woman of thirty-five, and you still have many fair years before this Age of Reason. But the husband you need is one like the man of Vignano.

In short, my dear one, give me thousands and thousands of details. For my part, I console my grief with the mesdemoiselles Pauline, like the girl who bathed in the Seine this summer, do you remember, in the letter from Alfred that you read? But all this is mere silver or even copper in comparison with what the sight of Sofia's pretty leg was to me once!

I have been spending a fortnight at Bee[3], quite close to you: the steamboat could have set me down at Leghorn in eighteen hours.

But when I saw the *Henri IV* weigh anchor, and this idea occurred to me, I thought of the rights of Signor Berlinghieri. What I fear is that you won't write to me often. You know how discreet I am, so speak to me with an open heart.

My last visit was perhaps less agreeable than the visit to Vignano, because there you spoke to me open-heartedly on all matters, even on your ideas of matrimonio *with*[4] Fracassetti. Whereas on my visit in February you made a demi-mystery of your disputes with Berlinghieri. Now, in love as in friendship, as soon as one of the couple shows distrust, or even reserve, the other is half paralysed, however little shy or delicate he may be by nature.

[1] Giulia. (The letter is addressed " to Mme Sofia, at Pietra-Santa, Tuscany".)
[2] Presumably Guilio Martini, Giulia's fiancé.
[3] Civitavecchia.
[4] In English in the original.

TO DI FIORE

Civitavecchia, the 30th of April 1833

Your excellent letter, which I received two hours ago, has already modified my resolve to the following extent. If I go to Paris, I shall spend only thirty days there, and shall go twenty-five times to the theatre. I shall enter no drawing-room but Mme de Tracy's. I shall make the immense effort of not displaying all the wit you ascribe to me—and the effort will not be painful: the idea of malevolence freezes me stiff.

On the other hand, life advances, the half-century is already past. Must I allow myself to die of boredom from excessive prudence? For six months I have been owed a month's leave of absence. I was expecting, as everybody does, to have it prolonged. Now I renounce it. Nay more, there lives at Naples a young and amiable woman: I shall write to her and ask her if she desires to benefit by my leave. If she accepts, I shall not come to see you—although I am thirsty for a conversation that is something other than a ceremony. Nowadays I never have a chance of hearing a single unexpected remark. I was expecting to live on *beauty* as my bread and butter, and this is impossible: two years of this diet have brought me to the end of my tether. I have been exerting every effort to speak to you with absolutely mathematical good sense: a month's stay in Paris will enable me to breathe freely for a year. You know that I am standoffish by nature: clearly in the space of a month I could not, even if I wished to, chatter too much in any dangerous drawing-room. I shall pay one visit, in duty, to my old colonel, who forgets a promise that he gave me without my even asking him for it.

. . . I have let a week pass, and I am still of the same opinion—forgive me if I vex you. Life is so short at my age that, when all is said, one must not deprive himself of all pleasure because it may contain some small, very small, danger. I am going to Lutetia to see the streets, the book-sellers' shop-windows and all the theatres whose plays and actors are new since two and a half years ago. Are you still dining at the Provençaux? Even if love—or rather, friendship enlivened by pleasures—were to hold me in Italy, I should not be making an advantageous exchange: the

[306]

mass of one's ideas needs occasional stirring. Bear in mind that everything I have heard in the past thirty months has seemed to me ridiculous, or, at best, dull. I fall asleep so heavily during these wretched conversations, which are my daily fare, that sometimes I find myself uttering stupidities worse than those of my partners, who are scandalised.

Farewell, my dear fellow, I much fear that I have scandalised *you* by my reasoning, which to you is bound to seem unreasonable. Remember that the anecdote is too long to write, and in any case is not applicable. If you absolutely forbade me to budge, I suppose that in that case I would have the strength to cling to the rock like an oyster: but then what would I have to think about during the long months of next winter?

Jules PARDESSUS.

—— 178 ——

TO MME GAULTHIER

Rome, the 1st of May 1833

Dear, kind Jules, I always love you to madness. I often think of you; but for eighteen months I have not written. When I write or speak to French people, I always perceive that I have infringed one of the two thousand conventions that reign despotically in Paris, and even at Saint-Denis. For example, how am I to give you an account of the life we lead?

. . . Nothing here is so dreadful as the months of July and August. At eleven o'clock in the evening, imagine a huge drawing-room, without lamps, all the windows open and each person occupying the half of a sofa. This life is not without sweetness, but it tends to deprive the people sprawling on the sofas of threequarters of the little wit that Heaven gave them. *Dolce far niente* enters into one through every pore. To write a letter is a great affair: I have taken up my pen in a transport of love for you. Try, sweet Jules, to have a similar transport: write to me at Marseilles, in care of M. Bazin, proprietor of the steamboat. But M. Bazin, as a prudent man, accepts letters only if they are franked.

The French who come here perish of boredom. They imagine that the larks will fall for them ready roasted. On the contrary, one needs the devil's own skill here, absolutely as great as *Julien's*. Forgive me for quoting that author. One must always appear to despise and shun the descendants of Caesar and Cicero.

A thousand friendly greetings.

Baron PATAULT.

P.S. A thousand affectionate regards to monsieur your brother. Where is he? In the Midi, I suppose . . . My folly is enamoured of his wisdom.

—— 179 ——

TO M. RABOT, HEAD ——¹
OF THE FRENCH CONSULATE AT CIVITAVECCHIA

Hotel Giacinta, 11*th of January* 1834

Have you read, Monsieur, the life of Descartes? Having the opportunity, like yourself, to quit the life of dissipation for a short while, he set himself to examine the forty or fifty things that he regarded as truths. He perceived that these pretended truths were merely fashionable twaddle.

Your stay at Civitavecchia may afford you the same sort of opportunity. Examine the twaddle that Parisian charlatanism passes off as truths. You will find a volume entitled *de l'Esprit* which can help you to perceive the falsity of three quarters of the things that the Paris charlatans call true.

You are aware, Monsieur, that it is part of our agreement that you are entitled to spend five days a month at Rome. At the office you will spend five or six hours daily in copying out either official documents or notes on the region. Never speak of what you have copied, either at Paris or here. For the rest, it is all one whether you work at the office from eight o'clock until two or from ten o'clock to four. Sometimes, on days when the steamboat is leaving, it may be desirable that you should come to the office before ten o'clock. You must arrange with M. —— for one of the two of you to be at the office from nine o'clock to four or five.

If a sailor or a traveller has business with the office, it is proper that he should find somebody there.

---

¹ Clerk? Beyle wrote to the Apostolic Delegate: " M. Rabot, aged 29 and a Bachelor of Law, is a member of a good Parisian family. He is destined for a consular career and is to remain for several months at Civitavecchia, attached to the French consulate."

I do not think you will be able to hold out against the boredom of a small town for more than two or three months. If you imitate Descartes, the time will not be wasted.

You might go to Rome from the 2nd to the 12th of February: the Carnival ends on the 11th.

You will be able to get in touch with the excellent Signor Manzi[1] and study the antiquities and the *probable* history of the tombs of Corneto. You might learn eight pages of Goldoni by heart daily.

I have the honour to be, Monsieur, your very humble and obedient servant.

(flourish)

——— 180 ———

TO THE DUC DE BROGLIE[2]

Civitavecchia, the 22nd of February 1834

Monsieur le Duc, in accordance with Article 6 of the Decree of the 24th of August 1833, I have the honour to solicit Your Excellency's consent in favour of M. Lysimaque Tavernier-Caftangiu, whom I propose for the post of chancery secretary at the consulate in Civitavecchia. M. Tavernier will receive approximately 1,056 francs a year; which is very little. Good commercial clerks in Civitavecchia earn from one thousand three hundred to one thousand four hundred francs. M. Tavernier will be paid mainly in prestige.

Several considerations have impelled me somewhat to postpone M. Lysimaque Tavernier's nomination. M. Tavernier, who supposes himself all-knowing and all-deserving, cannot keep the shipping accounts, and always delays by a month or two the completion of the financial report which it is my duty to make to the Ministry. As my own hand-writing is bad, this is an embarrassment to me. On the other hand, to appoint a successor to M. Tavernier would be to inflict a mortal blow upon him. I feared a tragic climax. M. Tavernier is very obliging to Frenchmen who arrive at Civitavecchia by the steam boats and whose passports are a continual subject of litigation with the local police. These considerations have caused me to overlook the inconvenience of myself keeping the shipping accounts.

[1] Cf. letter no. 175.
[2] Former colleague of Beyle's on the Council of State, and, in 1832, Minister for Foreign Affairs.

M. L. Tavernier, grandson of M. Tavernier, French consul at Salonika about 1798, gratuitously exercised the functions of chancery secretary under M. le baron de Vaux, my predecessor. M. de Vaux, who had replaced him some time before my arrival, advised me not to employ him, telling me that I should much regret it. M. Tavernier at present receives fifteen crowns a month, and I pay for his lodging. I would prefer to pay more for a more skilful and less uneasy assistant. I believe M. Tavernier to be beyond reproach as regards probity. M. le comte de Sainte-Aulaire was so kind as to address to Your Excellency several requests in favour of M. Tavernier. His Excellency M. le marquis de Latour-Maubourg will probably write to the same effect.

I could not find a man capable of replacing him—a man possessing, for example, half the exactitude and knowledge of Signor Poggi, of Leghorn—for less than one thousand three hundred to one thousand four hundred francs.

I am respectfully, Monsieur le Duc, Your Excellency's very humble and obedient servant,

DE BEYLE.[1]

―――― 181 ――――

TO MME GAULTHIER

Civitavecchia, 4th of May 1834

I have read the *Lieutenant*, my dear and amiable friend. You will have to copy it out again entirely, meanwhile imagining to yourself that you are translating a book in German. The language is, in my opinion, horribly noble and over-emphatic. I have scribbled cruelly all over it. You must not be lazy; for, after all, you write only for the sake of writing: for you it is an amusement. So, for example, turn all the end of the second manuscript volume into dialogue—all the part concerning Versailles, Hélène, Sophie and the drawing-room charades. All that is too heavy in narrative. The dénoûment falls flat. Olivier seems to be chasing millions —an admirable thing in real life, since the spectator says: " I might dine at that man's house."

[1] On May 12th, 1834, Mérimée wrote to Sutton Sharpe: " Not long ago Beyle deeply irritated his Ministry by proposing a chancery clerk and adding, at the end of his letter: ' By the way, the man is utterly incompetent.' Moreover, he sent in, signed by himself, a very well constructed report on the sugar-trade. The only trouble was that the said report, signed by a sugar-merchant, had already been in the Ministry for a week."

An abominable thing from the reader's point of view, however . . .
I have sketched another dénoûment . . . As you see, I have been faithful
to our agreement. I have in no way catered to your vanity . . . There
should be fewer *de's* amongst the names, and you should not mention
your characters by their baptismal names. When you speak of Crozet,
do you call him " Louis "? You say " Crozet ", or you should do.

You ought to cut out at least fifty superlatives in every chapter.
Never say: " Olivier's burning passion for Hélène."

The poor novelist must try to make the reader *believe* in the existence
of a " burning passion ", but must never mention it by name: to do so
is immodest.

Bear in mind that rich people have no passions, except that of hurt
vanity.

If you say: " The passion that devoured him ", you lapse into the
style of a novel for chambermaids, published in duodecimo by M.
Pigoreau. But the *Lieutenant* will not do for chambermaids: it has not
enough corpses, abductions and other things that are a matter of course
in old Pigoreau's novels.

LEUWEN
or
The pupil expelled from the École Polytechnique[1]

That's the title I would give it. It explains the friendship or liaison
between Olivier and Edmond. The character of Edmond, the " future
academician ", is the newest thing in the *Lieutenant*. The basic structure
of the chapters is true to life; but everything is spoilt by the superlatives
of the late M. Desmazures. Tell me the story as if you were writing to me.
Read Marivaux's *Marianne* and M. Mérimée's *Quinze cent soixante-douze*,
as one takes a black draught, to cure you of the provincial Phoebus.
When describing a man, a woman, or a place, always think of someone
or something that actually exists.

I am quite full of the *Lieutenant*, which I have just finished[2]. But
how am I to send you back the manuscript? I must find an opportunity—
but how? I shall seek.

Write me a letter full of proper names . . . Return from a holiday is
always a very sad moment: I could write two or three pages, and not bad

[1] College of Engineering.
[2] A few days later Beyle began writing the unfinished novel known under the title of
Lucien Leuwen.
Mme Gaulthier never published anything.

ones, on this subject[1]. One says to oneself: " Am I to live and grow old far from my fatherland? " Or from " *the* fatherland ", as is more fashionable. I spend all my evenings at the home of a nineteen-year-old marchesa who supposes herself to have friendly feelings towards your humble servant. To me she is like a comfortable sofa. Alas! nothing more, I go no further; and, what is much worse, I do not want to go further.

------- 182 -------

TO LYSIMAQUE TAVERNIER

Rome, the 7th of June 1834

I am surprised, Monsieur, by the tone of your letter of the 5th inst. You state, Monsieur: " Keenly hurt by the ingratitude and injustice of your behaviour, I have the honour to present my resignation."

I accept your resignation, Monsieur, the terms in which you offer it leaving me no alternative.

In 1831, on my arrival at Civitavecchia, I found you unemployed. M. le baron de Vaux, my predecessor, had withdrawn his confidence from you and had appointed as chancery secretary a gentleman named, I think, Signor Baldrini.

M. le baron de Vaux repeated to me twenty times over that if I gave you employment I would regret it. I enjoined you to obtain a recommendation from M. de Sainte-Aulaire, French ambassador at Rome, and you were unable to do so. You besought me with tears for the post of chancery secretary, and I yielded.

You satisfactorily discharge your duties towards French travellers, but you are incapable of keeping the most simple accounts. You muddled the Ancona accounts to such a degree that, against all the evidence, His Excellency M. the Minister of Shipping has just condemned me to pay two hundred and eighty francs. As soon as I leave you in charge of the least detail, I am almost certain to receive, a month later, a reprimand from His Excellency M. the Minister for Foreign Affairs.

Thus it came about that in his letter of the 19th of May last, concerning chancery expenditure, His Excellency the Minister for Foreign Affairs

---

[1] Beyle had returned to Civitavecchia in December, 1833, after a six months' leave of absence.

enjoins me " to acquire sufficient grasp of the decrees of the 23rd and 24th of August last, and also of the circular of the 2nd of September, to avoid further errors in their application ".

In the position in which you have put me, monsieur, I can but accept your resignation and invite you to reflect upon the ridiculous imputations of " ingratitude " and " injustice " applied to a man who, without knowing you and against the hundred times repeated advice of his predecessor, gave you an honourable post.

I have the honour to be, Monsieur, your very humble and obedient servant.

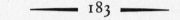

183

TO THE MARQUIS DE LATOUR-MAUBOURG

Rome, the 14th of June 1834

Monsieur le Marquis,

Your Excellency uses me with so much kindness that I cannot but yield.

But I do so not without foreseeing the labyrinth of unpleasantnesses into which I am about to enter. I have always regarded M. Lysimaque as a man of utter falsity; since the Decree of the month of August last he has ceased to give clear replies to threequarters of my letters; he considers himself a personage. Now that he finds himself reinstated by the Embassy, after having called me " ungrateful " and " unjust ", I must be ready for a hundred malicious little tricks, which will be repeated daily and with which I shall not dare to take up your time. Since your Excellency is well-disposed towards M. Lysimaque, I would willingly undertake to give him fifteen crowns a month for a year, on condition that he no longer had any part in my affairs. I had resolved to remain at Civitavecchia for several months, perhaps for ever. It seems to me that honour has spoken. One is given the lie, one must fight; a clerk is insolent, one dismisses him; either I am badly mistaken or M. L. is quite capable of making every kind of excuse.

The Greeks, whom Your Excellency knows better than I do, attach no importance to words, but only to facts. M. L. retains his post, and against my will. God knows what calumnies he will lay against me with Your Excellency and with the Minister.

M. Antoine Albert[1], who has been employed in my office for three years, and whom I sent as a courier to Your Excellency on the 22nd of April last, is a man of complete integrity. I was of service to him when he tried to kill his mistress, and himself afterwards. I have known his father and all his family for a long time. They are completely estimable people of whom there is only one opinion. I would prefer to give M. Lysimaque two hundred crowns and remain for six months at Civitavecchia with M. Albert as my clerk, rather than to be exposed to the calumnies of this Greek, who will feel that he is under high protection[2].

I am respectfully, Monsieur le Marquis, Your Excellency's very humble and obedient servant,

H. BEYLE.

―――― 184 ――――

TO ROMAIN COLOMB

Civitavecchia, the 10th of September 1834

. . . I am beginning to be very tired of the profession, and I deeply envy the man who at the age of fifty has an income of five thousand francs. Of what use is it, to a man who does not care for shooting, to be in a country rich in hares and partridges? Of what use is it to be able to play the second rôle at " Bee ", if self-important gossip, an air of self-importance, a serious manner of speaking of the morning's work and the correspondence by the last courier, if all these things are my *horror*? Nothing in the whole world seems to me so stupid as seriousness.

Here are two errands. Try to sell my post to somebody for four thousand francs a year. Insert advertisements in the *Débats* so that I shall be able to sell my manuscripts if ever I have the good fortune to be in a position to do so. Advertise, at my expense, the *Histoire de la Peinture en Italie*, the *Vie de Rossini* (that great man, the only great man besides you and myself, is dying at Bologna, 'tis said), the *Rouge et le*

[1] " M. Albert (Toto). A young man who has been working at the Consulate for six or seven years. He is gloomy, self-absorbed, taciturn: in 1833 he ran his sword through a young woman, and I saved him from the hulks." (Letter dated November 29th, 1839, to the comte de Latour-Maubourg, who had replaced his brother the marquis after the latter's death in office at Rome in 1837.) See also letter no. 219.

[2] In 1838 Beyle, on leave in Paris, wrote to his friend Donato Bucci: " Shall I be able to produce legal proof that the Greek forced the lock of my private office? He told M. Gal. that it was the wind that had forced the door." Lysimaque Tavernier Caftangioglu was decorated with the Légion d'honneur.

Noir, the *Vies de Haydn, Mozart et Métastase*. In short, do what ever you choose, provided that when the carriage-folk, the people who can read me, feel bored in the country, their newspaper will confront them with one of my advertisements.

I can tell you that there is not a single dreary English family visiting Rome but reads the *Promenades*. At the house of the Minister-Cardinal on St. Peter's day, when we were watching the fireworks, people spoke to me of it without knowing who I was. These fools think it lacks seriousness. But how happy I would be on a fourth storey, writing another such book, if I had bread! What a prospect, never to see again the wits of Paris, except perhaps two or three times before I die!

Yesterday I was at a charming dinner, the handsomest spot in the neighbourhood: trees, a cool wind and thirty-three fellow diners, who considered themselves honoured by the presence of a consul. But not a single subtle or vigorous idea amongst the lot of them. Must I die of suffocation by fools? It seems very probable. I am liked, respected, I had the best portion from a fourteen-pound fish, the best of its kind. I had an excellent horse, which covered five and a half miles in three-quarters of an hour. But I am perishing of boredom.

. . . .

—— 185 ——

TO SOPHIE DUVAUCEL

Civitavecchia, 28th of October 1834

In very truth I must thank you for your delightful letters: I keep them and re-read them in the long, solitary evenings I spend at Civitavecchia. Here a year has gone by since I last saw you, since I last saw Paris. Must I live and die on this solitary shore? I fear I must. In that case I shall die completely numbed by boredom and the non-communication of my ideas. Assuredly, I do not claim that they are good ones; but, such as they are, if all Civitavecchia were to club together, it could not understand the simplest of them. If only I were a glutton, or a sportsman! If only I were an antiquarian! But I love the *beautiful*, and not the *rare*; moreover, I believe only what is *proven*. Despite these disqualifications, I have joined a society that is about to stir up the Etruscans who had themselves buried in style two thousand seven hundred years ago. Two leagues hence there is a little town mentioned by Ariosto at the beginning of *Gioconda*; its name, Corneto, is very famous in Italy. Beside it lies a bare, abominable hill, with no tree or any outstanding feature. This is the *Necropolis*, the Père La Chaise of Tarquinie, whence came that Tarquin whose son was so famous in the annals of feminine virtue. Two feet beneath the surface of this bare, sterile soil—the dreariest in the world—one finds pretty little chambers eight feet wide by ten feet long. Here we have the "coupe". But do you understand the word? By "coupe" you will suppose I mean a *goblet*. Not a bit of it: the word means a *cut*, as in "coup de sabre". When you slice a Calville apple crosswise, you have a "coupe" of it. So here we have the "coupe" of these tombs, which are two thousand seven hundred years old: I shall not rebate a single century.

. . . But when this Etruscan gentleman was a great man—which meant a man of courage and skilful at everything—his chariot was burned near the entry to the tomb, at a distance of fifteen to twenty feet; and you, as a scientist, know that hard charcoal endures for ever. We seek amongst the "charcoal", crawl on all fours through the door and find that everything was broken by Roman antiquarians of the society founded by the late Trajan. These gentry, or else the barbarian Saracens of the Middle Ages, were looking for metals, and they broke the vases out of spite. We find ten broken vases to one intact. You will receive, Heaven knows knows when! three or four pieces of pottery that were part of my share for this year. The pottery is of a handsome black, and can be used for serving your tea. It has no value, and if, after lasting two thousand seven hundred years, it gets broken in the Jardin, I shall send you other pieces. Your scientists, who deny anything that they cannot explain, will say that my pottery comes from the factory, that it is a counterfeit, or that it was manufactured under Leo X or under Augustus. Don't believe a word of it. Stick to your two thousand seven hundred years. As for the site, I once took MM. Adrien de Jussieu and Ampère there—that was in my youth—when I was less wearied by my "greatness". I hope that these gentlemen—even although they do cleave to the Institute—will not lie on a matter of cold facts.

. . . .

TO DI FIORE

Civitavecchia, the 1st of November 1834

This summer, dying of heat, I said to myself more than a hundred times: "How glad I am that the best of flowers did not take my advice. How have I managed to avoid sweating to death?"

I am forgetting everything that is not strictly reasonable—even how to spell. On every journey I am obliged to re-learn fine Paris manners. For example, here is a problem that I cannot solve: may I send Madame la comtesse K——[1] three or four black vases (worth twenty-seven francs) which I found in my excavations? If the answer is *yes*, I enclose a letter for her, written in true traveller's style; for I dare not crack jokes with a woman who has doubtless been frozen by the manners of the faubourg Saint-Germain. Because of these manners, my letter was a heavy task to write; and actually it will be twice as heavy to read. So these so-called fine manners probably *diminish* the pleasure that still remains, in 1834, on this cooling planet: in other words, they are eminently *immoral.*

Virtue consists in adding to happiness; vice adds to misery. All the rest is but hypocrisy or bourgeois asininity. (One must always seize any opportunity to instruct the young.)

In my Will I am leaving my bust of Tiberius—its fame grows daily— to M. le comte Molé. My eyes have grown accustomed to this bust: all it gives me is a little thrill of vanity when a stranger comes to see it and offers to buy it. *L'ho comprato*[2] myself, for four crowns from the peasant who dug it up. For this reason, would there be any respectable method of inducing M. Molé to accept it during my lifetime? I should much prefer it to be in the home of that amiable man, whom I have never met *except to thank him for some favour*, rather than in my own. His behaviour forms such a remarkable contrast to M. Guizot's[3] that my gratitude increases daily. In any case, who knows where I shall die, or whether my servant won't steal the bust and throw my Will on the fire?

[1] The comtesse de Castellane.
[2] I bought it.
[3] Who had promised Beyle the Légion d'honneur, and had not yet kept his promise.

I tell you again, and your wisdom will already have observed it twenty times over, that with an Italian I behave naturally, but with a Frenchman I become entirely tangled up by Parisian refinement: I should be familiar with it, at my age, and I know absolutely nothing about it.

When I learn it, it often seems to me the height of absurdity; but, after all, it is like a country's language: one must either speak it or abandon hope of being understood.

I am perishing of boredom. I cannot have a conversation with anyone. I wish I had a post at Paris worth four thousand francs. My true post would be in the service of Mark-Michael Rey, a Dutch publisher, who would pay me four thousand francs a year for one or two octavo volumes. That is the only work that does not seem to me ridiculous. What, to grow old at Civitavecchia! Or even at Rome! *I have seen so much sunshine!*

I know that there is something ridiculous about my constant complaining; but can one ever complain too loudly of not having been born with an income of four thousand francs? (My father had an income of twelve or fifteen thousand, and ruined himself in 1818.) What a prospect, of living and slowly burning oneself out in this region, unable to speak of anything but money and shooting! Today, the 1st of November, there is magnificent sunshine, much too hot for a walk beneath its rays. I have just met the most agreeable man in Civitavecchia. He imparted to me the above-mentioned information, concerning the sun, and after that we knew how to talk to one another. . . . I was awoken at half past three in the morning by a courier whom I sent off at noon to Leghorn, by the steamboat. I hurried off to Mass, breakfasted with tea, and here I am all panting . . . My window is sixty feet above the sea, and into this sea I throw the scraps of paper left on the table, after packing them in an envelope. . . . How many chilly characters, how many geometricians, would be happy in my place—or, at least, peaceful and satisfied! But, for my part, my soul is a fire that sinks unless it blazes. I need three or four cubic feet of new ideas per day, as a steamboat needs coal.

People here are a hundred times more passionate than in France. Deep and abominable intrigues for a profit of two hundred francs are of frequent occurrence. The women of Rome live constantly in the presence of death. This summer, in the via in Lucina, a young woman—with a very well-made leg, in faith!—fell dead at my feet with a knife-thrust in her neck. She had sought to leave her lover.

A young woman said to one of my friends: " If the boat-owner with whom I am living knows that I have come to your house, the first time he goes to Fiumicino, he will stab me and push me into the Tiber."

This was perfectly true, yet she continues to visit my friend. This boat-master has already two or three times had the misfortune to lose his mistresses overboard from his boat.

But all this is not worth the new ideas I would garner at Madame de Ka's[1], if I went there twenty times on end; on Tuesdays to Madame Ancelot's; on Wednesdays to Gérard's; on Saturdays to M. Cuvier's; three suppers a week at the Café Anglais—and I would be abreast of all that Paris is saying. I would also have the salons of M. Joseph Bernard, Béranger's friend, and those of Mme Curial, etc. With all this, to speak like M. Hugo, I would have an " open window " upon life, and all morning I would enjoy working on my next octavo, which perhaps would be worth nothing. M. Guizot would have to appoint me professor of the history of fine arts (painting, sculpture, architecture and music), with a salary of five thousand francs. Nothing would do more to raise the standard of French taste, which constantly inclines towards subject-pictures and light comedy (it all has to do with vanity and love of the " piquant "). Every year I would impart wholesome ideas to two hundred young people, of whom several would be destined to have salons in Paris about 1850. I would be piquant and instructive, I would endeavour not to let the wise and good think me crazy. Is that not the impression my books made on M. le comte d'H——?

M. Ampère junior, who is a professor at the Collège de France, with a salary of five thousand francs, and is now in Rome, promised me his vote for the chair of History of the Fine Arts. What I want you to do now is to find me a " friendly " minister.

I sometimes hope that as I approach your age I shall become as wise as you. I have within me a soul that inclines to madness. I would be happy to be lodged with you on the fourth storey of the club, in the room next to yours, and served by one of the domestics of the said club.

The King of Bavaria, who came to visit our tombs at Tarquinie, gave not a baioco in tips. For my part, I give five paoli (fifty-five sous) to the man who walks a quarter of a league to open the doors of those tombs. The same King of Bavaria asked for fried eggs at the porta de Montecone. He ate six, and was asked for forty-five sous: a furious aide de camp threw thirty-five sous on the table, swearing that, *per Dio*, he would pay no more.

Your King of Naples, who is only twenty-three, was at Rome this winter and gave a tip of two paoli to the custodian of the Museo Borghese, which has eighteen rooms and four hundred pictures. For my part, I give three paoli.

[1] The comtesse de Castellane.

His Majesty Don Miguel gives sixteen crowns (eighty-two francs) to every woman of the streets. He makes great use of these women, and in every possible manner.

─── 187 ───

TO ROMAIN COLOMB

Civitavecchia, the 4th of November 1834

'Tis all very well for you to talk, my dear fellow, I can assure you that I have no scruples about writing a bad book, being convinced that, if it is bad, five or six years after it is printed the grocer will have used all the pages for wrapping currants for children. During the last ten years there has been quite another reason why I have been held back from writing many things—fear that some indiscreet lout might mock at me if he read them. But, praise God! I am informed on all sides that my handwriting is becoming so bad that it is impossible to read it. It has reached the condition of a " cipher ", I am told, and recently, when I wrote to M. Hérard, my banker, my letter was accompanied by a copy made by one of my employees.

I have become so absent-minded that often I forget the end of a phrase before I have reached it. At other times I write at night, without a candle, as I am doing now. After all, I have written, at horrible speed, twelve or fifteen octavo volumes, all of which have been published by M. de Stendhal. The result of all this is that at the age of fifty-one my hand-writing is illegible. The shame of seeing some Paul Pry reading my soul by reading my writings has prevented me, since the age of reason— or, rather, in my case, the age of passion—from writing of what I feel, or, rather, of the aspects under which I see things—the which aspects might perhaps seem interesting to the reader, if by chance he had the same sort of melancholic and crazy soul as mine.

Experience has taught me—but only during the last year or two— that I run no danger of being understood, for a third reason which I would explain in Greek, if I knew how to write it.

Like the Boeotians, I cast my nets *too high.*

[320]

TO MME GAULTHIER

Civitavecchia, the 8th of November 1834

Would you be so kind, my dear and lovable friend, as to have the *Lieutenant* withdrawn? M. Colomb writes to me that he cannot understand it and nobody is clamouring for it. I am sure I wrote to you: my letter must have ended its days in the pipe of an Austrian corporal.

If you have seen my revisions to the *Lieutenant*, you will have said: " Is that all? Was *that* really worth waiting a year for? " The fact is that it was simply a matter of putting: " Bring me my horse ", instead of: " Approach with my courser ". If you train yourself by reading twenty pages of Marivaux's *Marianne* every morning, you will realise the advantages to be had from exact description of the impulses of the human heart. Never make your characters too rich, and have your hero commit some little gaucherie, since, after all, we, too, are heroes and we, too, commit gaucheries. We run where a dull man walks, and that with difficulty and with a stick: that is why he does not fall.

Write me an eight-page letter, and send it to M. Colomb, who will despatch it to M. Bazin, proprietor of the steamboat at Marseilles. In this way one avoids the route via Hunmingen, or via Chambéry and Rome.

Plenty of proper names, I implore, and little society adventures in country-houses. 'Tis there, I think, that the most cuckolds are manufactured.

Why is there not a Paris newspaper which reports that a cat has fallen from a rainpipe in the rue du Martrois? These great boobies of political journals never descend to anecdote unless it contains bloodshed. This is how I came to read about the adventures you wot of: I know both husband and wife. What hero was the indirect author of all the disturbance?

When will you have a little, well-warmed drawing-room on the fourth storey in the rue de Hanovre, with me in this drawing-room from seven until eight in the evening, chatting with a few intimate friends who know how to take nothing seriously but friendship and love? Everything else is but a bad joke. Whilst waiting for the setting of the drawing-room, make ready its cast of characters. How is the cast that attends upon Mme la députée de Saint-Denis?

—— 189 ——

TO SAINTE-BEUVE

Civitavecchia, the 21st *of December* 1834.
(Superb sunshine. I am working by an
open window.)

You knew long before I did, my dear monsieur, that our friend J.-J. Ampère emerged all spick and span from a very pretty and very acute danger. On the 12th of December, in full moonlight, the *Henri-IV* was so mad as to shave Monte Argentario at a distance of forty metres. (Of course, the canal between this mountain, and the island of Giglio is only eight miles wide!) The unfortunate boat touched on a *secca* where there is only three feet of water. The result was an enormous hole, through which the water entered and put out the furnaces. Happily the boat was able to remain afloat as far as the shore, else those on board would have had to fight for the two or three little longboats. How I hate a Gascon braggart! This is an exact description of the captain of the *Henri IV*, who since losing his ship has been more vainglorious and boastful than ever. This man's folly has compelled me to write an infinity of official documents. I have to report and report. Perhaps the Marseilles insurance company will refuse to pay the eighty, plus forty, making a hundred and twenty thousand francs, the value of the boat. Nobody is trying to salvage it. I cannot conceive why a machine that cost eighty thousand francs should be left under forty feet of water.

Ampère wrote to me on the 14th from Porto Triola, six miles from the fatal reef. He enjoins me to write to you, Monsieur. His letter reached me on the 21st; a traveller had forgotten about it for four days.

I seize the opportunity of writing to a man whom I would like to meet—a thing that almost never happens to me. I never speak of our beloved literature without becoming an Ovid: *barbarus hic ego sum quia non intelligor illis.* I receive the *Revue des Deux Mondes*, the *Rétrospective* and the *Edinburgh Review*. Ah, monsieur, what styles! And, by way of compensation, what a lack of ideas! I find consolation in M. Loève-Veimars, and, in the current issue, in M. Magnin, even although he says: " The century *progresses*! " What a pretty word, rhyming with " greases "![1] But, after all, he has ideas. If you meet M. Magnin and have nothing better to speak of, remind me to him. But ask why he invents " progresses " and uses " hieratic " and other Greek words which God confound! One should leave these poor stratagems to those men of genius who are destitute of ideas.

I, and all Rome, know French literature only through the Brussels editions. I live as if I were in Borneo. I have not yet seen *Volupté*, although I have twice ordered it from Leghorn. But you and I are separated by an abyss, for I believe that there is a *God*[2]: he is wicked and malignant. I shall be very much astonished if I find him after my death, and if he allows me to speak I shall have plenty to say to him. If he existed—and were just—I would not behave otherwise. I therefore stand to gain by his existence, for he will pay me for having behaved in the manner that procured me the greatest pleasure. But let us not talk any more, monsieur, of what separates us. If ever you care to come and occupy a bed for two months or two years in my apartment at Civitavecchia, you will reign over my books and over the loveliest sea in the world, *Tyrrhenum*. I am engaged in excavation and have some black vases that are two thousand seven hundred years old, so I am told. In this matter, as in others, I have my doubts. Ampère will tell you that I have spent my savings in buying the right to make copies from the archives that are guarded here so jealously—for the simple reason that their owners cannot read. The result is that I have seven folio volumes, but with writing only on one side of the page, containing perfectly true anecdotes written by contemporaries in half-slang[3]. When I am once again a poor devil living on a fourth storey, I shall translate all this *faithfully*. In my opinion, its entire merit lies in its faithfulness. I have told you all this in order to lead up to the question: what title should be given to this collection? " *Historiettes romaines*, faithfully translated from accounts written by contemporaries (1400 to 1650) "? But can one use the word " historiette " of a tragic tale?

I in no way oblige you to reply, monsieur. You can express your opinion to our castaway. I have written a novel entitled *L'Orange de Malte*[4]. The hero, son of a rich banker who is later ruined, is an ensign at Nancy, then confidential secretary to a minister in Paris. The whole thing is written like the *Code Civil*. I have a horror of wordiness à la Chateaubriand. If you and I live to be old, monsieur, we shall see works

---

[1] *Progresse—graisse.*
[2] In English in the original.
[3] The source of *Chroniques Italiennes*.
[4] *Lucien Leuwen.*

in the style of Sand offered for sale at ten sous the volume like the *fashionable*[1] novels of Colman in London, and nobody will want them. After that they will be taken to Canada, where, since provincials always love over-emphasis, they will fetch thirty or thirty-six francs per hundred volumes.

Italy is no longer the country I admired in 1815. She is in love with a thing that she does not possess. The fine arts, for which alone she is made, are for her no longer anything more than a last resort. She is profoundly humiliated in her *excessive* vanity at not having a lilac robe like her elder sisters, France, Spain and Portugal. But if she had it, she could not wear it. First of all she would need twenty years of the iron rod of Frederick II, who would have murderers hanged and thieves gaoled. A young thief, a protégé of mine, had been sentenced to three years in the hulks here. He said: " Apoplexy seize the Madonna " (*Accidente alla Madonna*), and was sentenced to twenty years in the hulks. In Rome alone there are two hundred murderers, and two hundred corpses are found in the streets. On the first day of Carnival one man is guillotined and one man shot from the rear, and during the rest of the year like fates befall two or three others. Our messieurs Lucas could study the fine result of the abolition of the death penalty. I have had murderers give me an account of the inner debate that precedes a crime. The hulks, where life is very cheerful, are nothing. What frightens them exceedingly is the death penalty, for they believe firmly in the Madonna, and in God for the Madonna's sake, as her brother-in-law. Have the castaway tell you the secret story of the felon for whom I obtained the use of a place of convenience. Respectful greetings.

Adolphe de Seyssels.

P.S. My compliments to MM. Victor Hugo, Magnin, Loève-Veimars, Taschereau. Be sure to tell them that foreigners understand the styles of Voltaire and Rollin, but nothing at all of M. de S——. This is literally true. The length of this rambling discourse will prove to you, monsieur, how much I would enjoy consulting you. What an admirable style Tallemant des Réaux has! Imagine what it would be if translated by the gentlemen of the *Revue des Deux Mondes*.

[1] In English in the original.

TO MME DUCREST DE VILLENEUVE[1]

4th of March 1835

Madame, just imagine it, Verona contains certain austere philosophers, avowed enemies of the outpourings of friendship! These gentlemen light their pipes not only with my letters—a thing for which I willingly forgive them—but also with letters addressed to me. Perhaps everybody is treated in the same way, or perhaps the memory of my name, which has been kept alive since Trieste, still has some influence. What it is to have a name! Three months ago, suffering cruelly from this inconvenience, I asked my friends in Paris to address their letters to M. Bazin, at Marseilles. Ever kindly Heaven chose this moment to send the cholera upon the rude inhabitants of Provence, and in their panic they are keeping all my letters, probably supposing them to be a prophylactic. My little harbour is closed by a frightful quarantine. Marshall Marmont, who arrived yesterday from Malta, is in quarantine for ten days; and is as peevish as if his name were Catinat. This evening, at the ball, an amiable gentleman said to me: " I leave tomorrow for Paris." The result was that I left the ball at half past two and am writing you these lines, with my head full of the happenings of the Carnival, which I have found very amusing. To start with, I am no longer engaged to be married[2]. Monsieur the father-in-law wanted to spend his life with me; he thinks I am a very pleasant person. My character is so ill-disposed that I immediately broke off the engagement. Imagine a man of sixty-five attached to my poor person and regarding himself as my father! I would not dine every day with an old man, not if he paid me a hundred francs a dinner. What's an inheritance for which one has to pay court?

The great event of the Carnival is that the eight or ten noblest and richest of our ladies (all our ladies have titles, of course) have thought fit to sit on a sofa and not to return the greetings of any of the others. They stare at them fixedly and then avert their eyes. In short, exactly the same treatment as poor Mme de Sainte-Aulaire, whom you all regarded at Paris as a great lady, suffered at Vienna. And when *the husband*[3]

[1] After Cuvier's death, Sophie Duvaucel had married Admiral Ducrest de Villeneuve, in 1834.

[2] Beyle had proposed marriage to Mlle Vidau, aged twenty, granddaughter of J. B. Vidau, French consul at Civitavecchia, *ob.* 1789.

[3] In English in the original.

protested to the *husband of the most impertinent, the celebrated*[1] Prince Metternich, the latter laughed at him. The little manoeuvres of our local exclusives gave me constant pleasure throughout the Carnival. For the rest, I have not yet encountered a single woman, I shall not say, of wit, but of the strength of personality of Mlle Poingferré de Serres. Do you remember that M. Mouton of Mont-de-Marsan?

Give me a short description of this Orient of yours, if you want my imagination to follow you amidst your splendours[2]. Do you play the exclusive with the unfortunate wives of little naval lieutenants? Do you keep on saying that we are being " débordés " by democracy? Say rather: " désourlés "[3]. This was one of my repartees to a demi-exclusive who had repeated the word " débordés " in my hearing for the tenth time in an evening.

Mme la Directrice de la Poste in charge of the Oriental mail is opening your letters. There you have the vast maliciousness of little towns. Have them addressed by an Admiralty clerk. Sign them: " Augustine de Sève ", and have them put in the post at Nantes or Brest. Instead of " Lebrun who spoke so well of Corneille ", put " Brunle who spoke of Neillecor." That will suffice to put a stop to all provincial mischief. I am finishing a novel in which I depict (as the men of letters, your protégés, are wont to say) a country town of thirty thousand people in the region of Metz or Nancy. I call it Montvallier[4]. Here my hero falls in love. Tell me something of provincial life. You will interest me doubly or triply. Present my respectful homage to those who are dear to you. What news of pretty Mme Martial? Is *the husband*[1] jealous? At one time, when there was a question of his being appointed a Master of Appeals, he would not leave her behind in Paris. Write to M. Bel, Palazzo Conti, Roma. Nothing more. This gentleman will pass on to me the letters for which I burn—for I am very pleased to tell you, here and for the first time, that burn I do.

Anastase DE SERPIÈRE.

[1] In English in the original.
[2] Admiral Ducrest de Villeneuve was Maritime Prefect of Lorient.
[3] " Inundated "—" unpicked at the hem ":—untranslated play on words.
[4] Lucien Leuwen's garrison.

TO DOCTOR PRÉVOST[1]

Rome, the 8*th of March* 1835

Monsieur,

I am filled with gratitude for the good advice you gave me in December 1833. (I have gout and gravel, I am very fat, excessively nervous and fifty years of age.) You prescribed me wine of Colchis and complete abstention from acids.

When I returned here, I received a proposal of marriage. I postponed the major treatment and contented myself with abstaining entirely from acids. I take bicarbonate of soda or of potassium three times a week during six months of the year. I pass a gravel that is completely rounded, as if by friction: I think this is the effect of the bicarbonate. Instead of weighing six grains, the particles of gravel are of less than a quarter of a grain and cause no discomfort. I pass two or three grains (in weight) of gravel every week, in two hundred round particles. For eighteen months I have abstained from coffee, and the pains in my intestines have almost entirely ceased. Since I gave up coffee, they have not been violent enough to make me curse. When I take coffee again, the pain in the intestines returns, especially three inches to the left of the navel. I breakfast with tea and butter. I drink little wine: when I drink wine of Champagne, next day I feel much more cheerful and less nervous. Since December 1833 I have not taken six grains of vinegar or lemon-juice. I feel very well, for which I thank you. Is there anything I should do? If there is nothing, then I sincerely beg you, monsieur, not to trouble to answer: I would rather that you brought relief to one patient the more. I dine every day with that kindly and judicious man, M. Abraham Constantin, and we often speak of your humanity and the care with which you listen to your patients.

I am, monsieur, with the sincerest gratitude, your very devoted servant,

H. BEYLE.

---

[1] A Genevan physician, a friend of Abraham Constantin.

TO THE DUC DE BROGLIE[1]

Civitavecchia, the 8th of April 1835

. . . I shall end with a story that was widely current at the Roman court during the Carnival, and with whose hero I am acquainted. It has no basic significance, and I mention it here only because it is possible that the newspapers may get hold of it.

During the time of the French occupation, the Reverend Father Manci Capellari[2] left his monastery, which was on an island half a league from Venice, and entered the household of Signor Matinelli, a Venetian nobleman, to take charge of his son's education. The Father was very learned and had all the virtues: a tender friendship arose between master and pupil. When the Reverend Father Capellari left Venice, he maintained a regular correspondence with his pupil, Signor Matinelli junior. Recently he insisted that Signor Matinelli should come to Rome. The young man arrived about Christmas and left Rome on the second day of Lent. Signor Matinelli is perhaps thirty-six years of age, with an income of twelve or fifteen thousand francs. He has a sweet nature and much good sense. Incidentally, he is a perfect Venetian: he loves pleasure above all things and has a horror of all disturbance. He writes excellent historical works, which Herr von Metternich does not allow him to print; but the refusals are couched in most polite terms.

He was received by His Holiness like a son, and spent five or six hours daily in his company. Signor Matinelli detests the rôle of adroit and prudent courtier. It was despite his utmost efforts that he accepted the Cross of St. Gregory, which his old master insisted on bestowing upon him. Blunt frankness and " what do I care? " are His Holiness's basic characteristics. The Pope regards himself as a poor man who has won the top prize in a rich lottery, but is in no way dazzled by this stroke of luck. He would consider it humiliating *to his intelligence* to be unable to play the rôle of sovereign with ease and composure. During the ceremonies in the sacristy, His Holiness converses easily whilst quantities of monks come and kiss his foot. The Pope carefully applies himself to deriving from his position all that it can contribute to his health and

[1] At this time President of the Council and Minister for Foreign Affairs.
[2] Pope Gregory XVI.

happiness. He has the true character of a Venetian philosopher, who is dazzled by nothing, who loves the pleasures of life, and loves cold good sense first and last. The only trouble in his life are the liberals, and he hates them. His Holiness is primarily concerned with the government of the Church, disputes between monasteries and his care to award ecclesiastical posts to those most worthy of them. Secular cares take second place, and modesty, which is one of His Holiness's virtues, causes him often, when a secular question arises, to excuse himself on grounds of ignorance.

His Holiness used to take Signor Matinelli with him on his walks. The pomp with which sovereigns are accompanied embarrassed Signor Matinelli. " In truth, I know not how to speak to Your Holiness." " As of old: I am still the master and you the disciple."

When he was two miles outside the city, the Pope would dismount from his carriage, take Signor Matinelli by the arm and walk with him for two hours, leaving his suite fifty paces to the rear. The suite was much astonished, and even somewhat alarmed. People " in the know " claim that if Signor Matinelli, who is a widower, had wished it, he could have become a Prelate, Great Chamberlain and soon afterwards a cardinal. But nothing is more antipathetic to Signor Matinelli's frank and merry nature than the duties imposed by high office.

" This Rome of yours seems to me the gloomiest thing in the world," he said to the Pope, " and I am sure that not a day passes without Your Holiness's missing Venice." His Holiness often asked for news, spoke on all topics with the simplicity that a Venetian nobleman displays to his intimates, and often argued with Signor Matinelli.

The latter made it a point of honour in no way to alter his mode of speech. When speaking of a cardinal, he might quite well say: " That rascal of a Such-an-One! " And if the Pope dissented, Signor Matinelli would maintain his opinion, as he would have done with a private person.

" I never once lied all the time I was at the Vatican," Signor Matinelli would say. " To remind me of my duty, I never went to visit His Holiness except in a frock-coat. . . . Apart from the late Cardinal Albani," he would say to the Pope, " the majority of your Cardinals have not the strength of character to be sub-prefects. They are getting you quite gratuitously hated."

" So much the worse for whoever hates me. Nobody will come and pull me out of this armchair! And where do you expect me to find people with Albani's strength of character? What do you think of Such-an-One? "

"One of the most notable rascals at your court."

"And Ciacchi?"

"A man of the first merit: Your Holiness could find use for a dozen such."

His Holiness continually compared the personages whom he employs with the persons employed by Napoleon at Venice about 1810. During entire walks, His Holiness would talk with Signor Matinelli of astronomy and the progress this science has made since Lalande. His Holiness is the perfect type of a noble Venetian who has been made Doge, and he speaks of sovereigns just as though they had always been his peers.

"Besides, what can these people do either for or against us?" ("We" for "I" is a manner of speech which His Holiness has adopted with great ease.)

After his arrival at Rome several years before, Mgr. Capellari had written Signor Matinelli a letter criticising everything he had observed in the government. He had ended by expressing the keenest longing to return to Venice, and the keenest disgust at all he saw in Rome. Signor Matinelli mentioned this letter to His Holiness. "I would very much like to see it." Next day Signor Matinelli brought it. His Holiness laughed heartily when he read it.

"If you cared to sign it with your present signature, it would be a very curious piece in my library." His Holiness took the letter and laughingly signed it.

Having been a poor man all his life, the Pope has no idea of any very refined pleasures; but all others he relishes with true Venetian philosophy. His Holiness speaks of fifteen or twenty francs as if it were a considerable sum. He has a horror of dignity and of the "sublime comedy" that certain French Councils would have him play. His Holiness was reading the *Paroles d'un croyant* with great admiration: "What style!" "The style of that condemnation you have been made to sign is not up to it." "Chancery stuff!" the Pope replied. "Do you remember the official replies of Such-an-One?" (His Holiness named a Venetian nobleman whose name I have forgotten.) What is singular is that Signor Matinelli remained true to himself. On the eve of his departure, as he was returning from the Vatican, we saw that he was not wearing the Cross. "I have taken leave of His Holiness," he said. "I shall never wear it again. *Mi par mill' anni di riveder l'Opera a Venezia*[1]. I shall be there in seven days, God be praised!" His Holiness, who is aware that Signor Matinelli knows the Capellari family, did not say to him: "*Salutateli di mia parte*[2]." It is a custom that no Italian would have failed to observe.

[1] I am dying to see the Opera at Venice again.   [2] Give them my greetings.

[330]

Signor Matinelli and the rest of us were filled with the liveliest admiration for the naïve and sublime virtues of His Holiness.

193

TO DI FIORE

Civitavecchia, —— *April* 1835
Boring as the plague

I live here on the fringe of barbarism, I have gout and gravel, and I am very fat, excessively nervous and fifty-two years of age! Ah! had I known in 1814 that my father was ruined, I would have become a tooth-puller, lawyer, judge, etc. I am so stupefied by boredom that I have no desires; I am in black gloom. You will understand how excessive is my stagnation when I confess to you that I read the advertisements in the *Quotidienne*! Being reduced to such a diet simply bores me to death! In this bewitched sojourn I have no knowledge of anything.

The only unhappiness is a life of boredom.

Oh, to have a cottage or an income of fifteen hundred francs in the rue Saint-Roch! I am well, it is true, but I perish of boredom. The brute's real profession is to write a novel in an attic, for I prefer the pleasure of writing nonsense to that of wearing a laced coat that costs eight hundred francs. I go to Rome when I wish, but nevertheless, when all is said, one must stick to one's post. But what to do at this post? Here I become stupider every day. I find nobody with whom to play those games of shuttlecock and battledore which are called "displaying wit". I have reached such a point of decadence that as soon as I try to create possible characters, I become absurd: in the abominable absence of ideas in which I vegetate, I continually re-sift the same material.

Not a shadow of company—and Dominique is supposed to say that he is enjoying himself and is enchanted with his post! For I learn from Paris that I, too, must dissemble and refrain from saying that I am bored, and that on pain of being regarded as a fickle person who is never content with anything. Consequently, I have just written to Mme Azur that I would not write any more, but in order to keep my post. . . . Think of being obliged to tremble for the retention of a post at which one perishes of boredom!

Do see if there is no way of earning *two thousand*[1] (2000 francs) in Lutetia: a room facing south, on a fifth storey. Such a little room, with an income of five francs and five francs earned by a novel, would be supreme happiness. It is my natural bent to live with two candles and a writing-table; and now, as I write to you, I am happily doing just that. But how bored I become in my swallow's nest!

Farewell, I want to hang myself, to give up everything, for a room on the fifth storey, rue Richepanse.

L'ennuyé, Baron DORMANT.

 194

Rome, the 15th of April 1835

" It is useless, " you say, great philosopher, to find him " a room facing south and on the fifth storey." These are the very words of your letter. They are also the same words as were spoken by Paul-Louis Courier on that famous four-hour walk on Shrove Tuesday, tête-à-tête with myself—a walk that terminated in a dinner at Biffi's, which he thought too expensive, greatly to my pride. He was killed a week later. But my pride was not the result of this great man's death, but of seeing that he shared certain abominable weaknesses which the course of the conversation led me, on this occasion, to confide to him. Since he shared them, my account of them did not bore him. " I do not consider that Dominique is so badly off." So much the worse! A thousand times so much the worse! That little room, with an income of five francs and five francs earned by the *Bois de Prémol*[2], would be supreme happiness.

There is no music at Rome. Four years of solitude with learned dunderheads who answer you after quarter of an hour's thought, have knocked me stupid, even although every year of this solitude has been paid for, at first at the rate of eleven thousand francs, and now, since M. Victor's[3] decrees concerning the chanceries, at the rate of nine thousand eight hundred francs only.

I worshipped, and I still worship—or so, at least, I believe—a woman named a thousand years[4]. This passion was a mania from 1814 to 1821. I obtained in marriage her elder sister, named Rome: a woman of grave, austere worth, without music. I know her through and through. After

---

[1] In English in the original.
[2] *Lucien Leuwen.*
[3] The duc de Broglie.
[4] Mille ans—Milan.

[332]

four years of matrimonio there is no longer anything exalted or romantic between us. I would gladly forsake her for Señorita Valencia, of whom much good is spoken; but a young woman's character is always a problem. If, on thrusting my hand into the closed sack, I were to seize not an eel, but a serpent! . . . A year ago I refused to marry a tall young woman who was well-disposed towards me, because of the father-in-law, who was in love with the *furia francese* and claimed the right to live with me.

—— 195 ——

TO THE DUC DE BROGLIE

Civitavecchia, the 19th *of May* 1835

Monsieur le Duc,

I take advantage of the departure of the steamboat *La Méditerranée* to inform your Excellency of the impending arrival of His Holiness[1] in this port.

The Pope is expected tomorrow, the 20th of May. His Holiness will honour the town with his presence for three days: it is thirty-one years since a Pope last visited Civitavecchia. A triumphal arch has been erected in the middle of the piazza San Francesco, the principal square in the town. The harbour will be lit up. On the whole the inhabitants are apathetic. It has been difficult to recruit young men of the commercial world to take His Holiness's horses from between the shafts. Four years ago there would have been competition for this honour. The change has been brought about by the capricious administration of Mgr Peraldi, delegate (prefect) of this province.

What has made the strongest impression on the high commercial world, which is the local aristocracy, is the fact that His Holiness is accompanied by Herr Sebregondi.

. . . I think I spoke of Herr Sebregondi in my letter of the 5th of April (of which, as a precaution, I kept no copy, having no confidence in the persons around me). At the risk of repeating myself, I shall say that Herr von Metternich has admirably well understood that one cannot control the Roman court except by paying it or frightening it. But these men of imagination will never be scared for long by a man whom they know through and through—by an ambassador, for example. Herr von

---

[1] Gregory XVI.

Metternich always has at Rome a secondary agent who causes great uneasiness to the twenty or thirty persons who constitute this country's camarilla.

We first of all had Herr Prokesch, who in Rome was thought to be Herr von Metternich's natural son: a man without private means. Herr Sebregondi, the new bogey, fulfils his mission admirably. He scares everybody, even in the municipality of Civitavecchia. I know of nobody who sets himself up against him, except the Conte Moroni[1], an old man without talents and, moreover, at present taken up with the news from Spain.

The reigning Pope has all the virtues, but His Holiness does nothing in the wealthy part of his States, from Bologna to Ancona and from Spoleto to Rimini, without the consent of Herr Sebregondi.

196

TO THE DUC DE BROGLIE

(Civitavecchia, the 20th of May 1835)

His Holiness arrived today at one o'clock in the afternoon. His horses were taken from between the shafts at Casanuova, at five hundred paces from the town. The leading merchants of the town, Signori Gugielmotti, Defilippi, Alberti, etc. dragged the Pope's carriage to the gate. Here his Holiness dismounted and proceeded on foot all across the town to his palace. His Holiness paused to read the inscription on the triumphal arch that had been erected on the piazza San Francesco. He entered the church of this name to say his prayers. His Holiness appeared very grateful for the welcome he received, which, in fact, left nothing to be desired.

I have been confined to bed for two days by fever and gout. Today I was bled, and I hope to be able tomorrow to present myself in audience with His Holiness, together with the other consuls[2].

. . . .

[1] " The Conte Moroni, 68 years of age, a colonel of His Holiness's guards, a man below the mediocre in everything, and especially in the understanding of political matters." (Letter of April 5th, 1835.)

[2] " I had gout in May 1835 at Civitavecchia." (*Vie de Henri Brulard.*)

Yesterday His Holiness went to Allumiera, today he has gone to see the salt-works at Corneto. I hope that this evening he will honour the steamboat *Le Sully* with his presence. I arranged this with Mgr Fieschi, His Holiness's *maestro di camera*. His Holiness displays the vigour, strength and cheerfulness of a man of twenty. Herr Sebregondi is constantly with him.

. . . .

I was not able to see the Pope before his departure, being still confined to bed by fever and bleedings. His Holiness was most cordial towards everything French. I learn that his ten-league trip under the tricolour has produced a great effect at Naples. Throughout it all the Pope was a man cheerfully enjoying his position. On his departure he shook hands with everybody, provoking groans from Prince Massimo and the other etiquette-bound courtiers.

However strange it may seem in Paris, I regard it as an established fact that the government of this country views the arrival of steamboats at Civitavecchia with great disfavour. The diffusion of opinions which are not its own seems to this government the greatest of calamities. The ten-league trip that His Holiness deigned to take on the steamboat *La Méditerranée*, and the tokens of boundless respect which, at my request, were shown to His Holiness on board the vessel, have been a severe set-back to certain persons, and I hope to have fewer chicaneries to set aright during the next two or three months.

197

TO DI FIORE, AT PARIS

Rome, the 16th of August 1835

We witness the comic spectacle of fear in all its forms. It is enough to disgust one. Two drunkards died of the cholera at Florence, and as many at Bologna. Our French-born agents, in order not to be suspected of fear, deny the existence of the cholera, although they have it in their own homes; which tends to discredit our news with the people of the country.

Yesterday I was vividly reminded of you. I was in the largest church of the local Inquisition—and of all the Inquisitions in the world, for that matter. It was filled with the middle and upper classes, so that there was no more room. I crept beneath the ledge of a statue on a tomb, and gazed at all these faces animated by fear. My own was full of mathematical calculations: if things go here as they did at Paris, how many of these people will quit this world? Of nine hundred thousand inhabitants, Paris lost twenty thousand, or two in ninety, or one in forty-five. And there were at least eighteen hundred of us in that church!

Suddenly, at dusk, the Dominican, rather a good preacher, shouted in a voice of thunder: " Brethren, let us say a *Pater* and an *Ave* for who-ever shall be the first of us to die of the cholera." The women screamed at the tops of their voices: it was like a penance, and I shall never forget it. The *Pater* and the *Ave* were recited in tears.

I have sent six pages of writing to M. Dijon[1]. I spoke with the same sincerity as to you: the tone of his letter seemed to authorise me to do so. But souls who possess mansions are like the marble at their doors, very polished and very cold . . . Revolts and murders, and not the cholera, are what will set us all a dance here.

198

TO ALBERT STAPFER

Civitavecchia, the 27th of September 1835

Dear and obliging Friend,

I received your letter from La Rochelle with the keenest pleasure; I read it and re-read it. Three days later I went for a walk by the shore with two Italian friends, one of whom has done a good translation of Thucydides. We sat for a moment enjoying the fresh breeze from the roads—I speak in sailor-fashion to a Rochelais. Next day I had the deuce of a fever, and for twenty-seven days I took no dinner. After that came the great heats. I was bored stiff by my official correspondence, I relied on your friendship and waited until I should be in perfect health before replying to you. Today there is a sirocco-storm in the air, and I am

[1] The comte Molé.

shaking like an old man. I most sincerely congratulate you on having found a companion for life: marriage may have its moments of impatience, but never the deep, black boredom of celibacy! Your character is lofty, just and firm, and, without flattery to all the young men I know, 'tis you whom I would have chosen to be the husband of my daughter, if I had had one. Try not to take life reasonably: life is a woeful thing, and if one draws logical conclusions from events, one makes it much more disagreeable than if one tweaks its ears a little, *cras ingens iterabimus aequor*.

There is one thing about which I am sovereignly curious—the moral life of a small French town, such as La Rochelle, for example. Do you know a burgess of La Rochelle with an income of eight thousand francs and forty years of age? At what hour does he rise, and what does he do at each hour of the day? What does he think of Rousseau, of M. de la Mennais, and of Louis-Philippe? He doubtless takes Signora Pasta for a street-singer who throws herself at the head of every passer-by.

I am writing a novel in two octavo volumes, entitled *Le Chasseur vert*[1]. Have you read *Le Rouge*? Would you have the courage to tell me *exactly* all the faults you have detected in it? I shall try to avoid them in *Le Chasseur vert*, which I cannot publish as long as I live to a Budget[2]. I have a collection of twelve folio volumes of manuscript, which cost me two thousand francs. They contain original and completely true anecdotes written by contemporaries in the style of the period[3]. I have one thousand three hundred, one thousand four hundred or one thousand five hundred of them. This sort of thing did not become dull in Italy until the country became utterly corrupted, in about 1680. That was the era of false wit. A bastard of one of the greatest families had the idea of writing his life like J.-J. Rouseau. He never says: " The sun rose ", but always: " Phoebus emerged from the breast of the waves." It is stupefyingly boring. Despite this fault, I paid three hundred francs for the right to have copies made of these confessions. The author lived at Rome at the time of Christina of Sweden's entry in 1665, I think. . . . I have posed for the hands of Mirabeau's statue by M. Jaley[4]. I recommend both the work and its author to you; it is most scrupulously done. Do you not think that our

[1] The first edition of *Lucien Leuwen* appeared under this title in 1894.
[2] " As long as in order to live I have to adhere to a Budget, I shall not be able to *print it* " (in English in the original), " for what a Budget detests most is that one should make any show of having ideas." (Will of February 17th, 1835, incorporated in the manuscript of *Lucien Leuwen*.
[3] The source of the *Chroniques Italiennes*.
[4] " In 1834, M. Jaley, who was at Rome making his statue of Mirabeau, obtained permission from Beyle to draw his hands in order to give them to the prince of orators. Beyle was highly flattered, for everybody knows that Mirabeau had very beautiful hands." (Note by Colomb.)

Revolution had only three men: Mirabeau, Napoleon and La Fayette—
plus a clever Davus[1], M. de Randtalley?[2]

TO M. LEVAVASEUR, PUBLISHER AT PARIS

Civitavecchia, the 21st of November 1835

I am truly touched, monsieur, by the kind letter you took the trouble
to write to me. I am not by nature responsive: the majority of men bore
me. The result is that many people would be delighted to repeat: " He
pays no heed to his profession. See, he has time to write trivialities."
What would happen if these trivialities contained occasional jokes on the
sort of stupidities that serve the ends of the mighty? What would your
friend the *Journal des Débats* say? " You may write anything you like
provided you do not speak of this, or of that, or yet of that other thing,
which tends to lead us back again to the literature of the Empire."

I have therefore written a novel whose style is, I hope, less staccato
than that of the *Rouge*: two large volumes, or three small ones. If
literature could pay me three thousand francs a year, I would send you
the *Chasseur vert*; for I prefer the pleasure of writing nonsense to that
of wearing a laced coat that costs eight hundred francs.

I have bought, at great expense, some old manuscripts in yellowed
ink, dating from the sixteenth and seventeenth centuries. They contain—
in the semi-dialect of the period, which, however, I understand very well
—historiettes of eighty pages each, almost all of them tragic. I shall call
the book *Historiettes Romaines*[3]. There is nothing salacious in them, as
there is in Tallemant des Réaux. These tales are more sombre and more
interesting. Although love plays a great part in them, an intelligent man
would find them a most useful complement to the history of Italy in the
sixteenth and seventeenth centuries. This was the manner of life that
gave birth to men like Raphael and Michael Angelo—whom they are
so stupidly trying to bring back into our midst by means of academies
and schools of the fine arts. They forget that it takes a daring soul
to wield the most skilful brush, and all they produce are poor devils

---

[1] A sly manservant of Latin comedy.
[2] Talleyrand.
[3] These were the *Chroniques Italiennes*. Levavasseur had just published the first edition of
Tallemant des Réaux's *Historiettes*.

condemned to pay court to an head-clerk in order to obtain a commission for a picture.

But forgive me, monsieur, I digress, I am imitating Pindar too much. Do not show this letter to half-fools, and believe me that I would be delighted to give you a work which you, with your skill, would rapidly bring to the notice of good judges—an advantage I have hitherto lacked.

I am at present writing a book which may be a great folly: 'tis my *Confessions*—like those of Jean-Jacques Rousseau, apart from the style, only franker[1]. I began with the Russian campaign in 1812: I was furious with all the platitudes of M. de Ségur, who for his part is seeking to filch the great ribbon of the Légion d'honneur. Besides the Russian campaign and the Emperor's court, the book describes the author's love-affairs— a beautiful contrast. (By " beautiful ", I here mean " great ".) Perhaps the candour of this manuscript will make it too irritating to be published.

I hear you are publishing " a new novel by M. de Stendhal ". Capital! So if I ever come into an inheritance of three thousand francs a year, I shall send you the *Chasseur vert*, a work that will be quite proud of having been advertised for a space of two or three years. This novel can also be entitled *les Bois de Prémol*, if that suits you better. So now, monsieur, you know all my literary plans for the present.

TO MME GAULTHIER

Civitavecchia (Roman States),
the 14th of March 1836

Forgive me for my silence, my dear, kind friend: if I had been willing to force my nature, you would have become a task and a duty to me. I have not written two letters in the past three months. I consider " les convenances " one of the dreariest of stupidities, and that, thanks to this invention of fools, the duties which the world imposes give more boredom and vexation than its pleasures give pleasure. Had I forced myself to write to you, my letter would have bored both of us: it is like forcing

---

[1] " I resume only on the 23rd of November 1835. The same idea of writing *my life* " (in English in the original) " recently occurred to me during my trip to Ravenna. To tell the truth, I have had it many times since 1832, but I have always been discouraged by the appalling difficulty of the *I*'s and *me*'s, which get the author disliked. I do not feel I have the talent to get round it." (*Vie de Henri Brulard.*)

oneself to make love. I have just had the honour to write to Mme de Tascher, who lives in the faubourg Saint-Germain: perhaps Mme de Tascher will be scandalised by my slowness. Discover, I beg you, some passable excuse.

Let us talk of sad matters. I admired your conduct with Madame your mother, and congratulate you on it with all my heart. It was admirable of you to keep the fatal moment hidden from her[1]. I would give a year of those that chance has in store for me to meet my end in the same way. 'Tis the greatest possible service, a service in deed and not in word. Remind me to my old colleague, M. de la Bergerie, to M. Gaulthier and to Mme ——. À propos of old friends, I am very much surprised, and still more delighted, that M. le M. de —— still remembers so small a personage as myself. When next you see that excellent man, hand him the brief note which I have enclosed. I shall not repeat to you the account of the admirable death of Mme Laetitia[2]: I have said something of it to Mme Tascher. Since 1815 she had no feelings as regards rank. She was a soul worthy of Plutarch—the opposite, that is to say, of an ordinary princess. The atmosphere of Paris had in no way deprived her of the *faculty of will*, which no longer exists within a forty-league radius of Notre-Dame. The faculty of will ceases, in the Midi, at Valence, Dauphiné. Around Paris people are civilised, moderate, just, sometimes likeable, but as a pretty miniature is likeable. The thing most antipathetic, it seems, to anyone who has lived in Paris for more than ten years, is *energy* of any description. Fieschi[3] was an abominable creature, a man of the rabble; but he had more faculty of will in himself alone than the hundred and sixty of his peers who condemned him. Fieschi was the typical Italian, 'with four sharps' added by his insular quality. I shall tell you, if ever I see you, the story of the poisoning of four reforming archbishops who not long ago were expressly sent to Sardinia to reform the clergy there slightly. The story was told me by a priest who thought the poisoning very natural, and indeed very just. The gentlemen were poisoned at Sartène, and I saw the body of the first of them when it was brought back to Civitavecchia by a Sardinian warship. Cardinal Zurla, who is something of a scholar, very wicked, very fat and still more lecherous, went to Palermo eighteen months ago in order slightly to reform the morals of the Sicilian clergy. He was an intimate friend of the Pope, and was despatched in style by means of a cream-tart. The report is true that his body was subjected to the new embalming process, which is said to

---

[1] Mme Rougier de la Bergerie, Mme Gaulthier's mother, died in September 1835.
[2] Napoleon's mother died on February 2nd, 1836.
[3] Fieschi had just been executed.

be a perfect preservative. I went to see it with the noble contessa whom I mention in my letter to Mme la comtesse Tascher. She had the courage to take its hand in the coffin. Cardinal Zurla lay on his back, clad in his full robes. The lips and eyes were of the colour of lapis-lazuli: the whole face was sunken, and was a dismal sight. My devout friend remained flabbergasted by it for a fortnight. I also went to see it with my cousin, Mme la comtesse d'Oraison[1]. Once she had arrived at the lovely church of San Gregorio, on Mount Celius, she had not the courage to go and see the horror. The moral can be summed up as follows: remember that Fieschi is the typical Italian. As one ascends into the higher ranks, one finds men like the Duca de M —— who have no more character than a pistol clenched in the hand, and that because there is a formula for duels and nobody is afraid of *ridicule*. In 1300 all Italians were like Fieschi. The celebrated Benvenuto Cellini, who came to Paris in 1540 to make his *Diana* on the ground floor of the Louvre (under the clock, on the right), was a Fieschi. In 1530 Florence was taken, and from this moment *energy* was persecuted in Italy.

Really my handwriting is beyond endurance. This is because my chief pleasure is writing for printers. By writing as you see I succeed in covering twenty-five pages in three or four hours, after which I am dead with fatigue. I recently wrote the *Campagne de Russie* and the *Cour de Napoléon*, with less talent and greater candour than Rousseau. I am leaving these confessions to a Swiss friend, who will sell them ten years after my death, in 1856. All names have been changed, and, in any case, who will take an interest in '56 in the memory of my patrons who played out the comedy in 1812? Perhaps in 1856 no publisher will be willing to accept a manuscript in which I have shunned the emphatic style like the plague[2].

I have asked for leave of absence for next June. I wish some third person remembered our discussions on Shakespeare. But what a mocker I am, it seems; without knowing it. Any of my friends would give six francs to have somebody throw a glass of dirty water in my face when I go out in my best coat[3]. I am not at all angry about this. I shall not change during the ten or twenty years still left to me, not if I were to be made an officer of the Légion d'honneur[4]. . . . I have asked for the consulate at Carthagena, but this is a secret. I would like to see a people that takes action. What I would most wish would be to exchange my

[1] The comte Daru's eldest daughter. She had married the comte, later the marquis, d'Oraison.

[2] "I give and bequeath this volume and all the volumes of *The Life of Henri Brulard* to M. Abraham Constantin, chevalier de la Légion d'honneur . . . Rome, the 20th of January 1836. H. Beyle."

[3] Cf. letter no. 133, note 1.

[4] Beyle had been made chevalier de la Légion d'honneur by Guizot in 1835.

ten-thousand-a-year post for Monsieur your brother-in-law's post with the Audit Office. My post would spell happiness for a young man with any vanity. He would have the sixth salon and sixth rank at Rome, and, in point of amiability, the third or second. Twenty princes or grandees of Spain would throng to visit the French consul at Rome. But this jewel is still unknown in Paris, and for me it would be too heavy . . . Write to me, and be assured of all my eternal devotion.

P.S. What is become of Mme ———'s novel? Doesn't she know M. Ch—— or some other man of letters who could give her a puff? . . . What sort of a person is Mme la comtesse d'Oraison, M. le comte Daru's daughter? I was unable to read her character. Have you news of Mme la comtesse Curial? What sort of a person is Mme la comtesse B——, wife of M. le comte A—— B——, successor to that man of brains who was afraid of everything? . . . Tell me if a cat has died in your street. It is the little details that are precious to me. Society has changed since 1830, and I am not there to see the change. I want to hang myself and give up everything for a room on the fifth storey, rue Richepanse[1].

——— 201 ———

TO MME GAULTHIER

Paris, the 7th of October 1836

I would not pay the least attention, my dear friend, to the fact of Julie's being *envious*, if it were not injurious to her happiness. But the *sight* of another's happiness, compared with that of one's own wretched situation, at once engenders misery.

I have returned home specially to write to you: I am horribly busy, and very vexed at your absence. When do you return? I shall not leave until December, perhaps not until January. Send me an exact description of what you are doing. Above all, never think of anything sad: it spells old age.

I wanted to thank Mme D—— for the nice note she took the trouble to write me. But time, not the intention, has been lacking. I must dress

[1] In the margin of the MS. of the *Vie de Henri Brulard*, which he had been writing with feverish happiness since November 29th, 1835, the author notes: " 1836, 26th of March, announcement of my leave of absence in Paris. My imagination takes wings, and this task is interrupted."

for a dinner-party, to which I am invited together with some young ladies who earn forty francs whenever they dance. 'Tis the least dreary section of society, and therefore the best.

. . . .

Timoléon BRENET.

------ 202 ------

TO MME GAULTHIER

Paris, the 1st of November 1836

. . . Mme. Murat[1] is here: her fortune is quite meagre. She has obtained permission to spend the winter at Paris, and is paying a high rent for a furnished apartment. She found several at six thousand francs a month; but when the proprietors heard the name of the woman for whom the apartment was wanted, they asked for seven thousand, or made equivalent difficulties. Recently she found a handsome apartment in the rue Ville-Evêque for six thousand francs. The proprietor is Mme la comtesse de C—— V—— (the lady who blew out the brains of her husband's horse). When the critical moment arrived, of having to say: " 'Tis for Mme Murat ", the person who was performing the negotiations was very much astonished. " Why did you not say so sooner? " she exclaimed. " Mme Murat! For her, it will be only five thousand francs a month, and I shall leave behind for her all the little jewelled articles on the tables." Mme Murat refused them, for fear of their getting broken. In short, the ladies vied with one another in civility and good manners.

Mme Récamier is full of attentions for Mme de Lipona. The latter was at l'Abbaye-aux-Bois when M. Sosthènes de la Rochefoucauld was announced—the man who once tied a rope round the neck of the Emperor's statue on the place Vendôme. Mme Récamier offered to refuse him admission. " No," said Mme de Lipona. " The statue is back in its place. I have forgotten the people who pulled it down." It was better phrased, I have strangled this fine reply—one worthy of Plutarch.

Tell me where I can meet you; give me two days' notice. I expect to be here until December.

[1]Caroline Murat, former Queen of Naples, sister of the Emperor Napoleon. She was travelling under the name of comtesse Lipona (anagram of Napoli—Naples). (Note by Colomb.)

TO THE BARON DE MARESTE

Paris, the 9th of July 1837

So there you are at Lyons—yawning: 'tis the custom in that town.

Go into the vestibule of the Town Hall: you will see, on the left, the colossal statue of the Rhône, by Coustou. Behind it are the two famous tablets containing Claudius's speech to the Senate proposing the admission of the Gauls into the Senate-house. This speech was reported by Tacitus, *Annals* 11. We thus have a means of verifying a very curious fact. Tacitus did not invent this speech: all he did was to *correct* Claudius's words. Does the huge statue of the Rhône prevent one from reading Claudius's speech? This is what I wanted to ask you.

In my article, I poke fun a little at the Lyonnais. They could poke fun at me, if they proved that they have removed the colossal Rhône, and that one can now read the inscription quite easily. I need three or four anecdotes about love-affairs, each a page long[1]. Re-read your diary.

COTONET.

TO ABRAHAM CONSTANTIN

Paris, the 11th of July 1837

My dear friend, I have been away for six weeks. I found your letter on my return. You must think me either dead or very forgetful, or perhaps neither the one nor the other.

I remember very well that I intended to write to you on the day of the opening of the Exhibition; but I was so much harrowed by the dreary sight of such general mediocrity that I had not the strength. There was nothing I would have accepted as a gift, apart from a few landscapes: for example, the *View of Dinan*, by M. Dagnan. M. Delaroche's *Charles I* and *Strafford* are merely subject-pictures seen through a microscope. They had a great success in high society, the reason being that high

---

[1] For the *Memoires d'un touriste* which the author was writing at this time.

society recognised itself in M. Delaroche's characters. They are exquisitely clad, and their faces display no energy whatsoever. Energy, in all its forms, is the bête noire of good society, which was enchanted with the Exhibition because it found there none of those bold experiments that are signs of energy. What is always looked for is a certain elegance and wit. M. Signol's big picture was thought very dull: it is said that he is trying to win the votes of the devout.

M. Flandrin's *Saint-Clair* was thought to be a great come-down after his *Envieux de Dante*: I myself formed the same opinion at Rome. M. Tassy's immense picture was thought unworthy of a glance: an especial object of derision was his newly whitewashed portico of a restaurant. Court has done some good portraits. M. Dubuffe paints duchesses as if they were trollops: perhaps he is not mistaken. He has martyrised the face of General Athalin, which is, however, an excellent likeness. Never has paint been applied to canvas more carelessly: a blind man who passed his hand over the picture would think that somebody had been trying to paint mountains.

Three or four Germans were shown at the Salon. One of them, whose name is something like Winterhalter, has painted the *Decameron*: eight pretty women and two men sitting on the lawn at a villa near San Miniato. It resembles a fan: the landscape is very true to nature. M. Paturle bought it for eight thousand francs. The three other Germans won respect; but their colouring is too ugly, everything is grey. The same is true of M. Scheffer's *Christ*: it looks like a very grey and lustreless sketch by some pupil of Paolo Veronese. M. le duc d'Orléans bought this picture for madame la duchesse's Lutheran chapel at the Tuileries.

At present everybody is raving over the Spanish School. The Italian Schools are held in some contempt, and very high prices are being paid for Flemish paintings. M. Taylor[1] showed much address and resolution during his visit to Spain. At Barcelona the leader of the riot, who was in the street, offered to sell him for ten thousand francs the pictures in a church that was going to be burnt within two hours. The leader lent him fifty rioters to take down the pictures as fast as they could. When the staples supporting the frames were too difficult to break, they cut through the canvas near the frame and threw it down into the church. The rebel leader had so much respect for M. Taylor that when the latter wanted to pay him, he said: "You know that I have no time to accept your money now; I shall come back tomorrow."

I forgot to tell you that M. Taylor returned to the Louvre with a hundred and twenty Spanish pictures, of which twenty are masterpieces.

[1] Inspector of Fine Arts in 1838.

These are by Murillo, Velasquez and Cano: they have an austere truthfulness. These Spaniards are admirable at painting a monk in fear of Hell: the very folds of his habit give you the idea. Moreover, they make no attempt at " ideal beauty ". These pictures cost the King a million. 'Tis said that he offered M. Taylor a present of sixty thousand francs, and that M. Taylor refused it.

When M. Taylor bought these pictures in Spain, he had them packed in wool and told all the military posts he met that his bales contained wool. He paid tribute successively to the Christinos and the Carlists. When he reached the frontier he was obliged to have the bales carried across by smugglers.

M. Taylor says that three years ago one often found Spanish monasteries containing two hundred monks, but that nowadays they never number more than fifty, and these fifty are starving. The authorities forget to pay them their pittance, and they sell, without any scruple, the pictures in their churches.

Señor Aguado, who is now marques de las Marismas, has formed a gallery of pictures of which his janitor hands a list to people to whom Señor Aguado has given cards of admission. This list reads: six Correggios, eight Raphaels, etc.: what it means is that there is no Correggio or Raphael, but eight or ten highly remarkable Spanish paintings.

— 205 —

TO ROMAIN COLOMB

Paris, the 10th of January 1838

Here is some curious information that I collected yesterday evening at a gathering of intelligent people who are well informed of all that concerns England. I pass it on to you for your own and your family's profit.

The entire life of the English consists in preoccupation with rank. Their great task, of which they think ten times a day, is to try to penetrate, to insinuate themselves, into the rank immediately superior to that in which they live. It is only for this purpose that they love money.

Could anyone guess what was recently done by seven brothers, sons of a rich merchant who had six millions? In France, each of them would have devoted himself to his pleasures and would have calculated—

or, at least, whoever of them thought about money—that one day he would have a fortune of nearly nine hundred thousand francs. How different are the preoccupations of English brothers! The six younger ones wanted to be the "*younger brothers*[1]" of a great family, and begged their father to establish an entail of five millions in favour of the eldest.

The father was not at all surprised. But, as a reasonable man, he bade them go away, each in a different direction, scattering themselves amongst small towns thirty or forty leagues from the parental home, and then write him each a letter, after a week of reflection. All the letters, each containing a plea in favour of the entail, arrived on the same day, and next day the father began taking the necessary measures to establish it. The father has since died, and the eldest son enjoys a fortune of six millions. Each of the younger brothers has an income of seven thousand francs.

The human heart experiences a keen feeling of affection when it knows that the power which, with one word, could make it completely happy, is combined with every appearance of grace and weakness.

Hence the mad enthusiasm of the English at the sight of their Queen Victoria—a sentiment absolutely incomprehensible to the huge majority of Frenchmen. They judge by what happens in France, and suppose that an Englishman who is enthusiastic for the young queen must be a low and servile place-seeker.

Not a bit of it: such an Englishman may well be immensely rich, and would be nicely trapped if he were given a post worth thirty thousand francs in the Post Office or Customs.

Nevertheless, although he may have no hope of it, the Englishman feels that this young woman might change his rank.

During the last thirty years less importance has been attached to the title of "Sir", for a man who gives his wife that of "Lady". Rank has become a more complicated thing, more difficult to achieve.

Such-and-such a lord who is a *marquis* will be unhappy all his life because really in high society he has not the rank of another peer who is only a *baron*. It would take a long time to explain, and even then might remain incomprehensible.

[1] In English in the original.

TO M. G—— C——[1]

Paris, the 20th of January 1838

I shall repeat to you, monsieur, what Lord Byron once wrote to me: I shall give you my advice *though unasked*[2]. Mme Émilie was so kind as to read to me some pages of your *Don Juan*, which seemed to me very good.

I beg you to permit me to speak with utter candour, for I should like you to enjoy a success equal to your true worth.

A man whose name is Don Juan should not have commonplace adventures. The true Don Juan is the maréchal de Rais, or Cenci of Rome. He takes pleasure in things that give pleasure, only inasmuch as by so doing he defies public opinion.

It may be, monsieur, that your enterprise will be the less successful in that Lord Byron's Don Juan is a mere Faublas, for whom the larks fall ready roasted.

You will find in the *Mélanges tirés d'une grande bibliothèque* an analysis of the trial of Gilles, maréchal de Rais.

Lord Byron's reputation and the scintillating beauty of his verse have disguised the weakness of his *Don Juan*. Goethe gave Doctor Faust the devil as an ally, and with such a mighty auxiliary Faust did what all of us have done at the age of twenty—he seduced a shopgirl.

Seek, Monsieur, to discover actions that carry within them a deep sentiment of flouting bravado for all that the commonalty of men respects.

I was saying to Mme Émilie: Don Juan lived in France[3]. He happened to be in a certain room in the palace at the moment when, on the 5th of October 1789, the populace broke into the château of Versailles. Don Juan exposed himself to the greatest danger. He had about him a small pocket pistol. A patriot found him in the retreat where he was hiding. Don Juan put the muzzle of his pistol in the patriot's ear and killed him.

---

[1] M. G—— C—— had sent Beyle a translation of the first canto of, and an original sequel to, Lord Byron's *Don Juan*, asking for his observations and criticisms. This canto in the journal *L'Illustration* in May 1842. (Note by Colomb.)

[2] In English in the original.

[3] The Don Juan to whom Beyle alludes was the duc de Lauzun, condemned to death by the revolutionary tribunal on January 1st, 1794. At that time he bore the name of duc de Biron. His *Mémoires*, in a single octavo volume, appeared in 1822. (Note by Colomb.)

He stripped him, clothed himself in the patriot's garments and emerged from the hiding-place uttering the shouts of the rabble. Gradually he made his way to the gate of the palace and escaped.

It happened that a janitor had been murdered and robbed of four thousand five hundred francs which he had collected for the rents of the great house in the rue Saint-Honoré owned by the duc R——. Don Juan was mistaken for this ignoble thief: he was condemned, and received consolation from an hypocritical priest and a lascivious great lady. He went to the guillotine with great courage and simplicity: he was weary of flouting men, because he so much despised them.

To raise your voice to the tone worthy of the theme, you might re-read the article *Gilles de Rais* in the biography of the hypocritical M. Michaud, also Cenci and the trial of the aforesaid maréchal de Rais.

Employ the French used in the translation by MM. de Port-Royal, published about 1600. According to them, one should not have a passion "*au* coeur": they say "*dans* le coeur". It is the *Charivari* that says "*au* coeur". The *Charivari* is admirable when it makes us laugh, and not for its pretentious style.

All these arguments, which are written in haste, immediately after leaving Mme Émilie's, will demonstrate to you, Monsieur, how eager I am that you should enjoy a great success. Be convinced that Lord Byron's Don Juan is a mere Faublas: give to yours actions that are out of the common.

Pray accept, Monsieur, the homage of my most respectful regards.

DURAND-ROBET.

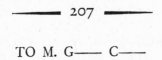

TO M. G—— C——

Paris, the 19*th of February* 1838

. . . I shall tell you frankly, monsieur, that to write a book which has the luck to find four thousand readers, one must:

1. Study French for two years in books written before 1700. I except only the marquis de Saint-Simon.

2. Study the truth of the ideas in Bentham or in Helvétius's *L'Esprit*, and in a hundred and one volumes of Memoirs: Gourville, Mme de Motteville, d'Aubigné, etc.

[349]

In a novel, from the second page onwards, one must say something new, or, at least, *individual*, concerning the setting of the action.

From the sixth page onwards, or at latest from the eighth, there must be adventures.

The newly rich lend energy to good society, just as the barbarians did in the eleventh century to what was left of Rome. We are very far from the insipidity of the reign of Louis XVI. At that time the style of narration could be more important than the contents, today the opposite is true.

Read the trial of Gilles de Laval, maréchal de Rais, at the Royal Library. Invent adventures of equal energy. A thousand compliments, Monsieur.

CAUMARTIN.

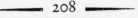 208

TO DI FIORE

Bordeaux, the 24th of March 1838

. . . For a week I have been persecuted by rain. By good fortune I found a friend here—not a serious friend, who is of no service, but a merry friend who invites me to dinner with the pretty women of the region. Before this journey I did not know what wine of Bordeaux really was. Before sending it to England or elsewhere, they mix it with a third part of wine of l'Ermitage. The true bordeaux has an amazing bouquet, it is less "full-bodied" than the wine we know by this name.

People say to me here: "What would you do at Bayonne in rain like this?" Every evening there is an agreeable performance at one of the two theatres . . . An excellent inn, *Baron's*, free from noise. When I arrived there at four o'clock in the morning, my street-carrier knocked rather hard. "Do not knock like that," said the porter. "It can be heard on the fourth storey as clearly as here". This gave me an excellent opinion of the maison Baron. It smells of burnt fat, for the kitchen is on the stairs.

Angoulême stands on a mountain: a superb view from the promenade. Here the women begin to have heavenly eyes, noses that are boldly designed without being too big, and admirable foreheads, smooth and serene. In short, the "Iberian stock" is obvious.

I amuse myself by making—by writing, I mean—my "travels in

the Midi ". If I continue to be reassured by your letters, I shall visit Toulouse, Montpellier, Avignon and Grenoble.

The people of Bordeaux are not at all hypocritical: they think only of the life of the body. M. Ravez has become a lawyer again, and is making a deal of money. Le P—— has again fallen into the contempt he enjoyed before his days of greatness: he lives in a damp château on the shore, two hours' journey from here . . . There are many rich Spaniards, who decorate the churches. Otherwise, nothing is done for the arts at Bordeaux. . . . Very pretty wenches: some of them can be had for two hundred francs, " as a favour ".

Farewell, dear fellow, be persuaded of my extreme gratitude. I often think of you and of the two twelve-year-old Spanish lasses[1].

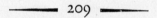

209

TO DI FIORE

Strasbourg, the 2nd of July 1838

If I had found here a single line from you, I would have left for Paris. My ardour for travelling has grown much cooler. Gout overtook me at Berne, and became raging at Bâle, where it made me prisoner. I wanted to see what is left of the famous *Totentanz*, the cathedral, and the admirable Holbeins. I made unheard-of efforts, followed by an abominable day in the diligence from Bâle to Strasbourg. . . . The weather turned hot today, after a week of winter. I went out, but it is quite impossible to climb the celebrated tower (the highest in the world—it is four hundred, thirty-seven and a half feet tall, and St. Peter's at Rome is only four hundred and twenty-eight).

The sight of me walking in the street, leaning on a stick and cursing when my left foot strikes on a pointed cobble, must make the people of Strasbourg laugh; but nobody knows me. As things are, I would be delighted to return to Paris. But I am so near the sublime cathedral of Cologne! Two days, and another by steamboat. The journey is damp, but at least it is not fatiguing! The clerks, helped by my natural improvidence, will end by relegating me to Civitavecchia—or, what is worse, relegating me to poverty. I shall never see Cologne. The thing about me is, I love *the beautiful*: it is my weakness, to which I sacrifice, as you

[1] The daughters of the Countess de Montijo.

see, both prudence and health. God knows what the humidity of the Rhine will do to me!

Tomorrow, the 3rd of July, to Baden. On the 5th of July I return to Kehl, where I take the steamboat. On the 6th, we sleep ashore, at Mainz. On the 7th, at Cologne. On the 9th I shall be at Brussels, by travelling twenty-seven leagues by railway from Liège to the said Brussels. A day for the pictures by Rubens, and on the 11th or 12th I leave for Paris.

The good Colomb writes to me that because of me you no longer dare to visit " that amiable man "[1]. Colomb takes this excuse for your idleness seriously, as if there were, or could be, any question of lying to a man whom one likes, under the pretext of his being a minister.

All one needs to say to M. Dijon[1] is: " He is at Cologne, and will be at Paris in a week."

The degree of play-acting that you, *rightly*, think necessary for visits means that they become laborious tasks for you, and you take your uncertainty as to what you should say about me as your pretext for avoiding them. To M. Dijon you should tell the truth: to the old marquis and other impotent ill-wishers you should say: " He has gone to Grenoble on important business, he has not been there for ten years." What does it finally matter to the " amiable man "—who, as you know, makes no use of the magnificent pen that Heaven bestowed upon me—what does it matter to him whether I squander my thirteen francs a day in the rue Caumartin or at Cologne? The malevolence of the clerks is so great that nothing can increase it. Therefore, etc.

I met the admirable Prévost at Geneva. He wanted to come and pay me a long visit of friendship, and prescribed Vichy and the occasional application of leeches. Fat men between the ages of fifty-five and sixty-five are tormented by plethora of blood. After that comes tranquillity, and life diminishes by a twentieth part yearly. My visit to this true philosopher gave me heart-felt pleasure.

What indiscretion will you find in the *Touriste*[2]? Any attempt to please fools by proving to them for seven hundred pages that they are foolish is doomed to failure.

[1] The comte Molé. [2] The *Mémoires d'un touriste.*

TO DI FIORE

Paris, the 13th of August 1838

Madame the widow Derosne, rue Saint-Honoré, at the corner of the rue de l'Arbre-Sec, will sell you for a hundred francs a lump, as big as two eggs, of " monesia " wood ground to a powder.

An American sea-captain who found himself on the South American coast, with dysentery on board, made himself popular with the savages; and these, when they saw his men continually taking down their breeches, said to him: " We will cure your crew in two days."

" Monesia " is an astringent that heals cuts. It is being kept secret because there is a hope of curing the cholera with it; and, if this were known, there would be a devilish amount of rumour-mongering and charlantanism.

In my eagerness to obey you, I have used the wrong side of the paper; which reminds me of Palaprat's quatrain. The duc de Vendôme locked him up in a small room and said to him: " You shall not come out until you have written a quatrain for my portrait.

Five minutes later Palaprat called out: " Monseigneur, 'tis done, monseigneur, 'tis perfect."

Lecteur, vois ce héros

. . . .

Qui prit la vérole et Barcelone
Toutes deux du mauvais côté.[1]

The Duke had taken Barcelona by forcing a bastion that was thought to be unassailable.

But perhaps you already know the quatrain.

CAUMARTIN.

[1] Reader, behold this hero . . ., who took the pox and Barcelona, both of them from the wrong side.

TO THE CONTE CINI[1]

3rd of January 1839

My dear Count,

M. le vicomte D——, a friend of M. Praslin's who has arrived from Rome, has given me a superb description of the great number of foreigners whom you are pleasurably welcoming. I can see from here the kindly contessa going to the ball twice a week, and I guess that she finds much more entertainment there than she did three years ago. She will be just as pretty as she was, but, now that she is obliged to fast during Lent, she will have lost some of that shyness which prevented her from being entertained by the laughable follies of this world. Have you still with you those young German barons who were starchier than their shirt-collars? Have you had the good fortune to meet and to hear the perorations of the silliest of all Frenchmen, a certain M. Fulchiron, Deputy, who was at Rome in November? Our weather here is even more abominable than usual, I am enrheumed through and through, as are all my friends here, but never were our evenings more agreeably spent. Our conversations turn upon whether the Government will be overthrown. Every day there is a step forward or back, and since both attackers and defenders are men of wit, the argument is very entertaining. There is a coalition in the Chamber of Deputies—which means that there is an alliance between M. Guizot (chief of what might be called the ultras, in so far as such beings have been capable of existing since 1830), M. Thiers, the eloquent spokesman of the moderates, and finally M. Odilon Barrot, chief of the Left.

M. Duvergier de Hauranne has published two excellent pamphlets explaining the gist of the matter to everybody. We are entertained and interested to such a degree that the best novel in the world, were such a thing to appear, would seem tedious.

Three thieves are in alliance to rob a man who possesses that

[1] The Conte and Contessa Cini were Beyle's warmest and most loyal friends in Rome, together with the princes Caetani mentioned in this letter. (Cf. note by Stryienski.) Beyle had tender feelings towards the charming Contessa Cini, with whom Don Filippo Caetani was also in love. On the margin of the manuscript of the *Vie de Henri Brulard*, he notes: " Sacrifice made—Contessa Sandra (8-17th of February 1836). Observe the beauty of the man's character, that the sacrifice was made at the Aliberti ball of Tuesday the 16th of February, when Don Filippo spoke to me. The quarrel with me had lasted since the English ball, 8th of February 1836."

handsome diamond called power. Once the man is on the ground, how will they set about sharing the diamond?

About the 12th of January there will be a battle in the Chamber of Deputies—that is to say, there will be a debate on the *Address*. MM. Guizot, Thiers, Odilon Barrot, Duvergier de Hauranne, Jaubert and Passy will attack; MM. Molé, Salvandy, Janvier and Barthe will defend. The attackers want the Chamber to vote for an amendment that will sharply criticise the Government's policy and may compel it to resign. But the funny thing about the affair—and I mention this to explain why I have been telling you this long story—is that the attackers cannot say to the Government: "Instead of doing *this*, you should have done *that*."

For, if they are successful, next day they will be ministers, and in that case would be obliged by their own speeches to do *that*.

The thing to do is to find an ingenious method of outrageously blaming the government without ever saying what it should have done— otherwise your words of yesterday will be exceedingly embarrassing tomorrow.

You can now understand, my dear Count, how amusing this battle is to these intelligent people. Note that the combatants are, as regards wit, the flower of the nation, and moreover they are speaking of our most interesting affairs.

There have never been so many great foreign noblemen in Paris; and what I have never observed before is that they take as much interest as we do in the debates in our Chambers. Yesterday and the day before there was the annual sale in aid of the Poles. Picture a very large hall on the boulevard, in the finest quarter. Fifteen small shops have been set up, and each shop is kept by the four prettiest women of a particular nation—for example, one shop is kept by the four prettiest Spanish women now in Paris, the next two by the eight prettiest and noblest Englishwomen, then come the French, the Germans, etc. Amidst these shops circulate all the handsome young men of all nations, all who regard themselves as noble, witty or rich. This would be the proper place for Don Filippo and Don Michele[1], with their air of noble distinction: I looked for them in vain.

[1] Don Filippo and Don Michele Caetani, who are repeatedly referred to in this correspondence. It was to Don Filippo that Beyle bequeathed his books in his Will of June 8th, 1836. In 1832 he was lodging within a few yards of the palazzo Caetani (a sixteenth-century palace, huge and dark, in a narrow street, the via delle Botteghe Oscure, and one of the richest palaces in Rome). "The three princes of this name," Beyle had written, "are my best friends. Their mother, a former friend of Paul-Louis Courier, used to offer me opportunities for a delightful evening's gossip" (letter of June 11th, 1832—cf. letter no. 170).

The Queen and the Princesses have sent many frames of embroidery and other little pieces of work made by themselves: you can imagine how eager people are to buy them. A single Deputy, M. Parant, bought a thousand francs' worth of them. I myself bought a bouquet of violets, which cost me five francs. This assembly, especially when I was there, is certainly the finest in Europe. The shopkeeping ladies flirt with the passers-by: imagine what singular dialogues arise—one must be graceful and witty or perish in the attempt—never has a sale been so brilliant. The day before yesterday they made four thousand nine hundred francs, and the value of the objects sold may well have been four or five hundred. There was much laughter at the expense of a foreigner who, to pay ten francs, proffered a gold napoleon, and then waited for his change as if he were in an ordinary shop. It is worthy of remark that, since the hall faces south and receives the best of the daylight, elderly women take care not to be seen there—perhaps that is why the place is so gay. Don Filippo, a past master in the art of turning the heads of fair English-women, will find that a morning spent there advances the affairs of a man of gallantry more than six ordinary evenings. À propos of evenings, this year those of the Countess Granville, wife of the English ambassador, are much frequented: there is no unnecessary stiffness, and that is all that need be said.

Mlle Rachel is a poor, scrawny little eighteen-year-old beggar-girl who plays tragedy as if she were herself inventing the words she speaks: she has created a revolution at the Théâtre Français, which takes in six thousand francs when Mlle Rachel is playing. Before her it used to take in one thousand five hundred francs. Mlle Rachel's especial triumph is in the rôle of Hermione in Racine's *Andromaque*. She is magnificent at expressing irony. Now that she is in fashion, a man invited to dinner may very well say: " This evening I cannot: I have a ticket for Mlle Rachel." The poor little Jewess will earn only twenty-six thousand francs this year: if she had known how to bargain, she would have had sixty. 'Tis true that she has an annuity of four thousand francs from the

Beyle visited them often and with pleasure. Even today his memory remains alive with Don Michele's son and daughter, who often heard their father speak of Beyle's manifestations of wit or of his sallies.

The family of the Caetani is one of the oldest in Rome: Boniface VIII was a Caetani. As supporters of the Italian Government, they retained their authority and fortune. The present Duca de Sermonetta was mayor of Rome. His sister, the Contessa Lovatelli, holds Rome's most literary and learned salon: she is herself a member of the Academia dei Lincei.

This family had a tradition of wit and culture, a somewhat rare thing in Rome, and Stendhal therefore had people to whom he could talk. . . . After Stendhal, Balzac was received there. He dedicated his *Parents Pauvres* to this same " Don Michele Angelo Cajetani, prince de Teano ". Still later, Taine was to receive hospitality from the family. (I owe this note to the kind help of my friend Paul Argelet.) (Note by Casimir Stryienski.)

Comédie Française. Mlle Rachel is the daughter of a German Jew who performed as a showman at fairs. She has a genius that confounds me with amazement every time I see her perform. Such a miracle has not been seen in France for two hundred years.

. . . If you wish to render me a service, my dear Count, for which I shall be most grateful, remind me to your amiable countess. Tell her that I ask news of her from all who come from Rome. Buy cakes from time to time and give them to the children, telling them it is M.B. who sends them from Paris.

. . . .

━━ 212 ━━

TO MME GAULTHIER

Paris, the 21st of March 1839

When you go to the Exhibition, my dear friend, it will perhaps be lent some novelty in your eyes by the scandals I shall describe. When you come to Paris do not fail to inform me in advance.

I have not yet paid a call upon that courageous woman whom I admire from the depths of my heart[1]. I am in what people call a *coup de feu*. In other words, I do not go to dine until eight o'clock, and at midnight I resume work until three; but by Tuesday I shall be free[2]. I am most impatient to see you.

LE SALON DE 1839

To a lady of Naples.

Scheffer's paintings, which send the fair ladies of the faubourg Saint-Germain into swoons, are a mere patchwork of certain paintings of the Venetian School—minus the colouring, of course. All his work is of the colour of wine and has a gloomy, rather dignified air. *Faust's Margarete*, which is regarded as this painter's masterpiece, is merely a fat German

---

[1] The comtesse de Tascher.
[2] On this Tuesday, March 26th, 1839, Stendhal finished correcting the proofs of *La Chartreuse de Parme*, which he had written between November 4th and December 26th, 1838.

woman with a protruding belly and heavy cheeks. The general appearance of this figure has a certain naturalness; but, whatever else may be said, it is the opposite of the ideal. Faust's loving gaze would do very well for a face in a subject picture; the Devil is not wicked enough, although very sardonic. The great fault of all these figures of Scheffer's is that, as I have said, they look like a decoction of Tintoretto and Paolo Veronese—or rather, a decoction of the works of their pupils, such as Carlo Veronese, Paolo's son. What entrances the ladies is the serious, dignified air which these figures admittedly possess.

This serious, dignified air is just what is utterly lacking in Vernet's three immense pictures, all of them dealing with Constantine. They are much less beautiful and less serious than nature. They present nature as seen by a man of vast talent but without any feeling for what is noble. For this reason the public, which as a whole is dull, much admires the faithfulness of these assaults. The soldiers look like horrible frogs: there is no flesh on their bones. The monarch, of course, is the centre of everything. The huge picture, which is in the middle, is the dullest; the little picture on the right is the least dull.

I saw a great number of dull Gudins and one admirable one: a church in Normandy by the sea, where the tide is beginning to ebb. I have never seen the sea so limpid on the Normandy coast.

I have not yet been able to see any of the fourteen Decamps. Yesterday evening, at the concert of the *Cercle des Arts*, the music was blaring and execrable, and received astonishing applause. Decamps' *Corps de Garde turc* and his *Supplice turc* were being lauded to the skies. The latter depicts men being hurled down from a high wall covered with iron spikes: each of them is caught on whichever spike the Devil chooses.

The devotional pictures, fabricated on Monte Pincio, have had no success. They are thought horribly dull: people do not do justice to their profound skill. For the rest, they bore me and I gave them only a passing glance.

For me, M. Flandrin's masterpiece is still his *Envieux du Dante*. His *Saint-Clair*, which I saw at Nantes, is very gloomy and arid.

There is one thing at the Salon that would make you die of laughter— an allegory by M. Mauzaisse. It is annoying that the painter has been allowed to profane the figure of an august and revered personage. In the foreground I noticed a naked woman of enormous physical charms with bandaged eyes. She holds a torch with which to set fire to everything: as you will have guessed, she is Liberty. This figure is good and well painted: I would like to cut it out with scissors. Another figure, of very farcical appearance, is presenting the Crown to the King.

There are some charming portraits of pretty women, painted in the style of Il Domenichino, by M. Court. I cannot conceive why this man is not a great painter.

My eyes were wearied by an enormous series of quite good portraits. M. Amaury Duval has painted a portrait in chocolate of an ugly wench, which is said to be a masterpiece of draughtsmanship: I could not find it so.

In general, all these painters seem to be skilful craftsmen, but lacking in perception and, above all, in soul: they see dignity only in affectation. I except, of course, Eugene Delacroix, three of whose pictures were rejected by those brutes at the Institut—out of envy, the curs!

—— 213 ——

TO HONORÉ DE BALZAC

Friday, 29th of March 1839

My janitor, by whom I wanted to send you *la Chartreuse*—as to the King of Novelists of this century—refuses to go to rue Cassini, no. 1. He pretends not to understand my directions: near the Observatoire, " and then ask ", is what I was told.

You sometimes come to a Christian country, monsieur, so give me a decent address—in care of a publisher, for example. (You will say that I seem to be searching for an epigram.)

Or else send somebody to fetch the said novel at rue Godot-de-Mauroy, 30 (Hôtel Godot-de-Mauroy).

If I hear from you that you are sending a messenger, I shall leave the book with my janitor. If you read it, tell me your sincere opinion of it.

I shall ponder over your criticisms with the greatest respect.

Your devoted

FREDERICK

rue Godot-de-Mauroy, no. 30

TO MME ROMAIN COLOMB

Paris, the 9th of June 1839

My adorable cousin,

Not being able to have a tête-à-tête with you, I have decided to write to you. I truly fear that Colomb is hatching an illness. That red complexion, the lassitude of which he complains, his changes of mood, are fatal signs.

I think that he is trying, out of vanity, to do everything at his office and not to leave a foothold, as they say, to his lieutenant.

Since Parisian women can do anything, compel him to ask for a week's leave of absence in which to take care of himself. When they look at his complexion, they will grant him it.

Take him to Chantilly and have fifteen leeches applied. A week spent there in the bosom of domestic bliss and amongst tall trees will completely restore him to his normal condition. Compel him to go to Saint-Germain every Sunday by the railway.

Lastly, take heart: if you lose him, I will marry you[1].

COTONET.

TO ROMAIN COLOMB

Rome, 4th of January 1840[2]

. . . All that the newspapers say about the rôle played here by a certain fat and very ill-built young man is ridiculously false[3]. The Ambassador of the King of the French has held a reception at which all the cardinals

---

[1] Colomb adds : " As all three of us had agreed."

[2] The comte Molé, his patron, having resigned from the presidency of the Council, Beyle had been obliged to return to his Consulate. He was back in Civitavecchia on August 10th, 1839. He had sketched out a new novel: " I dictated 310 pages of *Lamiel* at Rome during the first days of January 1840." (Note on a copy of the *Mémoires d'un touriste*.)

[3] The duc de Bordeaux, who had recently assumed the title of comte de Chambord.

were present. It was literally impossible to move in the two magnificent drawing-rooms of the palazzo Colonna. I never saw so many diamonds.

The young man in whose honour they have told so many lies is a large-scale copy of the duc d'Angoulême. He continually rocks from one foot to the other. When speaking to ladies he seems to be reciting a lesson, and keeps glancing at his tutor—which does not, however, prevent him from subjecting the latter to outbursts of somewhat rude impatience. He has acquired so many bad habits that M. de Genoude will have a deal of trouble in making him see the things of this world as they are. He lives continually in such an atmosphere of flattery that he is never confronted with any real difficulty.

As soon as he appears in a drawing-room, two of his courtiers approach all who are wearing gloves and instruct them to take them off—a thing that the young Romans find most shocking. He is invited out of curiosity: the intimates of his entourage ask for the list of persons invited, and always cross out five or six names—Italian names, be it remarked. This " effaçade " and the story of the gloves have caused people to judge the poor young man very severely. They do not realise that these things should be blamed solely on the blockheads about him.

The prince has a superb complexion and handsome fair hair. He is fat, squat and ill-built: his face much resembles Louis XVI's. He speaks in an odd manner, in an extremely high-pitched voice, and his expressions are not modern French. He has been taught the art of never expressing a decided opinion. He never says: " This is a good horse " or " a bad horse ". His eyes have no sparkle: 'tis by no means the glance of a future conqueror. I should rather say that his glance and manners are steeped in honey: everything about him is of a studied sweetness. In sum, the Pretender has a very kind and gentle manner; he speaks well on all topics; but he always has a slight semblance of reciting a lesson, without any admixture of improvisation. If he were a young duke from the faubourg Saint-Germain, adorned with an income of a hundred thousand francs, he would be a great success and would be the chevalier Grandisson of " right-thinking " persons. The poor unfortunate has never seen a palace or a statue without being surrounded by eight or ten officials, whose express mission seems to be to prevent all good sense from reaching him. In short, he has not the " diable au corps ". One always notices something honeyed and learnt by rote in his words and gestures. Rocking to and fro, bending now one knee and now the other, he says to all women: " Has madame been long at Rome? Does madame expect to remain here for some considerable time? "

He lowers his eyes as he utters these witty words, and seems to be much preoccupied with the hat he holds in his right hand. The Duchesa R. has said of him: " He is too much educated."

What greatly harms the Pretender is the open, natural, ardent amiability of the Hereditary Grand Duke of Russia, who was here a year ago. He was a most soldierly prince, unceremonious, merry and kind. There is nothing of the " barbarian " about him, but he never puts people in their places and seems to be the intimate friend of the officers in whose company he finds himself. In short, this young Russian is a complete contrast to the French Pretender. Both have German, kindly faces; but ours has a silly manner and the other a gay one. Moreover, all the people around the young duke are horribly ill attired and have a lumpish air. The ladies of Rome have even remarked that this suite smells unpleasantly.

────── 216 ──────

TO EUGENIA GUZMAN Y PALAFOX, CONDESA DE TEBA[1]

Civitavecchia, the 10th of August 1840

Mademoiselle,

Your letters are too short and are undated. Mine have the opposite fault. Because of you, I can no longer think of anything but of what is happening at Barcelona. I have long perceived that any State which changes its form of government is storing up trouble for itself for forty years. You will never enjoy peace in Spain until all offices are held by men who today are fifteen years of age, or four years older than yourself. You are eleven or twelve, are you not? Thirteen, perhaps?

Thus, all your life long you will find little accidents like that of Barcelona occurring once every four years. Would you rather have been born about 1750, under the ridiculous reign of—(a king so obscure that I cannot remember his name)? For my part, I give thanks to God that I entered Berlin, with my pistols carefully loaded and primed, on the 26th of October 1806. Napoleon wore for the entry the full-dress uniform of a Major-General. Perhaps this was the only time I ever saw him.

---

[1] Beyle assiduously frequented the Countess de Montijo's salon, of which his friends Mérimée and Di Fiore were intimates. When he wrote to this latter, on his departure from Paris: " I keenly miss my two fourteen-year-old lady friends ", he was referring to the Countess de Montijo's daughters. The elder, Paca, was to become the Duchess of Alba, and the younger, Eugenia, the Empress of the French.

He marched twenty paces ahead of his soldiers: the crowd, which was *silent*, was within two paces of his horse. He could have been shot at from any of the windows. Unter den Linden, by which he entered, is like the Rambla at Barcelona. Had I been born under the ridiculous Louis XV, on the 26th of October 1806 I would have been strolling proudly on the boulevard, in a grey silk coat striped with violet, playing the pompous ass.

I shall shortly send you a book by Varchi which I have been expecting for a fortnight. It is the *History of the Siege of Florence in* 1530. The Florentine National Guard held out for a year and killed ten thousand men. They had a hero, a genius comparable to Napoleon, a merchant named Ferruci. Out of hatred for rebellious towns, nobody has ever spoken of Ferruci. I have seen one of his letters, written on the eve of the battle in which he was killed. The city of Florence was betrayed by the infamous Malatesta, whom it had appointed Commander-in-Chief and who was a very brave man. He died in the following year, of *contempt*.

So do not take accidents like that of Barcelona too tragically.

I have found some bronze medallions of Augustus, Tiberius, Nero, etc. The twelve or fifteen first Roman emperors had a hundred and twenty million subjects. You will hear them spoken of all your life. Augustus was the subtlest of rascals; Tiberius, half mad with gloom, was a great prince; Trajan was the only man to be compared to Napoleon, apart from Caesar. Study their portraits carefully. I fear that your eyes, and those of mademoiselle Paquita, have been spoilt by lithographs and keepsakes. The half-effaced portraits of Roman emperors are generally masterpieces of design.

The revolution following the death of Ferdinand VII has reduced your fortune by a half. Try to accustom yourself to this sorrow. When I was in Russia, the frost made my hair fall out all over my temples. It took me a fortnight to accustom myself to this ugly spectacle, and after that I thought no more of it. Strive to habituate yourself to the million *reales* that the creation of a government of *mistrust* has cost you.

(Two Chambers discuss a budget, and say to the seven ministers appointed by the *King*[1]: " I distrust you. You tell me that a cannon costs four thousand francs. I think it costs only three thousand five hundred francs, and that you want five hundred francs for yourself, so as to become as rich as M. Talleyrand.")

It is not in your power to recover those million reales. The best thing would be to stop thinking about them. You will have to make

[1] In English in the original.

[363]

the same sort of effort when you are forty-five—that is to say, at the first assaults of old age. That is when women buy a little English dog, and converse with this dog. I would rather buy a thousand books: for my part, I intend to spend my old age, if I reach it, in writing the story of a man whom I loved, and hurling insults at those whom I do not love. If the book is tedious, ten years after my death nobody will know that I wrote it. But it is not proper for a woman to write. So invent an occupation for your old age. Think of all these things ten years before they happen. Think of the grief you will suffer at the hands of the Conde de Santa Cruz.

<hr/>

217

TO HONORÉ DE BALZAC[1]

Civitavecchia, 16th of October 1840

I was much surprised[2], monsieur, by the article you were so good as to devote to *la Chartreuse*. I thank you for your advice more than for your praise. You have taken excessive pity on an orphan abandoned in the street. I did not expect to be read before 1880. To be a somebody I would have had to win the hand of Mlle Bertin (who set the words of M. Victor Hugo to music).

I received the review yesterday evening, and this morning I have reduced the fifty-four first pages of the first volume of the *Chartreuse* to four or five.

I took the keenest pleasure in writing these fifty-four pages, I was speaking of things that I adore, and I had never thought of the *art* of novel-writing. In my youth I drew up plans for novels, and drawing up plans freezes me stiff.

I compose twenty or thirty pages, then I feel a need for distraction—

[1] On October 15th Stendhal had received the *Revue Parisienne* of September 25th, 1840, which contained a very long and important article by Balzac on *La Chartreuse de Parme*. It is no exaggeration to say that he was overwhelmed by it. Never had a colleague of this stature addressed such praise to him. On the following day he set about replying. He spent several days at the task, and his letter was not sent off until October 29th. Amongst Stendhal's papers are three different drafts of his attempts to reply, the first and last written entirely by himself and the second by a copyist, with manuscript corrections by Beyle. When Romain Colomb published the *Correspondence*, he amalgamated the third version with the second and added some phrases from the first, thus forming a very adroit little patchwork. In our ignorance of the exact text as received by Balzac, I reproduce the three drafts in order and sequence." (Note by M. Martineau.)

[2] A note in a corner of the first page: " Mention—Review received on the day before the reply.

a little love-making, if I can, or a little dissipation. Next morning I have forgotten everything, and when I read the three or four final pages of yesterday's chapter, today's chapter comes to me. The book you have taken into your protection was dictated in from sixty to seventy days. I was under a pressure of ideas.

I had no suspicion that there were rules to be observed. For La Harpe I have a contempt that amounts to hatred. As the book progressed, I formed my judgments upon it from the *Histoire de la peinture*. As for M. de la Harpe and his living disciples, I compare them to the glaciated painters after 1600. And, with the exception of those whom you love, I think that by about 1950 nobody will have any suspicion of the real names. Of those whom we have seen, there are none who seem to me to have a better chance than Prudhon and Gros's *Hospice de Jaffa*.

I shall have Rassi, Barbone, etc. appear in the foyer of the Opera. These gentlemen were sent to Paris by the Prince of Parma in the capacity of spies. The thick Milanese they speak catches Fabrice's attention.

Is that not a good method of introducing the characters?

In short, whilst putting down much of your kind praise to pity for an unknown work, I agree with all you say except about style. Pray do not think that this is overweening conceit. I know of only one rule: style cannot be too *clear*, too *simple*. Since ideas on . . . are unknown to the newly rich, fops, etc., they cannot be expressed too *clearly*.

Ever since 1802 I have thought M. de Chateaubriand's " fine style " ridiculous. It seems to me to give expression to a number of small false-hoods.

You will think me a monster of conceit, monsieur, for daring to speak to you of " style ". Here, you will say, is a little known[1] author whom I praise to the skies, and who now wants to be praised even for his style. On the other hand, one must conceal nothing from one's physician. I shall correct the style, and I shall confess to you that many passages of narrative were left as I dictated them, without any correction.

Lest you be horrified by my attitude, I am obliged to enter into a few details.

I read very little. When I read for pleasure, I pick up the *Mémoires* of Marshall Gouvion Saint-Cyr. He is my Homer. I often read Ariosto. There are only two books that give me a sense of " good writing ": Fénelon's *Dialogues des Morts*, and Montesquieu.

I detest the style of M. Villemain, for example, which seems to me adapted only to the polite utterance of insults.

[1] Stendhal first wrote " unknown ".

The essence of my trouble is that the style of J.-J. Rousseau, M. Villemain or Mme Sand seems to me to say many things that *should not be said*, and often tells many actual *falsehoods*. There, the big word has slipped out.

Often I ponder for a quarter of an hour whether to place an adjective before or after its noun. I seek to be (1) truthful, (2) clear in my accounts of what happens in a human heart.

I think that since a year ago I have realised that one must sometimes give the reader a rest by describing landscape, clothes, etc.

As for beauty of phraseology, its roundness, rhythm, etc. (as in the funeral oration of *Jacques le Fataliste*), I often regard it as a fault.

Just as, in painting, the pictures of 1840 will be ridiculous in 1880, so, I think, the polite style of the present day, fluent and saying nothing, will be very stale forty years hence; it will be what the letters of Voiture are to us.

As for contemporary success, I have told myself, ever since *L'Histoire de la Peinture*, that I would be a candidate for the Académie if I had been able to win the hand of Mlle Bertin (who set some of M. Victor Hugo's words to music).

I expect that in fifty years some literary botcher will publish fragments of my books which may possibly find favour as being free from *affectation*, and perhaps as being *true*.

Whilst dictating the *Chartreuse*, I thought that by publishing what I composed on first impulse, I was being more true, more *natural*, more worthy of favour in 1880—by which time society will no longer be paved with vulgar newly-rich, who esteem the "noblions" above everything, precisely because they themselves are *ignoble*. Bocalin's fable . . . *il Cuculo a piu metodo*[1].

I repeat, the perfection of *French*, in my view, are Fénelon's *Dialogues des morts* and Montesquieu. As for perfection of narrative, that is to be found in Ariosto. The pedants have ranked him below Tasso, who repeatedly falls flat.

I shall tell you an absurdity: many of the passages concerning the Duchess Sanseverina are copied from Correggio. M. Villemain seems to me to be Pietro de Cortone.

I have never met Signora de Belgiojoso. I have met many a Rassi, who was German.

I took the Prince from the court of Saint-Cloud, where I in some sort dwelt in 1810 and 1811.

I take a being whom I have known, and say to myself: with the same

[1] The cuckoo has more method.

habits, contracted in the art of going every morning "in pursuit of pleasure", what would he do if he had more intelligence? I have seen Herr von Metternich, who was then at Saint-Cloud, wearing a bracelet of the hair of Caroline Murat. I was at that time acting as a scribe for M. le comte Daru, who was obliged to tell me secrets so that I might lighten his enormous task.

Napoleon sent one evening to know why there was so much laughter in the chancery.

Napoleon is represented by N, M.D.'s drawing-room by C.[1]

I wrote the *Chartreuse* thinking of the death of Sandrino, an event which moved me in my deepest nature. M. Dupont deprived me of a chance to introduce it.

I had said to myself: to be at all original in 1880, after thousands of novels, my hero must not fall in love in the first volume, and there must be two heroines.

I had no thought of[2] Herr von Metternich's *non exequatur*. I have never had any regret for what was fated not to happen. I shall confess to you that my pride is based upon hopes of having some slight fame in 1880. By that time there will be little talk of Herr von Metternich, and still less of the small prince. Death causes us to exchange rôles with such people. They can do anything to our bodies during their lives, but scarcely are they dead when silence enfolds them. Who speaks today of M. de Villèle, of Louis XVIII? Of Charles X, rather more: he had himself driven out.

I will tell you what my misfortune is: find me a remedy. To work in the morning, one must find distraction in the evening, else in the morning one finds oneself bored by one's subject. Hence my unhappiness amongst five thousand dense merchants of Civitavecchia. There is nothing poetical here but the twelve hundred convicts, and to them I do not speak. The women spend their time dreaming of ways to make their husbands give them a hat from France.

Your remarks have caused me to re-read some passages of the *Chartreuse* with pleasure.

How to entertain you a little, in exchange for all the surprise and pleasure I had from the review? By sending you a sincere letter, instead and in place of a polite and showable letter into which I would have slipped my enthusiasm for Mme de Mortsauf (*le lys dans la vallée*) and for *Le Père Goriot*.

---

[1] The letters N and C refer to one of the numerous sketches of which Stendhal's manuscripts are full.

[2] Stendhal first wrote: "of avenging myself for".

Beware of a saying that I have heard concerning the charming Windermere. Beware of the moment when your writings will have *out written themselves*[1]. The savour of novelty is delicious in the first three numbers.

Walter Scott's style, which you have at Paris, is the bourgeois style of M. Delecluze, author of Mlle de Liron, which is not bad[2].

II[3]

Yesterday evening, monsieur, I had a great surprise. You have taken pity on an orphan abandoned in the street. I did not expect to be read before 1880, when some literary botcher would have found my over-simple pages in some old book.

Nothing would be easier, monsieur, than to write you a polite letter such as you and I well know how to write. But since your treatment of me is unique, I wish to imitate you and reply with a sincere letter.

I received the Review yesterday evening, and this morning I have reduced the fifty-four first pages of the *Chartreuse* to four or five. I had taken too much pleasure in speaking of those happy days of my youth. Indeed I felt some remorse at the time, but I consoled myself by thinking of the tedious first half-volumes of father Walter Scott, and the long preamble to the divine *Princesse de Clèves*.

There was a time when I used to draw up plans for novels—for *Vanina*, for example; but drawing up plans freezes me stiff. I dictate twenty-five or thirty pages, then it is evening and I need violent distraction. It is necessary that by next morning I shall have forgotten everything. When I read three or four final pages of yesterday's chapter, today's chapter comes to me.

I must confess to you that many pages of the *Chartreuse* were published as dictated. I believed that in this way I was being simple, not involved (I detest the involved). You have persuaded me to repent of this, and I shall say, like a child." I won't do it again."

I had sixty or seventy sessions of dictation, and I spoilt all the part about the prison, which I had to re-write. How can such details interest you? But I have the sinister intention of asking you for advice the first

---

[1] In English in the original.

[2] In a corner of this first draft, Stendhal wrote: " My handwriting is so bad when I write to a man of intelligence, my ideas awake so rapidly, that I have decided to have this letter copied out."

[3] At the top of the paper, in Beyle's handwriting: " This reply goes off on the 30th of October 1840—2nd reply lightened—first letter crammed with egotism—details concerning the writing of *la Chartreuse*—on the 29th, I cut out the egotism and wrote a less heavy letter.

" Appalling egotism, never send off such naked truth, 'tis ridiculous. Never be in haste to send off, distrust the truth."

time we meet on the boulevard. Should I keep Fausta, an episode that became over-long? Fabrice wants to prove to the duchess that he is incapable of love.

For people like La Harpe I have a contempt that amounts to hatred.

As *la Chartreuse* progressed, I formed my judgments upon it from the history of painting, with which I am familiar. For example, literature in France is at the stage of the pupils of Pietro de Cortone (in *peinture au trait*, expression proved a faster worker, and ruined all Italian painters for fifty years).

For example, the entire character of the Duchess Sanseverina is copied from Correggio (that is to say, it produces the same effect on my soul as Correggio does). I must be very confident of your good nature to dare to hazard such twaddle.

I believe we are in the age of Claudian, and I read few modern books. With the exception of Mme de Mortsauf and other works by the same author, some novels by George Sand and some newspaper articles by M. Soulié, I have read nothing of what is being currently published.

Whilst writing the *Chartreuse*, in order to acquire the correct tone I occasionally read a few pages of the *Code civil*.

My Homer, which I often re-read, is Marshall Saint-Cyr's *Mémoires*. My day-to-day author is Ariosto.

I could never, even in 1802—when I was an officer of dragoons in Piedmont, within three leagues of Marengo—I could never read twenty pages of M. de Chateaubriand. I almost had to fight a duel because I laughed at " the indeterminate crest of the forests ". I have never read *La Chaumière Indienne*, I find M. de Maistre insupportable. Doubtless that is why I write badly—from an exaggerated love of logic.

The only authors who give me the impression of good writing are Fénelon, *Les Dialogues des morts*, and Montesquieu. Less than a fortnight ago I wept as I re-read *Aristonoüs, ou l'esclave d'Alcine*.

I shall have Rassi and Riscara appear in the foyer of the Opera, sent there as spies by Ernest IV after Waterloo. Fabrice, returning from Amiens, will notice their " Italian " looks and " thick Milanese ", which the spies suppose nobody can understand. I have been told that one must introduce one's characters, and that the *Chartreuse* resembles a volume of memoirs: the characters appear as they are required. The fault into which I have fallen seems to me very excusable: is not this an account of Fabrice's life?

In short, monsieur, whilst putting down much of your excessive praise to pity for a forsaken child, I am in agreement with you on all matters of principle. I ought to end my letter at this point.

You will think me a monster of conceit. " What! " you will exclaim to yourself inwardly, " this brute, not content with what I have done for him—a thing without precedent in this century—wants to be praised for his style as well! "

I know of only one rule: to be *clear*. If I am not clear, all " my world " is annihilated. I want to describe what occurs in the depths of the souls of Mosca, the Duchess and Clelia. 'Tis a region scarcely penetrable by the gaze of the newly rich, of people like the Latinist Director of the Mint, M. le comte Roy, M. Laffitte, etc., etc.—the gaze of grocers, good paterfamiliases, etc., etc. . . .

If, to the obscurity of the subject, I add the stylistic obscurities of M. Villemain, Mme Sand, etc. (supposing that I had the rare privilege of writing like these coryphées of the grand style)—if to the fundamental difficulty I add the obscurities of this much-vaunted style—absolutely nobody will understand the Duchess's struggle against Ernest IV. The style of M. Chateaubriand and M. Villemain seems to me to express: (1) many little things that are agreeable enough, but not worth saying— like the style of Ausonius, Claudian, etc.; (2) many little *falsehoods* agreeable to the ear.

III[1]

Yesterday evening, monsieur, I had a great surprise. I do not think that anybody has ever been so treated in a review, and by the best judge of the matter. You have taken pity on an orphan abandoned in the middle of the street. I have responded worthily to such kindness: I received the review yesterday evening, and this morning I reduced the first fifty-four pages of the work whose worldly success you are so greatly fostering, to four or five pages.

The laborious kitchen of literature might well have given me a distaste for the pleasure of writing: I have postponed my hope of the satisfactions of authorship to twenty or thirty years hence. A literary botcher might then discover the works whose merit you so strangely exaggerate.

Your self-deception goes very far—*Phèdre*, indeed! I must confess to you that I was scandalised—I who am quite well disposed towards the author.

Since you have taken the trouble to read this novel three times, I shall have a deal of questions to ask you at our first encounter on the boulevard:

---

[1] At the top of the paper: " A copiar in bella carta. Vorrei mandar col bastimento del 29." (Copy out on good paper. I want to send it off by the ship sailing on the 29th.)

(1) Is it permissible to call Fabrice " our hero "? My object was to avoid repeating the name " Fabrice " too often.

(2) Should I omit the Fausta episode, which became too long in the course of writing? Fabrice seizes the offered opportunity of demonstrating to the Duchess that he is not susceptible of *love*.

(3) The fifty-four first pages seemed to me a graceful introduction. I did indeed feel some remorse whilst correcting the proofs, but I thought of Walter Scott's tedious first half-volumes and the long preamble to the divine *Princesse de Clèves*.

I abhor the involved style, and I must confess to you that many pages of the *Chartreuse* are published as originally dictated. I shall say, like a child: " I won't do it again." I believe, however, that since the destruction of the Court in 1792, form has daily played a more meagre part. If M. Villemain, whom I mention as the most distinguished of the academicians, were to translate the *Chartreuse* into French, he would take three volumes to express what has been presented in two. Since most rascals are given to over-emphasis and eloquence, the declamatory tone will come to be detested. At the age of seventeen I almost fought a duel over M. de Chateaubriand's " the indeterminate crest of the forests ", which numbered many admirers amongst the 6th Dragoons. I have never read *La Chaumière indienne*, I cannot endure M. de Maistre.

My Homer is the *Mémoires* of Marshal Gouvion Saint-Cyr. Montesquieu and Fénelon's *Dialogues* seem to me well written. Except for Madame de Mortsauf[1] and her fellows, I have read nothing published in the last thirty years. I read Ariosto, whose stories I love. The Duchess is copied from Correggio. I see the future history of French letters in the history of painting. We have reached the stage of the pupils of Pietro de Cortone, who worked fast and indulged in violently exaggerated expression, like Mme Cottin when she causes the ashlars of the Borromaean isles to " walk ". After this novel, I did not. . . .[2] Whilst writing the *Chartreuse*, in order to acquire the correct tone I read every morning two or three pages of the Civil Code.

Permit me to employ an obscenity. I do not wish to f——g the reader's soul. The poor reader lets pass such ambitious expressions as " the wind uprooting the waves ", but they come back to him when the moment of emotion has gone by. For my part, I hope that if the reader thinks of Count Mosca, he will find nothing to reject.

(4) I shall have Rassi and Riscara appear in the foyer of the Opera, having been sent to Paris as spies after Waterloo by Ernest IV. Fabrice,

---

[1] Beyle wrote " Mordauff ".   [2] Sentence unfinished.

returning from Amiens, will notice their Italian look and their " thick " Milanese, which these observers suppose nobody can understand. Everybody tells me that one most introduce one's characters. I shall devote much less space to the good Abbé Blanès. I thought it was necessary to have characters who took no part in the action but simply touched the reader's soul and removed the sense of romanticism.

I shall seem to you a monster of conceit. Our great academicians would have had the public raving about their writings, if they had been born in 1780. Their hopes of greatness depended upon the ancien régime.

As half-fools become more and more numerous, the part played by *form* diminishes. If the *Chartreuse* had been translated into French by Mme Sand, she would have had some success, but to express what is told in the two present volumes she would have needed three or four. Carefully weigh this excuse.

The half-fool cleaves especially to the verse of Racine, for he can tell when a line is not finished; but Racine's versification daily becomes a smaller part of his merit. The public, as it grows more numerous and less sheep-like, calls for a greater number of " little true touches " concerning a passion, a situation taken from life, etc. We know to how great an extent Voltaire, Racine, etc.—indeed, all except Corneille— are compelled to write lines " padded " for the sake of rhyme. Well, these lines occupy the place that was legitimately owed to such little true touches.

In fifty years M. Bignon, and the Bignons of prose, will have bored everyone so much with productions devoid of any merit except elegance that the half-fools will be in a quandary. Since their vanity will insist that they continue to talk about literature and make a show of being able to think, what will become of them when they can no longer cling to form? They will end by making a god of Voltaire. Wit endures only two hundred years: in 1978 Voltaire will be Voiture; but *Le Père Goriot* will always be *Le Père Goriot*. Perhaps the half-fools will be so upset at no longer having their beloved rules to admire that they will conceive a distaste for literature and turn religious. Since all the rogues of politics have the declamatory and eloquent tone, people in 1880 will be disgusted with it. Then perhaps they will read the *Chartreuse*.

The part played by " *form* " becomes daily more meagre. Think of Hume: imagine a history of France, from 1780 to 1840, written with Hume's good sense. People would read it even if it were written in patois: in fact, it would be written like the Civil Code. I shall correct the style of the *Chartreuse*, since it offends you, but I shall have great difficulty. I do not admire the style now in fashion, I am out of patience with it. I am confronted with Claudians, Senecas, Ausoniuses. I have been told for the past year that I must sometimes give the reader a rest by describing landscape, clothes, etc. Such descriptions have bored me so much when written by others! But I shall try.

As for contemporary success, of which I should never have dreamed but for the *Revue Parisienne*, I told myself at least fifteen years ago that I would become a candidate for the Académie if I won the hand of Mlle Bertin, who would have had my praises sung thrice a week. When society is no longer " spotted " with vulgar newly-rich, who value nobility above all else, precisely because they themselves are ignoble, it will no longer be on its knees before the journal of the aristocracy. Before 1793, good society was the true judge of books; now it is dreaming of the return of '93, it is afraid, it is no longer a judge. Take a look at the catalogue of a little bookshop near Saint-Thomas d'Aquin (rue du Bac, about no. 110), a catalogue which it lends to the neighbouring nobility. It is the most convincing argument I know of the impossibility of finding favour with these poltroons numbed by idleness.

I have nowhere portrayed Herr von Metternich, whom I have not seen since I saw him in 1810 at Saint-Cloud, when he wore a bracelet of the hair of Caroline Murat, who at that time was so beautiful. I never regret what was fated not to happen. I am a fatalist, and I hide it. I dream that perhaps I shall have some success about 1860 or '80. By then there will be little talk of Herr von Metternich, and still less of the small prince. Who was Prime Minister in England at the time of Malherbe? Unless by any chance his name was Cromwell, I am at a loss for an answer.

Death causes us to exchange rôles with such people. They can do anything to our bodies during their lives, but at the moment of death oblivion enfolds them for ever. Who will speak of M. de Villèle, or of M. de Martignac, in a hundred years? M. de Talleyrand himself will be saved only by his *Mémoires*, if he has left any good ones; whereas *Le Roman Comique* is today what *Le Père Goriot* will be in 1980. It is Scarron who keeps us familiar with the name of that Rothschild of his day, M. de Montauron, who was also, at a cost of fifty louis, the patron of Corneille.

You clearly perceived, Monsieur, with the insight of a man familiar with practical matters, that *La Chartreuse* could not attack the theme of a great State such as France, Spain or Vienna, because of questions of administrative detail. There remained the small principalities of Germany and Italy.

But the Germans grovel so before a ribbon, they are so stupid! I spent several years amongst them, and have forgotten their language in sheer contempt. You will realise that my characters could not be German. If you follow this train of thought you will discover that I was led, step by step, to an extinct dynasty, to a house of Farnese, the least obscure of these " extinct " lines by reason of its grandparents the generals.

I take a character well known to me, I leave him with the habits he has contracted in the art of going off every morning in pursuit of pleasure, and next I give him more wit. I have never met Signora de Belgiojoso. Rassi was German, and I have spoken with him a hundred times. I learnt to know the Prince whilst staying at Saint-Cloud in 1810 and 1811.

Ouf! I hope that by now you will have read this pamphlet three times over. You tell me, monsieur, that you know no English: the " bourgeois " style of Walter Scott is represented at Paris in the heavy prose of M. Delécluze, editor of the *Débats* and author of a work, *Mademoiselle de Liron*, which has some quality. Walter Scott's prose is inelegant and, above all, pretentious. He presents the spectacle of a dwarf who does not want to lose an inch of his stature.

Your amazing article, such as no writer has ever received from another, caused me—I now dare to confess it—to burst into laughter as I read it, whenever I came upon a somewhat excessive piece of praise, which I did at every step. I could imagine the faces my friends would pull as they read it.

For example, the minister d'Argout, when he was a commissioner on the Council of State, was my equal and, moreover, what is called a friend of mine. Comes 1830, he is a minister; his clerks, whom I do not know, believe that there are dozens of artists . . .

218

TO DI FIORE

Rome, the 5th of March 1841

At Shrovetide, in the magnificent palazzo Colonna, which is adorned with the tapestries Louis XIV gave to the High Constable Colonna, I found myself at a ball with two queens. My wife insisted on going, and furthermore on wearing her three little diamonds worth two thousand five hundred francs: a great honour for me.

The Queen of Naples[1] looks like a grocer's wife overcome with age. Her husband is handsome and stupid, and entirely hidden behind a wide blue ribbon.

The Queen of Spain looks good-natured and kindly, but horribly common. Nobody would suppose that she is thirty-four years of age. She seems forty. Throughout the evening I saw her at a distance of two paces, and during the masquerades on the Corso she was throwing *confetti* at her friends with a little air of affected grace which was in fact far from graceful.

The Queen of Naples[2] has the irritated air of a benevolent curmudgeon, and seems to me fundamentally kindly. Her daughter went to the ball wearing a little red felt hat. (Ask our friend Colomb to read this.)

The Queen of Spain was lodging at Serny's, the best inn, and spending, with her suite, four hundred and eighty francs a day. The Conde Colombi, her chamberlain, a former attaché at the French embassy at Constantinople, is her man-of-all-work. The Queen is a very good shot with the pistol and killed several *grelettes*—which are a sort of seabird—when travelling by steamboat a month ago.

Señor Munoz[3] has arrived at Rome. The Queen drove a bargain with Prince Borghese by which, for thirty thousand crowns (one hundred and seventy thousand francs) she sold him the principality of Castel-Ferrate, or most of it, which brings in four thousand five hundred francs. But the *Supremo Gerarca* refused to give this principality to Señor Munoz, who was thus unable to become Prince of Castel-Ferrate, near Rieti. The Queen has rented the château of Prangins, near Nyon, on the lake of Geneva, where Colomb went for the ball in 1808. It is a truly royal dwelling, selected once before by Joséphine Bonaparte. The avaricious proprietor refused seven hundred thousand francs for it, and the Queen was content to rent it.

In any case, it is much wiser, but for the climate, to be free at Prangins than a slave elsewhere: but the silly little women here do not see things in the proper light. The queens spent no great sums, and thus created no stir in Rome. The Roman populace believes only in *expenditure cash down*. . . . The Carnival was not brilliant: the visitors threw bouquets costing half a baioco and less, and sweetmeats made of plaster. Roman avarice is in mourning for the death of the Duchesa Torlonia and the

---

[1] Maria-Isabella, daughter of Charles IV, King of Spain, born on the 6th of July 1789, married, on the 6th of October 1802, to King Francis I, father of the reigning king, re-married to the Prince of——. (Note by Colomb.)

[2] Maria-Christina, born on the 27th of April 1806, widow of Ferdinand VII. (Note by Colomb.)

[3] Morganatic husband of Queen Maria-Christina.

Princesa Borghese: an excellent opportunity not to hold receptions. Those of monsieur the ambassador of France were admirable.

I have forgotten a large number of anecdotes concerning Naples. The balls there are very gay, and about two hours after midnight the King shuts the gates to prevent the dancers from leaving.

The admiration due to wealth has been paid to the marriage, at Florence, of the Grand Duke's daughter and Modena. The Grand Duke deserves admiration, especially for his great roads. The road from Rome to Florence will pass through Civitavecchia, without snow, avoiding the horrible mountains of Radicofani and without danger.

The cost of embassies and consulates should be cut by a half. For example, the ambassador at Rome receives emoluments of sixty thousand francs a year, six balls at three thousand francs each and a dozen dinners. With this receipt, anyone can be adored and kissed on the big toe. Ribbons and dignities are simply sneered at.

———— 219 ————

TO DI FIORE

Civitavecchia, the 14th of March 1841

I am re-reading with new pleasure your letter of the 17th of February.

If you chance to pass near the rue Croix-des-Petits-Champs, no. 34, go up to the counting-house and ask for M. Bonavie. He is a lad for whom for three years I have had nothing but praise. He was a soldier in the Indies: his sufferings there have made him naïve and colourless in manner. Would that God might please to let me have him here! He copied for me by the page, at twenty centimes per twenty lines. Say to him: " I shall send you by the local post some letters of M. Beyle's, which I find difficult to read with my bad eyesight. To spare my friends, make fair copies of the letters, at twenty lines a page, on pot-paper, and send the original and the copy back to me by post." A copy of my letters, by M. Bonavie or another, will be a great comfort to me. When I have to concern myself with how to form the characters, for the first page I can think of nothing but stupidities.

. . . Signorina Molica, a young singer, rather pretty and very passionate, who sings so that I could hear her across a piazza and two streets. She told me herself that she sings as she speaks, without any fatigue. Signorina Molica is twenty-two years of age, a baritone or contralto. Signor Molica papa is a Master Mason and lives in the palazzo where I have three rooms on the third storey, overlooking the sea, and three rooms at the back, for forty-four francs a month. I have seen Signorina Molica only once: I am too " great " to go to her home, which grieves me deeply. I have not seen her for six months: 'tis M. Dominique's second clerk who pays court to her, with the best of intentions. This clerk will one day earn twenty crowns a month (a hundred and twelve francs), and on this the couple will live. This Carnival there has been an opera sung by amateurs. By unanimous consent, Civitavecchia has never had such a prima donna. When the tenor strayed from the key, Signorina Molica brought him back again; she dominated even the orchestra. All the young women of the country detest her, for she is gay and likeable and can talk. She knows how to put passion into her parts. She understands French a little. She would make the Opera resound, and without ever screaming, which she has no need to do. What theatre would refuse to pay her six thousand francs in the first year, after two débuts? What doubt that after two years—unless in the mean time she fell a prey to some malady—she would be earning twenty thousand? She ought to marry M. Toto d'Alberti[1], who is of French extraction, writes well and earns, by following three or four different trades, from ninety-five to a hundred francs a month. Her father, a wheat-broker, is a highly respectable man who is wearing himself out with pretty peasant girls. Toto ran a dagger into his first mistress, who had been unfaithful to him: Dominique saved him. He was asked to what penalty he should be sentenced. " To three months' imprisonment." The young man was in the fortress for fifty-five days. Immediately after the crime Dominique stole the dagger, which has not been seen since. Carried on a sofa to Dominique's dwelling (the crime had occurred in the young man's lodging—the fair one lived in the house), Toto d'Alberti was a prey to frightful convulsions. Soon ten gendarmes came to guard him. Dominique was eloquent: he proved that there had been no crime—the wound had been inflicted upon the young lady's major charms. The gendarmes concluded that Dominique was the culprit's protector, and from that moment the affair took a turn for the better. Dominique had never spoken to the faithless fair one. On leaving the fortress, Toto, who is now the lover of Signorina Molica, spent some months in Barcelona. From then on he detested the faithless fair, and never spoke to her again. This passionate, sombre-eyed lover is a little, well-built Jew. All his family has a French appearance. But how is the

[1] Cf. letter no. 183.

idea of a stage career to be inserted into the head of Signor the Mason Molica? I am too lazy to become the ringleader in this affair. My opinion of this unknown talent is shared by Signor Blasi and four other very keen lovers of the stage, who sang at the theatre with Signorina Breadcrumb (Molica) all through the Carnival.

Lieutenant-Colonel Sodermarck has given up everything in order to paint my portrait[1]. He finds people willing to pay six hundred francs.

Interrupted by the accidents of the 15th of March.

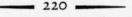

220

TO DI FIORE

Civitavecchia, the 5th of April 1841

I, too, have had a grapple with the void[2]. It is only the immediate experience which is disagreeable, and the horror of it comes from all the silly nonsense that is put into our heads at the age of three.

Say nothing to Colomb. I intended not to mention the matter in my letters, but I believe in the sincerity of the interest you will take in it. Well, then, to start with I had horrible headaches for six months: after that four attacks, as follows:

Suddenly I forget all French words. I cannot even say: " Give me a glass of water." I study myself with curiosity. Apart from the use of words, I have all the natural faculties of an *animal*. This lasts from eight to ten minutes. Then gradually memory of words returns, and I am left in a state of exhaustion.

Since I have little belief in physic, and especially in physicians, who are men of meagre gifts, I took consultation only after six months of frightful headaches. . . . Herr Severin, a homoeopath from Berlin, has performed some handsome cures at Rome. He uttered some phrases from which I gathered that this was a case of *nervous* apoplexy, not the sanguine sort.

I shall write to the excellent M. Prévost, of Geneva, but I have no belief in anything except the profound study that M. Prévost gives to this illness.

[1] Cf. letter no. 224.
[2] On March 15th, 1841, Beyle suffered the first attacks of the illness of which he died in Paris on March 23rd, 1842.

Herr Severin (spiteful, witty face, the outlook of a charlatan) has had me take aconite to stimulate the circulation, and proposes in the spring to have me take *sulphide*. The best drug would be that prescribed by M. Dijon[1]. I would go to Geneva and spend two days with the excellent M. Prévost, who rid me of gravel and gout by eliminating acids.

In the past year I have had four complete lapses of memory of French. A lapse lasts from six to eight minutes. The mind works satisfactorily, but without words. Ten days ago, whilst dining at the restaurant with Constantin, I made incredible efforts to remember the word " glass ". I continually have a latent pain in the head, which comes from the stomach; and now I am fatigued by having tried to write these three pages more legibly.

During the last attack but one, at dawn, I continued to dress myself to go out shooting. One might as well be knocked out there as any-where else. *Vale.*

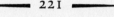

221

TO DI FIORE

Rome, the 10th of April 1841

Here is my first letter. I came to Rome on the first of this month to profit by the skill of the brusque Dr. Dematteis, who shows me marked kindness. He treated me for gravel in 1833.

The doctor refused to bleed me a third time. He denied the existence of a thick tongue, although yesterday this somewhat disagreeable phenomenon reappeared when I was with Constantin, whom I had gone to see at work on the portrait of Charlemagne which the Paris govern-ment has ordered from him for three thousand francs.

Dr. Dematteis is a man of strong views. He rejects homoeopathy, and insists that my trouble is a gout which, since it does not go to the feet, is carried to the head. Four or five times a day I am on the point of suffocation. But dinner half sets me right, and I sleep well. A hundred times I have renounced life on going to bed, being firmly convinced that I would not wake up. The labour of writing a letter of three lines causes spells of dizziness.

I have been fairly successful in hiding my trouble. I consider that there is nothing ridiculous about dying in the street, provided one does

[1] A holiday such as the comte Molé had already granted him.

not do it on purpose. Two days ago, at the exhibition (arch-dull) of works by the pupils of the Académie de France, whilst standing before a marble *Love* who is clipping his own wings, I had a sensation of utter suffocation; I was very red in the face.

I did not ask the doctor the name of this illness, in order not to put gloomy ideas into my head: so I cannot tell you what it is. Is it possible for homoeopathy, by preventing the gout from being active, to cause one to die of apoplexy, like the powders once taken by the Duke of Portland?

It was Doctor Dematteis who supplied me with this touch of erudition.

Imagine a handsome room, on the second storey, in the busiest street in Rome[1]. The landlord, a good man, lives there with Constantin. His name is Signor Frezza, and for two years he has been delighted to receive seventeen piastres a month. He has me looked after by his fat servant Barbara. She steals from me, and has just robbed me of a pair of boots. 'Tis all I can do to refrain from asking her for these boots, as I may be very sick in her house. In any case, it would be better than dying in a wayside inn.

Holy Saturday, 10th of April, at seven o'clock in the evening.

———— 222 ————

TO DI FIORE

Rome (Monday), the 19th of April 1841

Yesterday an exutory was applied to my left arm. This morning I was bled. The most disagreeable symptom is the clumsiness of my tongue, which makes me mumble.

The excellent Constantin comes to see me twice daily. M. Alertz, of Aix-la-Chapelle, physician to the Pope, also visits me. Constantin skilfully gilds the pill for me, which in any case is not too bitter. I have great hopes of recovery. Nevertheless I want to say farewell to you, in case this letter may be the *ultima*. I truly love you, and you are not one of a crowd.

Farewell, take events cheerfully as they come.

CONDOTTI 48.

The 20th of April, attack of weakness in the left leg and thigh.
The 21st of April, all goes well.

[1] Via Condotti.

[380]

TO ROMAIN COLOMB

Civitavecchia, the 19th of June 1841

We have had a great local mishap this morning, my dear fellow. It has caused all the inhabitants to turn pale and has stirred them from their lethargy.

Pollux has gone back to Hell. In the middle of the canale di Piombino, on the night of the 17th to 18th, at eleven o'clock in the evening, the *Mongibello* a Neapolitan ship, ran down the *Pollux*, a Sardinian steam-boat, and despatched it to the bottom of the sea. A sailor had the presence of mind to catch hold of the *Mongibello's* rigging, and the passengers of the unhappy *Pollux* were able to leap up into the rigging and save their lives. The only man to perish was a Neapolitan captain.

. . . The Neapolitan captain's name is Castagnola. He was a man of forty, rich, handsome, well educated. I knew him here in Civitavecchia, whence he took ship on the 17th.

The childishness of men is beyond belief. Passengers always prefer State-owned vessels, despite their slowness and the arrogance of their officers, who refuse to be taken for coachmen . . .

Despite everything, the sea is a hundred times less dangerous than a carriage. Besides, death is prompt—a great advantage . . . What makes the sea so terrifying in Italy is the thought of Hell: Dominique has never had such ideas for half a second. . . . I had lent a traveller my small travelling-case: that was the sum of my loss.

Did I tell you of all the mortifications of M. Lacordaire, who was compelled to leave his dozen disciples, and, instead of playing the colonel at the head of his dozen men, was obliged to live with the dirtiest, most jealous and most spiteful monks, at the Minerva in Rome? He is rightly punished, and M. de Lammenais will laugh to know that he is execrated because he washes his hands. The French "scandalise" the Roman priests. I believe that *La Vie de Saint Dominique* by the aforesaid de Lacordaire provoked the indignation of a powerful priest, one of the courtiers of the Dowager Queen of Sardinia, who in my presence lamented the "French ideas" in Lacordaire's book. The French were half "Protestant". I added: "because they permit *self-examination of conscience*, which is the worst of sins."

You will call me a liar: Cardinal Tosti said to —— that Ambassador L——[1] was afraid of your fat Dominique. Cardinal Tosti's confidante told this to a friend, who repeated it to me.

I have two dogs, to which I am tenderly devoted. One of them is a black English spaniel, a lovely dog, but sad and melancholic. The other, *Lupetto*, is café au lait, gay, lively—a young Burgundian, in short. I was being saddened by having nothing to love.

—— 224 ——

TO ROMAIN COLOMB

Florence, the 8th of October 1841[2]

My dear fellow, I shall leave here about the 22nd with Salvagnoli, a lawyer and a man of intelligence, who plans to spend a month in Paris. He is said to be malicious; but is that not said of me?

I have some hope of turning into a miser: all the Parisian pleasures of which Besançon speaks seem to me expensive. . . . From Marseilles I shall go to Geneva, to ask M. Prévost for instructions concerning my health.

The Grand Duke of Tuscany recently held a gathering of all the scientists. There were eight hundred and fifty *scienzati*, as they are called. At Boboli an excellent dinner was provided every day: a dinner for four hundred and fifty *scienzati*. Each of them paid fifty sous; but the Grand Duke secretly added two francs per dinner. As for science, not much of that was done; but the scientists no longer seem ridiculous to those Chinamen known as Tuscans.

I find everything too expensive. Can this, at last, be the dawn of avarice? Rossini has turned banker, and creates scenes, it is said, with Signorina —— over the most paltry gown. I am not talking nonsense when I compare myself to a man of genius.

The Toscana was admirable. In 1880 they will still speak of the congress of 1844: eight hundred and fifty scientists, with Orioli as the chief of them. Did I tell you that my portrait[3], painted by Colonel Sodermark,

[1] The comte de Latour-Maubourg, who became French ambassador at Rome after the death of his brother the marquis.

[2] " His state of health induced him to apply for leave of absence in order to go to Geneva and consult Dr. Prévost. Thereupon he set out for Paris, where he arrived on the 8th of November 1841." (Romain Colomb.)

[3] Reproduced as a frontispiece to this book.

a Swedish officer and artist, is a masterpiece? It was the king of the Roman exhibition at the Porta del Popolo.

The month of October is delightful in Rome: the populace goes mad with joy. It claims that in November all the old wine turns to vinegar: this is something that must be prevented. Hence the numerous libations on Monte Testaccio . . . Throughout the whole month, on Thursdays and Sundays, the villa Borghese is full of madmen. Strangers go to see the three Raphael frescoes, painted by his pupils at his country-house outside the Pincian gate.

—— **225** ——

TO M. BONNAIRE, EDITOR OF THE
REVUE DES DEUX MONDES

Paris, the 21st of March 1842

I have received, Monsieur, the letter you were so good as to write to me on the 7th of March. Apart from a few small details, I accept all your conditions.

You give me your word of honour that you will not change a single word of the manuscript (as with the " broken heart " in *L'Abbesse de Castro*).[1]

Within a year from now, I shall deliver to you the manuscript of two volumes of tales and novels, which will compose two volumes like *La Chartreuse de Parme*, about sixteen or seventeen pages of the *Revue*.

Payment for these two volumes will be five thousand francs.

Once every two months I shall send you a story, which will be signed " Stendhal ". You will be entitled to publish it in the *Revue des Deux Mondes*. You will have the right to assemble these novels in octavo volumes, of which seven hundred copies will be printed. After this octavo edition you will furthermore have the right to publish an edition in decimo-octavo, popular format, to the number of three thousand copies, the whole signed " Stendhal ".

For these divers rights I shall receive an immediate payment of *fifteen hundred francs*.

---

[1] *L'Abbesse de Castro* and the other stories composing the *Chroniques Italiennes* had appeared in the *Revue des Deux Mondes*. Stendhal had resumed work on *Lamiel*. The anecdote of the Wayfarer and that of the Dagger-stroke are dated March 1842.

As each story is published, payment will be made of five hundred francs. The total payment shall have amounted to five thousand francs up to the time of publication of the octavo edition.

At the time of publication of each of these editions, you will have sent me a dozen copies of each, or the sum of sixty francs.

With the purpose of correcting literary errors, I shall have the right, in each new edition, to excise one page and to add two or three.

I enclose my receipt for the fifteen hundred francs.

Pray accept, monsieur, etc. . . .

H. BEYLE.

P.S. If you publish advertisements or catalogues, I shall request you to include in them the titles of works by M. de Stendhal[1].

[1] This letter is probably the last Beyle wrote, since he was struck down in the street on March 22nd by the attack of apoplexy to which he succumbed in the night. On March 23rd, 1842, Romain Colomb signed " the death-certificate of the sieur Henri-Marie Beyle, French consul at Civitavecchia, aged fifty-nine, chevalier de la Légion d'honneur, bachelor, born at Grenoble (Isère) and deceased at Paris in his domicile, rue Neuve-des-Petits-Champs, no. 78, today at two o'clock in the morning."

Also published by The Soho Book Company:

THE DEAD SEAGULL, by GEORGE BARKER

George Barker was born in Essex in 1913 of an English father and an Irish mother. At an early age he came to London, where he set up a printing press in Shepherd's Bush (The Phoenix Press). His first poems were printed there. He was soon noticed as an extravagant figure around town and his work attracted the practical encouragement of T. S. Eliot and the admiration of W. B. Yeats. *Thirty Preliminary Poems* were published in 1933, followed by *A Vision of Beasts and Gods, Eros in Dogma* (1944), *News of the World* (1950), *The True Confession of George Barker* (1950), *Calamiterror* and other works. His *Collected Poems* were first published by Faber & Faber in 1957. His more recent works include *In Memory of David Archer* (1973), *Villa Stellar*, and *Anno Domini* (1983). Apart from verse, George Barker has written three books for children. He has lived in the United States, Japan and Italy, and now lives in Norfolk.

His novel, *The Dead Seagull*, was first published in 1950. It is recognisably the work of a poet being short, lyrical and strong. It is the closely-observed story of a love affair, sometimes brutally scathing, sometimes almost pornographical; above all it is an unparalleled description of the power of sexual love.

'I warn you that as you lie in your bed and feel the determination of your lover slipping its blade between your ribs, this is the real consummation. "Kill me, Kill me," you murmur. But it always surprises you when you die.'

ISBN 0948166 00 2   £4.95

Please ask for these books at your local bookshop. If unavailable they can be ordered direct from The Soho Book Company, Orders Department, 1/3 Brewer Street, London W1R 3FN. Please enclose £1 extra for each complete order to cover postage and packing.

MY HEART LAID BARE,
by CHARLES BAUDELAIRE

Charles Baudelaire was born in Paris in 1821. His passionate and almost unnatural love for his young widowed mother was shattered when she married General Aupick in 1828. He came to see Aupick as a symbol of the respectability and authority he loathed, and his loss of the love of his mother as a symbol of his destiny in the world. His parents opposed his determination to become a poet and embarked him for India but Baudelaire left the ship at Reunion and returned to Paris. He set up an apartment on the Ile Saint-Louis, which he furnished in decadent style, filling it with gilt and damasks and paintings by Delacroix. Here he set out to embody his ideal of the Dandy. He contracted dangerous debts and his life of desperate excess soon became depraved and sordid when he began the disastrous liasion with the mulatto actress Jeanne Duval, the *Venus Noire* of his poems. In 1857 he published *Les Fleurs du Mal*. He was prosecuted and fined for offences to public morals and a ban was imposed on the more obscene poems in the work which was not lifted until 1949. By 1864, Baudelaire's resources were exhausted and he fled to Brussels where his ruined constitution finally gave way. He was brought back to Paris in 1866 suffering from general paralysis and lingered on until 31 August 1867, when he died.

A characteristic theme of Baudelaire's is "l'horreur et l'extase de la vie." He found inspiration in the streets and the mysterious hidden life of Paris, and also in the spirit of evil itself. A sense of damnation provoked him to blasphemy; "*Enfer ou Ciel, qu'importe?*" he wrote. Beauty, to him, already contained the elements of its own corruption. *My Heart Laid Bare* and the other prose works published in this volume exhibit all Baudelaire's characteristic themes and are written with a disturbing blend of intellectual precision and romantic beauty, and with a sarcasm which merges into squalid decadence.

ISBN 0948166 07 X   £5.95

Also published by The Soho Book Company:

NAPOLEON'S MEMOIRS,
edited by SOMERSET DE CHAIR

Napoleon Bonaparte, the Emperor Napoleon I, appeared unexpectedly in a Corsican drawing room during the feast of the Assumption of 1769. He was born, he claimed, 'on an old carpet, on which were worked large designs.' He climbed rapidly in the French Revolutionary Armies and by 1796, aged 27, he commanded the Army of Italy which he led to victory against Austria. In 1798 he conquered Egypt but was thwarted in his hopes of destroying British Power in India by Nelson's naval victory at Aboukir Bay. In 1799 Napoleon took advantage of a political crisis in Paris to return there. His popularity was still high and he engineered the *coup d'etat du 18 Brumaire* from which he emerged as First Consul, effectively a dictator. In 1802 he was elected consul for life and was constituted emperor by the *senatus-consulte* of 18 May 1804, confirmed by plebiscite. He and his wife Josephine were crowned at Notre-Dame in the presence of Pope Pius VII.

He had no children by Josephine, and divorced her in 1809 to marry the archduchess Marie-Louise of Austria, who bore him a son. He restored order and civil unity to France and reconstructed the financial, educational, judicial, executive and legislative systems. At the same time he ruthlessly suppressed conspiracies and destroyed the freedom of the press. By 1810 his empire covered most of Europe, excluding Russia, but following his disastrous Russian campaign (1812) and defeat at Leipzig (1813) the allies invaded France in 1814. Napoleon abdicated unconditionally, and was granted sovereignty of Elba, a small island to which he was confined off the Mediterranean coast. Ten months later he escaped on the brig *L'Inconstant* and landed with 700 soldiers at Juan les Pins. Louis XVIII fled to Belgium and Napoleon made his way to Paris amidst scenes of exultation. The allied coalition regathered in order to destroy him, and he was narrowly defeated at Waterloo (1815). He abdicated for a second time and considered sailing for America, but finally gave himself up to the British government. He spent the rest of his life interned on the Atlantic Island of St Helena, where he dictated and corrected his memoirs. He died in 1821, probably of stomach cancer, but possibly of Arsenic poisoning.

Somerset de Chair (1911–) was a member of the House of Commons (1935–45, 50–51) and parliamentary private secretary to the Minister for Production (1942–44). During the war he served in the British Army in the Middle East in the Royal Horse Guards (1938–42). He is an author and poet.

ISBN 0948166 10 X   £7.95

DOMINIQUE, by EUGENE FROMENTIN

Eugene Fromentin was born at La Rochelle, on the Atlantic coast of France, in 1820. His family owned considerable properties in the area and his father was the superintendent of a mental hospital. He was sent to Paris to read for the bar but gave up law for painting. He was a successful artist of the school of Delacroix, and was highly esteemed by his contemporaries for his paintings of North Africa, which he visited several times during the 1840's and 1850's. *A Summer in the Sahara* (1857) and *A Year in the Sahel* (1859) are accounts of his wanderings there which at once established him as a literary artist of the first order. After the publication of *Dominique* he felt unable to satisfy his high literary standards and returned to painting. Shortly before his death he published *The Old Masters of Belgium and Holland* (1876), essays on the Dutch and Flemish painters. He died prematurely of an anthrax infection in 1876.

Dominique, his masterpiece, first appeared in 1862. The touching freshness of its landscapes would alone render it valuable, but it is remarkable as a sober analysis of delirious passion. While still at school M. Dominique de Bray falls in love with Madeleine d'Orsel, who is a few years older than him. She discovers this only after her marriage, and elects to cure him, but falls in love herself. Their moral distress rises to a climax when by accident, Dominique discovers this. The book offers a vision of chastity and pain which hints at the dark side of life, suggesting that there are other ends to existence besides mere happiness.

ISBN 0948166 06 1   £4.95

THE ENCHANTED WANDERER,
by NICOLAI LYESKOV

Nicolai Semyonovich Lyeskov (or Leskov) was born in a small village in Central Russia in 1831. His mother was of aristocratic birth and his father was a famous criminal investigator of seemingly supernatural abilities, who ruined himself by turning to farming. Lyeskov himself was brought up with the children of serfs. Both his parents died when he was sixteen and he was then looked after by his aunt, a quaker convert married to an Englishman. English influences, combined with the lessons of his early impoverishment and extensive travels through Russia can be detected in his work. As a minor official in the Orel penal court, he became thoroughly acquainted with the severities and inefficiencies of the penal system under Nicholas I. He went to St Petersburg in 1862, where he became a journalist and published several novels. It was during this period that he wrote his remarkable series of tales, including *Lady Macbeth of Mtensk* (1865) and *The Enchanted Wanderer* (1873), and culminating in *The Left-Handed Smith, The Lady and the Slut*, and *The Mountain*. His later tales became increasingly religious. Lyeskov refused to align himself with any political faction and was ill-treated by his critics. His reading public was large. Tolstoy wrote of him that "he has long followed the road which I am now travelling", and Maxim Gorky recognised him "as a literary artist, assuredly worthy of being placed on a level with such masters of Russian literature as Tolstoy, Gogol, Turgenev and Goncharov." He died of a heart attack in 1895 and was buried at St Petersburg.

The Enchanted Wanderer has been described as the high water mark of Lyeskov's narrative power, providing a Quixotic account of the Russian people through the eyes of an illiterate sage. As this wanderer travels from place to place, he recounts his restless history in a series of rustic episodes describing the essence of life under the Tsars. The adventures follow each other in breathless succession, and they are saturated with expressive and picturesque detail. They provide the reader with a delightful portrait of the Russia of the time, as well as a more sombre portrait of a strong and unschooled character searching for truth.

Translated by A. G. Paschkoff.

ISBN 0948166 04 5   £5.95

SELECTED LETTERS of FRIEDRICH NIETZSCHE

Friedrich Wilhelm Nietzsche was born near Leipzig in 1844, the son of a Lutheran pastor. His upbringing was very pious. He went to the famous grammar school of Pforta, and then to the universities of Bonn and Leipzig where he was powerfully influenced by his reading of Schopenhauer. His brilliance as a philologist was such that he was appointed to the chair of classical philology at the University of Basel at the age of 24, before he had taken his degree. While at Basel he made and broke his passionate friendship with the composer Richard Wagner and took part as an ambulance orderly in the Franco-Prussian war. Plagued by ill health, he was obliged to retire from the University in 1879. After this he lived a reclusive life in Switzerland, France and Italy, until in 1889 he became paralysed and went mad. He died in 1900.

Nietzsche became famous with *The Birth of Tragedy* (1872) which was of revolutionary importance, challenging the accepted tradition of classical scholarship. He achieved lasting fame with *Thus Spake Zarathustra*, mostly written between 1883 and 1885. His other works include *Untimely Meditations* (1873–6); *Human, All Too Human* (1878–9); *The Wanderer and his Shadow* (1880); *The Dawn* (1881); *The Gay Science* (1882 & 1887); *Beyond Good and Evil* (1886); *Towards a Genealogy of Morals* (1887); and, at the end of his working life, *The Twilight of the Idols*, *The Anti-Christ* and *Ecce Homo*. In seeking to analyse and redefine morality, Nietzsche was led to reject Christian ethics and affirm the "Superman" and the doctrine of power. His influence on modern German literature has been enormous.

This selection of his letters by Oscar Levy, the Nietzschean scholar, contains the essence of a vast correspondence spanning Nietzsche's life and work. It includes confessional letters to his mother and sister, alongside impassioned correspondence with great figures of the time, such as Strindberg, Burckhardt and Taine. In it we see "a writer of the most forbidding aspect, a prophet of almost superhuman inspiration, a hermit inabiting a desert of icy glaciers, coming down, so to say, to the inhabited valley, to the familiar plain, where he assumes a human form and a human speech." (O. Levy)

Translated by A. N. Ludovici. Edited with an introduction by O. Levy.

ISBN 0948166 01 0 £6.95

Also published by The Soho Book Company:

MARIUS THE EPICUREAN,
by WALTER PATER

Walter Horatio Pater was born in 1839 into a family of Dutch descent. He spent his entire working life at Oxford, where he received his B.A. from Queen's College in 1862. In 1864 he became a fellow of Brasenose College. He became associated with the Pre-Raphaelites, particularly Swinburne, in 1869. A volume of collected essays entitled *Studies in the History of the Renaissance* (1873) first brought Pater fame. It was followed by other collections: *Imaginary Portraits* (1887); *Appreciations* (1889), containing his judgements of Shakespeare, Wordsworth and other English writers; *Plato and Platonism* (1893); and two posthumous collections issued in 1895. *Gaston de LaTour* (1896), a story of the France of Charles IX, was left unfinished at Pater's death in 1894. It was as a critic and a humanist that he became a powerful influence on his own and succeeding generations, claiming disciples as diverse as Virginia Woolf and Ezra Pound.

Marius the Epicurean stands apart from the rest of his work, enshrining its values and presenting them in a more rounded and complete form. It has been described as "the most highly finished of all his works and the expression of his deepest thought." He gave up a considerable period, between 1880 and 1885, to its composition. It is the story of the life, at the time of the Antonines, of a grave and thoughtful man. Pater traces the reactions of Marius to the spiritual and philosophical influences to which he is subjected. These range from the *Golden Book* of Lucius Apuleius to the stoicism of Marcus Aurelius, and from the tranquil beauties of the old Roman religion to the lurid horrors of the Christian persecution. An excuse for the detailed examination of a series of human ideals, the book was written to illustrate the highest aim of the aesthetic life.

ISBN 0948166 02 9   £7.95

Please ask for these books at your local bookshop. If unavailable they can be ordered direct from The Soho Book Company, Orders Department, 1/3 Brewer Street, London W1R 3FN. Please enclose £1 extra for each complete order to cover postage and packing.

Also published by The Soho Book Company:

ARMANCE, by STENDHAL

Stendhal was one of the many pen-names used by Henri Beyle. He was born at Grenoble in 1783, and educated there. His mother died when he was seven; he detested his father and the rest of his family, and the devout, Royalist atmosphere in which they lived. In Paris by 1799, he procured an army commission in 1800 which took him to Milan. In Italy, he fell in love and discovered his spiritual home. Between 1806 and 1813 the victualling of Napoleon's armies in Germany, Russia and Austria constituted much of his work. He left the army at the end of this period, his health impaired largely through his own excesses. He refused office under the Bourbons and spent seven years in Italy, absorbed by a shattering unrequited passion which was the main event of his life. Unjustly accused of spying, he was forced to leave and from 1821 to 1830 he was mostly in Paris, living frugally, writing, and frequenting literary *salons*. He published *Of Love* (1822) and *The Red and the Black* (1830) during this period. Under the July monarchy he was appointed French consul at Trieste, but was soon transferred to Civitavecchia, a dreary, unhealthy port, 45 miles outside Rome. He held this office until his sudden death from apoplexy, in a Paris street in 1842. His masterpiece *The Charterhouse of Parma*, which he wrote in 52 days, appeared in 1839. Stendhal was not a conscious stylist, and was prepared to sacrifice harmony and rhythm to the lucidity with which he expressed his often complicated ideas. He had an ironical attitude to life, and the behaviour of his characters, and even their virtue, springs from their passions. His ideal was what he called Beylism; a worship of magnificent, all-conquering energy in the pursuit of happiness.

Armance, his earliest novel, appeared in 1827. It exemplifies Stendhal's style and attitude to life. Set in contemporary Paris, this charming love story conceals a powerful study of nobility of spirit. Armance and Octave are secretly in love: as clouds of passionate tension gather we are compelled to ask whether destiny will allow them to meet, and honour allow them to be happy.

Translated by C. K. Scott Moncrieff.

ISBN 0948166 03 7 £5.95

Please ask for these books at your local bookshop. If unavailable they can be ordered direct from The Soho Book Company, Orders Department, 1/3 Brewer Street, London W1R 3FN. Please enclose £1 extra for each complete order to cover postage and packing.

Also published by The Soho Book Company:

AXEL, by VILLIERS de l'ISLE-ADAM

Philippe-Auguste, Comte de Villiers de l'Isle-Adam was born at St Brieuc, Britanny, in 1838. He came of an ancient, impoverished and eccentric family, fervently Catholic and steeped in chivalric tradition. He lived mostly in Paris, making literature the sole object of a vagabond existence, and suffered atrocious poverty until his death in 1889. His writing has a powerful poetic quality, concealing a mystical philosophy beneath an ornate and extravagantly decadent romantic style.

Axel is the epitome of symbolist drama, and gave its name to the definitive work on decadence and symbolism, Edmund Wilson's *Axel's Castle*. "Count Villiers de l'Isle-Adam," wrote W. B. Yeats, "swept together words behind which glimmered a spiritual and passionate mood, as the flame glimmers behind the dusky blue and red glass in an Eastern lamp." Villiers started Axel at about the time he became acquainted with Wagner, in 1869, and worked on it during nearly two decades. Over this period his own metaphysical enthusiasms moved from occultism, through more orthodox idealisms and back to Catholicism, which he had never ceased to practice. Each of these positions is examined in turn by Axel, Count of Auersperg and by Sara, an escaped nun of heartbreaking beauty whom he discovers in the vaults of his storm-swept castle. Each is rejected and it is with the dramatic discovery of the highest ideal, amidst tumbling cascades of gold and jewels, that the work ends.

ISBN 0948166 05 3   £4.95

Please ask for these books at your local bookshop. If unavailable they can be ordered direct from The Soho Book Company, Orders Department, 1/3 Brewer Street, London W1R 3FN. Please enclose £1 extra for each complete order to cover postage and packing.

THE SOHO BOOK COMPANY

NAPOLEON'S MEMOIRS
A classic of military
and political autobiography.
(Observer)

ISBN 0948166 10 X/£7.95

STENDHAL'S LETTERS
You can read your way out
of anything with this. It
is another world and a better.
(Cyril Connolly)

ISBN 0948166 09 6/£6.95

**THE ENCHANTED
WANDERER,
by NICOLAI LYESKOV**
He deserves the privilege of
standing with Tolstoy. (M. Gorky)

ISBN 0948166 04 5/£5.95

**SELECTED LETTERS
OF FRIEDRICH NIETZSCHE**
Visions have appeared on my
horizon the like of which I have
never seen.

ISBN 0948166 01 0/£6.95

**DOMINIQUE,
by EUGENE FROMENTIN**
I feel myself a child before
a man who has reflected so much.
(George Sand)

ISBN 0948166 06 1/£4.95

**THE DEAD SEAGULL,
by GEORGE BARKER**
I warn you that as you lie in your
bed and feel the determination of
your lover slipping its blade
between your ribs, this is the real
consummation. "Kill me, Kill me,"
you murmer, but it always surprises
you when you die.

ISBN 0948166 00 2/£4.95

**MARIUS THE EPICUREAN,
by WALTER PATER**
The only great prose in
modern English. (W. B. Yeats)

ISBN 0948166 02 9/£7.95

ARMANCE, by STENDHAL
A neglected masterpiece. (A. Gide)

ISBN 0948166 03 7/£5.95

**AXEL, by VILLIERS de
l'ISLE ADAM**
Admirable, but mad. (J. P. Sartre)

ISBN 0948166 05 3/£4.95

**MY HEART LAID BARE,
by CHARLES BAUDELAIRE**
Enfer ou Ciel,
qu'importe?

ISBN 0948166 07 X/£5.95

*Please ask for these books at your local bookshop. If unavailable they can be ordered direct from
The Soho Book Company, Orders Department, 1/3 Brewer Street, London W1R 3FN.
Please add £1 extra for each complete order to cover postage and packing.*